IT'S THE BERRIES!

Life as a Co-Ed in the Roaring Twenties

ISBN 978-0-9977956-9-1

Published in the United States by **Yesteryear Publishing**.

Cover and page design by **E. Nan (Thompson) Edmunds**.

William S. Jackson, Contributor

Books are available at **www.amazon.com**.

Yesteryear Publishing
91 Grandview Road
Hummelstown, PA 17036

www.yesteryearpublishing.org

yesteryearpublishing@gmail.com

The Author

Dr. Judith Thompson Witmer is a prolific writer on a wide range of topics. Her professional books include the first guidebook written for women in pursuing advancement in educational administration, a book on service learning, and one on team-based professional development.

Her research passion, however, is **personal and social history** beginning with a biography of Rodrigue Mortel, MD (*I Am from Haiti*). This was followed by *Jebbie: Vamp to Victim*, the true story of Jessie Pifer, a young woman who went from being the stunning and stylish girl with all the gentlemen callers to becoming a town legend, until she fell prey to a family member who betrayed her.

All the Gentlemen Callers: Letters Found in a 1920s Steamer Trunk is a companion publication to *Jebbie* in the form of 100 narrated love letters from Jebbie's many suitors, offering a first-hand account of life in a gentler time.

Growing up Silent in the 1950s: Not All Tailfins and Rock 'n' Roll is an investigation of the factors that created the Silent Generation. Its historical framework is enlivened by personal reflections by members of this generation as well as the author's confirmation of the factors that created a generation that history has shown to be exceptionally responsible and productive.

Loyal Hearts Proclaim, the 500-page history of Lower Dauphin High School, is the first of its kind, containing anything one would want to know about this hidden treasure, unusual in its support of faculty offering innovative courses and approaches to teaching and learning. This is the only chronicle of *any* high school's *everything*.

The author's more recent books include a biography of her parents (*Kate and Howard*) and a narrative genealogy of the lineage of four sisters (*The Thompson Sisters*) from the time their ancestors landed here in the 17th Century. In 2016, she produced *Letters from a Son to His Father, WWII*, the story of a gentle, young soldier who spent three years in the Philippines, faithfully writing to his widowed father. *I Have Always Loved You* is the story of an enduring friendship of classmates. *The English Students* celebrates a set of Baby Boomers with uncommon energy, providing a fresh canvas upon which to create both art and history.

The Author

Eight of the author's 22 books, including *It's the Berries,* are set in Curwensville, Pennsylvania, each written from a different perspective, but all reflecting the author's high regard for this small town in the hills of Clearfield County. She has also published shorter pieces as blogs, maintaining a personal interest in what shaped several generations. One of these is the cheers and football songs used in the 1930s and 50s; another tells the story of how we (Curwensville High School) became the Golden Tide; and another as to how yearbooks originated.

Judith Thompson Witmer EdD.

In addition to the number of books she has written, Judith Witmer has published numerous articles in professional journals, a cover feature in *Penn State Medicine*, newspaper columns, monographs, national speeches, and book reviews. Dr. Witmer holds a B.A. in English Literature, an M.S. in Humanities, and a Doctorate in Ethics and Administration, as well as post-doctoral credits from Harvard University.

www.yesteryearpublishing.org

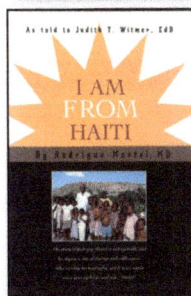

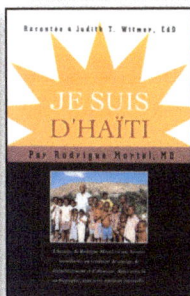

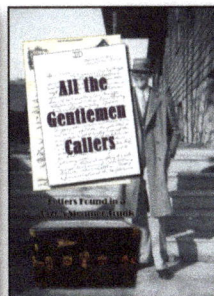

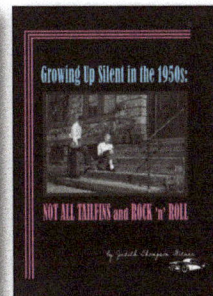

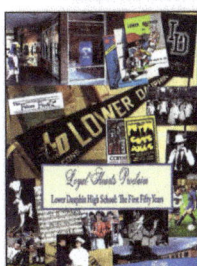

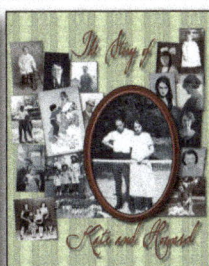

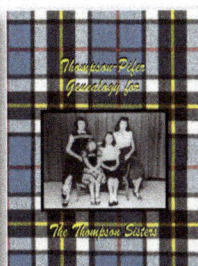

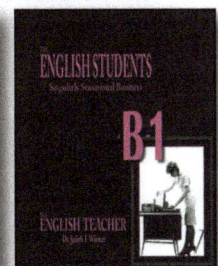

v

Coming Attractions

Coming Attractions

Dedication

to

My Aunt Mary Alice Thompson Jackson Crunk

It's the Berries is a slice of life, a glimpse into the college years of Mary Alice Thompson, a small-town girl who clearly exemplifies the 1920s Co-ed. Her life is full, her problems minimal, her outlook usually rosy, and her heart pure.

I did not know my aunt until ten years after the here-in Diary was completed, yet I found it enthralling that her sweet disposition had never changed from the autumn of her entering Drexel Institute through her final years. She was always pleasant, calm, and as kind as can be, even-tempered and never intrusive into her brother's occasionally unsettled family life. This is as I remember her.

Aunt Mary Alice's Christmas presents to us were the special gifts of each year. They were always beautifully wrapped and well-thought-through. I had always wondered how she knew what was "just right" every year, as she had no daughters and no sister, but she always selected something age appropriate and lovely. One year she gifted my sister and me sewing kits. I used the sewing kit for years, until it fell apart; I looked for a replica, but had to settle for a similar, but less interesting, style. However, I removed the pin cushion from the original sewing box and placed it in its ersatz container where it serves its purpose as well as being a reminder of the quality, but well-used original gift.

Another special gift from my aunt is a leather jewelry box, with a top tier that lifts by a hinge when the lid is opened; mine is rose-colored and Jo Ellen's green. This remains my favorite jewelry box of the several I have had during the many years since. How did she always know?

Peggy shown with her doll trunk, a few of her costumes and the sewing machine used to create them.

Aunt Mary Alice also gave me my first (and only) Madam Alexander doll that until a few years ago I had believed was Princess Margaret (but actually was Elizabeth) and had named Peggy. Seventy years later the dress is too fragile and tattered to place on Peggy, so here she is dressed in a once-new green velvet cape hand-sewn by Laura Bressler, a next-door neighbor who was blind, although no one ever told me what had caused the blindness and I had been reared to never ask questions that might appear to be rude. The weathered doll trunk

Doll clothes designed and sewn by the author on her child-sized sewing machine.

(shared with Jo Ellen) was repainted approximately 60 years ago and, while it is in a deteriorating condition, I cannot part with it. The child's sewing machine on the left is also a gift from my aunt on another occasion. I used it to make the clothes hanging on the rack and the ones I designed and made, replicas of my own outfits in some cases, particularly the plaid peplum dress which Mrs. Buterbaugh, a local dressmaker, had created for me. Note also the rolled-leg pink jeans and ankle socks.

Aunt Mary Alice was soft-spoken and a meticulous housekeeper. She was the inspiration for my desire to collect period furniture, particularly anything with a Victorian flair. I treasure the footstools she gifted my sisters and me; each is covered with needlepoint by "a great aunt" and had been on a set of dining room chairs. The piece de resistance, however, is a decorative Victorian bench, also covered in needlepoint created by, according to Mary Alice, this same great aunt.[1]

I remember Mary Alice's house—always trimmed with white painted woodwork—as spotless. And I recall in particular a trip to Pittsburgh being held for theatre owners. Her son Bill (my cousin and three years older than I) and I had been promised and were anticipating an "audience" with Roy Rogers, my favorite movie cowboy!! I was heartsick with disappointment when I was left in the lobby while my cousin was invited to the dressing room. I did not know until recently that the audience scheduled with Mr. Rogers was at the time the cowboy star was dressing for the second part of his performance and would not have been appropriate to be viewed by a little girl ……..

However, what I truly owe Mary Alice Thompson is my life from the age of eighteen when I, who had stood at the head of the class academically, had to face the fact that my mother had no means by which to send me to college. She was a single (divorced) parent with four daughters and a nominal income.

---

[1] Based only on recalling Mary Alice's brief mention that the needlepoint was created by her great aunt (or "my" great aunt), the best I could discern was the possibility of the needlework's being done by one or the other of her two maternal aunts, Martha Jane Bailey (1858-1945) who married Jonathan Ogden or, and more likely, Annie Gardner Bailey (1863–1919) who married Charles Boyd.

Then, a miracle happened. In the spring of my senior year in high school, the Superintendent of Schools contacted Aunt Mary Alice and asked her if she could see her way to help with the cost of my college education. In retrospect, I stand in awe of this gentleman, Mr. Harry Heil, taking this task upon himself. He had to have known the depth of the plea he was making. However, my aunt agreed to his request. Yes, she paid for the education at Penn State and provided me with spending money. I entered the freshman class and enrolled in Penn State's DuBois campus, as there had been no remaining dorm space in the main campus by the time this phenomenon occurred. DuBois Campus, as it turned out, was a perfect fit and my happiest year of the four.

I recall, in particular, the day when my aunt joined me on Penn State's main campus and offered to take me shopping for shoes—saddle shoes in particular! The style for "saddles" had recently changed to a "lighter" design profile than my cohort had favored, a version that had not particularly appealed until I saw them in the store. I was very pleased with her kind offer and I returned to the dorm with a pair of these new saddles, the traditional white but with a newer gray "saddle," still puzzled at my aunt's very evident pleasure in buying shoes.

It took reading her diaries to discover that we were kindred spirits when it came to shoes. She mentions shoes 27 times in her Drexel Diary and her delight in purchasing them was evident on that afternoon we spent together on campus. Little could she have ever thought that someday her diary would bring such delight.

In addition to this book's being a thank you from a grateful niece to her aunt, I further dedicate *"It's the Berries"* to the following:

- **William Spencer Jackson** (Bill), Mary Alice's son and a journalist, who devotedly retained the memorabilia of his mother, making this book possible.

- **William Kitson Jackson** (Kit), William's son, who is the fourth generation to carry the William Jackson name. Kit's son is the fifth name bearer.

- **Tracy Jackson,** Bill's daughter, whose features most resemble her handsome Grandfather Jackson she never knew, and who was the light of Mary Alice's eye.

- My sister, **Jo Ellen,** the beauty, the comparison others made to Mary Alice for her sweet disposition.

- My sister, **Elizabeth Nan,** the only one to carry the family-history name of Elizabeth, who is a skilled artistic designer, including the layout for this book and others in our publishing business Yesteryear.

My granddaughters:

- **Jordan,** Class Salutatorian and Dean's List Ace, who has signs of being the next generation's memorabilia keeper.

- **Jillian,** Dean's List Superlative, as well as the stylish co-ed everyone wanted to be.

- **Emily,** who begins her own journey as a college freshman this year of 2020.

- **Olivia,** the youngest, who likely will surprise us all, as still water usually runs deep.

Introduction

Mary Alice Thompson

What kind of future did they dream of, this Generation of the 1920s who had come out of the Great War and could look forward to creating whatever kind of life they chose? It is said they were seeking personal freedom, which they had not had as children. They were riotous in small ways and full of "le bon mot," looking to design their own style, their own view of work, and their own choices in whatever they faced.

This 1920s Generation also had come out of a heritage of the nineteenth century when people were "born into" their small towns much as generations in previous centuries were born into the church. Those of the nineteenth century had "belonged" to their towns by their very presence, and a home town was a community to which one belonged by birth—"one big family," according to Sherwood Anderson and Booth Tarkington.[i] Their social values, which are the basis for our personal and social behavior, were instilled in each by all other town dwellers, either implied or overtly.

Thus, these foundational tenets by which the new generation were to be guided in the twentieth century were set in the last decade of the nineteenth and then influenced the first decade of the twentieth century. Described as "the good years" by author Walter Lord and "the age of confidence" by editor and critic Henry Seidel Canby, the "turn of the century" set the tone for optimism with strong beliefs in the future, in progress, in technology, in God, and, above all, in America.[ii]

For the most part, members of this generation were with family and friends on every occasion imaginable, gathering in the two or three blocks of the shopping area on Saturdays, attending Catechism Classes or Sunday School, and church services on Sunday, marching in or watching parades on Memorial Day and the Fourth of July, swimming in the rivers and streams, knowing their parents and sometimes grandparents, and sitting on porches on summer afternoons while savoring the slow movement of the porch swing, iced lemonade, made from real lemons, quietness, and what some would call gentility.

This was made easier for many of the young people as middle and higher income parents were ready to give their young adult offspring opportunities they themselves had not had. More of the youth finished high school because they didn't have to help support the family (as many immigrants had had to), they had been exposed to music lessons (even in less wealthy families) and pastimes such as tennis, and many of both sexes welcomed the wider opportunities that their public school provided, particularly sports. Schools—and some communities—offered libraries, towns built tennis courts, and girls saw for the first time that they could lead more active lives, as the household did not depend upon their services.

This generation also traveled as families, as by the late 19th century the railroad connected most communities and the growing children saw more of the world. In Curwensville and other similar communities, enough affluent fathers could be part of clubs and lodges and could afford to support "private stone lodges" in which groups could hold parties or spend a weekend "camping" not too far from home. (Curwensville had Greenwood Lodge, privately owned.)

Satisfaction with life in small towns may have varied by degree, but it was still satisfaction, a kind of contentment and fulfillment. Most adults were employed, lived with intact families, and knew their place in the class structure. Families were somewhat stratified by the size of house, the make of car, and by the financial success of the father, but this was more accepted and not usually spoken of openly in terms of envy.

Gentility and propriety are the measures by which they lived, and "Please" and "Thank you" were well-worn words in their vocabulary.

Thus, it is to this small town, with enough business and professional men to make it possible for their daughters to have better opportunities, that we turn our initial attention.

It could be said that Mary Alice Thompson was born into privilege, but, if so, it was not one of inherited wealth. The financial capital came from her father, who could be described as a "self-made man," one who had had to "grow up quickly." Howard Jefferson Thompson was only fourteen years of age when his mother died, leaving five children to be reared by their father, Ignatius or, as he was known, "Nace."

This Ignatius Thompson (born Francis Ignatius), the eldest son of James Thompson, joined his uncle (John Thompson) in the family foundry which manufactured ploughs, stoves, and the like needed by a burgeoning community. Nace also engaged to a large extent in the lumber business and in 1890 purchased the budding Anderson Creek Electric Company where his sons learned the business.

Nace was enterprising and also served as Constable of Curwensville Borough for many years. Howard J. later would tell the story that he and his brothers were roused from their beds some nights because their father (as Constable) was paid $1 per night for lodging any arrestee in his home. (There were no beds in the jail for prisoners.)

There is no evidence that any of the five Thompson children (Walter, Howard, Maud Ann, Fred, and Francis) were graduated from high school, but that would not be unusual for the time and their circumstance. However, what was offered to their offspring was the privilege of being the product of what many small towns could provide to their children—a community that valued them.

H. J., as Howard Jefferson Thompson came to be known, carried a heavy burden of having to grow up too fast and taking on the work of an adult and perhaps that is why there are no photos of H. J. smiling, nor do any of his grandchildren recall his smiling, let alone ever talking to them. He was viewed as "a hard man," but very definitively a self-made success (see biographic summary from the county newspaper when years later he ran for a seat in the State Senate). He left the child-rearing to his bride, with their first child, a son, born nine months following the marriage of H. J. and Elizabeth. A year and a half later their daughter Mary Alice was born, with a fourteen-year gap between her birth and that of the baby brother of the family, Philip Bell.

Fortunately for the Thompson children, their mother was best friend to her only sibling, Grace Wall, a year younger, and her family of eventually five children, all relatively close in age to Howard, Jr. (better known as "Bubby") and Mary Alice. There were many opportunities to be with family and friends on every occasion imaginable, gathering in the two or three blocks of the shopping area in Curwensville on Saturdays, attending Sunday School and church services on Sunday, watching parades on Memorial Day and the Fourth of July, swimming in the rivers and streams, playing tennis, later learning to play pool at the Walls, frequently visiting their maternal grandparents, who lived a block away.

The Thompsons and the Walls, as well as other middle and higher income parents, were ready to give their young adult offspring opportunities they themselves had not had. All of the above eight children finished high school, with most attending colleges, because they didn't have to help support their families. They also had been exposed to music lessons and pastimes such as tennis, and welcomed the wider opportunities provided by their public schools, particularly sports. And, importantly, girls saw for the first time that they could lead more active lives because their households did not depend upon their services.

Mary Alice Thompson's history of growing up in the small town of Curwensville begins with the town itself, a town which developed elements of a paternalistic community and instilled these for several generations, providing a fundamental "good and decent life" for Mary Alice's grandparents (see Lavinia's Diary, included in this book), parents, and, in turn, the person Mary Alice herself would become.

Curwensville, Pennsylvania

In 1882 the Pennsylvania Railroad placed Curwensville on its list of summer resorts and the town was billed as "one of the most picturesque in the county with abundant natural resources, two banks, a building and loan association, two newspapers, seven churches, and six hotels."[iii] By 1912 there were 34 boarding houses and four hotels in the town.[iv]

White pine lumber found along the West Branch of the Susquehanna River was said to be superior in quality and the river provided a natural highway across the county for its passage, then on to Baltimore and Philadelphia by other means of transport where the lumber was readily sold. A Curwensville tannery became the county's leader in tanning.

It was the coal industry, however, that impacted the economy of the area—and likely much of the state—more than any other industry with the exception of lumbering and, once the lumbering industry slowed production, coal mining dominated, and Mary Alice's father owned interests in more than one mine.

Because of the demand for building stone, the stone quarries of Curwensville opened in the late 1800s. Curwensville supplied the stone for many local buildings as well as numerous other well-known structures of eastern United States, such as the largest viaduct railroad bridge in the world in Harrisburg, the foundation for the Cathedral of Learning in Pittsburgh, 80 bridges and underpasses in New York City, the steps of the Philadelphia Museum of Art, and the entire exterior of Princeton University's Chapel.

As early as 1874 Curwensville supported a number of businesses, including A. M. Kirk & Son, Jewelers and Optometrists, one of the longest standing enterprises in the history of the town, second only to Murphy's Drugstore. Running close in business longevity is Way's Stationery Store, established in 1896. Gates Hardware (1877) remains the "oldest family operated business in town."[v] Curwensville also had several general stores in the nineteenth and twentieth centuries.

On September 2, 1884 the cornerstone for a new school was laid, complete with Masonic ceremonies. Built of locally quarried sandstone with eight classrooms, four on each floor connected by halls and two stairways, the monolithic stone building with its 287 students was the pride of the townspeople who came out in full force to celebrate what also became the focal point of the town and the center for community ceremonies.

In the early twentieth century, a popular practice that lasted for a good sixty or seventy years began: the gathering of shoppers on Friday or Saturday night when the stores were open late. Streets were crowded, citizens were nicely dressed, and there was a sense of community with the assurance that one would see many friends and neighbors.

Even in towns like Curwensville with only one main block of stores, the atmosphere was one of an outing, especially between Thanksgiving and Christmas when there was an added air of excitement, including, after World War II, a local Santa Claus at Kantar's. Town bands occasionally added to the festivities, although these were difficult to maintain and periodically had to disband and later reorganize under a different name and sponsorship.

Traditions that everyone followed on holidays and in marking life passages became ritualized, the high points of each life often drawing the notice through announcements in the local paper—birth announcements, birthday parties, school and social activities, awards, graduations, trips, and marriages. Church, social, and fraternal organizations all held annual events. High schools offered literary societies, concerts, class plays, and commencements—along with a sports program attended by most of the townspeople.

Families also practiced their own traditions associated with civic holidays such as when and who decorated their Christmas tree and what relatives would be visited on Christmas morning; who hosted Thanksgiving; how the family cemetery sites were "decorated" for Memorial Day and who would plan the family picnics held after the town parade and/or public ceremony that day; and the flowers worn on Mother's Day.

Summertime celebrations focused on Memorial Day and the Fourth of July. Memorial Day, which had originated to honor the Civil War dead, had no prescribed format. An early morning cannon salute was often heard on the town square or cemetery, followed by a mid-morning parade that included the town and/or high school band(s), soldiers, veterans, politicians, occasional drill teams, and wagons (later automobiles) carrying local dignitaries.

Throughout the summer, particularly before the turn of the century, all could look forward to a circus or a carnival coming to town. Circuses were major attractions traveling by train to towns that had suitable railroad stops.[vi] Occasionally small carnivals came to Curwensville, typically sponsored by an organization such as the local fire company.

The Fourth of July was a celebration of patriotism, firecrackers, and pride of country. There were almost always family picnics and local parks would be filled with families, the picnic menu including hand-churned, home-made ice cream, followed by playing horseshoes, playing catch, and swimming in the Susquehanna River. The end of summer was marked in most communities by local, county, and state fairs, with the county fair likely the earliest "organized" communal event. In Curwensville an annual Labor Day program was provided by the Joshua Earl Sipes Post (VFW), which included activities all day, including a field meet, baseball game, exhibition by the Fireman's Drill Team, band concert, and in the evening Round Dancing at the American Legion Post and Square Dancing held in the Moose Hall.

The main holiday in a small town was Christmas, with fresh-cut trees that likely would have come from nearby forests, brightly colored packages, strung popcorn, carol singing through the streets of the town, school programs, church services, and many visits among family and friends.

For indoor events, there was the opera house, or academy of music[vii] intended for both homegrown and itinerant entertainment. Popular performances included traveling theatrical and vaudeville companies, lectures, graduations, and local talent events. In Curwensville, in the first third of the twentieth century, an annual town production of a musical comedy was staged, directed, and produced by a traveling production company, sponsored by a local fraternal organization, and cast with the town's citizenry.

Yet what is notable in all of this is that women had the most influence over family behavior. Thus, mothers had power in influencing all of the social and moral aspects of the next generation—**at least until after World War I by which time youth was becoming a recognized and separate "stage of life." Young adults then began their flings,** albeit less so in small towns, perhaps only enough to confound their parents. And, more importantly for the middle-upper and upper classes, daughters began to attend colleges.

By the 1920s those being graduated from high school were part of one of the most exciting times for young women to that date in history. They either sensed that things were changing for women or blithely took it for granted. Either way there was a sense of momentousness as they became a part of the "Roaring Twenties."

The H. J. Thompson family lived in Curwensville for several years after Howard and Elizabeth were married and both Howard, Jr. and Mary Alice were born there. However, always looking for wider opportunities, H.J. made the decision to relocate his family first to Clearfield, then to Philipsburg and to Bellefonte where he had initiated contacts. As such he became a pioneer in providing electrical service in a wide area. The family resided in Bellefonte for several years and that is where Philip was born in 1919.

Mary Alice attended several public and one private school:

> Grades 1, 2, 3 in Philipsburg
>
> Grades 4 – 11 in Bellefonte
>
> Private Prep School, Highland Hall, (1921–1922; traditionally this would have been her sophomore year, although there is a Bellefonte report card for these years.)
>
> Grade 12, Curwensville, graduating with the class of 1924.

Richard Wall, Mary Alice's cousin, later recalled that the Thompson family was away from Clearfield for about a half-dozen years. He further related that his grandparents (Vincent and Elizabeth Spencer), also the grandparents of the Thompson children, had moved to Bellefonte as well. There H. J. Thompson provided a clerking job for his father-in-law in his electric power company. The Walls and the Thompsons frequently traveled the distance between Curwensville and Bellefonte for family visits.[1]

Howard, Jr. worked for his father from the time he could remember. His 1920 Diary, written when he was fifteen, confirmed the many times he had missed school to read electric meters throughout Centre County. His father, a self-made man, allowed no frivolities and would not permit his son to waste time playing sports (although as a young adult he was an area champion tennis player) or even to join the Boy Scouts. His best friend was always his mother.

---

[1] Richard Wall wryly notes, "Our family. . .in our 1918 Buick touring car, with stops at roadside springs to refill the car radiator, (met) the Bellefonte relatives, who were travelling smoothly in Uncle Howard's Franklin (with its unique self-air-cooled motor) without needing to stop.

The following year the family moved to Clearfield. Family sources confirm that Bubby was not pleased to change high schools for his senior year, as his 1920 Diary reflects his devotion to Bellefonte sports. Graduated from Clearfield High School in 1922, he may have attended Williamsport Business College, as directed by his father, despite his strong desire to attend Penn State (at the time referred to as State College) where several of his classmates from Bellefonte had matriculated.

This move of residence by the family in the fall of 1921 may have been a contributing factor to Mary Alice's being enrolled at Highland Hall in Tyrone. She attended one year (1921-22), the year Bubby was a senior in Clearfield High School, and was very active in its many events. Programs from these events are in her scrapbook, including a formal school dance held February 25, 1922, having invited Bruce Norris from Curwensville. (See photo pages and note the post card showing the main building for Highland Hall; note the marked windows of which Mary Alice wrote, in typical young girl exuberance, "The places I marked are the windows of our room. We have a wonderful room; we see everything that goes on.")

Following her year at Highland Hall and her parents' return to Curwensville, Mary Alice entered Curwensville High School in the fall of 1922 as a sophomore, expecting to be graduated there in the spring of 1925; however, during her junior year 1923-24 it was realized that Mary Alice had fulfilled the required credits for graduation and would be granted a diploma with the Class of 1924 with whom she formed what would be lifelong friendships, including that of Jessie Pifer, maternal aunt of this book's author and sister of Katherine Pifer who later married Howard, Junior, Mary Alice's brother.

(Endnotes)

i   Lingeman, *Small Town America*, p. 281.

ii   Lingeman, *Small Town America*, p. 258.

iii *Curwensville in Celebration*, p. 17.

iv   Morgan, *Quarries*, p. 22.

v   *Curwensville in Celebration of 200 Years*, p. 109.

vi   Lingeman, *Small Town America*, p. 309.

vii These terms were used because the word "theatre" had a connotation suggestive of sinning where "opera" or "academy" sounded high-toned and cultured.

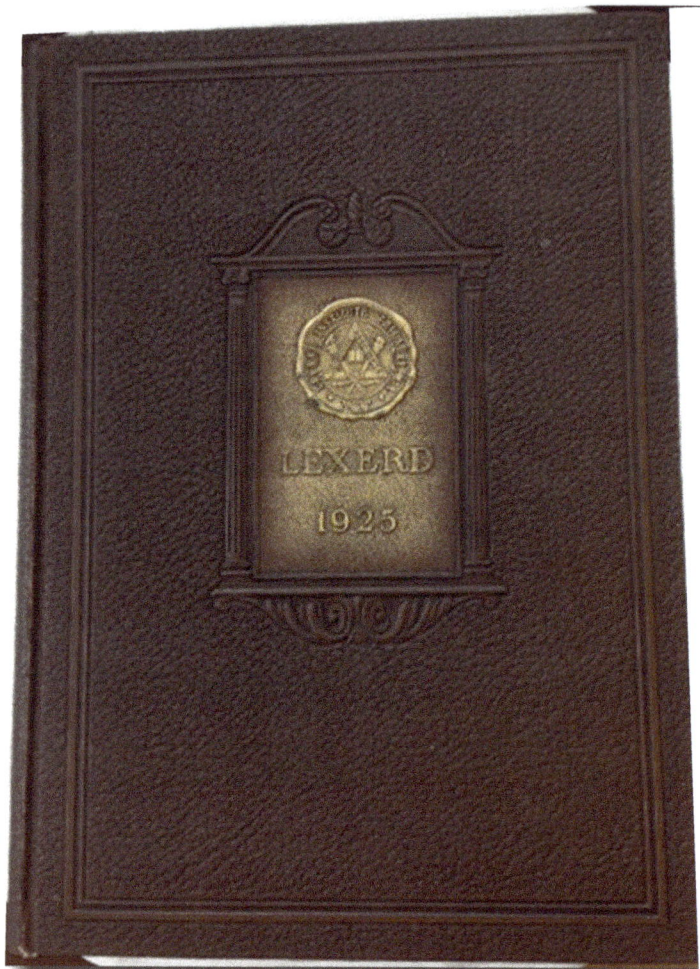

School diary

Sunday Sept. 21, 1924

... train gave me a book of fudge. ... up about 6.30. Cecil was up home for breakfast. Packed our lunch. Buddy went down to the train. Said goodby to Martin at the station. Got in W. Phila. about 5.10. Missed my big sister Florence Brierley. Cecil brought me out. Went to a tea room for supper with some girl. My one roommate Alice Kay came in eve. Talked awhile & took a walk. Florence lives in Ph... Alice & I all ...

... forded around

Monday July 27, 1925

Kate & I got up when Alice & I & ... Alice Murray went to work. Hiked & bundled ... ride to Lumber City. Got a ... boys & ed. Brandonville had. Dallied about 2 miles. After lunch we all hiked in town. Went home & took a bath. Cecil Kay brought us out. It rained real bad. I did get swimming. Drue, Hazel & Gabe came out in eve. Cecil Kay & I hiked in town spied a ... hunt ... awhile? But had to bring us out again ...

Tues. July 28, 1925

We all slept until real late. Forded around all day ... got ... had a real bulldog ...

... get ... of them.

Thurs. July 30, 1925

Alice Elizabeth & Adline & Alice Murray were all away most of the day. We all slept until about 11 o'clock. Got lunch. Bud Smith brought Alice Murray out for lunch. Forded around left ... The girls came back only ... Got dressed & helped with supper. Had so much company in eve. Alice's family. The cousins were out awhile. There were so many fellows come we didn't know what to do. I am to have a date with a fellow from Philipsburg. I did turn ... But Kinfore out & took me for a ride. Surely like him a lot. He kissed me for the first time we ... He is so sweet; the only thing he went home at 11 o'clock. Then I had Roy Dunsmore from Philipsburg. He was real ...

IT'S THE BERRIES!

Life as a Co-Ed in the Roaring Twenties

Author's note to the reader:

If I were limited to one word in describing Mary Alice Thompson it would be "unpretentious." In so saying I urge the reader to take the effort to know her, as a quick first read through her diaries might lead one to assume that Mary Alice's life at Drexel was uneventful and repetitive. It was neither.

What her diary does is what diaries do; it provides a "slice of life," an account in which the narrative is truncated. Don't make a mistake and gloss over her shortened sentences. This is the perfect story through which to read "between the lines."

The joy in the reading is in getting to know Mary Alice and her foibles, finding common ground even if you are not at all like her. The repetitions characterize her as being typical; accept that. And if you were ever a co-ed who lived in a college dorm, you will understand your own eye rolls as you read what she has written, never intending for us to intrude. Yes, she was naïve in many ways, but I guarantee you will find yourself identifying with her or, if like me you were not the typical crowd-runner, you will be confirmed in why you made the right choice!

Preface

In the 1920s in small towns across America, families were changing substantively. Young people were finishing high school and fewer were forced to leave school to help support their families. The designation of "classes" of people was slowly fading and group photographs of pupils (the term of the time) hinted that there were wide-spread levels of income.

The newly introduced "High School Yearbooks" (providing a high school had a yearbook prior to the 1920s)[1] help to clarify the differences between parents (pre-WWI) and their offspring (post-WWI). Youth enrolled in high schools and colleges after the Great War were involved with sports teams, music programs, literary clubs, and other activities not open to youth earlier. One can readily recognize those who were the class leaders, the popular ones, the ones with the income to support private music lessons, the ones "with a future"—and, of course, the ones with the recognizable family names.

By 1920 most Americans had put World War I behind them, fully assured that this had rightly been branded as "the war to end all wars," and most citizens did not expect that there would ever be another world war. Veterans of this Great War did not even entertain the *possibility* that their own sons would be called to bear arms in a war that would be larger in every way than the one just finished by their fathers.

Thus, the 1920s became a time of optimism, discovery, and independence. It was a decade for building a new social structure, in no small way led by youth. What is remarkable is that the young did not set out with a cause because there was nothing to "have a cause about." Rather, they viewed the world as their oyster with no war and no famine, but, instead, a sense of normalcy with a future that could be made into anything anyone wanted.

This was the same decade in which, for the first time, both women and men "went to college." By the end of the second decade, 20 percent of college-age Americans were enrolled in colleges, a rate unthinkable prior to the 1920s. In particular, this never-before influx of young women into "higher education" had a major impact and altered not only the make-up of college campuses, but also marked a definitive turning point in the lives of all young people.

The 47% increase in the number of women on campuses challenged the way both male students and faculty approached the classroom; further, it influenced many of the new activities found on the campuses, particularly social ones.

---

[1] The first high school yearbook, named "The Evergreen," appeared in 1845 in Waterford, NY. However, it was not until the 1920s that yearbooks began to include school activities and to cover more than just the graduating seniors. Sales campaigns began in 1925, supporting the cost of the publication through advertisements placed in the book itself. (*High School Yearbooks,* Witmer, 2014).

No longer was the young, post-high school female the typical Gibson Girl of yore who had been assumed to be attending "socials, taking music lessons, or playing tennis." Instead, a young woman "of means" would likely find herself as an active "Betty Co-ed"—depicted in drawings as an attractive, though cartoonish, slender being with shingled hair—who was dedicated to having fun more than studying.

On and off campus women were smoking openly, even though smoking in the 1920s was still highly frowned upon in most circles. On college campuses co-eds viewed smoking as a symbol of their new-formed *freedom*. The result was that this increase in smoking ultimately resulted in the creation of anti-smoking rules on many college campuses—and even expulsion for some. The rationale given was that such behavior as smoking would undermine the "approved expectations" espoused by many colleges. However, these rules had very little impact.

Worse than smoking, however, is that, according to many adults, these new co-eds were drinking prohibited alcohol and attending (gasp!) petting parties—all made possible with living far from home and family. Even though there were curfews and strict guidelines established by the colleges, these restrictions were nothing like what living at home had been and most of the young women were ready to enjoy their new-found freedom, and just "work around" the rules.

What might seem surprising to later college students—especially those who attended in the 1940s and 1950s—striving for high grades in the 1920s was not the main goal for most co-eds and a C was considered average, good enough for most of them. Many of the young women did not want to work for high grades, thus risk being viewed as a "grind" and, therefore, boring.

For most of these budding co-eds, "partying" itself was enough to demonstrate what they viewed as rebellion against their parents' Victorian guidelines. If that didn't work, they could blame life's uncertainty as a result of the World War. Best of all, they had the luxury of believing that they would not have to support themselves financially after college.

What was important in the 1920s was being viewed as *stylish*, women with bobbed and/or marcelled hair, short skirts, and rolled silk stockings. While men still wore jackets to class, "letter sweaters" were gaining popularity, along with yellow raincoats and, for the women, shorter skirts and open (flapping[2]) galoshes. Knickerbockers were worn on weekends by the men, some of whom found their roominess convenient for carrying flasks of "booze." And who could overlook **raccoon coats**, *the* mark of style for collegians—both women and men!

The most popular activity by which the collegians passed the time was at dances, both those sponsored by the colleges and in public dance halls, learning the Foxtrot, Lindy, Charleston, and, for some, the Tango, made popular by movies featuring Rudolf Valentino.

---

[2] It has been suggested that this was the origin of the term "flapper."

A typical dance hall

Most of the college crowd of the early to mid-1920s also flocked to the "silent" moving picture shows at least once a week, as the "talkies" didn't arrive in theatres until the late 1920s. Indoor pastimes included new games, with a craze among some young people for Mahjong[3], Ouija boards, and crossword puzzles.

Dating rituals took on new sexual boldness as petting parties became common, and, as one would expect, the newer enclosed automobile allowed for "joyriding"[4] as well as privacy in an enclosed car.

The 1920s has also been noted as the greatest decade in American literature with *Main Street* (Sinclair Lewis), *The Sun Also Rises* (Ernest Hemingway), *An American Tragedy* (Theodore Dreiser), and the lesser known, but rather captivating—especially if a reader enjoys an overdose of detailed commentary, *The Green Hat* by Michael Arlen.

---

[3] Mahjong is a free solitaire game in which the player is challenged to eliminate all pieces from the board by finding matching pairs of images from the end lines of the game's pyramid of pieces.

[4] driving fast and dangerously for pleasure.

Drexel Institute
Philadelphia, PA

Mary Alice Thompson
Home Economics
Class of 1928

September 1924-June 1928

"The 1925 Lexerd," the Drexel Institute yearbook of Mary Alice's freshman year, notes that "The graduating Class of 1928 entered Drexel Institute in September, 1924," while providing a photo of the 1925 graduating seniors from when they had entered in the fall of 1920 as freshmen; all were males. There is then a group photograph of the current freshman class (Class of 1928), also all males. This is quite disconcerting as we view it years later, noting that the hallowed Drexel was most definitely a male-dominated institution of higher learning at a time women were flocking to colleges and universities.

To make their statement even more clear, the following pages of the yearbook feature photographs of the sophomore, junior, and senior classes enrolled in the **Engineering** programs; again all are male.

Next is shown the **Junior College**, comprised of a Senior Class and a Junior Class, with accompanying text defining its purpose. These students are predominately males.

This is followed by a description of the **Library Class** and the **Business Administration Class**, followed by the **Drexel School of Library Science**. These photos show nearly all female students who would become librarians or work in offices.

The descriptions of program offerings then gives a nod to the **Junior Home Economics Class of 1926**. This narrative provides information that this is the first year on campus for a full Home Economics program.

Finally, there is a photograph of the **Girls'[5] Freshman Class**, followed by a qualifying paragraph whose language sends a clear message: "The morning of September 22, 1924,[6] *a rather timid appearing group of freshmen* begin a life to which they were destined ... matriculated in one of four programs: Library, Library Science, Business Administration, or Home Economics."

---

[5]   Note the use of "Girls" here after using the term "Men" in describing the other degree programs.

[6]   Cf. to Mary Alice's Diary entry following her first day.

Among these determined young women ready for launching is one who left a personal record by keeping a diary at this newly co-ed college whose reputation had been built on its challenging engineering curriculum in a 4-year degree program for men.

This enterprising freshman diary keeper was Mary Alice Thompson, from Curwensville, Pennsylvania, a town of approximately 1,500 residents. Mary Alice was to be one of a few women who took on the challenge of earning a degree in a program that while designed for females, was surrounded by all the traditions of a male-predominant university.

Remember, this was **ALL** new for our young, inexperienced co-ed.

Diary

of

Miss Mary Alice Thompson
Drexel Institute
Residence: 216 N. 33rd Street [7]
Philadelphia

September 21, 1924–December 31, 1929 [7]

Off to Drexel on the Train:

Sunday, September 21, 1924

At home. I got up about 6:30. Cecil[8] was up for breakfast to be ready to ride to Philadelphia with me. Packed our lunch. Bubby[9] went down to the train with us. Jessie[10] also went to the train with me and gave me a box of fudge. I said good-bye to Martin[11] at the station. Got in at the West Philadelphia Station about 5 to 10:00 a.m. Missed my "big sister" Florence Briseby who was supposed to meet me but she went to the wrong stop, so Cousin Cecil brought me out to the college. Went to a tea room for supper with some girls. My one roommate, Alice Kay, came in the evening. We talked awhile and took a walk. Florence lives in Philadelphia, not in the dormitory, but she stayed with Alice and me all night to make sure we were all right.

---

[7] Dates of the Diary: **September 21, 1924** through June 19, 1928 at which time a gap occurs. The diary resumes January 1, 1929 and ends **December 30, 1929,** exactly ninety years from the date of the transcription of its initial entries.

[8] Cecil Wall, her first cousin, oldest of four boys and a girl. Mrs. Wall and Mrs. Thompson were sisters. Cecil was an upper classman at the University of Pennsylvania. Cecil went on to prominence as the resident director of Mount Vernon, the home of George Washington.

[9] Mary Alice's older brother.

[10] Jessie Pifer, best friend and classmate in Curwensville High School.

[11] The local station master.

27

Monday, September 22, 1924

Went down to one of the houses[12] for breakfast and then went over to the school. Paid my money[13] and fooled around all morning. Went up to the Art Gallery. I danced[14] awhile, then went over to the Cafeteria for lunch. Came back up to the house. Went back to school at 2:00.

Wrote a lot of cards. Took a short exam in the morning. Dressed for dinner. Freshmen had a meeting at the house we take our meals in. They told us all the rules. Had another meeting at our house. I have to make another girl's bed for her until Xmas. Her name is Elizbeth Biddle. We also have to wear a card with our name on our backs for about a week.

Tuesday, September 23, 1924

I didn't hear the bell, so didn't go to breakfast. Had classes all morning and only one in the afternoon. June Frankenfield and I went down town in the afternoon after class. Our first trip. Bought stockings, hat, umbrella and a wedding present for Bobby. Had a freshmen meeting after dinner. Wrote to Jimmy[15] in the evening. Went over to a drug store.

Wednesday, September 24, 1924

Went to breakfast. Had classes all morning. Everyone had to go to assembly. Had a house meeting after dinner. Studied a little in the evening. Talked to Marjorie[16] at West Chester.

Thursday, September 25, 1924

Had classes every period. Fooled around before dinner. Studied in the evening and later we freshmen had to entertain the upperclassmen. I was in a "wedding" fashion show, wearing pajamas in one and rompers in another. The upper classmen then served hot dogs and we danced awhile. Stayed up late and shared a box of candy sent to me from Jimmy. We had fun.

Friday, September 26, 1924

Went downtown after lunch. Bought some things. Went up and saw Mrs. Kittelberger.[17] Wrote to Mama after dinner and goofed around all evening.

12 These houses were specifically designated for those in the Home Economics program. These were dormitories in the sense that the house contained a number of students, most of whom shared a bedroom. As in traditional dormitories, these also provided common areas on the first floor, including a kitchen, dining room, and large common room.
13 Tuition.
14 Dancing prevailed, as will be noticed.
15 Jimmy Strickland. Mary Alice had saved a dance card from Curwensville High School, April 2, 1923 in which his name appears as first on the program.
16 Marjorie Wall, first cousin to Mary Alice, sister to Cecil Wall; the only girl of 5 children. Same age as Mary Alice. Attended West Chester Normal School.
17 George Kittelberger (Curwensville High School Class of 1886) had moved to Philadelphia where he married Marcia Henderson in 1895. Their son is George Frederick, Jr. who apparently was born in Curwensville in 1896 and was graduated from Curwensville H.S. in 1914. He returned to Philadelphia as there is a draft registration for George Frederick Kittelberger, (b.March 20 1896) in Philadelphia. The residence in Philadelphia is given as 4529 Locust Street in 1942. There is evidence that George, Sr. remained or returned to C'ville where his headstone marks his remains. Apparently Mrs. Kittelberger had independent financial security in Philadelphia and remained there.

Saturday, September 27, 1924

Hadn't any classes all day. Went up to the library and studied all morning. Alice Kay and I went downtown in the afternoon and bought our drapes. I got a white belt. In the evening we had a party down in the court. The upperclassmen gave it for the Freshmen.

Sunday, September 28, 1924

We turned our clocks back today. Gained an hour. Went to a Presbyterian church with some of the girls. Wrote letters after dinner. Studied in the evening. Cecil called me up. Talked to him a long time.

Monday, September 29, 1924

Had a special delivery letter from Bubby this morning saying Jimmy was in an accident and hurt bad, but had another letter later saying he wasn't hurt much. I worried all morning about him. Hadn't any classes in the afternoon. Made our curtains and got our lamp today. Heard from Alice, Marjorie, and Frances.

Tuesday, September 30, 1924

It rained nearly all day. Katherine (roommate) and I went downtown after lunch. Went to my first movie at Fox Theatre. It was great. "Daughters of Today!"[18] The best orchestra played.[19] After study hour was at a feed in Betty Biddle's room. Ethel Buckley had a box from home.

Wednesday, October 1, 1924

Had classes all periods. Went to football game between Drexel and Penn. Penn won 46-0. Studied all evening. Wrote to Jimmy (Strickland).

Thursday, October 2, 1924

No mail all day. Had classes every hour. Didn't do much studying in the evening. Went over to drug store.

Friday, October 3, 1924

Didn't have classes in the afternoon. Came home and played 3 sets of tennis with Ann Robinson from Virginia. She beat me. In the evening a bunch of the girls went down to the Episcopalian Church to a dance. Saw Ty Cobb and Mahlon Roberts. They are freshmen at Penn. Ed Walton and Bill Kern. Came home about 11:30.

Saturday, October 4, 1924

Went down to the library and studied nearly all morning. Reba Frank and I went to the Drexel football game in the afternoon. Played Ursinus and lost 6-0. Stayed in all evening. Wrote an English comp. All the other girls are out.

---

[18] Mabel Vandergrift moves from the country to the city and enrolls in an upscale college. She starts to hang around with a "fast" crowd, and one night at a party a young man picks her for his "conquest..."

[19] A reminder that the movies did not yet have sound, so a live orchestra would play appropriate music. In small towns, a piano sufficed.

Sunday, October 5, 1924

Went to church with Alice and Katherine. Wrote letters and fooled around all afternoon. Alice's sister Helen was up with a bunch of girls who go to Miss Fellman's School of Kindergartners. Studied in evening.

Monday, October 6, 1924

Had a basketball meeting at 3:00. No mail all day. June had a big feed in her room. Almost all the kids in the house were there. Stayed up after lights and studied.

Tuesday, October 7, 1924

Went down town after classes with Katherine. Got a pair of gym shoes. After study hour Katherine and I went over in Ethel's room, when Mrs. Dorsey came in. (Ruth A. L. Dorsey, Dean of Women). We were supposed to be in our own rooms. I hid in the clothes closet. Was scared to death. Katherine was in the other room and beat it upstairs. and down again to our room. Had a special[20] from Jimmy. Guess he is trying to line things up.

Wednesday, October 8, 1924

Had classes every hour. Went to a tea dance in the art gallery after classes from 4—6. Had a real nice time. Danced with the cheer leader (Tommy Mather). Studied all evening.

Thursday, October 9, 1924

Had classes every period. Took my physical exam today. Studied all evening. Wrote to Mama & Jimmy.

Friday, October 10, 1924

Sewed all afternoon. In the evening I went down to Jack Hart's[21] to dance. Cecil was there. Also met Mitch Akers. Had a real good time.

Saturday, October 11, 1924

Made up some chemistry experiments in morning. Went out to lunch with Miss Dashiell. Went to the Copper Kettle for lunch. Saw Jack Thompson from Philipsburg. Was surprised to see him. Went shopping down town with Miss Dashiell. Went over to the Penn gym to a dance in the evening. Danced with two Japanese. One was from Hong Kong. Gee, they were funny looking and they probably thought I was.

Sunday, October 12, 1924

Didn't go to church. The other girls went. I stayed home and wrote letters. Had a date with a fellow in the afternoon. Kathleen Hill got him for me. He came up from Newark. His home is in Lancaster. Lester something was his name. Fooled around all evening.

Monday, October 13, 1924

June and I walked downtown. Went down Chestnut Street. Went all over the city and to a lot of stores. Studied hard all evening.

20 Special delivery letter.
21 Jack Hart's was a popular public dance hall. Hart was a musician-songwriter in the 20s and 30s.

Tuesday, October 14, 1924

Had a letter from Jimmy. It was so sweet. Made up chem. experiments in the afternoon. Went to basketball practice. So glad I was on our high school team at home. Studied all evening.

Wednesday, October 15, 1924

Wrote Mama. Had classes every period. There was a court dance[22] from 4 to 6. Had a pretty good time. Studied in evening until 12:00.

Thursday, October 16, 1924

Practiced basketball after school.[23] Didn't get up to house until after 5:00. Wrote a couple of letters and studied. Went over to drug store at 9:45. Saw an awful cute fellow.

Friday, October 17, 1924

Didn't have classes in afternoon. Washed my hair and fixed a dress. Went down to Jack Hart's in the eve. Had a pretty good time. A fellow by the name of Chester Snively brought me home. He belongs to Sigma Alpha Rho[24] fraternity.

Saturday, October 18, 1924

Went down to school in the morning to see Miss Dashiell. Wrote letters until lunch time. In the afternoon June and I went out to the football game. Drexel played George Washington and they won 13-0. In the evening I went down to Wrightman Hall. Had a real good time. Same fellow brought me home as did last night.

Sunday, October 19, 1924

Got up early. Went out to George School with Marian Newgold and Sarah Thompson. Miss Dashiell left about 8:30. Had breakfast at the station. Had to rush and eat our sandwiches as we went to the train. Took about an hour to get out to Newtown to a Friends Meeting. The boys and girls eat together in the dining room. In the afternoon a male teacher took us for a walk. A teacher invited us to her home for coffee after dinner. Got back about 6:30. Talked almost all eve. Wrote a letter.

Monday, October 20, 1924

June and I were downtown all afternoon. Got a wreath for my hair. Wrote Chemistry in the evening. Had some cake in June's room after study hour.

---

[22] Court dance originally meant formal dances done in royal courts. Later, and in the 20th Century they still implied a formal dance. However, at Drexel the dances were held in the large interior "court" area of the building and sometimes held during the day.

[23] Basketball for women (especially in a college with a predominance of men) was mostly intramural, with a number of girls considered a part of the team. As the program grew the *Lexerd* provided more than a full page describing the program in addition to a picture of the "squad" of nine who played varsity games. Mary Alice, who had played interscholastic basketball at Highland Hall, was part of the team at Drexel, but not part of the squad. At 5' 4" she held her own.

[24] This fraternity is not listed in the *1925 Lexerd* because it is a high school fraternity, albeit the oldest, continuously run, independent Jewish high school fraternity in West Philadelphia, Pennsylvania.

Tuesday, October 21, 1924

Met Alice Dorsett and Elinor Coen at Wanamaker's at 3:00. Went to 326 15th Street to see Mae Crider and Edna Kilpatrick. Stayed there a long time. Studied all eve. Wrote some letters.

Wednesday, October 22, 1924

Had classes every hour. Studied all evening. Nothing much doing.

Thursday, October 23, 1924

Decided last night to go to the dance Saturday night. Invited Cecil for Alice Kay. Played basketball after school. Went over to 214[25] for a while to study chemistry. Hope I get a nice man to take to the dance.

Friday, October 24, 1924

Our textile class went on a field trip to the McClelland Knitting Mills. Saw how silk stockings were made. Got back about 5:30. Met Katherine's mother and brother, William. Then Kay and I went down to Jack Hart's. Had a grand time. A man from Allentown walked me home. He was awful nice. I met a couple of very cute men.

Saturday, October 25, 1924

Four teachers from West Philadelphia High took Lois Hamilton, Sarah Bennett, Sarah Ann Sutliff, June Frankenfield, Eleanor Coen and me to Valley Forge. We were at Washington's headquarters and Memorial Chapel. We had our lunch with us or rather *they* did. Left at 10:30 and came home at 4:30. Had a wonderful time. Rushed to get ready for the dance. Had to shorten my dress, fix my nails. Didn't get to dinner. Cecil went with Alice Kay. We went to Overbrook Golf Club.[26] Had the best time I have ever had at a dance like that. Went with a Freshman from Penn, Paul Lutz from Altoona. We all went out in a big bus.

Sunday, October 26, 1924

Didn't get up until 10:00. We ate some pimento cheese sandwiches in our room for breakfast. Took all morning to clean the room up. Took a walk through Fairmount Park in afternoon with the girls. Wrote some letters and studied.

Monday, October 27, 1924

Only had classes until 12:00. Came up to the house and sewed and fooled around. Wrote up chem. experiments in the evening.

Tuesday, October 28, 1924

Studied in the library awhile after lunch. Edna Kilpatrick and May Crider were up for dinner. Didn't do any studying.

---

[25] One of the dorm houses. Mary Alice's was 216.

[26] Overbrook was one of the earliest Country Clubs in the country. Today it ranks among the best.

Wednesday, October 29, 1924

Came up to the house and studied in the afternoon. Went over to the drug store in the evening. Had lights out.

Thursday, October 30, 1924

Had a test in cooking; it was hard. At 4:00 I went to a tea in the art gallery for freshmen. Had a real nice time. Dr. Matterson and Mrs. M. gave it. Met a cute fellow from New Jersey (Mr. Wells). Had a special from Jimmy. I answered it. Esther Bucklew had a box from home. We had a big feed in our room after lights. Took a special lights out. Had olives, pickles, rolls, beef loaf, olive butter, saltines and cakes. Everything was wonderful.

Friday, October 31, 1924

Went downtown and got my fur coat in the afternoon. Made up some chemistry experiments. Went down to Jack Hart's in eve. Had a grand time. We had another feed in our room after lights. Pickles, chicken, ham, Maryland biscuits, jelly and cake. Didn't get to bed until 1:30.

Saturday, November 1, 1924

Fooled around all morning. Went out to West Chester after lunch. Got there about 4:15. Had to wait for about an hour and a half and then Marjorie Irvin took me up to the Normal[27] and I saw Marjorie Wall. She surely was surprised. Stayed there for dinner, went down to her room and then back up to school for an entertainment in eve. Met a lot of girls, went down to a couple stores, then up to Marjorie's room. We talked a long time.

Sunday, November 2, 1924

We got up about 9:45, ate some buns and cream puffs and coffee for breakfast. Went to church and then up to the school for dinner. Was up in some girl's room awhile. Went back to the house. The girl next door to Marjorie W. took Marjorie and me for a ride in her Ford coupe. Met this girl's brother, George Irwin, who goes to Swarthmore. Gee, I am crazy about him, but suppose I will never see him again. The girls took me out to meet the trolley to return to Philadelphia. Got back by 7:00. Went over to the Tea Rose with Katherine and got some supper. I was all undressed and studying when Sarah Bennett got a telephone call and a man was coming out to see her and bringing a couple more with him. Alice and I went with her. She had a terrible time getting permission. She told Miss Dorsey she was going out to Germantown. We went out at 8:45 and stood around on the corners and walked up and down the streets until 10:15. The boys couldn't find the house, so that ended. When we came in we laughed like fools. Of course, we told the other girls we had a grand time.

Monday, November 3, 1924

Wrote Mama. Went to a carpet factory in aft. It was very interesting. Went to a Methodist banquet at the Rittenhouse Hotel. Had a grand time. A man from Meadville brought me home. Jack Prather. He graduated from Allegheny and knows P.A.Z.[28]. He is also Leo's roommate. I liked him a lot. We came in and danced awhile.

[27] Normal School for Teacher Education. West Chester in this case.
[28] This seems to be Paul Zetler, who appears throughout in the Diary. See Cast of Characters.

Tuesday, November 4, 1924

Went to the football game today between Dickinson and Marien. D. lost 14-0. Hugh Norris [high school classmate, a student at Dickinson] took me. We had the best time. Met some cute Dickinson men. After the game we came up to the house and I got permission to go out until 8:00 p.m. Went down town to a movie and then went to "Buhl's" for dinner. We walked up Broad St. and through City Hall. I like Hugh a lot and he is going to invite me to a fraternity dance at Dickinson. I asked him to come up here to a school dance on Presidential Election Day.

Wednesday, November 5, 1924

Had classes every hr. Studied in eve. Elizabeth Biddle's two sisters were in our room all eve. They are real cute. Had lights out.

Thursday, November 6, 1924

Wrote to Bubby. Had classes every hr. Came home and fooled around. Studied in eve. Kathleen Hill had a friend up in her room. Had chicken and cake, bread and jelly.

Friday, November 7, 1924

Went over to Miss Illman's after school. Had gym for first time. Saw Betty Boyd. Had my first visit since I left home. I went over to Jack Hart's in eve. Had a date with Jack Prather. There was a fellow over there I liked so much. Wilson Norfleet. His home is in Cuba. He went to some school in Tenn. before coming to Penn.

Saturday, November 8, 1924

Had a special from Jimmy this morning. Went down town in morning with June. Got a black belt. After lunch a gang of girls from our house went out to Drexel Lodge near Wayne. They were Alice Dorsett, Alice Kay, Katherine Howd, Ethel Buckley, Mildred Larkin, Eliz. Biddle, Sarah Bennett, Mary Taylor, Dot Larkwood, Ruth Stout, Edith Knabb, Marie Hobbs, Ida Bromley, Mary Churchill, Ruth K., Kathleen Hill, Ann Robinson and Sarah Ann Sutliff. Went down to West Phila. Station and went out to Wayne, then to the Lodge in a "taxi."[29] Fooled around all aft., eve. Smoked, played cards, and danced. Helped get supper and had baked beans, hot dogs, rolls, potato chips, and coffee. Everything tasted so good. We never went to bed until 1:30 and nearly everywhere someone was awake. Slept with Kathleen in a little cot, but slept on the floor most of the night.

Sunday, November 9, 1924

Got up about 6:30. Went out and got some wood. It was snowing! I felt like I was at Greenwood Lodge at home. Helped get breakfast. Took a walk to a little store about ½ mile away. Got some stuff to eat. Fooled around the rest of morning and aft. Came in about 4:30. Everyone looked at us as we came out of the station. No wonder. Some dizzy man called up to me and wanted a "blind date."[30] I didn't give it to him. When we came into Wayne, Edith

---

29 Taxicabs were still fairly new and likely not familiar to Mary Alice; hence, her use of quotation marks.
30 Likely this was not a completely familiar term to her.

Knobb and I walked. Had date in evening with Jack Prather. He brought a couple of dates for Grace and Ethel. Those men were so cute.

Monday, November 10, 1924

Came up to house after lunch and washed my hair and fooled around. Studied in eve.

Tuesday, November 11, 1924

Armistice Day. We had school all day. Stayed for b.b. practice. Grace Johns gave a feed in our room after lights. Had beef loaf, potato chips, saltines, cheese, jelly, pickles, little cakes and grapes.

Wednesday, November 12, 1924

Had classes every hr. Studied and wrote letters in eve. Wrote Mama.

Thursday, November 13, 1924

Went to a court dance at 4:00. Had classes every hour. In the evening we had a feed in our room. Had loads to eat. Pickles, potato chips, buns, jelly, cheese, cake and saltines.

Friday, November 14, 1924

June and I went down town in aft. Fooled around in the stores. Stayed in in eve. We were not allowed to go down to Jack Hart's.

Saturday, November 15, 1924

Fooled around all morning. Met Cora and some girls at Wanamaker's at the "eagle."[31] Went to Chestnut Street Opera House. Saw "Battling Butler."[32] It was the first show I had seen here. It was real good. Went out to Beechwood[33] in the evening and got there about 6:00 p.m. Went to dinner. In the eve. I saw "The Confidence Man"[34] at the school. Played some bridge and ate.

Sunday, November 16, 1924

Didn't get up until 12:00. Went to dinner. Fooled around all day. Had the best time. Came back about 8:30. Had a date with Jack Prather.

Monday, November 17, 1924

Came home and studied all aft. Saw Jack Thompson when June and I went up to "Sophie's" for lunch. He didn't see me.

---

[31] This was a large statue near the entrance to the store. "Meet me at the eagle" became a catch phrase.

[32] "Battling Butler" is one of Buster Keaton's lesser known films, it is considered a great and hilarious film.

[33] Beechwood in Jenkintown was a private academic "finishing school" as described by a current online seller of a 1919 Yearbook. It must have been more than that since Alice had been graduated from high school in 1924. Considering what information is included in this Diary, my best guess would be that she had been accepted, arrived, and there was no rooming available for her for a few days, since she was told to return in a couple of weeks. Additional research led to the discovery that from 1925 to the mid-1960s, a campus of Beaver College, originally a girls-only college, was located on the site. This likely is what occurred.

[34] "The Confidence Man" is considered a lost silent film.

Tuesday, November 18, 1924

Played b.b. Went to a dance from 4–6. Had a real nice time. John Wandall from Allentown was over with June. I like him a lot.

Wednesday, November 19, 1924

Had classes every hour. Had a "special" from Jimmy. Oh, boy! A week from tonight!

Thursday, November 20, 1924

Went to the b. b. game after school. Freshmen (girls) beat the Seniors, 23-14. Got a box from home with a cake and some other things. Had a feast in Ethel's room.

Friday, November 21, 1924

Today is my birthday. Katherine & Alice gave me writing paper and Eleanor gave me a compact. Was at a court dance and rally for the Drexel-Temple game tomorrow. Met a couple of nice fellows. Had a good time. In the evening Cecil came in and I went out to Sharps. Bill Thorpe[35] was there. We played 500. Margaret Sharp was there also.

Saturday, November 22, 1924

Met Elinor Coen's brother Stanley. He is so sweet. I am crazy about him. Danced with him down in the parlor. Dottie Larkwood took him to the Junior Prom. In the afternoon, Alice and I went downtown. Got a pair of shoes. Lost my little pocket book and $1.00. Studied in the evening.

Sunday, November 23, 1924

Wrote to Bubby. Didn't go to church. Studied and wrote letters in the afternoon. Studied in evening.

Monday, November 24, 1924

Wrote some letters and studied in apt. Got a big box of candy from Aunt Maude. Studied all evening.

Tuesday, November 25, 1924

Had a letter from Jimmy and one from Marjorie. Came home after lunch and washed my hair.

Wednesday, November 26, 1924

Had classes from 9:00 until 3:00. Didn't get any lunch. A lot of the kids left today. Met Marjorie and Jimmy.[36] Went down to the train with Alice to see Ethel off. Was standing at the entrance of the station and saw Jimmy down by the cabs. I ran down and got him. He kissed me when he saw me. I didn't know if he would or not.

---

[35] from Clearfield.

[36] Just a reminder that this is Jimmy Strickland from Curwensville, not a student at Drexel. He was someone she cared for deeply, but who didn't meet the expectations of her parents.

In the evening I got Jack Prather to come over for Marjorie and we all went down to dance at the "Palace of Amour." Marjorie was all for going and so was I. There was an awful tough crowd there. The music was terrible. Danced awhile. Got something to eat at Hyler's and came out on the elevated. Went to a big feed up in Edith Knabb's room. Everyone in the house was there. Had chicken, nut bread and everything, celery, cake, candy, and filling.

Thursday, November 27, 1924

Went over to breakfast. Marjorie stayed in bed. Fooled around all morning. Took Jimmy and Marjorie both over for dinner. Had a wonderful dinner. In aft. we fooled around awhile and then Marjorie went out to Germantown. Jimmy and I took her to the station. I took them in the school. We came up. I went up to Jack's and then he and Jimmy brought me back to the house and they went to get something to eat. I didn't want anything. In the evening Jimmy and I went down to the Stanley Theatre. Saw Dick Barthelmess in "Classmates."[37] It was so good. Jimmy S. is so sweet. I wonder if I will still like him when I go home?

Friday, November 28, 1924

Met Marjorie at West Philadelphia Station about 12:00. We went out to Sharps. Cecil and Arthur[38] came in. We were there for lunch. Mrs. Sharp was there. Later Marjorie's Uncle Vern and Aunt May Wall came. We stayed until about 4:00. Then she went out to visit Chester and I came back to the house. Jimmy[39] and Jack came over. I went over to the Tea Rose for dinner with them. In the evening Jack Prather had a date with Edith Knabb and Ida Bromley had a date with her man. He (Steve) has a car and we took a ride, dear knows where. Bub King called me up and asked me over to his house[40] to a dance. Gee, I only wish I had gone. I am only hoping he will call sometime again.

Saturday, November 29, 1924

Jimmy came over after lunch. Was here all aft. We just talked and played the vic.[41] Went over to the Tea Rose with him for dinner. Went down in eve. It was pretty good. Came home in a taxi. He is so sweet to me and tonight he said he thought I didn't care for him as much as I used to. I really do not believe I do.

Sunday, November 30, 1924

Jimmy came over about 2:00 p.m. Was here all aft. We just sat in the parlor and talked. He was so wonderful to me. Went over to the Tea Rose for supper. Went down to the train with Jimmy. I didn't get caught. Kissed him good-bye.

---

[37] *Classmates* is a lost 1924 American silent drama film starring Richard Barthelmess, produced by his company Inspiration Pictures, and distributed by Associated First National Pictures. He is noted on the Hollywood Walk of Fame and was twice nominated for an Academy Award.

[38] Cecil's brother and, thus, cousin to Mary Alice.

[39] A reminder that transportation by train made it easy for traveling almost anywhere.

[40] Fraternity House.

[41] Victrola.

Monday, December 1, 1924

Gee, it was hard to go back to school again. Had a chem. test first period. Went down town in afternoon with Katherine. Got a new pocketbook and hat box. Studied in eve. Went over to drug store.

Tuesday, December 2, 1924

Had our tea in afternoon. Everything went pretty well. Didn't get to the dance until late. Studied and wrote to Bubby in the evening. Got a "special" from Jimmy.

Wednesday, December 3, 1924

Had cooking all afternoon. Studied in evening. Nothing much doing.

Thursday, December 4, 1924

June and I cut cooking class. I went downtown. Got a dress. Studied in evening.

Friday, December 5, 1924

Went downtown. It rained all aft. Got Mama a pen and something for Philip for Christmas. Went to Jack Hart's in evening.

Saturday, December 6, 1924

Sewed all morning and aft. Went to Wightman Hall[42] (Penn's gymnasium) in evening. Penn beat Drexel in basketball, 34 to 11. Stayed and danced afterwards. Met a cute fellow from the South. Bill Peavey.

Sunday, December 7, 1924

Wrote letters in the morning. Didn't go to church. Went out to Mrs. Foster's tea and then to Epworth League afterwards. Met an awful cute fellow. Dewitt Rosendale, a "Pitt." Ate with him at tea and walked to League with him.

Monday, December 8, 1924

Took a field trip in aft. to Quarter Masters Depot. Saw where they make all soldiers' uniforms. Studied in eve.

Tuesday, December 9, 1924

Played B.B. from 4 to 5. Came home and took a bath and studied after dinner. Boys from the fraternity came over and were initiating their new members. We had a lot of fun out of it.

Wednesday, December 10, 1924

Had classes every hr. Didn't get home until late. Studied in eve.

Thursday, December 11, 1924

Had cooking class until late. I was at the court dance with Jimmy awhile. Studied all eve.

---

[42] Originally constructed as a field house, this building is now part of the west edifice of Franklin Field.

Friday, December 12, 1924

Freshmen Home Ec. had a "Fair" in aft. I baked cakes and worked all aft. We had a big Xmas dinner over at the dining room. Had chicken and everything. Then confetti. In the eve. I went down to Jack Hart's. Danced with Bill Brown from Clearfield. A cute little boy brought me home. Mr. Zeck, or something like that.

Saturday, December 13, 1924

Sewed in the morning. Studied in aft. and eve. No mail. All the girls were down on our floor singing Carols and carrying on until 12:15. Stayed up until 1:00.

Sunday, December 14, 1924

Stayed in and studied all day. Wrote to Jimmy.

Monday, December 15, 1924

Had English exam in morning. Studied Chemistry in afternoon & evening.

Tuesday, December 16, 1924

Took Chem exam today. It was terrible. Don't think I passed. Fooled around all afternoon. Studied textiles in eve.

Wednesday, December 17, 1924

Had textile exam in the morning. June and I went down town in aft. Did a lot of shopping. Fooled around all eve. Studied cooking after lights.[43] Gene's birthday.

Thursday, December 18, 1924

Took cooking exam in morning. Found out my Chem grade. Got 53. Just got a Conditional grade,[44] but I think I will repeat the course. Had assembly in the morning at 11:00. There were a lot of Xmas trees in the court, all decorated. Every class had their own tree. Came home & fooled around all aft. and eve. getting ready to go home. Packed.

Friday, December 19, 1924

Left at 10:30. Met Cora at West Philadelphia Station. Julia Bullock got on in Lancaster and Sidney Korb in Harrisburg. Margaret Leitzinger and Ellen Johnson were on and five girls from Beechwood. Had a real good time. Had lunch on the train. Libby King and Helen Kephart got on at Tyrone. Jessie and Alice and Bubby were down at the train station to meet me. Fooled around all eve. Saw Jimmy.

Saturday, December 20, 1924

Went to see everybody. Was up at Mama Spencer's. In aft. I went to Clearfield with Alice, Jessie, Elizabeth Wall, Kate Smith, Genevieve and Cora. Went to all the stores. Went to the LR to a dance in eve. Had a grand time. Was with Jimmy awhile. He is so nice, only I want to break off with him. Saw a lot of the fellows. Gene Mc was up. Bubby brought me home.

---

43   Co-eds were expected to have the lights in their rooms out at a certain hour and be asleep in bed.

44   A grade given until the student did additional work or other demonstration of mastering the material.

Sunday, December 21, 1924

Mama and I went to church. Eliz. King was with us. Marjorie and Cecil came home last night. All of us girls fooled around all aft. Marjorie had a date with P.A.Z. in eve. We all went to church. Wrote Xmas cards after I came home.

Monday, December 22, 1924

Was down street in the morning. Mama and I shopped in Clearfield in aft. Was talking to John Leitzinger. Nothing doing in eve. Jessie and I fooled around awhile.

Tuesday, December 23, 1924

Got breakfast. Made candy all aft. Went down and helped trim the tree at the Children's Home. Jessie, Alice, Mildred Leib, Mrs. Satelle and I went. Was up at Jimmies in eve. Talked to Jimmy.

Wednesday, December 24, 1924

Went to the stores. Fooled around. Made some more candy. Was with Jimmy over at Pifer's. He gave me a wonderful looking dinner ring for Christmas. Was up at church to hear Philip's little speech. Jessie came over [The Thompsons lived on Thompson Street across from the Pifers.] and helped trim the tree. Went down to Uncle Charley's; took the presents down. Papa and Mama know about Jimmy being down to Phila. and about my writing to him and everything. I am going to have to give the ring back.

Thursday, December 25, 1924

Went to all the girls' houses in the morning and afternoon. We had our dinner alone this year. Went to the dance in the eve. Had a real good time. Jimmy Grant from Clearfield wanted to bring me home. I told J.S.[45] that I was not going to have anything more to do with him. He wouldn't take the ring back. I don't know what I am going to do about it.

Friday, December 26, 1924

Worked in the morning. Washed my hair and went down the street in the aft. Frances Custer came over on the evening train. Played pool awhile at the Walls[46] and listened to the radio.

Saturday, December 27, 1924

Worked in the morning. Took down the Xmas tree. Frances fooled around all day. In aft. I went to Clearfield with Alice and her mother and Jessie. In eve. we all went down to the dance. I had to come home at intermission. Frances stayed all night with Marjorie. They left the dance early and went up to Kings and played cards. Hugh Norris brought me home.

---

[45] Jimmy Strickland

[46] The Walls had a small pool table in their third floor, a finished area that was a playroom. (Some years later it was this author's bedroom.)

Sunday, December 28, 1924

Got dinner. Mama and Papa and Katy[47] & Philip left after dinner for Florida. Cecil went with them as far as Harrisburg. In eve. all the girls were here for supper. We all fooled around.

Monday, December 29, 1924

Frances went home at noon. Went to Clearfield with Marjorie in aft. We went to a shower for Perdita Ardery in the afternoon at Marjorie Murray's house. Margaret Kelley, Alice M. Wall, Mary Shirk, and another girl were there.

Tuesday, December 30, 1924

Washed up the kitchen floor in aft. Alice and I went to the movies in eve. Jimmy met me afterwards and came up on the porch and talked awhile.

Wednesday, December 31, 1924

Went down to the Walls for dinner. Frances came over again on the evening train. Eliz. came up and Kenny and Murray and Orville Johnson were there.

1925

Thursday, January 1, 1925

Marjorie and Zetler[48] were up for lunch. Walked around all day. We all went up to Mama Spencer's for supper. In eve. I went to the New Year's Dance at the Dimeling Hotel with Hugh. Had a wonderful time. Got home about 1:30. He came in for a while.

Friday, January 2, 1925

Frances left on the morning train. Worked all day. Had a party in the eve. Alice, Bob H., Jessie, J. Holten, J. Strickland, Elizabeth King, Murray Clark, Catherine, Marjorie, and Zetler. Jimmy stayed until almost 3:00 a.m.

Saturday, January 3, 1925

Worked most of the day. Marjorie was up at Aunt Mary's for supper. In eve. Jimmy was here. Winfield Sykes,[50] Josie, Bubby & Catherine (Pifer) also stopped by.

Sunday, January 4, 1925

Worked all morning. Went up to Mama Spencer's. Was at Marjorie's for dinner. All the kids were at the train. Hugh and Bruce were on as far as Harrisburg. They took Marjorie and me into the diner car, which was the only place we could find to sit. Some fellows from Clearfield were along. Bill Brown, Saul Merkin, and Laurence Howe. At Harrisburg I met Leo Sutton from Altoona. Marjorie stayed all night with me. Cecil met us at the train. He and Leo brought us up in a taxi. We did a crossword (the newest craze) puzzle that I saved.

---

47 Today Katy would be referred to as an au pair. She lived with the Thompsons, likely did light housekeeping, but Philip would have been her primary responsibility.

48 aka P. A. Z., a science teacher at Curwensville High School.

50 Winfield Sykes, a Curwensville friend, appears in "All the Gentlemen Callers" and is on the cover.

Monday, January 5, 1925

Got up for breakfast. Went down to school and registered, and then Marjorie and I went downtown. We both got evening dresses. She went out to dinner with John and then went out to West Chester in evening. I wrote to Mama and redd things up a little.

Tuesday, January 6, 1925

Went down to school at 9:00. Had chem. lab. And English. Came up to the house. Wrote letters in eve.

Wednesday, January 7, 1925

Didn't have any classes until assembly. Had classes part of the afternoon. Came up and took Cecil's checkbook down to Hotel Bartram. Went down to basketball practice, then came back in the eve. Drexel boys and girls played Osteopathy Hospital and danced afterwards. Had a dance with Tommy Mathers and one with a Bowers fellow who plays on the team. Had a good time.

Thursday, January 8, 1925

Had classes every hour. Changed from Chem. 2 to Chem. 1. Went to B.B. practice. Studied in evening.

Friday, January 9, 1925

Didn't have classes after 2:00. Came home and fooled around. Went down to Jack Hart's in eve. Had a good time. Cecil was there for a while.

Saturday, January 10, 1925

Got up about 10:00. Fooled around all morning and aft. Went down to school in eve to a sorority party. Had a real good time. Got home about 12. Saw a little of the BB game. Drexel lost. Jack called up for a date.

Sunday, January 11, 1925

We all had breakfast in Ethel's room. Miss Corsey came up and found us using the grill and we got the devil.[49] Fooled around all aft. and eve. Jack called up for a date but I told him I was busy. I couldn't stand him much longer.

Monday, January 12, 1925

Wrote Mama. Had classes until 4:00. Came home and wrote a letter. Studied in eve. and talked about the house dance. Invited Bub King.[50] I only hope we have a good time.

Tuesday, January 13, 1925

Had classes every hr. Came home and got dressed. Went down to the Aldine with Cousin Anna.[51] Saw "The Ten Commandments." It was real good. She brought me clear up to the house.

---

49 See accompanying note of reprimand in the Scrapbook collection.
50 A friend from Clearfield who dated M.A. a number of times.
51 Cousin Anna Robinson, a possible 2nd cousin of Marjorie Wall. See Cast of Characters.

Wednesday, January 14, 1925

Got a box of candy from Jimmy. This is awkward. Wrote him a short note, the first I have written since I came back from Christmas vacation.

Thursday, January 15, 1925

Had classes until 4:00. Went to B.B. game. Drexel girls played Temple and won, 22 – 21. Some game! Studied in evening.

Friday, January 16, 1925

Cut English and Chem in morning. June and Edith & I went downtown. Came home and June and I had lunch in the bathroom. Had baked beans and cheese and crackers and pickles. In the evening Cecil took me down to the Stanton and saw Harold Lloyd in "Hot Water." We then came up to Jack Hart's. Had the best time. Had some good dances with Bill Brown. Wilson Norfleet brought me home. Gee, he is so sweet. I am crazy about him. I only hope I see him again sometime. Hope he liked me.

Saturday, January 17, 1925

Had 2 hr. classes in morning. Got some pans and things for school. Kathleen and I carried them up to the house. Went downtown and had my hair waved. Got some buckles for my shoes. Came up to the house and helped make sandwiches. Took a bath and fussed around and got dressed. We had a formal dinner at the dining room. Had an orchestra. It played for the dance afterwards at 3305 and 3307. We had our house dance. Bub King came for me. Had a wonderful time. They are having a big fraternity dance at Jefferson[52] soon. I wonder if he will invite me? I am not expecting him to.

Sunday, January 18, 1925

Got up about 11:00. Our room was a wreck. Tried to redd things up a little and went to dinner. Wrote 4 letters in aft. Had a blind date in eve. Not so hot. Kathleen Hill had some also. The crazy things brought us lollypops and pretzels. Had to stay up after lights to write Chemistry Experiments.

Monday, January 19, 1925

June and I had lunch in our room. Washed a lot of the party dishes. Got my permission from Mama and Miss Dorsey to go to Dickinson College on February 6 & 7. Wrote Mama & Hugh in eve.

Tuesday, January 20, 1925

All slushy. Had classes until 4:00. Played BB. Studied in eve.

Wednesday, January 21, 1925

Didn't have classes until 11:00. Had cooking from 12:00 to 4:30. Made bread. Alice and Kate and I made cinnamon toast in our bathroom after lights.

---

[52] Thomas Jefferson University was a private university in Philadelphia. Established in its earliest form in 1824, the university later combined with Philadelphia University.

43

Thursday, January 22, 1925

Today is Jimmy's birthday. I got the sweetest letter from him; also got a letter from Hugh. Went to the B.B. game after school. Drexel girls lost to E. Stroudsburg Normal, 20-27.

Friday, January 23, 1925

Went down town in the afternoon. On the subway we ran over a man. They put him in our (subway) car and took him downtown. Went down to Jack Hart's in eve. Had a wonderful time. Thornton Morris brought me home. He is a wonderful dancer. He cut in all the time. Norfleet was not there. Danced with a cute fellow from Drexel, Henry Stetina.[53] He cut in a lot and asked to bring me home. Hope he does tomorrow night from the game.

Saturday, January 24, 1925

There was an almost total eclipse of the sun this morning. We could see it very well. Was talking to Miss Dashiell down at school. Wrote letters and fooled around all aft. Went down to Drexel to the B.B. game in eve. June and Kathleen were along. We lost 30-33. Danced afterwards. Had the best time. Thornton Morris from Penn was there. He brought me home. We went into the corner drugstore and got some ice cream. Kathleen and Albert Mathers were along. Danced with Powers, met Jack Roberts. Henry Stetina is so sweet. I hope I get to see him down at school sometime soon.

Sunday, January 25, 1925

Studied up in Kathleen's room all aft. Nothing doing today.

Monday, January 26, 1925

Came up to the house 2 hrs. at noon. Went to the B.B. game after school. Played Philadelphia Textile School. It was an exciting game. We won 25-23.

Tuesday, January 27, 1925

Only had classes until 2:00. Came home and read. Fooled around in eve. Worked a crossword puzzle. Wrote a letter.

Wednesday, January 28, 1925

Had cooking from 12:00 to 4:00. Talked to Stetina for about an hour. Gave him one of my cinnamon rolls. They were good.

Thursday, January 29, 1925

Saw Stetina at noon and after school but not to talk to. Our cooking class went through Abbots Dairy in aft. Went up to Kathleen's cousins after school and to The Copper Kettle for dinner. It rained terrible. Had a party here in the house in eve. Farewell party for Eleanor Coen and Alice Dorsett. Alice is going to the practice house and Eleanor home. Elected Edith Knabb new house chairman.

---

[53] Member of the fraternity near the Home Economics building and a BMOC.

Friday, January 30, 1925

Wrote to Mama. Kathleen and I made fudge after school. It was real good. Went down to Jack Hart's in eve. The music was awful. Didn't have as good a time, but had some good dances. Eleanor left today.

Saturday, January 31, 1925

Went down town after classes at 11:00. Ate lunch at Horn and Hardart Automat. Was all alone. Got some new galoshes. Studied awhile in apt. Kathleen and I went out to her Cousin Susie's over the weekend. Had a grand dinner, steak and everything. Went to the movies. We were supposed to have dates afterwards, but the fellows had to work until so late they didn't go over. Susie and a girl who stays there and the girl next door, Frances and Kathleen, and I fooled around.

Sunday, February 1, 1925

Susie went down and brought us something to eat. Had breakfast in bed. Coffee, rolls, and bananas. Got up about 12:00. Fooled around all aft. The one fellow Bob who lives next door came over before supper and then after supper he brought Clarence over. Clarence and I danced a little. They had to leave early as they had dates. Kathleen and I left shortly afterwards. Stopped in drug store by the station and got something to eat. Studied in eve.

Monday, February 2, 1925

Washed some stockings. Fooled around. Had 2 letters from Hugh.

Tuesday, February 3, 1925

Had classes every hr. Was talking to Wells and Powers today. Wrote Bubby.

Wednesday, February 4, 1925

Miss Jones was not there today. We had a test and then left. Went up to see Susie with Kathleen. Got the things she gave us to take along. Packed some of our things. Studied in eve.

Thursday, February 5, 1925

There is a little boy down at school I would like to meet. I don't even know what his name is. Washed my hair and packed to go to Dickinson.

Friday, February 6, 1925

Didn't go to any classes today. Packed everything up and checked Kathleen's and my suitcase at the station. Had my hair curled at 10:30. Came back up to school, then went over to the drug store and ate some lunch. Kate, Alice, and Ethel went to the train with Kathleen and me. Helen and Irene and another girl who goes to school in New York went down along. Arrived at Carlisle about 4:16. Bruce, Hugh (Hugh Grant Norris, Delta Theta, from Curwensville and her date for the house party), and Raybold took us to Kauffman's where all the college girls and fellows hang out. Had something to drink. Went up to hotel Molly Pitcher. Got dressed and fellows came for us about 6:00. Went up to Hertzler Hall where the dance was. "The Merrymakers" from Lebanon played. They were wonderful. Went through the receiving line, then got a favor. Danced until 12:00. Had our picture taken. Threw confetti and had crazy hats. There was a roof we could go out on and the moon was wonderful. Was out there with Hugh and Bruce. They both kissed me. Hugh was drinking a little, but just enough to make him feel good. We carried on high, acting crazy, etc.

Saturday, February 7, 1925

Had our breakfast brought up to our room. The boys came up for us and took us up to Chapel. We sat in the balcony. All the girls and fellows looked back up at us. They gave Hugh a cheer. Went up to Kauffman's and had something to eat. Got a copy of *Dickinsonian*, their weekly school paper. Hugh had to go to a class, so they left us at the hotel. We went over to Metzger Hall, the girls' dorm, to see Isabelle Ward. She didn't come for a while, so we talked to her roommate. Was there for lunch with her. Met some cute girls.

Danced awhile afterwards. The fellows came for us and we went up to the house. Fooled around all aft. Was up in their room three times before dinner and once afterwards. Hugh took me down to see the dining room. We sat downstairs for a long time. I drank about a half glass of gin. It was not so good tasting but pretty "hot." Had more fun at dinner. Some of the fellows were rather "tight." Danced at the house. Went down to the hotel and dressed. Fellows went up to the house again and dressed.

Came back about 9:00. We went over to the "Wellington"—some joint. All the kids there were drunk except a few. Helen Mumford passed out (almost). Bruce was there with his girl. Went back over to the hotel. Had a good orchestra there. Had tables sitting around. All the Phi Delta Thetas had a room alone. All the fellows had something to drink. I had some ginger ale and something else. Sure did make me feel good but, oh, so dizzy. I felt the same in the aft. but not so bad. Had another drink of something up in the boys' room after dinner. Some of them were feeling pretty good.[54]

Sunday, February 8, 1925

Got up about 11:40. Hugh came up for us. Went down to some little restaurant and got something to eat. Went up to the frat house and fooled around. Was there for dinner.[55] Had to rush right from dinner to the hotel for our bags. The train left at 2:01. Gee, I hated to come back. Got in about 6:00. Went over to tea. Came back to house and talked all eve. Put things away and studied.

Monday, February 9, 1925

Had classes every hour. Came up to the house and fooled around. Hard to get down to school work again!

---

[54] Someone once said that Mary Alice is blunt. At the time I thought perhaps this was meant unkindly. Now I see it was not, but that the person who knew her perhaps should have used the word "candid," which is an apt description as it can include a sense of innocence, a characteristic Mary Alice retained.

[55] The term "dinner" is being used as the noon meal, a colloquialism; supper, the evening meal.

Tuesday, February 10, 1925

Had a Home Ec. meeting in afternoon from 3 to 4. Miss Bain, head of the National Home Ec. Club, spoke. We are going to start a club here in school. There was a tea afterwards.

Wednesday, February 11, 1925

Went down town in the morning. Spoke to the little light-haired boy today. Had a letter from Bruce (Norris); was so surprised. Jack Roberts asked me to the fraternity some Friday night at Drexel. Another surprise. Two in one day. Kathleen and I went up to see Susie and stayed with her for dinner at The Copper Kettle.

Thursday, February 12, 1925

Had a letter from Hugh this morning; also one from Bubby. (Wrote to Bubby in eve.) Card from Mama. (Wrote Mama.)

Friday, February 13, 1925

Didn't have any classes in afternoon so June and I came up to the boys' fraternity Phi Kappa Beta with Bob Fox and helped decorate. Had the best time. Sammy Jones was helping out. I am crazy about him, but he goes with Ruth McCullough and is crazy about her, so no hopes for me. Went down to school again at 4:00 to a party the Senior girls gave for the Freshmen. Had an orchestra, danced and had refreshments. Went over to the fraternity dance with John "Jack" Roberts. Had the best time. There was the sweetest boy who played "traps" in the orchestra. He looked almost exactly like Gene McKenzie. I would love to meet him. After we all came home, about 1 o'clock, we were all making so much noise and Miss Dorsey came up and bawled us all out. It was funny, but we all have to report ourselves to student government.

Saturday, February 14, 1925

Went out to West Chester in aft. and had dinner with Marjorie. Danced over in the gym until 7 o'clock. Went down to Irvine's. Went down to the drug store. Met a lot of fellows. Went back up to Irvine's, and a cute fellow Bill (Patterson) came up. We all danced. He sure could dance.

Sunday, February 15, 1925

Got up about 10:30 and got some breakfast. Ruth Parker was there; she graduated from Drexel. Went up to school for dinner, Marge Irvin came up for us, drove downtown, got some candy. Walked down again with some fellow. Bill was up again in aft. Came back at 7:45. Had a date in eve. with Wilton Wright. He goes to Drexel and lives over in the Phi Kappa Beta house. He is real nice.

Monday, February 16, 1925

Cut Art Class and went down town. Came home then and fooled around.

Tuesday, February 17, 1925

There was a court dance at 4 o'clock. Danced with Wilton Wright, two with Jack Roberts, Burr, and Joe. Had a real good time. I would give anything to go out with Stetina. He is so sweet. Hope I see Norfleet at Jack Hart's Friday night. I am only hoping I get a bid to the "Ivy Ball" at Penn next month.

Wednesday, February 18, 1925

All departments had their assembly together today. Miss Dashiell spoke to the Home Ec. girls. She came in our cooking class awhile afterwards. She is the sweetest person. I am just crazy about her. Went out to Suzie's after school. Patty Kirk called up and is expecting me out over Saturday night.

Thursday, February 19, 1925

Went to girls B.B. game. Played Penn. Lost 30-31. Game was up in Armory.

Friday, February 20, 1925

Went downtown in aft. Went to Johnson Art Museum.[56] Met May Crider and Louise Taylor down on Broad St. She is married. Miss Dorsey wouldn't let me go out in eve. Stayed in and sewed on a blouse.

Saturday, February 21, 1925

Met Marjorie at West Philadelphia station and we went out to Kirks. They have the sweetest house. In the evening we went to a party. The first part of the eve. was a Christian Endeavor party, then we went out and rode around the block and came back again and danced until 12:00. There was a cute fellow there by the name of Bob. The boys were all young and Patty and Jane seem older.

Sunday, February 22, 1925

Got up and went to Sunday School and church. Cecil was out at Kirks for dinner. We talked all aft. Came in about 7:00 and Marjorie stayed all night with me. I had a date with Jack Roberts. We sat in the house until 10:00, then went out and walked around until 12:00. Marjorie stayed with the girls. Have a date with him Friday night.

Monday, February 23, 1925

Marjorie and I went down to the movies to the Stanley. Saw Thomas Meigan in "Comin' Through."[57] Came back up to the Tea Rose for lunch. Smoked over there. Marjorie went out to West Chester and I went out to Susie's. Kathleen was out there. Had dates in eve. until 3:00 a.m. Went to the movies first. Kathleen was with John Wandall and I was with John Joseph, an awful nice fellow from Penn. He lives in Ohio and his father is Vice-president of Goodrich Rubber Co. or Fire Co. or something like that. Only trouble is I found out he is a Catholic. I was never with a fellow like him; he was so different. I just wonder what he thought of me. I am going to find out sometime.

---

[56] When Attorney John Johnson died in 1917 he left his enormous art collection to the city — nearly 1,500 pieces, the vast majority Renaissance and Dutch Masters paintings.

[57] "Comin' Thro the Rye" is a 1923 British silent drama film.

Tuesday, February 24, 1925

Had classes every hour. Was talking to Jack Roberts at noon. Had practice at 4:00 for Friday night. Went to girls BB game; we beat Ursinus 35–25. Powers was down talking to me. Wrote to Bubby.

Wednesday, February 25, 1925

Went down to Assembly. Cut cooking class. Came up to the house and washed some things. Slept for about an hour and a half. Went down to school after dinner to practice for the Vaudeville show Friday night. Sammy Jones was there. He is the sweetest boy.

Thursday, February 26, 1925

Wrote to Mama. Had an English quiz today. Don't think I passed. Went to a lecture on "Milk" at 4 o'clock. Went down to school in eve. to practice. Had a telephone call from Joe, the fellow I was with Monday night. He is so sweet. I hope I see him again soon.

Friday, February 27, 1925

June and I went down town in aft. Went to the Art Museum. Then had my hair washed and curled. Went down to school. Had our vaudeville show ("Cap and Bells") in eve. Had pictures taken afterwards. Had a date with Jack Roberts. Talked to Stetina a couple of minutes.

Saturday, February 28, 1925

Had our house bridge party in aft. In the evening Cecil and Bill Thorpe came over and took Florence Kreutzer and me to the Penn State BB game. It was a wonderful game. State lost 36-24. Saw Mahlon and Nev. Robb, Edna Kirkpatrick, Tommy Mensch, Ty Cobb, Bill Brown, and a fellow from Clearfield over there.

Sunday, March 1, 1925

Studied all day. Didn't do much else. It rained all afternoon.

Monday, March 2, 1925

Came up to house for 2 hrs. at noon. Studied all eve. Alice, Kathleen and I threw some doughnuts out the window to some fellows and talked to them a long time.

Tuesday, March 3, 1925

Went to Penn-Drexel girls BB game after school. We won 15-14. It was terribly exciting. Studied all evening. At 9:45 Kathleen and I went down to 210, Joe Liese's apartment. I was with another fellow. They have the cutest place down there.

Wednesday, March 4, 1925

June and I went down town in the morning and got flowers for our luncheon. Went back to school and prepared my luncheon. Had it at 1 o'clock. Had Kate, Alice and Kathleen. Went off pretty well. Had cream tomato soup—croutons, stuffed egg salad, potato chips, olives, baking powder biscuits, oatmeal crisps and tea. Had cooking class all aft. Went to first half of Boys' BB game. They lost 37-25. Went to a tea given by Miss Chapman. Studied all eve.

49

Thursday, March 5, 1925

Had cooking until late. Had two telephone calls in eve. John Joseph called me and Bud somebody from 210.[58] Wrote to Mama.

Friday, March 6, 1925

Kathleen and I went downtown in aft. Went to a million stores. Got a jumper dress. Stayed in at night. Eleven girls on our floor are campused for 2 weeks ago for when we were all up at 1 o'clock and raising the devil and Miss Dorsey came up and bawled us out. The restriction is over Monday night.

Saturday, March 7, 1925

Marjorie, Zetler, Cecil and Marge Irvin were here for a while in the afternoon. Kathleen, Ann and I went up to the Tea Rose and had some ice cream and smoked. Walked around until 7:15. Studied in eve.

Sunday, March 8, 1925

Kathleen and I went up to Jack Hart's for church. It was real nice. In the afternoon we went for a ride in a cute little Ford with Joe Lease and Bud Minner. They both live in 210 right up the street. Took some pictures. Joe called me in the evening.

Monday, March 9, 1925

Gave my report in "Art." Studied all evening.

Tuesday, March 10, 1925

Was dead tired after school. Took a bath and dressed before dinner. Had a date in eve. with John Joseph. He was so sweet. I wonder though when I will have another date with him.

Wednesday, March 11, 1925

Had an indoor gym meet after school. Freshmen won. I was in the Marching and Obstacle Race. Studied all evening.

Thursday, March 12, 1925

Got out of cooking 1 hour early today. Talked to Mathers and Charles Arthur before coming home. Studied in eve. Went over to drugstore. Joe didn't call me. I am disappointed, as I thought he would. Cecil called me tonight.

Friday, March 13, 1925

Went to the court dance. Danced with Albert Mathers, Jack Roberts, and Eddie Powers. Powers asked me to go to a high school fraternity dance with him. I like him a lot. Went down to Jack Hart's in eve. Bill Brown from Clearfield brought me home. Had a dance with Norfleet.

---

[58] This would be the address of one of the fraternities.

Saturday, March 14, 1925

Kathleen and I went down town all aft. Fooled around at all the stores. Had a formal dinner over at dining room. Kathleen and I went for a ride with Joe Liese for a while, then went down to Drexel BB game. We lost 17-23. Played Junior Varsity Penn. Someone called me three times while I was out. I wonder who it was?

Sunday, March 15, 1925

June and I went to church at Walnut Street Presbyterian. Started to study chem., then Joe and Bud came for Kathleen and me and took us for a ride. Went way beyond Norristown. John Joseph called me before tea. He is so sweet. I can hardly wait until I have another date with him. In eve. Bud called and also Wilton Wright. Wright wanted a date. I studied chem. all eve. until late.

Monday, March 16, 1925

Took Chem exam in morning. Only hope I passed. It was awful hard. Came up to house and fooled around and studied a little English. Had a card from Mama; they expect to be here tomorrow. I am only hoping they will wait until Friday and take me home along.

Tuesday, March 17, 1925

Took English exam in the morning. Found out I passed my Chem I. Got 69 in exam and 75 as average. Sewed on blouse part of the afternoon. Was looking for Mama and Papa all aft. Papa called me up and I went down to the Bartram Hotel where they are staying. Mama came back up here with me for dinner. I am going home along. Gee, I am so anxious to go. In the eve. Mama & Papa & I went down to the Broad Street Theatre and saw "New Brooms."[59] It surely was good. Came home and studied bacteriology.

Wednesday, March 18, 1925

Went down to the hotel after breakfast and Mama, Katy, and Philip and I went downtown. Chased around to all the stores. Got a coat, dress and slicker. Had lunch at Wanamaker's. Came up to school and took bacteriology exam. Went back down town and met Mama. Got a school dress and Mama got some things. Had our dinner then went up to the hotel. Called Cecil. Brought Philip up to the house awhile. Papa came up for him. I studied cooking after he left.

Thursday, March 19, 1925

Took exam in cooking this morn. It was simply terrible. Went up to hotel and went to lunch at the Blue Lattice Inn with Mama, Katy, and Philip. We went downtown then and met Papa and Mrs. Kittelberger. Got a new hat and gloves. Went to Stanley; saw Dick Barthelmess in "New Toys."[60] It was very good. Went and got dinner, went up to the hotel.

[59] William Churchill de Mille, the older brother of Hollywood legend Cecil B. DeMille and father of Tony Award-winning choreographer Agnes de Mille. was an American screenwriter and film director from the silent film era through the early 1930s. He also specialized in adapting Broadway plays into silent films.

[60] A noted actor with a star in the Hall of Fame walk, Barthelmess also was a founder of the Academy of Motion Picture Arts and Sciences.

Mama & Mrs. Kittelberger came up to the house with me. I am not going home along. Am going down to Kathleen's. Grace and I took Kate down to their train at 11:30 p.m. Came home and June and I studied. Alice went home today.

Friday, March 20, 1925

Took Art exam in morning. It was not so hard. Went down town in aft. and had my hair waved and washed. Kathleen and I went to the flower show. Were a little late for dinner. Jack Roberts called for a date. Went down to Jack Hart's. Came home with Kathleen and John. Joe went up to New York to see his Mother & Dad.

Saturday, March 21, 1925

Went down to train with Kathleen, then went over to the Tea Rose for breakfast. Had the best cinnamon toast. Came over to house and fooled around. Wrote letters in aft. Joe came around and took me out in the car. I drove it part of the time. Had loads of fun. He came over in the evening and I went out to the movies with him. Was supposed to have gone out with Grace and Betty Biddle.

Sunday, March 22, 1925

Got up at 6:30. Started for Kathleen's at 7:15 with Bud and Joe Lease in the Ford. Went through Elkton. They live near Kennedyville. Went to SS. Met some of K's cousins. After dinner we went up to Chestertown. Drove all around. Met Elizabeth Dukes. Came back to the house and fooled around. The boys left for home about 9 o'clock. Kathleen and I ate chicken sandwiches, then went to bed.

Monday, March 23, 1925

Sewed in the morning. Went into Chestertown in aft. Went up town and fooled around. Met some of the kids. Went to bed early.

Tuesday, March 24, 1925

Sewed in the morning. Kathleen and I drove by horse and buggy into a little town. Came back and baked a cake. Packed suitcases in eve.

Wednesday, March 25, 1925

Got up about 6 o'clock and Mr. Hill brought us into Elkton. Got back at school about 10:45. Registered and came up to house. Fooled around, unpacked. June, Kathleen, and I went up to see Susie. In eve. had a date with Joe Joseph and Kathleen had one with John Wandall. Joe is so sweet. I am just crazy about him, if only I thought he liked me.

Thursday, March 26, 1925

Had classes every hr. Talked to Bud awhile. Stetina looked so sweet today. Joe didn't call me. I was supposed to go about at 9:45 and see Bud, but couldn't be bothered.

Friday, March 27, 1925

Went downtown in aft. Got flowers for coat and some things for Philip. Went down to Jack Hart's in eve. It was awful dumb. No one there.

Saturday, March 28, 1925

Sewed and fooled around all morning. Went out to West Chester after lunch. Went up in Maud Allen's room after dinner. Margie Irvin and I went downtown after dinner.

Sunday, March 29, 1925

Didn't get to see Bill Patterson. Marjorie and I slept until 12:00. Went to the Overton for dinner. Then went over to Marge's awhile. Went over to her room and wrote to Hugh. They took me into 69th Street in Margie's Ford. Went down to the train with Grace, Kate, and Florence to meet Alice. Studied after lights. Wrote to Bubby.

Monday, March 30, 1925

June and Edith and I went downtown after classes. Got material for pajamas and a scarf. Wrote letters and studied in eve.

Tuesday, March 31, , 1925

Went in the library awhile and studied before coming home. Studied in eve. Nothing much doing. Don't know if I will go home for Easter or not.

Wednesday, April 1, 1925

Had cooking all afternoon. Went to Home Economics meeting at 4 o'clock. We had our dinner served backwards on account of its being April Fool's Night.

Thursday, April 2, 1925

Went through Reading Terminal storage section of the market in afternoon. The best looking man took us through. He was so nice. Mr. Carroll. I don't see why Joe doesn't call. I would like to ask him to the Senior dance, but I won't if I do not hear from him soon.

Friday, April 3, 1925

Came home at 1 o'clock and dressed. Went down to a Tea Dance. Had a real nice time. Wilton Wright walked up with June and me after the dance. Went down to Jack Hart's in eve. Had a wonderful time. John Joseph was there. He didn't ask to bring me home until after another fellow did. I came home with a Mr. Johnston. He is very nice. Said he could call me up. I just wonder if he will. He belongs to a fraternity. Jack Prather also asked to bring me home. Danced with some nice fellows, Paul Johnston, Kappa Sigma.

Saturday, April 4, 1925

Didn't have any classes. Sewed all morning. Had a date in the evening with Bud Minner and Kathleen was with Joe Liese. Went down to the Fox and then went over to Bud's Uncle Frank's house for about an hour. J. J. called me up in aft. He is coming over tomorrow night. I am going to ask him to the Senior Dance.

53

Sunday, April 5, 1925

Alice and I went to church up at Jack Hart's. They were having Communion services there. Studied after dinner. About 5 o'clock Kathleen and I went for a ride with Bud and Joe. Paul Johnston called me up. Also Cousin Anna and Marjorie. Marjorie is going home Tuesday In the evening I had a date with John Joseph. He is so sweet, but I cannot yet quite make him out. I don't believe though that he cares much about me; he is different though.

Monday, April 6, 1925

Wrote some letters. Am not going home for Easter. Could not study in eve. Hurt my neck in gym class. Strained a nerve and I cannot turn my head. It hurts awful at times.

Tuesday, April 7, 1925

Didn't go to school all day. Stayed in my room most of the time. Laid down nearly all morning. Studied some in aft and evening. Went down to the 3:33 train to see Marjorie off. Cecil called me after dinner; he is going to hike home tomorrow.

Wednesday, April 8, 1925

Had classes every hour. Dot and Alice and I went to Miss Dorsey at noon about keeping the house open. After dinner we all went in to Miss Dorsey's office. The house is going to be open so we can stay.

Thursday, April 9, 1925

The girls must all have gone away today for vacation. Had classes until 4 o'clock. Went down to station with Jane, Alice, Edith, and Dot and I fooled around after dinner and then went up to the Waffle Shop. Smoked and ate. Walked around awhile and came home.

Friday, April 10, 1925

Alice and I went down town after breakfast. Went up to see Peg Alexander at her apartment. She and two other girls have a darling place together. She invited Alice and me down. Alice and I went to Ventura Gardens for lunch and smoked. Came up to house again, dressed and went out to Jenkintown. Her cousin Mrs. Stone and Bunny and Eleanor met us. Went out to their place. When Mr. Stone came we went for a ride. Talked after dinner. Alice's Uncle Joe came. They all brought us home in the car. Had a feed in our room after we got home. Mama sent me a box. Cake, pickles, cheese, nuts, candy and cookies. Got bread and made sandwiches. I had 3 telephone calls. I think Hugh Norris is in the city. I only hope so. I am dying to find out who all called.

Saturday, April 11, 1925

Was fooling around after breakfast when Hugh Norris came and surprised me. I was so glad to see him. His little cousin was along. We took a walk out through the park. It was wonderful out. After lunch we went out to Alice's cousin's with her. We didn't stay very long. Hugh called about 5:30 and then he came over in the eve. about 8:30. Alice and Hugh and I went down to Peg Alexander's apartment. Alice and I stayed there all night. Hugh and I went up to the Mandarin Café and ate and danced, then went back to the apartment.

Jack Prather had called me last eve. for a date. I got him and another fellow again this morning. Went out to 63rd St. and played tennis. Marjorie was here when I came back. Went down to the trolley with her. John [Shearer] was supposed to meet her, but missed her somehow. He came up here for her. He is so crazy. I have a date with him tomorrow night.

Wednesday, April 15, 1925

Wrote some letters after school. Had a date in eve. with John Berryman Shearer. He goes with Marjorie sometimes. He is rare. Brought me a box of candy and 2 magazines. Told me all the time how nice he thought I was, how much he adored me, etc. Such craziness.

Thursday, April 16, 1925

Sewed all eve. and night. Had classes until late afternoon.

Friday, April 17, 1925

It rained all afternoon. Went up to Johnson & Johnson. I had my hair washed and curled. Dressed for the dance after dinner. John Joseph, John Wandall and Carl Hoffman all came together for June, Kathleen and me. They came late so we taxied all the way out to the Pelham Club in Germantown.[61]

Had the best time. John is so sweet, I don't know if he cares much for me or not. We all came back in a taxi also. Just got here at 1 o'clock. Had the most wonderful time.

Saturday, April 18, 1925

Got up late and went over to the Tea Rose for breakfast, then June and I walked out to 63rd St and came back on the El.[62] Sewed all aft. Went down town with June, then sewed in eve.

Sunday, April 19, 1925

Got up late and fooled around. Sewed all afternoon. Studied and wrote letters in the evening.

Monday, April 20, 1925

Came up to the house at 2 o'clock. Went down to the court dance at 4:00. Had a real nice time. Had a couple good dances. Powers[63] was not there. I only wish Stetina would dance with me. That old John Joseph has not called yet.

Tuesday, April 21, 1925

Through with classes at 2 o'clock. Went out to Miss Jones' apartment with Jane Heath and Marian Newgold. Miss Jones and Miss Stephen and Miss Michaels have the cutest apartment. I have to cook my demonstration dinner there the 20th of May. Had a house meeting after dinner. Wrote Mama.

---

61 The Pelham Auto Club was Pelham's social institution, "with billiards, a bowling alley, a dining room, a ballroom, card rooms, and a garage with a full-time mechanic." 28 Sep 1936 Pelham Club Became the First Home of Germantown Jewish Centre. The Centre leased the auditorium for $200 a month.

62 El is short for "elevated," and refers to the train, which takes riders from the Frankford Transportation Center to 69th Street; the track is elevated above the city except between 2nd and 40th streets, where it runs underneath Market St.

63 Eddie

Wednesday, April 22, 1925

Cut cooking class and came home at 2 o'clock. Wrote letters and finished laundry. Studied in eve. Had a big feed in our room in eve. Grace got a big box from home. We carried on until real late.

Friday, April 23, 1925

Was awful hot out today. Had classes every hr. Fooled around after school. Took a walk out in Fairmont Park after dinner. Studied in evening.

Friday, April 24, 1925

Had classes until 2 o'clock. Came up to the house and fooled around. After dinner John Wandall called up and Jim and Kathleen & I went out with him and John Joseph and Ted somebody June was with. Went down to the Stanton and saw "Charlie's Aunt."[64] It was a scream. Went up to the Rittenhouse and danced. Edna Kilpatrick was there. Was so surprised to see her. Had the best time. We all went out to Sue Krusens and stayed all night. The boys stayed until 2 o'clock. Joe is so sweet, I am crazy about him, but I hardly think he cares much for me.

Saturday, April 25, 1925

Got up about 8 o'clock. Came down to school with Kathleen. June and I came up to the house and went over to the Tea Rose for breakfast with Edith. John Scherer called me up after lunch. June and Edith and I went downtown in aft. Went to the stores and then to see Cullen Landis in "Cheap Kisses."[65] Rained in eve. June, Ann Robinson, and I went out on supposedly blind dates and here it was John Scherer. I never felt so cheap, as I had told him I could not have a date. I made the best of it. We went up to this one fellow's apartment. June was with Bill Simmons. He is a Senior and belongs to A. T. O. fraternity at Penn. I am crazy about him. Lost 1 hour tonight. Daylight saving begins.

Sunday, April 26, 1925

June and I went to church at Jack Hart's. John Scherer came up about 2:30. Went out for something to drink, then we three, he & June & I, went out to his home at Kirklyn.[66] Met his mother and dad and sister. They are all lovely. I cannot stand John, though I am supposed to have a date with him on Friday night, but I am going to break it. We got the car and went for Bill Simmons, but he was not home. Came into Tea Rose for tea, then went back out and got Bill & rode to 8:30. Joe Joseph, John Wandall and Ted were here twice in a Hudson Coach to take June and Kathleen and me for a ride.

---

[64] "Charley's Aunt" is a farce in three acts centering on a college undergraduate whose friends persuade him to impersonate the aunt of one of them. A popular play, then movie in 1925.

[65] ...a 1924 silent drama film starring Jean Hersholt as a famous sculptor. By C. Gardner Sullivan Productions, it was described as "a virile, fast-moving, jazzy story of the present day and age."

[66] A suburb of Philadelphia near Upper Darby.

Monday, April 27, 1925

Cut sewing class. Was vaccinated up at the infirmary[67] in the morning. Came home at 2 o'clock and fooled around, sewed, and then Kathleen and I took a walk in eve. Called Joe to ask him to the house dance, but he was not in. Left word for him to call tomorrow night.

Tuesday, April 28, 1925

Wrote a letter after school. Sue came over in evening and asked for permission for Kathleen and me to go to the dance tomorrow night with Joe & Bud. We are going to go stay at her place all night. John Joseph called up tonight. I asked him to the house dance but he cannot come. He is going to Allentown with John Wandall. Guess I will ask Paul Johnston. Hope he can come.

Wednesday, April 29, 1925

Had classes until 4 o'clock. Came home and took a bath. After dinner called up Paul Johnston to invite him to the dance, but he was going to Princeton and couldn't come. Kathleen and I went to a Phi Gamma Sigma fraternity dance with Bud Minner & Joe Lease at the Majestic Hotel. The music was wonderful and that was all. Stayed all night at Sue's.

Thursday, April 30, 1925

Came in from Sue's to school. Cut cooking and went down town with June. Got my dress pattern. Called Ty Cobb in eve. to come over to dance and he couldn't come. I am having a hard time and Kate is having Bill bring someone over for me. I hope he succeeds in getting someone. Leo Sutton is coming for Marjorie, Cecil for Florence, and Bill Shope for Mildred.

Friday, May 1, 1925

Didn't get anywhere in eve. Stayed in and helped decorate. Had a good time. Most of the girls were in. Bill, Kate's man, is bringing a fellow for me for the dance.

Saturday, May 2, 1925

June and I went down town right after breakfast. Got my dress material. Chased all over looking for cheap flowers. Got corsages for Mrs. Scott and Miss Dorsey. Marjorie called after lunch. Went up to dining room and helped fix tables and ice cakes and cut up chickens. Had a real good time working. Came back to the house and dressed. Marjorie came about 5:30. Went over to the formal dinner. After dinner we had our house dance. I was with Bob Way. He was real little. I didn't care much about him. Marjorie was with Leo Sutton and Cecil was with Florence.

Sunday, May 3, 1925

Got up about 10 o'clock. I went up to help tear down the decorations at the dining room. Went over to the Tea Rose and ate some breakfast. Then went over again with Marjorie. She and Kathleen and I walked out through the park. Came over and took pictures after dinner.

---

[67] Likely a requirement to be vaccinated before spending any length of time or even to visit schools; this would be a regulation for college students in the Home Economics Education program.

Marjorie left about 3 o'clock. Fooled around. Reba came with her cousin in a Pierce-Arrow car and took a gang of us for a ride. We all went over to the Tea Rose for tea when we came back.

1925 Pierce-Arrow

Monday, May 4, 1925
Came home at 2 o'clock and sewed. Wrote letters and studied in eve. John Joseph called. He is so sweet. Have a date with him tomorrow night.

Tuesday, May 5, 1925
Played tennis at 63rd St. with Ann Robinson. Rode a bicycle after dinner. Had loads of fun. Had a date in eve with John Joseph. I like him better every time I am with him. June was with Leonard Bland.

Wednesday, May 6, 1925
Had classes until 4 o'clock. Fooled around before dinner. Studied in eve.

Thursday, May 7, 1925
Had class until 5 0'clock. Went to a Jell-O demonstration[68] for 2 hrs. in aft. Studied in eve. Was looking for a call from J.J., but didn't get it.

Friday, May 8, 1925
Played my tennis tournament at 4 o'clock. Edna Forney beat me first set of 6-4, 6-0 and 6-4. June and I were at the horse show for a couple of hours. Saw some beautiful horses. Went down to Jack Hart's in eve. John Joseph was there. He brought me home. We got out early, then took a little walk. I never saw him so wonderful. The moon was out beautiful. Paul Johnson was there. We took a little walk. Had the best time. Had a big feed in Ethel's room after lights. **Miss Dorsey was out so we had a good time making a lot of noise.**

Saturday, May 9, 1925
Was supposed to meet Eliz. Wall at 8:30 at Reading Terminal. Missed her somehow. Got ready to go out to Drexel-Paul[69] after lunch and left for there about 2 o'clock. Had more fun going out on the train. Sat on platform of last car. Walked out from Wayne. Took several walks during the afternoon. Smoked some and picked some flowers. Helped get supper. Cooked weiners.

---

[68] After an inauspicious beginning in the late 1800s this undeveloped product finally emerged into the Jell-O Company in 1923. Two years later it merged with Postum Cereal, and eventually, that company became the behemoth known as the General Foods Corporation. Very likely General Foods would have been promoting this product in nascent—and captive!—Home Economics colleges.

[69] Possibly part of the Drexel Paul estate, later to become Gulph Mills Country Club near King of Prussia and Wayne. The Drexel-Paul Mary Alice is describing is the same place, but before the estate was first (1929) given to Drexel Institute to use for a camp for football and events for the students. Prior to 1929, the "lodge" would have been more primitive, but still very serviceable and appealing to the students.

Walked again after supper. Went in and played cards a while with Miss Dorsey. June and Reba and I started out for a ride with 3 fellows from Wayne. They took us too far away and then we got a tire puncture and at 12 o'clock were 8 miles from camp. I was scared to death. We asked some man to bring us back; we were lucky to get back without Miss Dorsey finding out!

Sunday, May 10, 1925
We all slept until 9:30. Had breakfast and fooled around. Read and walked. After dinner we started back. Started to walk but got a ride all the way into Wayne. Had more fun coming in. Had the best time. Studied awhile. Joe called about 8:15. He couldn't get me any earlier. He was so sweet. I like him so much.

Monday, May 11, 1925
Came home at 2 o'clock. Sewed after dinner and studied in eve.

Tuesday, May 12, 1925
Stayed in Chem. lab until 4 o'clock. Took bath before dinner. Studied all eve.

Wednesday, May 13, 1925
John Joseph called about 8 o'clock. Had a date with him, but I was not supposed to have a date as I am reported (deficient) in two subjects. Miss Dorsey called me in and bawled me out. Liz Fontaine told her I had a date. Don't know when I will see Miss Dorsey again as Mama and Papa will be here this weekend. Had a letter from Mama in the morning.

Thursday, May 14, 1925
Worked hard at school all day. Sewed until a quarter of six. After dinner went down town and met Mama & Papa at Broad Street Station. Went to hotel with them, then came back home and sewed. Wednesday they went to the Stanley (Theatre at 19th and Market Street).

Walnut Street Theatre in Philadelphia

Friday, May 15, 1925
Had classes until 2 o'clock. Met Mama at Wanamaker's at 2:30. Got a pair of slippers. Fooled around at the stores then went up to the Robert Morris Hotel. Had dinner there after Papa came. Alice Kay came down then and we went to the Walnut St. Theatre[70] and saw "Broke."[71] It was real good. Mama and Papa are leaving in the morning and are going to stop at Bellefonte for the day.

Saturday, May 16, 1925
Ann Robinson had a date with John Joseph last night. I should worry. Went downtown after lunch. Got dress material. Had a lawn fete over on 34th Street from 4 to 10. I asked Joe to come over but he was going out.

[70] The oldest theatre in the United States. This vintage photo is circa 1925.
[71] *Back Home and Broke* is a lost 1922 American silent comedy film.

Sunday, May 17, 1925
Didn't get up until after 11. Had a date with Joe in afternoon. June had one with George somebody. Took a walk through the park and took some pictures. I do not think Joe cares much for me anymore. I am so worried that I will not get to the dance on Friday. Studied in evening.

Monday, May 18, 1925
Went down town about 3. Got pattern and material for blouse. Came up to school to the Court dance. Had a dance with Eddie Powers. He is so nice. Went to Kathleen's dinner at 5 o'clock. It was awful good. Studied in eve. Was brought up before Student Government tonight about having a date Wednesday night. Do not know the verdict yet.

Tuesday, May 19, 1925
Went out to 63rd St. at 2 o'clock to practice for gym meet tomorrow. Got a box of candy from Jessie. Studied in eve. The Fellows from the fraternity were over here initiating some of the boys. One of them had to propose to me.

Wednesday, May 20, 1925
Had classes every hr. Went out to 63rd St. to track meet at 4 o'clock. Freshmen won. Was talking to Powers a couple of minutes. Had late dinner. I was in the relay and jump. Joe Joseph called me in eve. He is going to call again tomorrow night.

Thursday, May 21, 1925
Had classes every hr. Got out late. Sewed in eve. Joe was supposed to call but didn't.

Friday, May 22, 1925
Talked to Paul Burr about an hour at noon. Had my hair washed and curled up at Johnson & Johnson after school. Went down to the Freshmen-Senior dance at the Girard Craftsman Club.[72] Took John Joseph. Had a wonderful time. Kathleen was with John Wandall.

Saturday, May 23, 1925
I am campused from tonight until next Thursday. Sewed and fooled around all morning. Went downtown in aft. It surely was hot. Had a chance for 2 dates, one with Jack Prather and one with Bob Way. I would like to have had a date with Jack.

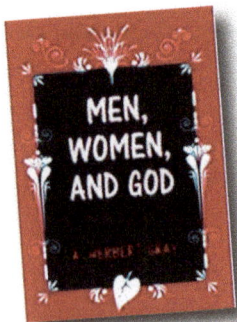
MEN, WOMEN, AND GOD

Sunday, May 24, 1925
June and I went to church in morning to Walnut Street Presbyterian. It rained in aft. I stayed in and studied and also in eve. Had an hr. interview with Miss Dorsey at 10:15 at night until 11:15. She was telling me about how Joe acted at the dance the other night. She read me some more stuff out of a book, "God, Men & Women." I would never say so, but I don't think she should have done this.

[72]   incorporated July 11, 1921.

Monday, May 25, 1925
Talked to Paul Burr quite a while in aft. after Eng. Class. He invited me to the Soph. Hop at the Belleview Strafford Hotel on Saturday night. June and I went downtown. Got things ready for the birthday dinner. Joe has not called me since the dance Friday night.

Tuesday, May 26, 1925
Came home at 2 o'clock and made favors to decorate the table for the birthday dinner. Our table looked real nice. Went down to school in eve. to practice for Thursday's play and the fashion show the Home Ec. department is giving.

Wednesday, May 27, 1925
Cut cooking in aft. and studied for English Composition. Think I passed English. Went down to school in eve and practiced for the Home Ec. play tomorrow. Got home about 11:15. I am supposed to be campused.

Thursday, May 28, 1925
Had the Home Ec. play in afternoon. Had a tea in the Art Gallery afterwards. In eve. Joe called for a date but I couldn't have one. He and John Wandall came over and brought June's scarf over. I stood at the top of the steps and talked to him for about 20 minutes.

Friday, May 29, 1925
Went down to Jack Hart's in eve. Had a grand time. John Joseph brought me home. Paul Johnston asked, too. Mama sent my new dress today.

Saturday, May 30, 1925
Sewed all day. In eve. went down to Belleview Strafford to the "Sophomore Hop" with Paul Buss, a fellow from Drexel. He lives in Princeton, NJ. The dance was on the Roof Garden.[73] It was up 18 stories. It surely was wonderful up there. Had a grand time.

Sunday, May 31, 1925
Worked on cooking notebook nearly all day. Had a date with John Joseph in eve. John Wandall was over with Kathleen. We took a walk out through the Park. They got us Cokes over at the drug store and June brought us each some cake.

Monday, June 1, 1925
Finished my cooking notebook. Went to a big fire, down on Chestnut St. almost across from Drexel, after dinner. It burned down 2 large buildings. Studied in the evening.

Tuesday, June 2, 1925
Had 2 hrs. of chem. class in aft. It was terribly hot all day. I about baked. Joe called after dinner. He's going to call again on Thursday or Friday. Worked all evening.

---

[73] The hotel is still offering the rooftop.

Wednesday, June 3, 1925

Had a lot of things in Assembly. Today was "Institute Day." Didn't have school in aft. R.O.T.C. marched out at 63rd St. I had to go out to Overbrook to Miss Jones' apartment to cook my dinner. Had potato salad, cheese and nut sandwiches, pineapple sandwiches, olives, cherry ice cream, and iced tea nut wafers. It was pretty good. Came in at 10:00.

Thursday June 4, 1925

Turned in Chem apparatus in morning. Sewed all aft. until 4 o'clock tea. Papa is here and called after dinner. I talked to him. He wanted me to come down to a show tonight but I had too much to do. Worked on my blouse all night. Went to bed about 2 o'clock.

Friday, June 5, 1925

Had classes every hr. at school. Last day of classes. Had a date in eve. with Piggie Burr. He never left until 10:45. No one rang the bell. He is going to write to me.

Saturday, June 6, 1925

Went down to school awhile in the morning. Went down town, got a hat and some things. In aft. went out to Kirks in Germantown to a Tea. It was real nice. Had a date with John Joseph in eve. Last date this freshman year. He was so sweet. Asked if I would write if he did. Papa called again for me to go down to a show with him. But I couldn't.

Sunday, June 7, 1925

Terribly hot all day. Packed trunk. Studied Chem in eve. Am scared to death of it.

Monday, June 8, 1925

Took Chem exam in morning. Only hope I passed it. Went down town in aft. Got dress material for Alice Wall and myself. Was down on 4th St. Some rare places. John Joseph called in eve. Have date with him tomorrow aft. Hugh Norris called me from Harrisburg.

Tuesday, June 9, 1925

Didn't have any exams today. In morning Paul ("Piggy") Burr came over and took me for a ride. In aft. had a date with John Joseph and Kathleen with John Wandall. Went down to the Stanley. They stayed until 8:30. Cecil called me.

Wednesday, June 10, 1925

Had Cooking and English exams. Passed Chem. Talked to Burr. Met Harold Tatman, a fellow I have been speaking to in passing for a long time but never actually talked to. John Joseph called me up before his train left. He wanted to know if I would forget him. How could I? I think he is the sweetest boy I ever met. Went out to Mrs. Kittelberger's all night. Frederick[74] came for me. Fooled around all eve.

Thursday, June 11, 1925

Trunks left this morning. Had sewing exam in aft. Went up to say goodbye to Cecil. Had a date in eve with "Piggy" Burr. He is coming down to the train tomorrow to say goodbye.

[74] See story on the Kittelbergers in separate section.

June 12, 1925 – September 18, 1925

Friday, June 12, 1925, Curwensville

Went down to the station. June and Kathleen went down along. "Piggy" Burr came just as the train was leaving. Came with 4 girls from Punxsutawney. Pauline Snyder's mother and brother met us in their car. They brought me home along. In evening we chased the streets. J. Holten took Marjorie, Marge Davis, Jessie and Alice and me for a ride. Libby King came home tonight also.

Saturday, June 13, 1925

Put some of my things away in the morning. Went down to the stores in aft. I went down street for a while in eve. Uncle Charley (Wall) took us all over to the dance at the Park.[75] Libby, Marge, Marjorie and Jessie and I. Had a real good time. Came home at 11:30. Alice was with Hugh Norris. I danced with J. Strickland.

Sunday, June 14, 1925

Went to church with Mama. Was up at Alice's. They discussed the soldiers monument[76] in afternoon. Didn't do anything in eve.

Monday, June 15, 1925

Unpacked my trunks in the morning. Worked around house. Was up at Aunt Mary's for supper. Went to movies in eve. with the girls.

Tuesday, June 16, 1925

Played 3 sets of tennis with Hugh Norris in aft. over on Irvin Hill.[77] Alice had the car in eve. Rode to Clearfield and on towards Grampian. Went over to the dance awhile. Not many there. Didn't stay long. Went to bed early.

Wednesday, June 17, 1925

Papa took Marge and Marjorie and me up to Mahaffey to the coal mine.[78] Went through the whole mine. Martin Ardrey and John Wright took Jessie and me up on the hill to see the Beacon Lights, lit for the airplanes to see by night.[79] Saw Strickland's baby; it is the sweetest thing; I could love it to death.

---

[75] Four years earlier in 1921 Mr. and Mrs. Hugh Irvin gave the town a large property along the Susquehanna River on the South Side of Curwensville. It was known as the Pee Wee's Nest, later Irvin Park. It became a natural center for town events and a pavilion was built for dancing.

[76] Erected in the area in front of the Dr. Elmo Erhard property. This "Doughboy" monument, or Soldiers' Memorial, was donated by Col. Edward A. Irvin and dedicated on Flag Day 1925.

[77] The tennis court was downriver from the Log Cabin used by the football players as a field locker room. This was flat land as the football field was located at the flat area (perhaps excavated and perhaps already flattened by nature along the Susquehanna River used for logging). We considered Irvin Hill itself as the residential area on top of the hill.

[78] This would be one of the mines owned by her father, Howard J. Thompson, president of the Cassidy Coal Company, among other holdings.

[79] Typically the term is used to describe a tower with a light that turns or in some way attracts the viewer; its purpose is to warn, in this case, airplanes to be aware of the terrain or buildings or for an airplane which is picking up a canvas bag containing mail.

Mary Alice visiting one of H.J.'s coal mines at Mahaffey

Thursday, June 18, 1925

Had letter from A. Kay today. Went over to the "Park"[80] in aft. Stayed for supper. Danced in aft. Billy McClure took me in to dance. Danced with Bruce. Had a date with Billy in eve. Bob Daugherty had a date with Alice. He has a big Nash car. They took us for a ride to DuBois. Didn't go to the dance there. Just went over and looked in.

Friday, June 19, 1925

Got up early and went over to Bellefonte. Saw Bobby, Louise Taylor, Marg. They are all married. I feel so old! Was up at Hall's awhile. Mark Hunter took me and got me a sundae. Talked to Joe Katz. Was down at Marjorie's after I came back. Dave McKinley and his friend were down there. They walked up with me.

Saturday, June 20, 1925

Went out to Greenwood Lodge after dinner. Took our suppers out. Aunt Grace went along. Also Aunt Mary and Verne Wall. Marge Irvin was with them. Took a walk to "Bear Run."[81] Went over and talked to Bruce. Was going to stay and let him bring me home, but didn't.

Was up on top of tower. Sidney Korb took the Marjories and myself over to the dance for a minute. Went in and danced once with Bill McClure. Sidney took me for a short ride. I drove his car a little.

Sunday, June 21, 1925

Jessie left for Clarion today.[82] (Described in *All the Gentlemen Callers.*) Went to church with Mama. In afternoon Bill Snyder took Libby and me for a ride. Had a date with Billie McClure in eve. Went up to Alice's most of the eve. Came down the street and J. Holten took us for a ride to Grampian. Got home pretty late. Billie wants me to go with him steady. **Nothing doing.** I'm not going steady with anyone.

Monday, June 22, 1925

Sewed all afternoon. Hugh came up and wanted a date but I had one; then he wanted one on Tuesday and I have one then so he asked for Wednesday. I am afraid Alice might not like it so well. Mama will have a fit when she finds out I have another date Wednesday. Had a date with Sidney Korb tonight. Nothing doing again. I drove his car all around. I would have died if I hadn't had something to do.

---

80 This would be Irvin Park on the south side of the town along the Susquehanna River. There was a pavilion there for dancing.

81 Bear Run is a stream that runs through parts of Clearfield County, including the area on which sits Greenwood Lodge. Its reservoir was easily accessible at Elliott Park, outside of Clearfield.

82 Jessie, as most young women who found themselves with few choices in life, had joined these ranks and attended Clarion State Normal School which offered courses for those who chose to be teachers. The Normal Schools offered summer programs which led to a certificate to teach grades 1-8.

Tuesday, June 23, 1925

Was down at Walls and Kings for a while. Had a date with Billie McClure in eve. Alice was with Bob Daugherty. We took a ride first, then went over to the dance at the Park for a while. Billie makes me tired. I don't want any more dates with him. He is getting tiresome already. There are hardly any fellows around here I can stand to go with. I hope I have a date with Hugh tomorrow night. The Richlens from Bellefonte were here.

Wednesday, June 24, 1925

Sewed in the morning and aft. Packed suitcase to go to Bellefonte. Had a date with Hugh Norris in eve. Went to the movies at Clearfield. Saw "A Thief in Paradise."[83] It was real good. It just poured rain here.

Thursday, June 25, 1925

Left early for Huntingdon. Went over to Commencement at the Reformatory.[84] Was there for dinner and supper. Left for Bellefonte about 6:30. Mrs. Heverly took Mama and me down to Heckla Park to dance.[85] Had a real good time. Danced with Phil, Ray, Jim Bower, Bill, and John.

Friday, June 26, 1925

Pressed dresses and went down to stores. Wrote to Kate & Howd. Was down at Richlens and in at Katz with Mary & Louise. Mama and Papa went home. Came up to Hills for supper. In eve. had date with Joe Katz. Bill Seig asked me for a date tomorrow night. Went for a ride. Was up at the aviation field. Saw 5 planes come in and go out at night. The field looked beautiful. Joe is so nice. I like him a lot.

Saturday, June 27, 1925 (still in Bellefonte or perhaps State College)

Stayed with Marjory Fri. and Saturday nights. In morning went downtown with Eleanor. In afternoon went out to American Line office with Marjory. She had to work awhile. I went shopping. Got a new hat. In eve. had a date with Bill Seig. He is very nice. I am crazy about him, but I doubt if he likes me much. I would love to hear from him.

Sunday, June 28, 1925

Eddie Miller and Marjory brought me home in the coupe. Left in the morning and stayed at Custers for dinner. Got them a lunch and they started back. M. Wall and I walked up to Cousin Dema's in eve. awhile. Jimmy Johnson, Bob Wright, and Hugh Norris took Alice and Marjorie and me for a ride. We were up in Lumber City and Bells Landing. Some ride!

---

[83] *A Thief in Paradise* is a 1925 American silent film, produced by Samuel Goldwyn, adapted from Leonard Merrick's novel *The Worldlings*. One of many lost films.

[84] H.J. was on the Board of Corrections (later, the Board of Trustees) and the family always attended the graduation for those who completed the requirements for a high school diploma. At this time it was known as the Huntingdon Reformatory for Young Offenders, later as the Huntingdon Industrial School. M.A.'s scrapbook contains the Commencement Programs.

[85] In Centre County, a small amusement park with a dance pavilion.

Franklin Sedan

Monday, June 29, 1925

Helped here at home some. Had a date with John Wright in eve. First date ever with him. Libby was with Leonard Kantar. He had the Franklin.[86] They took us out to Seldom Inn.[87] Had something to drink. Some time! Came in to Jim Booth's (restaurant in Curwensville) and got something to eat.

Tuesday, June 30, 1925

Sewed in afternoon. Took Philip and Mary Rider (his au pair) to the movies in evening. Listened to radio awhile.

Wednesday, July 1, 1925

Cut the grass in the morning. In aft. Marjorie took Mama, Aunt Grace, Mama Spencer and me down to Clearfield. Did a little shopping. Had a date with Billie McClure in eve. There was a dance in the Park. We went in and danced until they as much as put us out. Gee, I was mad. They might have told us initially that it was *private*.

Thursday, July 2, 1925

Sewed all day. Went down to the Presbyterian Church festival for some ice cream and cake. Alice and Marjorie and I went to the movies.

Friday, July 3, 1925

Went up to Ebensburg with Uncle Francis, Aunt Roxie, Darl, and Bobby. Had our lunch with us. Went in and danced some. Came home about 8:30. Frances Custer came over from Philipsburg. Marjorie and Alice met her. I didn't see her until the next morning. She and Marjorie went to Dubois with Kay Wrigley and Byron McDowell. I went downtown with the girls awhile and came home and went to bed early.

Saturday, July 4, 1925

Went down to the parade at Clearfield in morning. It was real good. In aft. Alice Wall took us down to the Park at Clearfield. Danson and I went on some of the rides at the Carnival. Merry-go-round, Whip, Caterpillar, Airplane, and Ferris Wheel. Had loads of fun. Came up to Marjorie's for supper. Went down to the dance in the evening with Marjorie, Byron, and Russel Price. Had a pretty good time. Went on the swings and Ferris wheel. Kay Wrigley brought us home. Alice and Hugh were along. Got home at 1:30 after taking some kids home to Grampian.

Sunday, July 5, 1925

Had a picnic dinner over at the Park. Katy's sisters were down from Sykesville. Mary Rider went home with them. Went to bed early.

---

86 America's most successful air-cooled automobile, with its first innovative air-cooled motorcar in 1902 and continued production until 1934. A status car, and the same make as the car later owned by H.J.!

87 Tionesta, Forest County, PA. The restaurant is still in business near Cook Forest.

Monday, July 6, 1925

Worked in the morning. Marjorie and I went down to Clearfield to the dentist in afternoon. Wrote 3 letters in eve. and went down to the movies.

Tuesday, July 7, 1925

Went to Clearfield with Marjorie in afternoon. Saw John Leitzinger to speak to. In eve. Alice and I went to the movies. Talked to J.S.,[88] the first in weeks.

Wednesday, July 8, 1925

Alice and I went down to Clearfield. I had a marcel. Went to the "Chatterbox" for supper. Had date with George Wrigley (first date) in eve. Alice was with Hugh. Went over to the Park to the dance. Wright's Colored Orchestra played. I surely had a good time. Never felt more like dancing in my life. The boys had something they gave Alice and me a taste of to drink. It didn't taste good, but it made my head dizzy.

Thursday, July 9, 1925

Pulled weeds out of the driveway all morning. Was over at the Park a while with Marjorie. Had date with Jimmy Holden in eve. First one in a couple of years. Took a ride. Had trouble with the car and had to be towed into the Bigler Garage. We waited for an hour or more.

Friday, July 10, 1925

Helped clean upstairs in morn. Packed our lunch and went out to Greenwood for supper. D. P. Wall[89] and C. M. Wall families and Fredrick Conklin were along. Had a real good time. Was up at the top of the beacon light, 80 feet.

Saturday, July 11, 1925

In the eve. Alice and Marjorie and I took John Wright's car and rode to Clearfield. We were over at the Park and had a flat tire. Billy McClure and Howd Milligan fixed it for us. I came back over to the dance with Billy. Danced with J. Strickland.

Sunday, July 12, 1925

Mama and I went to Church. Alice got Fredrick Conklin's Franklin in aft. and we rode around. Marjorie was with us. Raymond called for a date, but I had one with George Wrigley. Hugh was with Alice.

Monday, July 13, 1925

Marjorie, Dick, and I went swimming over at the riff raffs in aft. In evening George Wrigley, Hugh Norris, and Alice and I took our suppers out. George had their Franklin. Ate up near Bells Landing. Had a nice lunch and some whiskey to drink. I had 2 cups mixed with ginger ale. I was deathly sick, never hope to be so sick again. I believe I was clear gone a couple of times. The rest of them were scared. We stopped up at the school house. I tried to walk but couldn't. It was a terrible feeling. Never again for me. Got home at 11:30. Was scared

---

[88] Jimmie Strickland.
[89] Dillwyn Parrish Wall and Charles Miles Wall, brothers, sons of Miles.

to come home. Mama was on the front porch. I went to bed and she came up and talked to me. I felt a little better then. We rode up Bloomington Hill and got out and walked a little.

Tuesday, July 14, 1925

Went to Clearfield with Marjorie in aft. I didn't feel good all day. Mama and Papa left for Philadelphia in aft. Took Philip to movies. Marjorie went along.

Wednesday, July 15, 1925

Heard this morning that J. Strickland had another accident with his car. He and Orvis were coming down Bloomington Hill and ran into a freight train. I guess they were both drunk. If Jimmy could only behave himself. For some reason I was worrying about Jimmy the night before. Guess I must still like him. Marjorie, Libby, Dick and I went swimming at riff raffs. Had date with Bruce Norris in eve. He came in and took me out to Greenwood with him. Never again. I didn't like the looks of things. He surely is rough. I don't care much for such stuff when I am not crazy about the fellow. I like Bruce, but I don't like to have anyone act like that towards me. I just wonder what he thinks.

Thursday, July 16, 1925

Made some candy and sent it to Kenneth. Went out to Greenwood for supper with Aunt Grace. Dema and Lew were there and the McKendrick girls, Beth and Catherine. Had a date with George Wrigley when I came home. Alice was with Hugh. We took a ride to DuBois in George's Ford. Some car.

1925 Ford

Friday, July 17, 1925

Bobby (Stevenson) Keller came in and surprised me. Mama and Papa came home also. Had date with George Wrigley in eve. Alice had their car, she was with Hugh. Bubby was with us. We all took a ride, then went over to the dance at the Park. Mason and Dixon played. They were very good. I got home about 1:10.

Saturday, July 18, 1925

Went shopping in morning. Went to Clearfield in aft. Irene King came today. Bubby and I went to the movies. Talked to J.S.[90]

Sunday, July 19, 1925

Mama, Bobby, Marjorie and I went to church. We had early dinner and Mama & Papa went to Pittsburgh with Mr. and Mrs. Richlen from Bellefonte to select the picture (movie) to be shown the opening night of the new theatre[91] in Bellefonte. Marjorie & Bubby and I were here for supper. Alice and Adeline Barber came in eve. Also George Wrigley and Hugh. Alice Dorsett and Fred Wright came for a while. George stayed until about 11:00. I don't care a darn thing for him.

[90] Likely Jimmy Strickland.
[91] Richelieu Theatre.

Monday, July 20, 1925

Sewed some in afternoon. Bubby and I were down at Aunt Grace's for supper. Mr. and Mrs. Richlen stayed all night on their way home from Pittsburgh. Bubby and I slept at Marjorie's.[92]

Tuesday, July 21, 1925

Marjorie and I took Bubby over to Woodland to her aunt's. She expected to go on back to Snow Shoe today. It rained hard all day. Went to the dance over at the Park with George, Alice, and Hugh. I cannot stand George much longer.

Wednesday, July 22, 1925

Sewed in the morning. Bubby took Katy and Philip to Sykesville. Papa went away today. Didn't do a thing in eve.

Thursday, July 23, 1925

Sewed in aft. Went out to Groffe Acres for dinner. Alice entertained. There were 12 of us. Alice and Hugh, Adeline Barber and Dave McKinley, George Wrigley and myself, Marjorie and Ed Howard from Clearfield, Francis Schenley and Libby, John Wright and Eileen King. Took a ride to Dubois afterwards, then went up to Alice's where Shenley played his violin for us. He surely is wonderful.

Friday, July 24, 1925

Wrote to Kathleen. Worked all morning. We girls were planning on going camping tomorrow. Marjorie and I went to the movies. Sat beside J. S. I haven't had much of a talk with him since I have been home. Bub King came home tonight.

Saturday, July 25, 1925

Worked all morning. Got ready to come camping. Went out to Idlewild Lodge up at Humphrey's. It belongs to Jack Irvin. Burt King took us out at 4:30. Got all settled. George and Hugh came out and brought Alice and me into town and we got some candy and things. Went over to the dance at the Park. "Mira Mars" orchestra from Florida played. It was real good. Had a nice time, but can't stand George. All the girls were asleep when we got back. The Fellows stayed until 1:15. Marjorie was out but got sick and went in the house.

Sunday, July 26, 1925

George and Hugh were starting for Greenwood and got stuck in the mud on Saturday after they left here. They slept in the car all night. It just poured rain. They came out here for breakfast. Stayed nearly all morning. We had lots of visitors during the day. Joe Hipps, Bob and John Wright, Leonard Kantar, Mr. and Mrs. D. P. Wall, Mr. and Mrs. Fred Robison and Bobby. They brought ice cream along. Hugh and George came out again in aft. They didn't stay in eve. Thank goodness! Kay Wrigley and Schenley came out in eve. Also Bub King and a gang from DuBois. Danced and fooled around.

---

[92] Evidently so that the Richens could use their rooms.

Monday, July 27, 1925

Kate and I got up when Alice Wall and Alice Murry went into work. Hiked a ride to Lumber City and back. Walked about 2 miles. After lunch we all hiked in town. Went home and took a bath. Orvil King brought us out. It rained real hard. Dave, Hugh, and Jake came out in eve. Lib King and I hiked in town again.

Tuesday, July 28, 1925

We all slept until real late. Had a pain all day. Was lying down nearly all the time. Read a book. After supper Alice had the car and she and Kate and Lib Wall and Marjorie and I went down to Clearfield. After we came back Alice and I took the car and went into the dance.[93] Went uptown and got the kids some marshmallows. They were sore because we had left without them.

Wednesday, July 29, 1925

Sarah King was here all night. She and Eileen and I hiked up and back to Lumber City. Walked all but 2 miles. Bud Smith brought Alice out for lunch. Got dressed in evening and J. Holden came out. He took Alice and me to Clearfield. Looked for George but couldn't find him. Came out to camp. George and Hugh were here. Went into town later and got some ice cream. About 2:00 just Marjorie, Alice and Eileen and I were up and Tom McG. and Bob Brunetti came walking right in. They were drunk and were carrying some red lanterns they hooked from the streets in Clearfield. They stayed quite a while. We couldn't get rid of them.

Thursday, July 30, 1925

Alice, Elizabeth, Adeline, and Alice Murray were all away most of the day. Got lunch. Bud Smith brought Alice Murray out for lunch. The girls came back early. Got dressed and helped with supper. Had so much company in eve. Alice's family and Mary Conklin were out awhile. There were so many fellows arriving we didn't know what to do.

Bub King came out and took me for a ride. I surely like him a lot. He kissed me for the first time ever. He was so sweet, the only thing was that he went home at 11 o'clock.

Then I was with Don Dunsmore from Philipsburg. He was real good looking. Dave came out. John and Leonard, Hugh and George. Kate Smith had a date with Fred Redden and Marjorie with a Mr. Beezer from Philipsburg. We had about 4 fellows too many. Lib Wall was with Jake (Kantar) and Alice came with Clark and Alice Wall with Hugh.

Friday, July 31, 1925

It rained nearly all night. After the girls went into work we all slept late. Got lunch and sat around and read all aft. It was an awful day. Marjorie got our supper. Just made sandwiches and coffee, fruit salad, cheese and pickles. We all sat around the fireplace and ate. In eve I had a date with Bill Brown from Clearfield. He is real nice. Lib Wall was with Jake. Libby

---

93 Possibly at the PeeWee's Nest.

King with Leonard (Kantar), Marjorie with John and Adeline with Dave. We had made some sandwiches. After the fellows left some of us girls stayed up until 3:30. I made some biscuits for our breakfast at 3 o'clock. Went to sleep about 4 o'clock, just as it was beginning to be daylight.

Saturday, August 1, 1925

We got up about 8:30. Everyone left but Elizabeth and Eileen King and Marjorie and I. We had the whole camp to put in order. Mother and Alice came to help work. We at last got everything cleaned up by 12 o'clock. Bubby and Uncle Charley came out for us. Took all aft. to put my stuff away and get a bath and dressed. I felt so clean. Didn't go over to dance. Alice and I went to the movies. Marjorie had a date with P. A. Z.

Sunday, August 2, 1925

Went to church with Mama. Alice and Elizabeth Wall were here for dinner. Then we went up to Dubois to see a girl friend of Eliz. Went over to the Park and got Marjorie and listened to the band concert. We four went down to the Chatterbox for supper. Came up to Alice's. John Stamp & Ralph Fleming came up. We got them some supper; they had dates with Helen Shirk and Mabel Dale. Alice had a date with Hugh and Eileen with George. Marjorie and I went for a ride with Harold Strickland. Went out to Greenwood.

Monday, August 3, 1925

Fooled around all morning. Marjorie got the car and we went out to camp to see if she could find her pillow. I would love to have stayed. It was wonderful out there. Was down at Kings awhile in eve. Martin and John Wright took Eileen and me for a ride.

Tuesday, August 4, 1925

P.A.Z. came for me at 9:30. We went up to Clarion. Was at school cafeteria for lunch with Jessie. Saw Margaret Rhodes and Margaret Kelley who also are taking courses. Frances Sell from Drexel is working up there. I was so surprised to see her. Rode down town and got something to drink. Got home by 4:30. Had John Stamp and Ralph Fleming here for supper, also Marjorie. They took us for a ride, then we came home. I went over to the dance with J. Holton. Had the best time. Danced with Billie McClure and Ralph.

Wednesday, August 5, 1925

Cut the grass in the morning. Marge Irwin and Kenneth came today. Marjorie and Uncle Charley went to Tyrone to meet them. Eileen had a date with Billie McClure tonight. I hope he doesn't think he is spoiling me. Alice, Marge, Marjorie and Kenneth and I went to see "The Song of Love," a movie with Norma Talmadge."[94] Went up to Jimmies. Rufus and Harold took me over to Stricklands and I got a letter Jimmy sent me. I hope to have a date with Bub King sooo very soon; he is so good looking.

---

[94] 1923 American silent adventure drama film.

71

Thursday, August 6, 1925

Wrote 4 letters in the morning. Slept awhile in aft. Got dressed and went down to Marjorie's. Went to a Masonic Dance at Clearfield with John Wright. J. Holton came looking for me. Had a real nice time. Danced with Jimmy Grant.

Friday, August 7, 1925

Worked in the morning. John Stamp and Ralph Fleming were up in Uncle Fred's car with Jane, Mary Elizabeth, and Maude Ann. They were up again to say good-bye. John gave me my ring and I gave him his. They are leaving late tonight. Had a date with J. Holten in eve. Went out to Greenwood. Was up on top of the beacon light. Was over at Park awhile. The Redmen[95] had a big time over there.

Saturday, August 8, 1925

Fixed dress. Alice came up for me to go to Clearfield. Went down street awhile. Took Philip to movies in eve. Jane Kirk came today. Harold Strickland came up to take me for a ride. Was up street awhile with the Margies. Bub King was home when I was in to see Libby. If he would only ask me for a date.

Sunday, August 9, 1925

Went to church in morning with Mama. Alice came up in the car in aft. Went up to R. Strickland's with her while she had her hair cut. Went over to the Park awhile. Came home and slept awhile. Went to church at Presbyterian in eve. with the Margies and Jane Kirk. J. Holten asked for a date tonight, but I didn't give him one.

Monday, August 10, 1925

Worked all day. Washed and pressed clothes. Packed suitcase. Went to movies in eve with Margie and Libby King. Wanted to go over to Midway but wasn't allowed.

Tuesday, August 11, 1925

Got up about 5:30 and Mama and Papa and I went to Bellefonte. About 12:00 Catherine and I decided to go up to Buffalo and around that area for a trip. I was going down to stop at Wellsboro but Kate Howd was sick in bed. We got ready anyhow and went down to the train and it was late and we couldn't have made connections in Lock Haven, so Mr. Heverly took us down. Got in here at 8 o'clock. Called up Aunt Maude so Gertrude Stamp came down to the station and met us.[96] Sat and talked until late.[97]

---

[95] A non-profit fraternal organization devoted to "inspiring a greater love for the United States of America and the principles of American liberty." Also sponsored a women's auxiliary, the Degree of Pocahontas.

[96] Very likely there is a family connection here somewhere of the Stamp family and Estella Buckley and family in Curwensville.

[97] Based on what I surmise and remember, Aunt Maude Davidson worked for the Stamp family. (At Mrs. Stamp's death, Aunt Maude continued in the family's service) Gertrude is the daughter of the family. John, a son, named for his father, from all indications.

Wednesday, August 12, 1925

Didn't see John until this morning. He had stayed with Ralph Fleming all night. We had breakfast late. Ralph and John took Catherine and me for a ride in the Ford in aft. and was over to see Estella[98] and we went all around the Park. They took us out to The Glen[99] to dance. It was awful nice there. John stayed all night again with Ralph.[100]

Thursday, August 13, 1925

Went down town in aft with Mr. and Mrs. Epworth. Catherine and I went around to the stores and then went to the movies. In eve. Tom Humpheys came over and he and John and Catherine and I went out to the Green Mill. I danced and then we went down to The Glen and danced. Had a real good time.

Friday, August 14, 1925

Went out to see the boat races in the river in aft. In eve Tom and John took us over to Crystal Beach.[101] Danced and went on the Scenic Railway.[102] Went on the boat. Danced on the boat in morning. Estella came over.

Saturday, August 15, 1925

Estella took Catherine and me all through the Buffalo City Hospital. Wrote to Piggy. Gertrude took us down to a movie in aft. It was very good, I thought. In eve. Mrs. Stamp, Aunt Maud, John, Gertrude and Catherine and I drove up to Niagara Falls to see the colored lights on the Falls. Walked up and down the Canadian side. Looked in The Prince of Wales dancing hall.

Sunday, August 16, 1925

The Stamps took us down to the station. Left for Bellefonte on 9:10 train. Got into Bellefonte at 3:10. Long, hot ride. Got dressed, went up to Dim Lantern[103] with Heverlys for supper. Sat on Katz's porch awhile with Mary, Edna and a girl friend of Edna's.

Monday, August 17, 1925

Got up about 9 o'clock. Had lunch at 11:00. Wrote letters in aft. Catherine Reese and I went swimming in Hughes' pool when she came from work. The place was awful dirty. Had dates with Bill Seig and Cecil Walker in eve. Went up to Dim Lantern and got something to eat. I like Bill a lot.

---

[98] Estella Bulkley, a classmate of Mary Alice, was in a nursing program in Buffalo.

[99] Likely the Glen Tavern, constructed in 1887, has been operating as a restaurant and pub ever since.

[100] Likely so that the guests could have his room at home. That was the practice at the time.

[101] Built in 1888, Crystal Beach Amusement Park operated until 1989.

[102] Still in operation at the time this book was written.

[103] Very likely the Dim Lantern Restaurant was so named for its style of Chinese cuisine, prepared as small bite-sized portions of food served in small steamer baskets or on a small plate.

Tuesday, August 18, 1925

Was up at Catherine Allison's in morning. Saw Miss Dashiell whose home is Bellefonte. She is leaving for Drexel today. Went down to Schlows[104] and got a new dress. Was up at Marjory Hills for supper. We prepared the meal. Eddie Miller took us for a ride.

Wednesday, August 19, 1925

Didn't get up until 10:00. Mrs. Heverly went on a picnic in aft. I got supper for Mr. H. Catherine was here. In eve. we went down to see Maud Ann. Went to movies, saw Dick Bartholomew in "Shore Leave."[105] It was real good.

Thursday, August. 20, 1925

Went up to Louise Taylor's in aft. Mr. Heverly took Catherine and me down to the dance. Mrs. H. was along but she didn't go in. Had a real good time. Don and Ed Meyers were both up from Lock Haven. Danced with them. Danced with Dick Neil, Mahlon Robb, Carl Gray; Mahlon walked home with us. Came up from Paul's on the bus.

Friday, August 21, 1925

Marjorie Wall came over to Bellefonte today with Papa. We chased all around. Talked to Sam Waite and Hev Noll. Saw Phil Johnson. I wish I could have arranged a date with him. Also saw Bill and Cecil Walker. Went up to see Louise again in aft. Was up at Edna's and Blair's. Came home after supper. I was to have a date with Sam Waite.

Saturday, August 22, 1925

Unpacked and put things away. Was down street in aft. Jessie and Alice and I then went over to the dance with Bill Kelley and J.S. David and then Jimmy and I took a walk. This is the first he has kissed me since Xmas. He was so sweet. Stayed until the dance was over. Came home with Sidney. Cecil came home from Penn today.

Sunday, August 23, 1925

Went to church with Mama. Went out to Greenwood in aft. Cecil, Kenneth, Arthur, Dick, and Marjorie.[106] Took Alice with us. The Verne Walls[107] were there too. Margaret Sharp and Jane Teats were with them. Walked the streets awhile after we came home.

Monday, August 24, 1925

Cut the grass in the morning. Played tennis all aft. down at Shrots' farm. Hugh took Marjorie Murry and me down. Cecil, Kenneth, Jane Kirk and David McKinley came down. Had a good time. Marjorie and Jessie and I went to the movies in eve. "Triumph"[108] was on.

---

104 A popular upscale shop. The family donated generously to the community, including the Schlow Library.

105 The film was much-admired in its day. Barthelmess' performance in "Shore Leave" was one of the "Motion Picture Magazine" best of the year 1925, alongside honors also for Lon Chaney, W.C. Fields, and John Gilbert.

106 All of the Wall siblings.

107 Verne Wall is a brother of Charles; his children would be cousins of the five Walls aforementioned.

108 1924 American silent drama film directed by Cecil B. DeMille.

Tuesday, August 25, 1925

Went out to park for supper. Aunt Grace, Jane Kirk, Thornton Hile, Cousin Dema and Lew, and Mr. Rice. Went to the dance in eve. Billie McClure brought me home. Had a real good time. I only hope J. S. isn't cross. He didn't come in and dance.

Wednesday, August 26, 1925

Chased around all afternoon and morn. Getting a crowd together to go out to Greenwood. Got about 40 people together—all the girls and fellows around. Took our supper out and danced. Mama went as a chaperone. I was with Bub King most of the time. Had a grand time. What an evening.

Thursday, August. 27, 1925

Went to Clearfield all morning with Marjorie. Fooled around all aft. here at the house. Went to a dinner dance at Clearfield's Crystal Springs[109] with Kay Wrigley. Had a very good time. Danced until 12 o'clock. Met a lot of Clearfield fellows. The Clearfield Junior Board of Trade sponsored the party.

Friday, August 28, 1925

Fooled around all aft. Wrote letters. In eve. went down to Presbyterian Church for cake and ice cream. Gordon Kephart took Alice and Jessie and me to Clearfield. Came home early.

Saturday, August 29, 1925

Went to Clearfield shopping in afternoon with Alice. Got a pair of shoes. In eve. Alice and Jessie and I went over to the dance. Stayed until it was over. Came home in Bill Kelley's car with J.S. Had a good time at dance.

Sunday, August 30, 1925

Went to church with Mama. It was very warm today. Alice had the car so we gathered Jane and Marjorie, went swimming about 5:30, then came up here for supper. John Wright and Hugh wanted to take Alice and me for a ride, but I didn't want to go.

Monday, August 31, 1925

Worked all morning. Took a little nap in afternoon, then went to Clearfield with Alice and Marjorie who got a new hat. Took a ride in eve. with Alice. Came home early.

Tuesday, September 1, 1925

Sewed awhile in aft. Went for a ride with Bill Kittelberger in eve. Didn't get home until a quarter to 12:00. Libby and Gordon Kephart were along.

Wednesday, September 2, 1925

Played tennis down at Schrots in morn. In the aft was with Marjorie, Jane, Arthur, and Don Rexcord, a 2nd cousin of Marjorie's. There is a brother by the name of Kenneth in that family, too. Took Philip to movies in eve. J. S. sat behind me. He is going away Saturday. Wonder if I'll see him before he goes.

109 A private "camp"/dance venue in Clearfield County near Plymptonville

Light Tower at Greenwood

Thursday, September 3, 1925

Wrote letters in morning. Made sandwiches and got ready to go out to Greenwood in aft. Went out about 5 o'clock with John Wright. Had a date with Raymond Maurey. He is so passionate. I never was with anyone so much so, unless it was Bill Seig. It was beautiful out at Greenwood. The moon made it as light as day. Took a walk. Didn't go over to the light tower as Alice said J. S. was over there and I just didn't want to see him. I don't see why he came out tonight. I hope he isn't cross. He leaves on Saturday, and I do want to see him before he goes.

Friday, September 4, 1925

Cleaned all the upstairs in morning. Mama & Papa went over to Huntingdon early to meet with Gov. Pinchot at the Reformatory. Went to movies in eve. with Marjorie and Libby to see Norma Talmadge in "Secrets." It was real good. Went down to Walls and helped Marjorie serve Aunt Grace's Club.

Saturday, September 5, 1925

Took a nap in aft., then went down the street. Talked to J.S. a minute. Was supposed to see him in eve., but I had to go to Clearfield with Marjorie. Didn't get back until 9:30. Went up to Jimmies with Marjorie, and Don Rexcord walked up with me. He stayed until 11:30. I couldn't get him to go home. He wants a date Monday night. I don't want one with him but doubt if I can get out of it.

Sunday, September 6, 1925

Went to church with Mama. Jessie and I were at Libby's all aft. sitting on the porch. Raymond and Bob were there. Jessie and I stayed for supper. Had a date with Raymond in eve. Bob would have asked for one I think if I hadn't had one with Raymond. Bob brought me up home in the car from his place. We acted like fools down there. Bill Kittelberger was up to take me for a ride. Thank goodness I already had a date.

Monday, September 7, 1925 (Labor Day)

Big day today. Worked all morning. Went over to the Park in aft. Danced all afternoon. Had a real good time. Didn't go home for supper. Alice took us for a little ride. Came home and got dressed. Was supposed to have a date with Don Rexcord, but told him I was going up to Alice's. Then I went over to the dance with Alice and Hugh. Had a date with Bill McClure. Don and Marjorie came in. I felt terrible. I hope Marjorie isn't cross at me for I didn't even talk to her. Alice and Hugh left before I did. Now I won't see her until Xmas because when we went up she had gone to bed. Danced several times with J. S. Danced with Kirk Hile. Gee, he surely is good-looking. Billie had their maroon car. I had a real good time. Danced with Pete Barney, Blair Mann.

Tuesday, September 8, 1925

Washed dresses and ironed all morning and part of aft. Took a little nap in aft. Sewed a little. Mama and I went to the movies in eve. Rudolph Valentine was in "The Sainted Devil."[110] Bill Daugherty was up to see me about Hugh's fraternity pin for Alice.

Wednesday, September 9, 1925

Sewed in morning. Didn't get dressed until late. Stayed home most of the eve. Put Philip to bed, then made some fudge. The girls were up for a while. Jessie came over and we went down street. Jessie told me Bub asked where I was. He came up the next morning and I was out front and he stopped and told me he had looked for me last night.

Thursday, September 10, 1925

Wrote a couple of letters in the morning and sewed. Hugh came up for me and we went down to Shrots and played tennis. He won 6-4. Took a ride. Mama and Papa got up early and went to Bedford Springs. Aunt Grace and Uncle Charley went along. Was sitting out front after supper when Bub and Libby came up and took Bessie and me for a ride. Then I sat down on King's porch and Bob got the car later and we took a ride. Just wonder though what he thinks of me and if he likes me just a little bit. He said he would have me down to some of their good parties this year at the Phi Chi house.

Friday, September 11, 1925

Helped clean in morning. Marjorie and I went up to school awhile in aft. Was in Philip's room for a few minutes and up at the high school. Went up to Hepburnia where Jessie teaches. Stayed until she dismissed. Didn't do a thing in eve. Went to bed early.

Saturday, September 12, 1925

Sewed and fooled around all morn. and aft. Rained in eve. Sat down on King's porch awhile. Came home early.

Sunday, September 13, 1925

Went down to the train to say goodbye to Marjorie who is going to Kirks' home tonight. Didn't go to church. Packed trunk. Sat down on Kings' porch awhile in aft. Bob Daugherty and Pete Barney took Jessie and me for a ride. Libby and Jessie were here for supper. It seemed so quiet without Marjorie and Alice. Said goodbye to Hugh. Had a dumb date with a fellow from Clarion in eve. I wouldn't have gone, but Jessie would have been cross. Bill Somebody was his name.[111] They left at 10:30, thank goodness. I wonder if I will see Bub before he goes Wednesday? I hope so.

Monday, September 14, 1925

Mama and I went to Clearfield after dinner. Got a new hat, evening dress, and shoes. Came home on the bus. Was down at Libby's in eve. Said goodbye to her. She leaves in the morning

---

[110] His 29th film, late 1924. Said to be the best Valentino film to that date.

[111] Possibly Bill Fowler whom Jessie dated; Bill Fowler was Class President at Clarion, a High School letterman in three sports, and typically was self-assured.

for school. Had a date with Billie McClure. Went for a ride in Bob Daugherty's car with Virginia Murray and another fellow. Came home early.

Tuesday, September 15, 1925

Didn't get dressed until late. Stayed home with Philip awhile. Was talking to J.S. Think I saw him later with a girl in Bill Kelly's car—don't care in the least. Came home early.

Wednesday, September 16, 1925

Wrote Alice. Sewed and washed and pressed all day. Got dressed just before supper. Wrote some letters. Mason and Dixon orchestra played at the Park, but I didn't get over. Came home early. The town was dead, hardly a soul around. Bub was down street.

Thursday, September 17, 1925

Washed dresses and packed all morning & aft. Went down to the bakery after supper. Saw J. S. and had a date with Raymond in eve. He surely is hard to manage. So passionate. He and Bill Seig and Burt King are just alike, but I believe Bub is the worst when it comes to passion, though I can hardly tell. Thank goodness I am not that way. Wonder who I will date tomorrow night. Hope it is Bub. Only wish he would go back on the same train with me.

Friday, September 18, 1925

Fooled around here at home all day. Jessie wanted me to have a date with a fellow from Clarion, but I didn't want to. Bub has gone and he didn't even say goodbye to me. I wonder why? Perhaps he doesn't like me after the other night. Edith Sawtelle and I went to the movies. Colleen Moore in "So Big." It was real good.[112]

Saturday, September 19, 1925

My last night home until Christmas. Mama and Papa came home from Bellefonte today. Baked a cake in the morn. Katie went out to Sykesville in the afternoon. Her brother-in-law died. Had my hair washed and fooled around all aft. While I was eating my supper Jessie came over and told me Jimmy was over at her house and wanted to say goodbye to me. He left for Buffalo tonight. I was scared to death, didn't know whether to go over or not, but I went and kissed him goodbye. To think I didn't have even a date with him this whole summer; maybe it is the best thing though. Jessie, Kate, and I fooled around all eve. Went up to Grampian Park awhile. Came back and went in Jimmies. Was talking to Kirk Hile and Blair Mann. Kirk is so good looking. I am crazy about him. Blair Mann is going to write to me this year. I wonder who else will write to me. I wish Kirk would, but hardly any danger of that.[113]

---

[114] **Commentary:** Colleen Moore's role in "So Big" was quite different from her usual jazz baby/flapper parts. Because Moore's part in the film was so different from the roles she had become known for following "Flaming Youth," there was an outcry against her.

[113] **Author's note:** At the end of this first Diary is a listing of young men's names, perhaps with the number of times Mary Alice dated them: Billie McClure IIII; Sidney Korb I; John Wright II; Jimmy Holton III; Bill Seig II; Joe Katz I; George Wrigley IIII; Russel Price I; Hugh Norris I; Martin Ardery II; Bruce Norris I; Bub King III; Bill Brown I; Don Dunsmore I; Harold Strickland I; John Stamp III; P. A. Z. I; George Lyon I; J. Strickland III; Kay Wrigley I; Bill Kittelberger I; Raymond Maurey III; Don Rexroad I. This is followed by several other names in light pencil without the numbers: Bill (Clarion), Phil Johnson, Gene Kenzie, and Bob Daugherty.

September 1925 – June 1926

Sunday, September 20, 1925

Got up and helped Mama get breakfast. Katy went to Sykesville on Saturday. Finished packing, got dressed, and went up to Mama Spencer's. Helped get dinner. The Wall boys were up. Left on 1:35 train. Had a terrible tiresome trip down; no one I knew. Some of the girls, Kathleen and Florence, were at the train. Alice Kay was on the same train. Met my new roommate Jane Clark from Johnstown. She is real nice. Went over to the practice house awhile and fooled around.

Monday, September 21, 1925

Went to breakfast. Then went down to school up to Bartram and to the station. Got my suitcase and talked to Cecil on the phone. Went up to the house awhile, then back to school and registered. Took terribly long. Went to lunch about 2:30. Came up to house and unpacked a little and fooled around. Cecil came over awhile after dinner. Then Bill Brown came over and another fellow and I got June. Wrote letters (wrote Mama).

Tuesday, September 22, 1925

Went to classes all day. They didn't keep us the full time. Had Miss Turner and Miss Burdett today. Not so bad. Finished unpacking. Had an upperclassman meeting after dinner at dining room. Wrote letters all eve. Going to waken freshmen at 12:00 tonight. Initiated Freshmen. Took them to the cellar.

Wednesday, September 23, 1925

Got up for breakfast. Had assembly today for first. Didn't see anyone I knew. Wonder where they are? Got out about 3:00. Came home and fooled around. No mail today. Studied awhile in eve. Wrote Alice. Had lunch at some Greek place up near the University.

Thursday, September 24, 1925

Only had 2 hrs. of classes today. Kathleen and I went down town to Ventura Gardens for lunch. Had the best time. Purchased a dress, can't quite decide if I like it or not. Got a lot of little things. Was over to practice house awhile. Bill Brown called and made a date for tomorrow night. Right after he called, Joe dear called. He came right over. I was tickled to death. He just came in this morning. He is so sweet. He is the first fellow down here to kiss me this year. I am crazy about him. I don't care much for Bill.

Friday, September 25, 1925

Went down town at 11 o'clock and got my new dress. June was with me. We got our lunch at Horn and Hardart Automat under the Earl Theatre. Had classes until 4 o'clock. Had a date with Bill Brown in eve. I don't care much about him. Didn't do a thing. Walked all around and came in early. Wasted my first 12 o'clock privilege on him and did not do a thing.

Saturday, September 26, 1925

Had Nutrition class this morn. Only stayed 2 hrs., supposed to have three. Just as I was leaving school "Piggie" Burr came. He walked up to the house with me. Went down for my medical exam in aft. Took nearly all aft. Went down to Jack Hart's in eve. Saw some of my old friends. Bill Brown was there but I didn't pay much attention to him. Paul Johnston came home with me. Knew him last year. He is from Pittsburgh and a Kappa Sigma and is a Lutheran. He is a friend of Grace Niles. Also saw Leonard Bland ("Speed") from Bellwood. **The Freshmen were every kind of dumb.**

Sunday, September 27, 1925

Gained an hr. today. Clocks turned again to standard time. Went to church at 34th and Chestnut, Asbury M.E. Church. Wrote letters, read all aft. Studied in eve.

Monday, September 28, 1925

Had classes all day. Came home and fooled around (Wrote to Mama) before dinner. Had letters from Mrs. Heverly and Bubby. Joe came over at 8 o'clock and brought Dan somebody and I got Dot Oaks for him. Joe was sweeter than ever. He is so cute, such blue eyes. I hope to have a date with him Saturday night.

Tuesday, September 29, 1925

Went down town in morn. with Kathleen and Ann Robinson. Looked for a dress pattern and material. Didn't get either. Got letters from Hugh. Wrote Jessie. Took bath before dinner. Studied in evening. Then the Freshmen entertained the upper classmen with sandwiches and lemonade.

Wednesday, September 30, 1925

Went over to the cafeteria for lunch today for the first time. Fooled around after school. Had letters from both Piggie Burr and Billie McClure. Studied and wrote letters in eve.

Thursday, October 1, 1925

Only had classes 2 hrs. Kathleen and I went downtown. Had lunch at Wanamaker's 8th floor Tea Room. The Crystal Tea Room. Had the best lunch: Chicken Salad, Fried Oysters and French Fried Potatoes. An orchestra was playing and broadcasting. Got material for a dress to make at school, red duvetyn fabric. Met Jane at The Eagle and went down to the Fox. Saw "The Iron Horse."[114] It was real good. Had a letter from Raymond today. After dinner the Drexel boys came up to the dorms. We all went out. They were having a mass meeting for the football game. Wrote letters and studied in eve.

Friday, October 2, 1925

I wrote Alice. Had classes until 4 o'clock, then helped with programs for house warming. Went to each house in evening, then got something to eat up at the dining room. Miss Ruth

---

[114] Starring George O'Brian. "The Iron Horse" is a 1924 American Western silent film directed by John Ford. It was a major milestone in his career, and his lifelong connection to the western movie genre.

Dorsey gave us special permission to go to Jack Hart's in eve. Mrs. Phillips chaperoned us. Had the best time, only no one came home with me. Cannot imagine where Joe was. I wish someday I could make a hit with some of the most popular fellows down there; it just seems I can't.

Saturday, October 3, 1925
Had 3 hrs. of Nutritional Cooking Class. Had my first letter from Mama. Was going to the game, but didn't. Stayed home. Had a date with Piggie Burr in eve. Went down to go to a movie and there was a lineup for all of them. Came back and went up to Huston Hall to a dance. Had a pretty good time. Piggie didn't like all the cut-ins, but I couldn't help it.

Sunday, October 4, 1925
Went down to Jack Hart's church with June and Kathleen. Jane washed my hair in aft. Had a date at 4:30 with Wilton Wright. Went over to the Tea Rose with him for tea. Studied and wrote letters in eve.

Monday, October 5, 1925
Didn't get home until 4 o'clock. Fooled around. Had a letter from Miss Dashiell. Studied in evening.

Tuesday, October 6, 1925
Wrote Bubby. Had 3 hrs. off in morning. Had lunch at Tea Rose. Joe Joseph called about 5 o'clock. Studied awhile before dinner. Joe and John came over in eve. Kathleen and I had dates. Joe never was so sweet. I first wonder how much he likes me. I like him so much now. He makes me like him, then he turns around and acts so indifferent that makes me wonder. Jane Clark, Edna Forney, Ruth Rarsary, Sarah Ann Suttliff and Kathleen and I had a feed up in Kathleen's room, onions and everything. After lights.

Wednesday, October 7, 1925
U.S. Senator Pepper, representative from Pa., spoke in Assembly today. Took laundry down. (Wrote Mama) (Wrote Alice) Wilton Wright called for a date but I went to the Food Fair with the girls. Had more fun. Have a date with Wilton tomorrow night.

Thursday, October 8, 1925
Went downtown in aft. looking for dress material. Didn't get any. Hope to get it before class on Monday. Went to the Alpha Epsilon Tea Dance after school. Had a pretty good time. In eve. had a date with Wilton Wright. He is all right, but nothing thrilling. Wrote to Jessie and Kate.

Friday, October 9, 1925
Fooled around after school. Went down to Jack Hart's in eve. Fellow from Virginia brought me home. Had a real good time. Ate onions up in Kathleen's room afterwards: Jane, Kathleen, and I. Was supposed to go to the Drexel Fraternity dance, but Piggie couldn't get here for it.

Saturday, October 10, 1925

Had a three hour class in morning. Got ready to go out to Drexel-Paul[115] after lunch. Went downtown with June and Nancy; got material and pattern for a dress for sewing class. 13 of us went out to camp about 6 o'clock. The others had dinner all ready, hot dogs and spaghetti. It was terribly cold out. The coldest 10th of October for years. It snowed a little in aft. Wrote letters and walked to the store in eve. Got some candy. Went to bed about 1 o'clock.

Sunday, October 11, 1925

Slept with Kathleen. We were so nice and warm. Got up about 9 o'clock. Took a hike in morning. Smoked and went to another little store. Left for home about 4 o'clock. Betty Biddle left her pocketbook at Wayne station so we all had to get off at St. Davids. They found the pocketbook and sent it down to us on the next train an hour later. Took a bath and studied in eve.

Monday, October 12, 1925

Had classes until 4 o'clock. No mail today. Fooled around after school. Studied in eve.

Tuesday, October 13, 1925

Letter from J.S. today. Don't know what to do about it. Aunt Maude sent me a cute handkerchief doll today. Studied in eve.

Wednesday, October 14, 1925

Fooled around after school. Wrote letters and studied in eve. Had a feed up in Kathleen's room after lights.

Thursday, October 15, 1925

Studied in library awhile after my classes were over. Had lunch up in Kathleen's room. Played tennis with Wilton Wright and beat him 2 sets out of 3. Had a date with John Joseph in eve. He was so nice. I invited him to the house dance on the 31st, then he asked me to go to the Penn-Illinois football game that Saturday afternoon.

Friday, October 16, 1925

Ann Robinson and I played tennis over at the hospital court with a couple of Drexel fellows after school. Had a lot of fun. 13 girls from our house went down to the Shubert in eve. to see "Rose Marie." It was very good.

Saturday, October 17, 1925

Had classes all morning. Jane and I went downtown to get Philip a birthday present. Met Cora Wolf up at Wanamaker's. Was so surprised to see her. Had a date with Wilton Wright in eve. Six couples of us started down to the Earle but we left the rest. They were all Drexel girls and fellows. We went down to the Rittenhouse and danced and ate. I am afraid he is getting too hard a case on me. I can always tell. It is useless for him for I am tired of him already. Had a real good time, but OK if I had only been with someone I was crazy about. I was bored most of the time.

115 The lodge/camp mentioned above and used by Drexel for special events.

Sunday, October 18, 1925

Can you imagine I went to church with Wilton Wright? Went down to the Methodist Church. Sewed and worked all aft. In eve. June, Kathleen, and Jane and I went down to Christian Endeavor, then studied.

Monday, October 19, 1925

Saw Piggie down at school today. Talked to him awhile. Fooled around after school. Studied in eve.[116]

Tuesday, October 20, 1925

Came home for an hour at noon. Had classes until 4. Studied awhile in eve, then wrote letters, including to Alice.

Wednesday, October 21, 1925

Haven't heard a word from Mama yet. Have been expecting letters all week. A lot of scandal around school today. Mary Cunningham was sent home for stealing money. This is her 3rd year here at Drexel. There also is a big time about Marie Hobbs' being suspended indefinitely. Her father, sister, and uncle were here tonight. Miss Dorsey is raising the devil about it. Marie went up to the Penn-Yale game last weekend and Miss Dorsey found out all about it. She had signed out to her Aunt's in New York.

Thursday, October 22, 1925

Had 2 hr. class in Costume Design in morning. Stayed down in the library awhile. Came up to the house and went over to the Tea Rose for lunch with Ann, Milly & Kathleen. While I was over there Mama called me. Stayed at home all aft. Studied and got dressed. Had just finished dressing when Mama, Cecil, Marjorie, Marge, Uncle Charley and Aunt Grace came in Walls' car about 5 o'clock. They had been in the city. They didn't come around here before as I had told them I wouldn't be home until 5 o'clock. I went with them, only Cecil went back to the hotel. We had dinner at 69th Street. Went out to West Chester. Took Marjorie up to school. Aunt Grace, Uncle Charley and Mama and I went to the movies. Saw Harold Lloyd in "The Freshman"[117] It was very funny. Slept with Mama all night as Papa didn't come.

Friday, October 23, 1925

Cut all my classes today. Went to Chapel and Sociology with Marjorie. We went into the city and had lunch at the Tea Rose. Came over to the house awhile. Went in the practice house awhile. Got Cecil. We all went down town. Mama and I met Mrs. Kittelberger at Wanamaker's. Did some shopping, then went to the movies. I had seen it before. Went over to Friends Hotel. Marjorie went back to school. The rest of us went to see "Models

---

[116] This was also the date of the opening of the new theatre in Bellefonte, "The Richelieu."
[117] *The Freshman* is a 1925 comedy film that tells the story of a college freshman trying to become popular by joining the school football team. It remains one of Harold Lloyd's most successful and enduring films.

and Artists"[118] at Chestnut St. Opera House. It was real good. Had dinner at Friends Hotel. They are staying at the Commodore, right across the street from Friends. They are leaving in the morning, taking Mrs. Kittelberger along. Cecil brought me home. He and Murphy had dates after they left me.

Saturday, October 24, 1925

Had 3 hr. class in the morning. Stayed home all aft. and wrote letters. It rained all day. Joe came over in eve. We didn't go out. We were the only ones in the parlor. He was so wonderful, I wonder how much he likes me. Have a date Tuesday night. Talked to Cora after lunch. Wrote Jessie and Bubby.

Sunday, October 25, 1925

Went over to Tea Rose for breakfast, Jane and Betty and I. Started to study after dinner, but John and Joe came over. We took a walk. John asked Kathleen to go to the game and he is coming to the house dance. Got some ice cream over at the drugstore. Walked out through Fairmont Park. Joe was so crazy, just like a kid.

Monday, October 26, 1925

Stayed at school until 5 o'clock and sewed. Had letters from Piggie and Alice. John Deitz[119] dropped in a couple of min. to see me. He is from Clarion, a friend of Jessie's. I think he heard something about our dance on Saturday and came over thinking he might get a bid.

Tuesday, October 27, 1925

Kathleen and I went downtown for 3 hrs. in the morning. She got a coat and I got some silver slippers. Had class until 4 o'clock. Joe called before dinner. He and John came over in eve. I am beginning to love him, I believe. He is taking me to dinner and to a show or something on Friday, then the game and dinner Saturday. I only hope I can get all my lessons done O.K. Stayed up and studied and sewed until 3:00. Jane and I each got a box of candy from Abe, a friend of Jane's. Wrote to Alice.

Wednesday, October 28, 1925

Had classes until 4 o'clock. Washed Joe's scarf. Made out dance programs after dinner. Wrote a couple of letters and studied in eve.

Thursday, October 29, 1925

Went down town with Kathleen. She got a hat and shoes. Mama and Papa may be down again next week. I hope so. Jane washed my hair in eve.

---

[118] *Artists and Models* [1924] (Original Musical, Revue, Broadway) opened in New York City Oct 15, 1924 and played through May 23, 1925.

[119] John Deitz, who was attending the University of Pennsylvania, also plays a notable role in *All the Gentlemen Callers*, by the author of this book, about Jessie Pifer and all of her gentlemen callers.

Friday, October 30, 1925

Had classes until 4 o'clock. Went up to Johnson and Johnson and got a marcel. It snowed all day and was awful sloppy out. Got my feet wet, too. Came home and got dressed. Joe came for me before I had my hair combed and I kept the taxi waiting, couldn't help it. Went down to Kobler's for dinner. Had oysters. Went over to Broad Street Station and telephoned the house to have someone put my card out. Went down to the Forest Theatre and saw the "Ziegfeld Follies," the first time I ever saw them. They surely were good. Came up and stood on the porch awhile, got home a little early. Joe is so sweet.

Saturday, October 31, 1925

Had classes until 12 o'clock. After lunch we went to the game. (Penn 2, Illinois 24). It was real cold. Wore my galoshes. Kathleen and John sat right in back of Joe and me. The place was packed; the new stadium is not quite finished. The field was just awful muddy. The boys were just covered with mud. It was terrible. It was the most wonderful game, had the best time. Was up at their apartment for a while. It is the cutest place. They have a little kitchen, bedroom, and living room. We were up before the game and awhile after. Got dressed for the formal dinner our house gave. It was so nice. After the dinner I came home and got dressed again for the dance. Joe came over. He looked so sweet, had the best time.

Sunday, November 1, 1925

Got up late. Washed, put laundry away, and took some pictures in afternoon. Sewed on dress. Studied in eve.

Monday, November 2, 1925

Had classes every hour. Got home late. Went to the Methodist Banquet. There was the best speaker, we got home about 15 min. late and Miss Dorsey was along so I think we are all right. The other girls are cross but I didn't think we will get a demerit for it.

Tuesday, November 3, 1925

Wrote Alice. Sewed on dress from 10 to 1 o'clock. The class sewing was from 1 to 3. Got dress all finished and pressed. Had a date with Joe in eve. Don't know when I will see him again.

Wednesday, November 4, 1925

Stayed late to work on design for art. Went downtown at noon and got check cashed. Had letter from Mama, and they are coming down the end of this week. Wrote Kate.

Thursday, November 5, 1925

Came home at 11 o'clock. Studied all aft. Went down to Court Dance, didn't dance at all. They're mostly dumbbells. Had a telegram from Mama, met her at Broad St. Station and had dinner with her at Friends Hotel. Talked to her awhile, then came up to the house. Went up to see Cecil after I came from seeing Mama. If only I could have sent word to Joe I could have been out with him until 12 o'clock. Leo Sutton was here when I came back. He was calling on Mildred Starner. Wrote Jessie and Hugh.

Friday, November 6, 1925

Had classes until 12 o'clock. Got up and took a bath before breakfast, getting ambitious. Met Mama at Wanamaker's at 1:15. Frederick Kittelberger was with her.[120] He left and we went to the movies. Went back to the hotel; Papa had been there, but we didn't have time to wait and see him. Met Frederick at 5:45 at the Adelphia Hotel.

He took us to the Piccadilly for dinner. Danced and smoked. Mama did also. I don't know if I was surprised or not. They had some fancy dancing and singing. "California Night Hawks" played. Harold Knight from Clearfield runs it. He came up and spoke to us. I had met him once before at Tyrone. He kept smiling at me all evening. I thought I knew him. Went up to the Stanley to the movies. It surely was good. Corinne Griffith[121] in "Classified." Fred brought me home, only hope he doesn't call me up for a long time.

Saturday, November 7, 1925

Had 3 hr. class. Met Mama and Papa at 1:30 at Wanamaker's. Went over to Hotel. Mr. James Norris came for us and took us out to his house for dinner. They have a cute little girl Dorothy. **Met Mr. Norris's sister Mrs. Jackson.[122] They have a son going to Penn State. And he is a Delta Upsilon. William Jackson is his name.** Went to the Nixon Theatre. Got home at 10:30. Kathleen had a feed up in her room.

Sunday, November 8, 1925

I affiliated with Asbury M.E. Church this morning. There was a large crowd of girls and fellows joined. Kathleen & Betty Bell both joined. Haven't heard from Joe since Tuesday. Wonder when I will hear from him again. I am hoping he takes me to the Penn-Pitt game Saturday, but there isn't much danger of it. Had a big feed in Ida's—the whole house was there.

Monday, November 9, 1925

Slept on a piece of wedding cake. Didn't dream a thing. Talked to Piggie down at school today. Stayed awhile and worked on crafted pattern. Went over to the Practice House for dinner. Kate Howd is cook this week. June had a feed in eve. Wrote Bubby and Jessie.

Tuesday, November 10, 1925

Went down town and got some dress designs. Got a pocketbook. Played basketball after school. Studied and wrote letters in eve.

---

[120] Frederick is the son of Mrs. George Kittelberger.

[121] Widely regarded at the time, she was as one of the most beautiful actresses of the silent film era.

[122] Maiden name was Grace Norris from Curwensville. Mr. Jackson died at age 72, (interred in Arlington Cemetery) only several months prior to the death of Mrs. Jackson at age 67 from a heart attack. He had a brother, Frederick. Mary Alice served as Executrix for the estates of her former in-laws.

Wednesday, November 11, Armistice Day

Had formal assembly today. Came up to the house at noon. Stayed at school until 5:30 working on design. Got it all finished. Joe called after dinner. He and John came over. Joe has so many girls, I wonder if he likes me much. I don't seem to care anymore if anyone likes me or not. Bob Fox called me tonight and asked me to the Drexel Alumni Dance on the 21st. Told him I would tell him tomorrow. I have to make up a good excuse. Talked to Piggie awhile; he and Wilton are both going. The ones I really would like to go with don't ask me so then I don't care if I go or not. Wrote to Estella Buckley and Alice.

Thursday, November 12, 1925

Was through classes at 11 o'clock. Came up to house awhile, then went downtown. Met Kathleen and we went to the Stanley. **Saw Rudolph Valentino in person;** he is better looking than in his pictures. He had real black hair and speaks a broken English. He has a wonderful build. Also saw him play in "The Eagle."[123] It was wonderful.

Friday, November 13, 1925

There has been a detective around here for the last 3 nights. He is looking for a man who has been chasing around here exposed. He comes and sits in the parlor awhile while we are at dinner. Our Food Economics Class went through the Campbell Soup Factory in Camden, NJ. Met Jane downtown after school and we got our draperies. Jane worked on them all evening. I finished them when I came home. Kathleen and I went over to the apartment with John and Joe. Had the best time. Joe is so sweet, he told me how much he liked me. We took our 12 o'clock privilege. Dan, their roommate, came in and he was so funny; he had been drinking.

Saturday, November 14, 1925

A bunch of us went out to the Drexel-Upsula[124] football game. We lost 14-0. It was a wonderful day. Penn lost to Pitt 14-0. Stayed in this evening and wrote to Mama and studied some.

Sunday, November 15, 1925

Went down to the M.E. Church. Stayed for Sunday School in the Women's University Class; there is also the Men's University Class. We met together this morning; there was an outside speaker. After dinner Jane and I went down to Jefferson Hospital to see a girlfriend of Jane's. I also looked for Lucinda; neither of them was there; they were on duty. They live just across from Bub's fraternity "Phi Chi." Went up to Miss Illman's to see Harmie and she wasn't there. She was out with Willis Hile. Stopped in to see Cecil awhile. Studied in eve.

---

[123] It is said that Rudolph Valentino delivered one of the most nuanced and powerful performances of his career in this epic romance set in 18th century Russia,

[124] ...a Lutheran-affiliated, private college located in East Orange, New Jersey (1899–1995). After years of declining enrollment and financial problems, Upsala College closed in May 1995.

Monday, November 16, 1925

Wrote Marjorie. No mail today. Was at school all day. Studied in eve. Wish Joe had called tonight for a date. Maybe he will call tomorrow night?

Tuesday, November 17, 1925

Was downtown in morning. Got doily all finished and am going to send it to Mama tomorrow. Studied in eve. I wonder when Joe will call. I hope not Thursday night, for then I have one with John Deitz. Maybe tomorrow night. Wrote to Jessie; wrote to Mama.

Wednesday, November 18, 1925

Was down at school all day, studied in Library. Got 4 letters today. Jessie and Kate will be here next Thursday morning. I have so much work to do before Xmas; don't see how I will ever do it all. I guess Joe isn't going to call me anymore. I only hope he takes me out sometime this weekend. Wish I didn't have a date with Deitz tomorrow night. Only hope Joe doesn't call then. If he does.......

Thursday, November 19, 1925

Wrote to Kate. Studied all aft. Went down to Basket Ball practice at 4 o'clock. Had a date with John Deitz in eve. He brought another fellow over and I got Jane for him. Got a box of food from Mama today. Had a big feed up in Kathleen's room—pickles, meat loaf, cakes, pimento cheese and peanut butter.

Friday, November 20, 1925

Took trip through Abbott's Ice Cream today. Got the best ice cream. Met Jan at Wanamaker's after school and got tickets for "Sky High."[125]

Did some shopping. Went down to Jack Hart's in eve. Had a real good time. A cute little red-haired boy brought me home. He is from Schenectady, New York, and goes to Penn School. His name is William S. Hutchins. Joe was out at Beechwood on a blind date. Guess he is tired of me.

Saturday, November 21, 1925

I am 20 years old today. Cut my nutrition class in the morning. Studied in morning. Stayed in for the afternoon and studied then, too. I wrote to Mama in evening and studied. Joe hasn't called all week. I wonder why?

Sunday, November 22, 1925

Didn't go to church, fooled around until about 12 o'clock. Went out to George Rumsey's for dinner at Stenton out near Chestnut Hill. Talked nearly all aft. Had dinner about 4 o'clock, then took a ride in their car to the Stenton Country Club.[126] Got back at the house about

---

[125] Tom Mix movie, 1922.

[126] Today's Cedarbrook Country Club is a direct outgrowth of Stenton Country Club, which was founded in 1909 and played its golf on leased ground near Stenton Avenue and Washington Lane in the Chestnut Hill section of the city. In 1915 nine charter members of the Stenton Country Club applied for and received a corporate charter creating the legal entity known as Stenton Country Club. The charter and the names of the nine original members are currently displayed over the fireplace in the club's Grille Room.

7 o'clock. Had a date with John Joseph[127] in evening. He is going home Tuesday. Wish he would call me up before he leaves.

Monday, November 23, 1925

Wrote letters after school and had a committee meeting after dinner up at the dining room. I am on the Gift Committee. Washed hair, mine and Kathleen's, and had some food up in Kathleen's room.

Tuesday, November 24, 1925

Got my hair curled at 10:30 a.m. Came back to school and studied. Played basketball after school. (Grace Johns called from Scranton.) In eve. did my block printing on some handkerchiefs for art. Studied and wrote to Mama.

Wednesday, November 25, 1925

All the kids were leaving for home and there are only about 12 left here in the house. Marjorie called and said she wouldn't be in until tomorrow. She is staying at Norrises for their Thanksgiving dinner and then coming in here. Stayed in this eve. and wrote letters. Edith Knoble had me over in her room at 12 o'clock for some food.

Thursday, November 26, 1925

Thanksgiving Day. Jane and I got up at 6:15 and went down to Broad St. Station. Met Jessie and Kate.[128] Went over to Dining Room for breakfast. Took a walk up around the University. Went in to see Cecil. Jessie went to the Penn-Cornell Game with John Deitz.[129] Penn won, 7-0. Marjorie came about 5 o'clock. We all went over to the dining room for dinner. Had the most wonderful dinner. John Deitz and a Mr. Brown were here in the eve. Marjorie and Kate went to a fraternity dance at the Acacia Fraternity[130] with Bill and Cecil.

Friday, November 27, 1925

Got up about 10 o'clock. Went down town to Ventura Gardens for lunch. Shopped all aft. Went on Chestnut St. and Market St. through Gimbels, Wanamaker's, and about all the 5 and ten cent stores. Had more fun. Kate got a hat. Came up to the house. Marge Irvin came in from West Chester. We all went down to the Cathay for dinner. Had chicken chow mein. Jessie, Kate, Marjorie, Marge, Jane and I went to see "Sky High" afterwards at the Chestnut Street Opera House. It was pretty good. Marjorie stayed all night.

Saturday, November 28, 1925

Got up about 8 o'clock. Went over to the Tea Rose for breakfast then went down town. Got Kate's watch at Broad St. Station. She had left it on Friday morning on the Pullman. Went

---

[127] This adds to the confusion of Joseph who really was John Joseph but referred to as Joe.

[128] This is Jessie's sister Kate (my mother). It is very possible that Deitz invited Jessie and Jessie talked Kate into going with her.

[129] We are not surprised. They dated when Jessie attended Clarion Normal School in John's hometown of Clarion..

[130] Acacia is a social fraternity founded in 1904 at the University of Michigan in Ann Arbor, Michigan. The fraternity has 28 active chapters and 4 colonies throughout Canada and the United States. The fraternity was founded by undergraduate Freemasons, and was originally open only to men who had taken the Masonic obligations.

down to see Independence Hall. Walked up Chestnut St. Got a sundae at Whitman's. Went around to the Forest Theatre and got tickets. Went to the Automat for lunch. Went down to the Stanley in afternoon. Saw Gloria Swanson in "Stage Struck."[131]

Went over to the dining room for dinner. Went down to see "The Coconuts" in evening. It was very good. (This must have been a pre-Broadway show in November in 1925 as it opened in New York in December 1925.[132]) Jessie went with John Deitz. Marjorie went out to West Chester in the morning.

Sunday, November 29, 1925

Got up and went to church at the Asbury M. E. Church.[133] Went up to the dining room for dinner. Kate and Jessie went for a ride with John Deitz and a Mr. Thorpe. Didn't go to tea. Met Kathleen at 6:50 at West Phila. Went up to the Waffle Shop. Jessie and Kate had dates with Deitz and Thorpe in eve.

Monday, November 30, 1925

Jessie and Kate went over to the dining room for breakfast. I went down to school. They packed and went down to the station. Was excused from Economics and went down to the train with them, along with John Deitz. Their train was late. I couldn't wait until they left. **I hated to see them go as we had had such a good time.** Went up to the Waffle Shop at noon and got Joe's scarf he had left there last night. Studied in the eve.

Tuesday, December 1, 1925

Had a basketball meeting after school. Went to the boys' game between Drexel and Textile.[134] Drexel won. It was so exciting. Reba and I went over to the practice house for dinner. Had a date with Joe in eve. He was so sweet. I wonder if he likes me better than he used to?

Wednesday, December 2, 1925

Took laundry up before dinner. Got check cashed at drug store at 10 o'clock. Studied in eve. Wrote to Mama.

Thursday, December 3, 1925

Stayed down in library today and wrote my term paper on "Cheese" for Miss Burdett. Played basketball at 4 o'clock. Studied in eve.

---

[131] "Stage Struck" is a 1925 American silent comedy film starring Gloria Swanson, Lawrence Gray, Gertrude Astor, and Ford Sterling. The film was released by Paramount Pictures with the opening and ending sequences notable for being filmed in the early two-color Technicolor.

[132] "The Cocoanuts" opened at the Lyric Theater in New York City on December 8, 1925 and ran for 276 performances starring The Marx Brothers, Margaret Dumont, and Billy De Wolfe, with songs by Irving Berlin. The movie by the same name and actors was released in 1929.

[133] (Author's Note: This information parallels Jessie's memorabilia of her trip to Philadelphia which is in this author's possession. Jessie kept the church program, among many more programs and souvenirs from Philadelphia. Jessie is the author's maternal aunt and Mary Alice is the author's paternal aunt. Jessie and Mary Alice were high school classmates and good friends, and, of course, Kate later married Bubby, M.A.'s brother.)

[134] Philadelphia Textile school, part of Philadelphia University at the time.

Friday, December 4, 1925

Took trip through Wilbur Chocolate Factory today.[135] It has been raining almost all week. Had date with Joe in eve. Kathleen was with John and June with Dan Hennery. We were over at the apartment. Had the nicest time. Joe is still as sweet as ever.

Saturday, December 5, 1925

Wrote Alice. Stayed in all afternoon. Washed some things and sewed. In eve. had a date with Newton Clark McCullough. There was an Alumni Bazaar down at school and a dance. Jane with Al; I don't know his last name. We went down to school and danced awhile. Newt is awfully nice. He has light hair and blue eyes.

Sunday, December 6, 1925

Didn't go to church. Worked all day. Didn't go out at all, only to dinner and tea.

Monday, December 7, 1925

Wrote to Jessie. Worked on sewing awhile after school. Watched the court dance for a short time. Studied and sewed in eve.

Tuesday, December 8, 1925

Wrote to Kate and Marjorie. Last class in sewing this term. It is a great relief. Had B.B. practice after school. Studied in eve.

Wednesday, December 9, 1925

Had date with Joe in eve. Gave him his handkerchief I made for him. Hope he likes it. Painted some things for art after he left.

Thursday, December 10, 1925

Wrote Mama. Kathleen and I went down town all afternoon. Did a lot of shopping. Got some Xmas presents. Had lunch at the "Cathay." Studied in evening.

Friday, December 11, 1925

The Jordon "Playboy"

Wrote Bubby. Worked on Sewing notebook and finished it after school. Wilton Wright brought me home. He had a fellow's car from New Jersey. It is a Jordan Playboy. Had the best ride.[136] The top was down. Joe called after dinner. He and John wanted dates tonight, but Kathleen and I were too busy. Have dates tomorrow night.

---

135 This would have been part of the Home Economics program.

136 "Playboy" was the moniker that Jordan gave his rakish two-seat roadster when it debuted in April of 1919. The Jordan Playboy was an undistinguished automobile, but one thing set it apart from the competition—the advertising used to market the car.

Saturday, December 12, 1925

Had my last class in the morning for this term. June and I went downtown in the aft. Got my own Xmas present from Mama. An overnight bag. The stores and streets were packed. We had our Xmas party over at the Dining Room. Had a date with Joe. Have a date with Joe on Wednesday night. He gave me his picture tonight. It is so good of him. We went to the movies at the Arcadia. Milton Sills is in it.[137] Then we went up to the apartment awhile. No one else was there. Joe was so sweet. We didn't have long to stay.

Sunday, December 13, 1925

Wrote Jessie. Didn't go to church. Wrote some letters in the morning. Studied some in the aft. and again in eve.

Monday, December 14, 1925

Took Nutrition Final in aft. Studied all morning. Cecil called in eve. Studied English in eve.

Tuesday, December 15, 1925

Had English exam in the morning. June and I went down town in aft. Did a lot of Xmas shopping. Studied Art in evening.

Wednesday, December 16, 1925

Had Art exam in the morning. It was awful hard. Last night Miss Dorsey gave us a dorm party in her room We had hot ginger bread and coffee and candy canes. I drank 3 cups of coffee and could not get to sleep. Didn't even go to bed until 3 o'clock. Was up in Kathleen's room. I packed my suitcase and sent my laundry in afternoon. Had a date with Joe in evening. Last time I will see him before or until after vacation.

Thursday, December 17, 1925

Studied for Sewing exam in morn. Had formal assembly and sang Xmas carols in the court afterwards. Took Sewing exam in aft. Think I passed it. Also passed English and Art. Studied some. Joe called me up from the North Philadelphia Station. He was on his way home. I won't see him for 2 weeks or more.

Friday, December 18, 1925

Took Food Economics exam in morning. It was hard. Jane and a lot of the girls left for home for Xmas vacation in morning. The house seems so lonely. Studied Economics awhile. Also studied some in eve. Kathleen and I talked a blue streak. Suppose Joe is home now having a big time. This time tomorrow night I will be home maybe.

Saturday, December 19, 1925

Got up early to study some more economics. Took exam in morn. Took me 2 hrs. Came up to house and took a bath and got dressed. Went over to lunch. Did some sewing for Miss Dorsey in aft. Left for home at 3:33. Met Marjorie at the West Philadelphia station. Frances Light was along. Bub was on the train also. I do hope he asks me for a date while I am home.

137 Probably "The Sea Hawk."

Mama and Papa met us at Tyrone. Got home about 10:30. Alice and Kenneth were up. Fooled around and unpacked before going to bed.

Sunday, December 20, 1925

Uncle Fred came up in the morning before we were dressed to tell us Aunt Belle had died. We went down to Uncle Fred's in aft. Stayed at home in eve. Hugh and Alice were up. Was up at Aunt Mary's awhile, also down to see Libby.

Monday, December 21, 1925

Went down to Uncle Fred's in morn. to help Aunt Maude. Made beds, cleaned the house up and dusted. Mama came down about 4 o'clock so I came home. Jessie, Alice, Marjorie, Kate, Alice M. and Edith Satille were here awhile. We went down to Jimmies. Have seen hardly anyone since I have been home. Wonder how Joe is? Hope he does write to me, but no danger. Wrote some Xmas cards in eve.

Tuesday, December 22, 1925

Went down to Uncle Fred's in the morning to help Aunt Maude. Made the beds and worked around. Came home about 4 o'clock with Papa. Mama went down then. Went to the stores, got some Xmas cards and sent them. Went up to Alice's awhile in eve.

Wednesday, December 23, 1925

Worked all morning. Went down to Aunt Belle's funeral in aft. It was well attended. Uncle Walt and Lottie were here for supper.[138] Had a date with Raymond Maurey in eve. Alice took us to Clearfield where she bought Hugh's Xmas present, a pair of cuff links. Raymond stayed until about 12 o'clock. The fire whistle blew at 2:30. It wasn't much.

Thursday, December 24, 1925

Wrapped some of my presents. Katy went out to Sykesville. Was down street in eve. Talked to J. S. awhile in Jimmies. Was up to Alice's. Trimmed the tree. Got to bed real late. Got a lot of nice presents.

Friday, December 25, Christmas

Helped Mama all morning. We were all at Aunt Grace's for dinner. Had a big dinner. Went all around in aft. Saw Bob for the 1st time since I have been home. If he would only ask me for a date. Alice and Hugh, Marjorie and John Wright, and George Wrigley and I were down at the Masonic Temple in the evening and danced. Had a good time.

Saturday, December 26, 1925

We girls all went down to the dance at the Legion Rooms in eve. Had the best time. Billie McClure came home with me. Danced with J.S., Orville Johnson, Lee Smith, Theo Jordon, George Wrigley and Hugh. Billie invited me to the Charity Ball Monday night.

---

138 Walter Thompson, brother to H. J. Lottie is Walter's wife, formal name is Charlotte.

Sunday, December 27, 1925

Didn't go to church. Uncle Fred and all the kids and Aunt Maude were up for dinner and supper. Billie McClure came up and took me for a ride in afternoon. Charley Halfred was along so we got Kate Smith. Had a date with George Wrigley in eve. Was up at Alice's.

Monday, December 28, 1925

Worked around in the morning. Went down town awhile in aft. In eve went to the Charity Ball with Billie. Had a real good time. Bub and Raymond were both there. Had a lot of good dances. Didn't get home until 3:15. Got something to eat up at Booth's afterward. If only Bub would ask me for a date. I don't know why I like him. I wished he liked me. There doesn't look like there is much hope for me to get a date with him.

Tuesday, December 29, 1925

Helped Mama in the morning. Bubby brought Katy[139] back from Sykesville. Jessie and I went to Clearfield with Marjorie in aft. Went to the dentist. Had my teeth cleaned. Billie was up awhile in eve. Bob Daugherty was with him. Stayed in most of eve. Went down to Jimmies with Libby and Marjorie.

Wednesday, December 30, 1925

Was in the house all day. Had date with Billie in eve. Went to the movies. Mama and I went up to Jimmies after 11:00. Listened to radio.

Thursday December 31, 1925, New Year's Eve

Did some sewing in the morning. Went to a formal dance at the Acorn Club at DuBois in evening with Billie. [140] It was a "wet" party and the dance didn't begin until 10:00. Got home about 3:30. Stopped at Booth's. Raymond was there.

1926

Friday, January 1, 1926

Served awhile in the morn and aft. Went out with the girls in eve, then Leonard and John took Marjorie and me up to Groffe Acres. Came home early.

Saturday, January 2, 1926

Marjorie, Jessie, Kate, Alice, and I went down to Clearfield. Went to the stores. Talked to Allen Petace for a long time. We were down at the "Pig and Whistle." Went to the "Chatterbox" for dinner. Alice and I went over to Strickland's to see the baby after we came up from Clearfield. He is the sweetest thing. Went down to the Legion Rooms to the dance. Had the best time. Made Billie real cross at me because I wouldn't let him bring me home. Blair Mann was there. Danced with J.S. and Kirk Hile. Jessie and I took Alice home then we went up to Jimmies. Kirk Hile and another fellow wanted dates with us. Kirk is so good-looking.

---

[139] A reminder that Katy is the woman who helps with Philip and, I would presume, house chores.
[140] Could have been a copycat or affiliate of the Acorn Club in Philadelphia, a women's social club.

Sunday, January 3, 1926

Packed my bags and Mama and I went to church. Had dinner right after church. Went up to say goodbye to Mama and Papa Spencer. Went down to the train. Alice, Jessie, Kate and Al Murray were down at the train, also Bubby & Uncle Charley. Bub King got on the train but he was with some other girl. Didn't know her. Didn't see him at Tyrone. Was talking to John Leitzinger awhile. Saw Billie McClure at Clearfield. Said goodbye to him. Guess he wasn't cross about last night. Marjorie got off at Harrisburg to see the Principal of the schools about teaching there next year.

Came up to 216 N. 31st Street house in taxi with Betty Biddle and Jean Whitney. Talked to Bill Brown. Hope he doesn't call me and if he does, hope I am busy. There are hardly any girls here yet. About 8. Jane is coming tomorrow. It's too quiet.

Monday, January 4, 1926

Got up late. Jane came in about 7:30 and awakened me. The other girls kept coming all morning. Went down to register. Took me until 2 o'clock. Had to choose around, trying to get my roster made out. Came up to the house. Jane and Kathleen and I went down to see "The Merry Widow"[141] at the Stanley. It was real good. Joe called up about 5:30. He and John came over in eve. We had 10:30 permissions. Kathleen and I went over to the apartment. We had a big time.

Tuesday, January 5, 1926

Had a 9 o'clock class with 3 hrs. of sewing. It was terrible. Came up to house. Kathleen and I had lunch up in her room. Had to go back down for gym class. Came home and worked on Memory Book.[142] I got one today. Studied awhile.

Wednesday, January 6, 1926

Had classes every hr. Three hours of sewing just kills me. Saw Piggy today to talk to, the first this term. Wrote some letters in eve. and did some work for sewing.

Thursday, January 7, 1926

Didn't have a class until 9 o'clock. June and I came up to the house and got our lunch here. Made toast and had some cheese. Had class from 1 to 4. Went on a trip for Food Economics. Went to Park's Tea Co. Kathleen and I then went to see Douglas Fairbanks in "Don Quixote" at the Stanton. It was real good. Got home just in time for dinner.

Friday, January 8, 1926

Didn't have any classes until 11 o'clock then came up to house and got my lunch in Kathleen's room. Made some toast and tea. June and Kathleen and I went down to Jack Hart's in eve. Had the best time. Danced with a fellow who rooms with Dick Leopold from Clearfield. Bill Hutchens brought me home. He is a real cute little boy with red hair. Am going out with him next weekend.

---

141 "The Merry Widow" (1925 film). Released by Metro-Goldwyn-Mayer, the film stars Mae Murray and John Gilbert, with pre-fame uncredited appearances by Joan Crawford and Clark Gable.
142 Presuming this is the one that came to my possession.

Saturday, January 9, 1926

Had classes 3 hrs. Sat morn. June and Kathleen and I went shopping in the aft. Got a lot of things. Jane and Kathleen and I had dates in eve. with Joe, John, and Danny. Went over to the apt. Don't think we are going over there anymore. Joe made me so mad tonight. He is so foolish about some things. He always wants his own way and I won't give it to him.

Sunday, January 10, 1926

Didn't get up until 10:30. Pressed dresses and sewed all aft. Had date with Piggie in eve. June had one with Bob Fox. Studied after they left.

Monday, January 11, 1926

Wrote Bubby. Today is John Joseph's birthday. He is 19. Sent him a card last night. Went to school at 10 o'clock. Only had 2 hrs. today. Didn't have any physics lab. Came up to house. Did some studying. Sewed and studied in eve. Wrote to Alice.

Tuesday, January 12, 1926

Had 3 hrs. of sewing. Cut out my dress. Got 5 letters today. Mama, Bubby, Arthur Wall, A. Murray, and Louise Taylor. Alice Wall is coming down to Beechwood to school in just a couple of weeks. Went downtown in aft. Got frame for Joe's picture. Had lunch in Gimble's Tea Room. Came up to school to Basketball practice at 4 o'clock. Have a game out at Swarthmore on Friday aft. Don't know if I will get out or not. Wrote to Mama.

Wednesday, January 13, 1926

Had classes every hr. Ate lunch with Piggie. He is working in the cafeteria both at noon and in the eve. Studied in eve. Wonder when Joe will be over again. I don't expect to see him for a while. Studied in eve. Bill Hutchens called me. I have a date with him on Friday night.

Thursday, January 14, 1926

June and Kathleen and I went downtown at 2 o'clock. Got collar and cuffs for new black dress. Was talking to Don Rowe, our head waiter, after breakfast this morning. He is very nice. He asked me if I was going to the Junior Prom. Wonder why; guess he hadn't any reason. Kathleen had a date with John in eve. Joe didn't come over. Said he had some work to do. I wonder. I expected this, though, after Saturday night. This is the first week this year I have not had a date with Joe.

Friday, January 15, 1926

Cut English class on Fri aft. Came up to house, then went out to Swarthmore to see the Drexel girls play basketball. We lost 67-10. They had a wonderful team. Had a date in eve with Bill Hutchens from Schenectady, New York. Went down to see "Souls for Sale"[143] then went up to the Cathay Tea Garden Restaurant where we danced.

---

[143] This was the closest title I could find, although the word looks more like "Fables."

Saturday, January 16, 1926

Went out to West Chester after lunch. Got out there about 4 o'clock. Marjorie (Wall) and Marge Irvin met me. After dinner there was a play by the Moore Literary Society, called "The Imaginary Invalid.[144] It was really good.

Sunday, January 17, 1926

Got up about 10 o'clock. Went down to some tearoom for breakfast. After dinner went down to see Cornelia Smith from Hollidaysburg.[145] Went up to Marge Irvin's for a while. Bill Patterson was there; I had met him last year. He is real cute. He went down along to the trolley. Got back about 6:15. Studied some in eve. Wrote some letters. Wish Joe had called. Wonder when he will. Guess he doesn't like me anymore.

Monday, January 18, 1926

Finished a book for English in eve. "Far From the Madding Crowd." It was good. Thought maybe Joe would call tonight, but no luck. I wonder when. Wrote to Jessie.

Tuesday, January 19, 1926

Didn't have any classes in aft. Stayed down in the library and studied. Had basketball practice at 4:00. June and I had dates in eve. John didn't come over; he sent Kathleen a note.

Wednesday, January 20, 1926

Wrote Mama and Marjorie. Piggie walked down to school part way with me this morn. Had classes every hr. Had a telegram from Alice to meet her tonight at 9:35. Jane and I went down to Broad St. and met her. Got some ice cream over at the drug store. Talked a long time. Jane gave Alice her bed and slept over in Betty and Jane's room.

Thursday, January 21, 1926

Alice and I went over to breakfast. Went down to school and showed Alice around. Went down town. She got a hat. We each got cards and sent to J.S. Tomorrow is his birthday. Went up to the Stanley. Saw "His Secretary."[146] It was real good. Went up to the "Cathay" for lunch. Had Chicken Chow Mein. Alice went out to Jenkintown on the 4:02. Came up to the house. In eve. June and I went down to the basketball game. Drexel fellows played Susquehanna and won 32-20. It was a wonderful game. Piggie brought me home.

Friday, January 22, 1926

Jimmy Strickland is 21 today. Had classes until 4 o'clock. Alice came back in from Beechwood today. They didn't have room for her. She goes out again a week Tuesday. Called Cecil up and he came over awhile in eve.

---

[144] Moliere.

[145] Likely a classmate from Highland Hall.

[146] "His Secretary" is a 1925 American silent comedy film directed by Hobart Henley. The film starred Norma Shearer and Lew Cody. It is now considered lost.

Saturday, January 23, 1926

Alice didn't go down to classes with me. Called her Dad up at home. I had classes all morn. After lunch we went downtown. Did some shopping. Went to see "Dark Angel."[147] It was great. Met Cecil, Marjorie, Marge Irvin, and Bill Thorpe's cousin in Wanamaker's about 5 o'clock. Had a regular family reunion. After dinner Alice and I went down to the Stanton. Saw "That Royle Girl."[148]

Sunday, January 24, 1926

Went to church. Took a walk up around the University. It was awful cold. After dinner Alice and I went out to Beechwood. Met some darling girls. Alice found her trunk and got some clothes out. Went over to the Tea Rose for tea. Had a date with Piggie in eve. Alice had a date with Bob Hartman and June with Bob Fox. Wrote English theme before I went to bed.

Monday, January 25, 1926

Alice went out to Arthur Robinson's this morning to stay until Friday. She called me up tonight. I had classes all day. Did some washing after school. Edna Forney had Kathleen and me over to the Practice House for dinner tonight. Sewed a dress in eve.

Tuesday, January 26, 1926

Wrote Mama. Worked on dress awhile in apt. Went down town to get a buckle for it. Went to basketball practice. Studied in eve. Called Alice.

Wednesday, January 27, 1926

Stayed down at school until 5:30 and finished dress. Sewed and wrote some letters in eve. Wonder when I will ever hear from Joe. He is in love with some girl in Detroit. I suppose by now he is out there with her during his vacation. Maybe someday he will like me again. Wrote Kate. Wrote Gertrude Stamp.

Thursday, January 28, 1926

Wrote Jessie. Wrote Bubby. Had only one class today. Went down town with June. Had lunch at the Automat. Came up to house and did some work. Went back down to school for basketball practice. Studied in evening.

Friday, January 29, 1926

Studied in library in morn. and aft. Took trip to a good bakery at 4 o'clock. Was late for dinner. Alice came in from West Chester. She spent yesterday there with Marjorie. Jane took her over to dinner. Alice and Kathleen went down to Jack Hart's. Joe and Danny were there. Joe was walking with some awful girl. I don't care if I ever see him again. Guess he doesn't like me anymore anyway since I haven't heard from him for so long. June and I went over to the Drexel Phi Kappa Beta dance. I was with Allen Gilbert. He is terrible. Had a rather good time. Piggie was with Peg Hartel. Wonder who I will ask to our house dance? Haven't the least idea.

---

[147] "The Dark Angel" was a 1925 silent film starring Ronald Colman and Vilma Banky, now a lost film.
[148] "That Royle Girl" is a 1925 American silent comedy film directed by D.W. Griffith and released by Paramount Pictures.

Saturday, January 30, 1926

Kathleen, Jane, Alice and I all slept over in Jane's room. Betty and Jane were in ours last night. We ate a loaf of bread and a cake before going to bed. Got it at the bakery. Didn't go to breakfast. Got out of class early. Alice and I went down town. She got some shoes. Went to the Russian Inn for lunch. Fooled around downtown. Called up Miss Dashiell. Got a sundae over at Whitman's. Got dressed for the formal dinner. Miss Dashiell was here with me and also Alice. Danced awhile afterwards down in the parlor. We all went down to the train with Miss Dashiell. Stopped at school, saw the end of the basketball game. We lost 28-16 to St. Joseph's (boys). There wasn't any dance. Came up to the house. Miss Dorsey came up about 12:30 and bawled us out for not being in bed.

Sunday, January 31, 1926

Didn't go to church. It was raining. Stayed in all aft. Had a date with Joe in eve. He brought a fellow (John Spentel) with him. Got Edith Newton for him. Didn't know if I like Joe anymore or not.

Monday, February 1, 1926

Didn't go to breakfast. No mail today. Had quiz in Physics. Was through at 3 o'clock. Alice was down at school today. We came up to the house. Studied in eve. Finished my book "The Nigger of the Narcissus."[149] Didn't like it much.

Tuesday, February 2, 1926

Wrote Mama. Had sewing class all morning. Alice came down about 10:30 and came into class with me. We came up to the house after lunch. She parked and took the 2:17 train to school, I went downtown along. Got a check cashed at the Franklin National; Papa sent it today. Went back to school to basketball practice. Went down to the court dance awhile. Some boy came up on 3rd floor and took me down to dance with him. Don Rowe cut in. I was so tickled. Wonder who I am going to invite to our house dance? I cannot make up my mind.

Wednesday, February 3, 1926

Had classes every hr. Talked to Piggie awhile after school. I stayed and sewed awhile. Alice called after dinner. John Wandall was here this aft. to see Kathleen. Guess I have a date with Joe on Saturday night.

Thursday, February 4, 1926

Wrote Alice. Studied in the library today. Stayed down for basketball practice. The Freshmen had a big dinner up at the dining room.

Friday, February 5, 1926

Studied in the library some today. Alice called up. She came in after dinner. June and I went down to meet her. We went to Jack Hart's in eve. Had the best time. John Wandall came home with me.

---

[149] The book was based on Conrad's experiences while serving in the British Merchant Navy.

Friday, February 6, 1926

Got up for breakfast. Alice went down along to first class then came back to house with Jane and Kathleen. Elizabeth Dokes, Kathleen's girlfriend, came today. Alice and I went downtown after lunch. Met Kathleen and Elizabeth at Wanamaker's. I got a hat. Kathleen fooled around looking for an evening dress. Came up to house, got dressed and we all (Alice, Edith Newton, Kathleen, Elizabeth and I) went down to the Cathay for dinner. Met John, Joe, Mim Spardle, Jerry (the new roomie) and Chick. Went up to the apt. and fooled around. They all went down to the Dance Box to dance except Joe and I. Jane wouldn't go. Had more fun going up to get on trolley car. Some fellow was drunk. Joe and I fussed until about 11:30, then made up. He couldn't be too nice then.

Sunday, February 7, 1926

Didn't go to church. Fooled around all morning. Alice went out to school in aft. The day went so fast. Kathleen and I took her down to the train. Had a date with some fellow in eve. Linn Gramer brought him over. Jane had a date with Linn.

Monday, February 8, 1926

Wrote Mama and Papa Spencer. Finished classes at 3 o'clock. Came up to house and did some washing. Studied in eve. Fraternity boys were over tonight as part of their initiation.

Tuesday, February 9, 1926

Wrote Mama. Came up to house about 12:30. Didn't have any classes in aft. Did some studying and wrote a letter. Did some ironing and sewing. Studied in eve. Wonder if Joe will call tomorrow night or is he cross or does he like the girl he had a date with Sunday night too much or the girl in Detroit? I don't care if he is cross about anything I did, for I didn't do anything that should make him cross.

Wednesday, February 10, 1926

Had classes in evening. Dr. Plummer didn't come to Economics class this morning, so we left. Talked to Piggie after school. Studied in eve. Wonder when Joe will call; guess I was wrong in thinking he had changed on Saturday night.

Thursday, February 11, 1926

Mailed laundry in morning. Went down town in the afternoon. Came back to school for Basketball practice and then there wasn't any. Studied in eve. Eleanor Coan came down for the weekend. She is staying with Florence Kreutzer.

Friday, February 12, 1926

Got hair washed and curled up at Johnson and Johnson in morning. Had telegram from Papa. Met him at West Phil. Station at 5:43. Had dinner at the Tea Rose. Mama expects to come down on Monday. Got a room for them right next to the Tea Rose. Went down to school to Cap and Bells. Stayed awhile. Went down to Jack Hart's. Had the best time. Karl Rowles from Clearfield brought me home. Bill Brown, Mamie Higgins, Margaret Ardary were there.

Saturday, February 13, 1926

Alice came after lunch. We were to meet Papa at Wanamaker's at 2:00, but missed him. Fooled around awhile and came back to house and helped decorate for the dance. Got dressed for the formal dinner. Had our Valentine House Dance in eve. John Joseph was here with me. Alice had a blind date. I didn't care much for him. Kathleen had John. June had her Joe from home. Kitty Betz, June's friend was here. Frank Graner was here for her. John Spentel was with E. Newton. Eleanor Coen was here with Harry. He is a wonderful dancer. I had a valentine box of candy from Blair Mann.

Sunday, February 14, 1926

Wrote to Kate and Alice. Didn't get up until 10:30. Got dressed and went over to see Papa, but he wasn't there. Alice and I went out to Arthur Robinson's for dinner. Had a wonderful meal. Alice then went out to school at 4:45. I came back to the house. Left a note over at the house for Papa. Wrote letters and studied in eve (Delta Sigma Phi fraternity).

Monday, February 15, 1926

Stayed down at school until almost dinner time, working on forms. Finished it. Heard that we are going to be brought up before student government for going to The Dance Box a week ago Saturday night. Some fellow told a girl and she reported Edith and Kathleen. I wasn't with them and I am not going to say that I was. I was supposed to have seen "Bluebeard's 7 Wives" at the Stanley and they saw "Hands Up"[150] at the Karlton. Had a box of candy from Aunt Maude. Mama called right after I got home from dinner. Jane and I met her and Papa down at Broad Street Station. Papa went to a meeting and we went to The Stanley. Saw "The Duchess and The Waiter."[151] Had the best dancers and orchestra.

Thursday, February 16, 1926

Saw Mama and Papa after breakfast. Had sewing class all morning. Went downtown all afternoon. Got material for a dress for sewing class. Went back for girls' basketball game with New York University and lost 15-22. Helped serve cocoa to the girls afterwards. Called Cecil in eve. Studied.

Wednesday, February 17, 1926

Saw Mama and Papa after breakfast. Wrote to Marjorie. Had classes every hour. Went to a little retail grocery store after school with Mildred Starner. Studied in evening.

Thursday, February 18, 1926

Went down town with June and Kathleen in afternoon. Went back to school at 4 o'clock for basketball practice and there wasn't any. Came up to house and slept awhile. After dinner I went to a dance with Mama and Papa at the Benjamin Franklin Hotel. Harry Gates got me a date, Sutton Hamilton from Punxsutawney. He is down here at Penn Medical School. He

---

[150] American silent comedy, 1926.

[151] 1926 silent romantic comedy directed by Mal St. Clair and starring Florence Vidor and Adolphe Menjou. The film is based on a 1925 Broadway play of the same name.

lives in the "Mask and Wig" dorm. He was real nice and a good dancer; wonder if I will ever see him again. It was a dance for the Hardware Convention. John Joseph called me after I had gone.

Friday, February 19, 1926

Wrote Jessie. Saw Mama and Papa after breakfast. Came over to the house and did some work. Helped Jane with some things for her luncheon. Girls had Basketball game and beat Juniata College 18-20. I am so glad they won. Stayed in for evening.

Saturday February 20, 1926

Had classes all morning. Went downtown and had lunch at Wanamaker's with Mama and Papa. Met Alice and Cecil. Alice went with us to the movies at the Earle Theatre. It was real good. We left Mama and Papa and did some shopping. We went out to school and I came up to the house for dinner. Went downtown and met Mama and Papa at Broad St. Station. Went to The Broad Street Theatre and saw "Ladies of the Evening."[152] It was real good.

Sunday, February 21, 1926

Got up about 10:30. Went over to see Mama and Papa. They went out to Underwoods while I went to Abigale's with Kathleen. She lives at Frankford. Went to the Tea Rose and got something to eat. Cecil and Mr. Dennison came over to see Mama and Papa. I was over awhile, but came to the house. I hope to have a date with Joe tomorrow night.

Monday, February 22, 1926

Had breakfast at the Tea Rose with Mama and Papa. Went downtown and did some shopping. Met Mrs. Kittelberger. Papa left us and we had lunch at the Cathay. Went to the Palace and saw "Infatuation."[153] It was real good. Came up to house for dinner. Stayed in in eve. Just one year ago tonight I had my first date with John Joseph. John Wandall and all brought him out to Sue Krusens for me on a blind date. No date with Joe tonight, however. He has deserted me for good now. I will not be able to see him any night this week. I have so much to do.

Tuesday, February 23, 1926

A slow day. Saw Papa and Mama, wrote to Alice Murray, made a quick trip down town, got back for basketball practice.

Wednesday, February 24, 1926

Papa went to Parksburg today so I went over to see Mama after breakfast. Had classes every hr., 2 quizzes today, economics and sewing, then Mama and I were over at Cecil's fraternity to dinner—the Acacia Fraternity. We then went to see "May Flowers" at Chestnut St. Opera House. It was real good. Wrote Marjorie, Grace Johns, and Jessie.

---

[152] Norma Shearer and possibly Joan Crawford.
[153] Silent film adaptation of the 1919 play *Caesar's Wife* by Somerset Maugham.

Thursday, February 25, 1926

Went over to see Mama and Papa after breakfast. Mailed laundry. At school all day. Stayed for basketball game with Osteopathy; girls won 40-4. Studied in evening.

Friday, February 26, 1926

A full day. Saw Mama and Papa in morn, Mama came down to school for lunch in the cafeteria and met Piggie. Then after school I pressed some dresses for her. At that point Cecil called and invited me to their fraternity dance tomorrow night with George Eishner. After the call I went to Jack Hart's and had the best time with some wonderful dancers. Pete Pross was there; he is going to call me up sometime. Charley Moses wants a date with me. Matt Storey danced with me. He was a wonderful dancer and tall and good looking. He asked to bring me home, but I came home with Bill Brown. Danced with a cute fellow from Clarion, also with Mr. Kochler. Joe was there as well, but I didn't pay much attention to him. Guess he is tired of me, but what's the diff. It isn't worrying me any.

Saturday, February 27, 1926

Didn't go to classes in the morning. Stayed up at house and studied. Took a break when Alice came at 12:30. Went over to Tea Rose for lunch. Met Mama, Papa, Cousin Anna, Marjorie, and Marge at Wanamaker's. Alice and Marjorie and I went to the Fox. Saw "The Outsider."[154] Marge and Marjorie and I had dinner at the Tea Rose. Alice went out to school. In evening Cecil, Mr. Collins, and George Eichner came over. Went down to the Karlton and saw "Clothes Make the Pirate."[155] Then went up to the Acacia Fraternity and had the best time. I like George Eichner a lot. Two great full days in a row!

Sunday, February 28, 1926

Wrote Kate. Wrote Aunt Maud and Patty Kirk. Got up and had breakfast at the Tea Rose. Went in to see Mama and Papa. Marge and Marjorie went out to West Chester. Studied in aft. and eve. Wrote some letters. Took some pictures of myself and Jane after dinner.

Monday, March 1, 1926

Saw Mama and Papa and Orlie Norris in morning. Was at school all day. Talked to Piggie. Sewed on dress in eve.

Tuesday, March 2, 1926

Papa and Mr. Norris went to Springfield this morning. Mama stayed in the hotel, then came down to school at 4 o'clock. Went to basketball game; Ursinus girls beat us 55-13. She went over to the house to dinner along. Then she went down town to meet Mrs. Kittelberger. Studied all eve. Had a party for Mrs. Scott. She is going to her sister's tomorrow for a month or so. Have a new house mother while she is gone. (Miss Bergen).

[154] Silent film with Walter Pidgeon.
[155] 1925 American silent film starring Leon Errol and Dorothy Gish.

Wednesday, March 3, 1926

Saw Mama in morning. She was alone last night, but I had to be here. Had classes every hr. today. Got pictures we took on Sunday. Not so bad.

Thursday, March 4, 1926

I was glad that Mama and I could spend this morning shopping. I had to go back to school at 1 o'clock. Went to basketball practice. Studied in evening.

Friday, March 5, 1926

Another long day. Had classes until 4 o'clock. Went over to see Mama before and after dinner. Talked to Cecil. Went to Military Dance at the Adelphia with Al Mathis from Drexel. It was a Drexel dance. Had a real good time. Best orchestra. Had 1:30 permission. A gang of us left early and went down to Childs and ate. Coming home our taxi was hit and punctured a tire. We had to get out and get in another one. Got home just in time.

Saturday, March 6, 1926

Saw that Mama, Papa, and Mr. Norris came back, but didn't see them. Met Alice downtown in afternoon. We went to the Stanley to see May Murray in "The Masked Bride." The Gimbel Fashion show was on. Dottie Ake was in it. Stayed home in eve.

Sunday, March 7, 1926

Mama went home this morning, but Papa still has business appointments. Went over at noon and saw Papa. Sewed in afternoon. Had date with Piggie in eve.

Monday, March 8, 1926

Mailed a couple pkgs. in the morning. Washed both of Joe's scarves and sent them to him. Went down to Reading Terminal to learn about cheese. Took my overnight bag down to Gimbels to have my initials put on it. Studied in eve.

Tuesday, March 9, 1926

Wrote Bubby. Finished a book for English. Read in library all aft. Went over to Penn to girls' basketball game at 4 o'clock. We lost 38-11; the game was in Bennett Hall, the Girls New Dorm. Studied in eve.

Wednesday, March 10, 1926

Stayed after school and sewed on dress. Studied and sewed in evening. Wrote Jessie.

Thursday, March 11, 1926

Wrote Marjorie. Mailed laundry, got tickets and Pullman sleeper for Kathleen and me to go home. Was at school all day. Studied and sewed on dress in eve.

Friday, March 12, 1926

Wrote to Alice Wall. Finished dress today. Worked at school all day. Studied in eve. Piggie called me up.

Saturday, March 13, 1926

Wrote Mama. Classes all morning. Stayed home all afternoon. Fooled around. Had a date with Piggie in eve. Went down to school. The girls and boys varsity played the Alumni in basketball. Both varsity teams won. Went up to the Waffle Shop afterwards.

Sunday, March 14, 1926

Got up for breakfast on Sunday for a change. Piggie went to church with me. Went down to Asbury Methodist. Took some pictures after dinner. Piggie and I had ours taken together. Saw George Eichner at church and asked him to tell Cecil to call me which he did in the evening.

Monday, March 15, 1926

Studied English all morning. June, Betty Bell, E. Newton, Milly and I ate lunch over in June's room. Had cheese sandwiches, peas, cakes and oranges. Took Food Ec. exam in aft. Came home from it and studied some. Went up to Shoemaker's after dinner. Studied English and Sewing in eve. Stayed up in Kathleen's room until 1:15. Ate onions and drank coffee.

Tuesday, March 16, 1926

Took English 5 exam in morning and sewing in aft. Slept awhile then studied until 3:30. Drank some more coffee.

Wednesday, March 17, 1926

Got up at 6:30 to study. Only got 3 hrs. sleep last night. Had 2 hard exams today, English and Economics. Slept about an hour before dinner. Studied Physics in eve.

Thursday, March 18, 1926

Got up at 6:30 and studied Physics. Took exam in morning. Met Kathleen at noon. Went to Wan Kew for lunch. Chased around at stores all aft. Fooled around all eve. No more exams to study for.

Friday, March 19, 1926

Went up and had my hair washed and curled. Went down to school for lunch. Saw Piggie. He walked up to the house with me. Slept awhile in aft. Met Alice at Reading Terminal at 4 o'clock. Chased around to the stores. Was up at the house for dinner. Went down to Jack Hart's. Had the best time. Kathleen and I left at 11:30 to catch our sleeper at West Phila. First time either one of us was ever on a sleeper. Had more fun in dressing. Got up and looked out every time the train stopped. Didn't sleep much.

Saturday, March 20, 1926

Porter called us at 6:30. Got dressed as we got off at Tyrone at 7:05. Went down town and got breakfast. Papa and Mama met us at 9 o'clock. Went over to Bellefonte. Went all through the new Richelieu Theatre. Was at Heverlys for supper. Started home about 6 o'clock. Called all around after we got home (to Curwensville) and saw a bunch of the kids.

Sunday, March 21, 1926

"First day of spring." Kathleen and I went to church with Jessie. Took some pictures in the afternoon. Had a whole gang of kids. Libby King is home. Had a date with Raymond in eve. and Kathleen with John Wright. They stayed until after 12 o'clock.

Monday, March 22, 1926

Fooled around all morning. Went down town. Was in the bank and saw Bruce. Went in to see J. Holten. Went to Clearfield after dinner. Got a dress pattern. Chased around with the girls in eve. Even went down to see Aunt Grace.

Tuesday, March 23, 1926

Went out for errands and was so surprised to see Jimmy Strickland home from Detroit. Went to basketball game at high school in eve. High School played Independents and won 18-19. It was a real good game. Burton, Bruce, Martin, Bubby all played on Independents. Went up to Jessie's after the game. Jimmy was there, first date with him for about a year. I still love him, I guess. Kathleen was with John Wright.

Wednesday, March 24, 1926

Sewed some after breakfast, then we went to some of the stores. Went up to the High School in the afternoon. John Wright took Kathleen to the dance and I went with George Wrigley. Had a real good time. Jimmy Strickland was there. We stopped in at "The Sweet Shop" at intermission. Catherine (Pifer) wasn't working there at the time, but I'll see her tomorrow. Did a little parking after we got home. Went to bed at 2 o'clock.

Thursday, March 25, 1926

Got up and was ready to leave by 7. Bubby drove us over to Altoona to get the 10:02 to Philadelphia, to take the Limited extra fare train. Mama and Catherine were along with us and we were up at Gables store a couple of minutes in Altoona. Our train to Philadelphia was an hour late. We hit a big truck on the other side of Lancaster. Guess the driver was stuck. Stayed in all eve. Kathleen had a date with John Wandall.

Friday, March 26, 1926

Had classes every hr. until 2:00. Went to Jack Hart's in evening. Had a real good time, But I am beginning to get tired of it. Just the same old thing. If I could only get a nice boyfriend, but I don't seem to be able to. Wrote Mama. Wrote Piggie.

Saturday, March 27, 1926

Had classes all morning. Alice came up to the house after lunch. Went downtown shopping and went out to school with her. Was down in Libby Barnes' room most of the time. Went to the movies in eve. there at school.

Sunday, March 28, 1926

Didn't get up until 11:30. Got dressed in time for lunch. Did a little sewing for Alice. Came back in at 4:10. Jane hasn't come back yet. Studied in eve.

Monday, March 29, 1926

Wrote M. Hill. Had classes every hour. Started in Chem. again today. Here's hoping I pass it. Had letter from Cathryn Reese telling me Marjory Hill and Eddie Miller were married Friday. Was up in a room to a chicken feed. Oh, boy!

Tuesday, March 30, 1926

Was in Chem lab nearly all day. Got Group I done and all correct. Yeah!!! Studied in eve.

Wednesday, March 31, 1926

Had classes every hour. Rained all day. Nothing exciting. Alice is going home tomorrow.

Karlton Theatre lobby in the 1920s

Thursday, April 1, 1926 (April Fool)

Went downtown. Went to Broad Street station to see Alice off and missed her. Saw the McDonald twins from DuBois. Got a hat and dress and a birthday present for Joe. Had a class at 2 o'clock. Fooled around after school. Went down to the Karlton Theatre in eve. Chaperoned 2 freshmen girls.

Friday, April 2, 1926

Didn't get up for breakfast. Washed some things and fooled around all day. Only went to dinner. Stayed in in eve. Mrs. Kittelberger and Cecil called me. (Mrs. Scott came back.)

Saturday, April 3, 1926

Got up for breakfast. Sewed all morn. Had lunch in Alice Kay's room. Ruth Sutherland and I went down town awhile this afternoon. Stayed in this evening and sewed.

Sunday, April 4, 1926, Easter Sunday

Got up for breakfast. Jane, Sally and Helen Ellsworth went to Atlantic City in the morning and came back in eve. I went to church. Studied all aft. The kids came back in eve.

Monday, April 5, 1926

Had a letter from Marjorie. Classes every hour today. Studied in eve.

Tuesday, April 6, 1926

Didn't go to school until late. No mail. Had classes (Chem. lab) until 5 o'clock. Studied in eve.

Wednesday, April 7, 1926

Went downtown at noon and got a tie for Bubby for his birthday. Wrote some letters in eve. Alice called me.

Thursday, April 8, 1926

Came up to the house at 10 o'clock. Studied until 2:00. Went back to school. Fooled around all eve. Studied. Wrote Mama.

Friday, April 9, 1926

Was at school until 4 o'clock. Went for a walk through Fairmount Park after dinner. Went over to Hotel Pennsylvania to a Penn Dental Freshman dance. Gene Gomanski asked me to go on a blind date. He was terrible.

Saturday, April 10, 1926

Practiced some tennis in gym in morning. Met Alice at Wanamaker's at 1 o'clock. We went down to Ventura Inn for lunch, then went up to the Stanley and saw Dick Barthelmess in "Just Suppose."[156] It was real good. Went to a dance here in the house in eve. The Drexel Staff gave it. I was with Al Mathis. Had a good time. I was the only girl from "216" there.

Sunday, April 11, 1926

Didn't go to church. Washed some things after breakfast. Slept awhile after dinner. Kathleen and I went down to the Phi Chi Medical Fraternity for dinner followed by some movies afterwards. Had a real nice time. Was not so crazy about my assigned date. Mr. Kegerise or something like that. I had not met him before.

Monday, April 12, 1926

Wrote Papa. Wrote Bubby. Wrote Piggie. Had classes every hour. Received a letter from Papa. First one I ever received. Wrote some letters and studied in eve.

Tuesday, April 13, 1926

Wrote Mama. Wrote Tony. Wrote Alice. Was in chem. lab. nearly all day. Have to go all over my unknowns again. Letters from Mama and Julia Bullock. Pete Pross called me in eve. He can go to the Sophomore dance on Saturday and is bringing someone for Alice. So that is done.

Wednesday, April 14, 1926

Wrote Marjorie. Served at a luncheon Dr. Matterson gave for the Seniors. Jimmy Gillen was in the group I served. Studied and wrote a letter in eve. Alice called me.

Thursday, April 15, 1926

Worked in chem. lab again all morn. Didn't get unknown right. Am going to work on it again tomorrow. Sewed in eve. Roller skated after dinner.

Friday, April 16, 1926

Had classes up until 1 o'clock. Spent the rest of aft. in Chem. Practiced some tennis after lunch. Went to Jack Hart's in eve. Had the best time. Bill Brown brought me home. Matt Florey was there again. I like him a lot. Harry Brown was there also. He's a wonderful dancer.

Saturday, April 17, 1926

Had classes all morning. Talked to Wilton Wright down at school. Alice was up at home for lunch. Went up to have my hair curled, but didn't get it done. Went down to the Fox. Saw

---

[156] "Just Suppose" is a surviving 1926 American silent drama film with Barthelmess, a lead very popular at the time.

a good movie. Went to the Pagoda for dinner. Had the best time. Went to the Sophomore Hop in eve. Took Pete Pross. Had the best time I have had for a while. He is a Phi Delta. Brought Bill Meade with him, also a Phi Delta.

Sunday, April 18, 1926

Wrote Jessie. Alice and I went down to the Methodist Church. Alice went out to school[157] in aft. Went down to the train with her. Studied in eve.

Monday, April 19, 1926

Wrote to John Wright. Classes every hr. today. Quiz in Physics. It was terrible. Hope I passed it. Washed some things after school. Studied in eve.

Tuesday, April 20, 1926

Wrote to Mama. Had hair washed and curled in morning. Had classes all aft. Studied in eve.

Wednesday, April 21, 1926

Wrote to K. Smith and Marjorie Wall. Had classes all day. Jane and I went down town after school. Got a dress pattern. Studied in eve.

Thursday, April 22, 1926

Wrote to Mama Spencer. Came up to house at 10 o'clock. Mailed laundry. Went downtown with Jane. Got a pair of shoes. Ran into Lucinda Clark. Was so surprised. Studied in eve. Packed to go home with June tomorrow.

Friday, April 23, 1926

Had classes up until 2 o'clock. Came up to house. June, Kathleen, and I left for Allentown. Met John Wandall at 69th Street. Took us 2 hours on the trolley. Chased around awhile. June had a big party in eve. So much food.

Saturday, April 24, 1926

Got up late. Fooled around all morning. John came about 2 o'clock and took us to Bethlehem to see Vonkellers who have a hot house. They gave us a lot of flowers. It rained in eve. Had a real good time. Was with Joe Lainer. After the dance we took a long ride and stopped somewhere to eat.

Sunday, April 25, 1926

June, Kathleen, and Mrs. Frankenfield went to church and Sunday School. I was sick all day. I stayed in bed until 12 o'clock. In the afternoon a bunch of us took some pictures and went for a ride. It was awful cold. There were Kitty Butz, Tommy, Franklin Steine, John W., Joe Larnier, Jane, K. and I. We all had dinner at Frankenfields. Left for school at 7 o'clock. Mr. and Mrs. Wandall took us to the trolley.[158] Met June's Dad. Got back about 10:32.

---

[157] Beechwood/Beaver
[158] Presumably Wandalls also lived in the Bethlehem area.

Monday, April 26, 1926

Had classes every hr. Did some pressing after school. Alice W. called me in evening. Worked on a poster for Art in the eve. Wrote to Bub King and invited him to the Senior Ball. Hope he can come.

Tuesday, April 27, 1926

Papa called me after breakfast. He and Orlie are on their way home. They were up in the New England states. Worked on Home Ec. 30 posters all morning up at the house. Studied in eve. Bob King called. He cannot go to the Senior Ball. Don't know who I will ask now.

Wednesday, April 28, 1926

Wrote Mama. Had classes every hour. Did some studying in eve. Called the University and got Henry Bixler's address. Invited him to the Senior Ball.

Thursday, April 29, 1926

Finished my 3rd unknown in Chem. I got 100 on it. That's a great relief. Fooled around after dinner. Took a bath and got ready to go to the dance tomorrow night at West Chester. Henry Bixler called and he can come to the dance. I am so glad. Alice Wall called. Her Mother and Father are coming tomorrow and maybe Mama is coming along. I do hope so.

Friday, April 30, 1926

Left for West Chester at 2 o'clock. Missed Marjorie; she didn't meet me. Went on out to the school. She went to Norristown that night to see about a school. I went to their Junior Prom with Bill Patterson. Had a real good time.

Saturday, May 1, 1926

Got up and came back into school for a 11 o'clock class. Got a special from H. Kocher. She is coming next weekend. Met Alice (Wall), her Dad and Mother, Bea and Stella Robinson and Marguerite Riechenbaugh. Shopped. Had a sundae at Whitman's. Alice and Marguerite came up to the house awhile. The rest went out to Robinsons. Went down to the Mandarin for dinner. Went to see "No, No, Nannette"[159] in evening.

Sunday, May 2, 1926

Wrote Catherine Pifer, Marjorie Wall, Aunt Grace. Didn't go to church. Wrote some letters. After dinner, fooled around awhile. Went out to 69th St. to meet Alice. Was so surprised when I met John Joseph and Wasson at West Philadelphia station. They rode out to 69th St. with me. I would like to have a date with him one of these days. Alice, Marguerite Reichenbach, Margaret Sharp and I went out to Jenkintown (Beechwood/Beaver) and had one grand ride. Came back and studied.

Monday, May 3, 1926

Had classes every hr. Got laundry in aft. Did some washing after dinner, then studied. No mail today.

159 *No, No, Nanette* (Philadelphia Production) opened February 1925 in the Garrick Theatre.

Tuesday, May 4, 1926

Was in Chem lab nearly all day. Got 100 in both Groups 4 & 5 in my unknowns. Studied in eve. Worked on house plans.

Wednesday, May 5, 1926

Wrote Mama. Came up to house at noon. No assembly today. Kids were practicing for May Fete. Wilton Wright walked up to the house with me. Had class all aft. Got a dress but it is too big. Wrote letters and fooled around in eve.

Thursday, May 6, 1926

Came home at 10 o'clock. Mailed laundry, took bath and fooled around after dinner and slept awhile. Got ready for the Senior Ball. Took Harry Bixler. He is a wonderful dancer. The Court looked beautiful. Had a grand march, then went through receiving line. Had 2:30 permission. Got cute favors.

Friday, May 7, 1926

Had to go down to a 9 o'clock class. Helen Kolhner came up to house for me, then came down to school with Jane. Hadn't seen her for about 3 years. It was so good to see her again. Had a concert in the auditorium from 11:00 to 12:00. Kathleen and Helen and I went to the Tea Rose for lunch. Went downtown and right back. Had May Fete at school in aft. Alice Wall came in. She went down with Kathleen, met her there. Helen went back to the hotel; don't know if I will see her again or not. Had formal dinner at house. Went to Jack Hart's in eve. Had the best time. Harry was there and feeling good.

Saturday, May 8, 1926

Had a class at 11 o'clock. Alice went downtown; I met her at 1:30. Went to the Stanley and saw Coleen Moore in "Irene."[160] Went down to Plantation Inn at school for dinner. Held the pageant in eve. at school. Danced after. Jack Roberts brought me home. Wonder if he will invite me to their Spring Formal? Henry Stetina brought Alice home.

Sunday, May 9, 1926 (Mothers' Day)

Cecil and Alice and I went to church. Saw George Eichner. Didn't do a thing in aft. Went out to school. Studied in eve. Went to Vespers at 214.

Monday, May 10, 1926

Wrote Mama. Classes every hr. Started 1st General Unknown in Chem. today. Studied in eve. **Wrote to see about a job this summer.**

Tuesday, May 11, 1926

Wrote Grace. Went downtown after breakfast. Got some things. Was in chem. lab for 4 hrs. today. Studied in eve.

---

[160] A silent romantic comedy, partially filmed in Technicolor based on the stage production of "Colleen."

Wednesday, May 12, 1926

Had classes every hr. Was up at house at noon. Dottie Clymer called for me at school at 4 o'clock. Went up to fraternity and got Cecil. Went out to Dottie's for dinner. Had the nicest time. Dave, her husband, is very nice and she has the cutest little girl, "Doddie." Talked and then came home about 10:30.

Thursday, May 13, 1926

Wrote Mama and Alice. Went in Chem lab for 2 hrs. again today. Hope to finish Group I General tomorrow. Played tennis at 63rd St. after school with Edna Forney. Beat her; only hope I can keep the good work up.

Friday, May 14, 1926

Wrote Jessie and Marjory Hill. Had classes until 2:00. Came home and did some sewing. Took Mimsey Book over to the Practice House to get the girls to put their names in. John Wandall came and put his name in. Went down to Jack Hart's in eve. Harry Brown, Matt Storey, the boy who used to dance with Charlotte Starke—pink hair and some more. Had the best time.

Saturday, May 15, 1926

Had classes all morning. Talked to Jack Roberts. He asked me to the Phi Kappa Beta formal on the 28th. He had asked Harriet, but she told me to be sure and go if he asked me. Went down to the Kapolk House in aft. with Alice and Ethel. It surely is wonderful. Grace Johns came in eve. Went down to the Karlton and saw the Drexel Pageant in the news. E. Newton and I led the gang (Betty Biddle, Geare Johnson, Lib Hanes, Kate Howd, Dottie Oaks, Alice Kay, Ethel Buckley, E. Newton and myself). Went and took a #3 car. Stopped at some drugstore and got something to eat. A couple of men stopped and one of them talked to us.

Sunday, May 16, 1926

Wrote Marjorie W. Didn't get up until 11 o'clock. Jane got up early and went to Valley Forge with the Sorority. Wrote a letter. Grace Johns was here all day.

Monday, May 17, 1926

Had classes every hr. Kathleen and I went down town at 4 o'clock. Went around to the Part-Time Work Employment Agency. We might get a job in the Tea Room for this summer at Bay Head, NJ. Studied in evening.

Tuesday, May 18, 1926

Wrote Mama. Wrote English theme in morning. Worked in Chem. lab. After dinner Kathleen and I went out to Chestnut Hill to see Miss Cruise about working in her Tea Room. We got the job at $50 a month, but work from 15th of June to 15th of Sept.

Wednesday, May 19, 1926

Was going to play tennis after school but couldn't. Came up to house. Packed my laundry.

Thursday, May 20, 1926

Wrote Mama, Alice, Catherine Pifer. Cut Class. Came up to house. Alice called in eve. She is coming in tomorrow night. Did some sewing. Played tennis with Edna Forney at the 63rd St. court at 4 o'clock. Stetina was out there again.

Friday, May 21, 1926

Came up to house about 2:30. Alice came in about dinner time. Went to Jack Hart's in eve. Had a good time. Bob Drake brought me home. Bill Beam came home with Alice.

Saturday, May 22, 1926

Wrote Mama. Wrote Jessie. Alice went out to Arthur Robinson's in the morning and came back after lunch. Had classes all morning. We went down and saw "Queen High"[161] in aft. It was real good. Alice had a date with Bill Brown in eve. Stayed in and sewed.

Sunday, May 23, 1926

Got up and went to church. After dinner Alice and I went over to Miss Illman's to see Marian Horn. Went down to train with her. Marjorie Wall called me before ten. She was out at Kirk's over the weekend and called me from 69th Street Station. Studied in eve.

Monday, May 24, 1926

Had classes every hr. Studied in eve. Worked on Physics' experiments.

The Leader Theatre

Tuesday, May 25, 1926

Worked on color schemes up at house all morning. Finished up Chem lab in aft. Worked on Chem chart in eve.

Wednesday, May 26, 1926

Wrote Kate. Fooled around after school. Talked to Jack Roberts today. In eve. June and I took our first mid-week privilege and went to the movies up here on Lancaster Ave. at the Leader.[162] Saw Gloria Swanson in "The Untamed Lady."[163]

Thursday, May 27, 1926

Had my hair washed and curled in morning. Went downtown. Got a new white hat. Came back to class at 2 o'clock. Studied in eve.

Friday, May 28, 1926

Fooled around after school. Got ready for the dance after dinner. Went to the Phi Kappa Beta Spring Formal with Jack Roberts. Had the best time. It was at the Overbrook Country Club. Got cute favors, the best orchestra. Had 2 o'clock permission.

---

[161] 1926 stage musical *Queen High* that Buddy DeSylva, Lewis Gensler, and Laurence Schwab had adapted from Edward Peple's 1914 farce *A Pair of Sixes*.

[162] Originally a legitimate theatre, the Leader Theatre later became a movie house. It was remodeled in the early-1920s and again in 1935.

[163] This is a lost 1926 American silent drama film directed by Frank Tuttle.

Saturday, May 29, 1926

Jack called me up after lunch. June and I went down town in aft. Ruth Stout and I were the only girls in the house in the eve. Some of them went out to Drexel to the Freshman-Senior Dance. Did some sewing. Nice and quiet.

Sunday, May 30, 1926

Wrote Mama, C.A. Wall, and A. Murray. Didn't go to church. Fooled around all aft. Had a date with Jack Roberts in eve. Went out to the Arthur Robinson's home and stayed all night. Jack stayed until 1 o'clock.

Monday, May 31, 1926

Got up about 9:30. Fooled around all day until about 3:30. Came back to house. Sewed and fixed things all evening. Could have gone out, but didn't.

Tuesday, June 1, 1926

Had 1 hr. of class today. Worked on H. Ec. 30 at house all day. Didn't get to talk to Jack.

Wednesday, June 2, 1926

Talked to Jack a little. Didn't have any school in aft. It was Institute Day. The ROTC marched at 63rd St., but I didn't go out. Jane and I went down town. Had lunch at Ventura Gardens and ate outside. Got a blue flannel jacket. In eve. Cecil came for me and we went out to Mrs. Kittelberger's. Played bridge. Cecil and I each won prizes.

Thursday, June 3, 1926

Wrote Mama. Came up to the house at 11:00. Mailed laundry, wrote to Mama. Had class in aft. Got the kids to write their names in my Memory Book.

Friday, June 4, 1926

Worked on H. Ec. 30 all aft. Kathleen, June and I went to Jack Hart's in eve. Last time this year. Not very exciting tonight, Ronald Feioli brought me home. He said he was Spanish.

Saturday, June 5, 1926

Talked to Jack and Jerel Twiner at school in morning. Studied and worked around all aft. Had a date with Jack Roberts in eve. Went down to Stanley. Then I went up to the fraternity house, went in the back way. Danced. Was there over an hr.

Sunday, June 6, 1926

June and I went to church with Miss Dorsey. Two boys came home with me, including Carl Gregory. He is so very nice. Marjorie and Marge were here for a few minutes after dinner. Studied all aft and eve. Went to bed early at 11:00.

Monday, June 7, 1926

Wrote Mama. Wrote Alice. Studied all morning on Eng. and Chem. June and I ate lunch in her room. Took Physics exam in aft. Came to house and studied Eng. Studied Chem. all evening. Am scared to death about both of them, only wish they were over.

Tuesday, June 8, 1926

Wrote Bubby. Had my 2 hardest finals today: Chem and Eng. Passed Physics. Fooled around after school. Studied Ec. in eve.

Wednesday, June 9, 1926

Took Economics exam in morning. It was rather easy. Kathleen and I went down town. Had lunch at the Cathay. Did some intensive shopping. Met Miss Cruise at the College Club at 2:30. Made arrangements about going down on Tuesday. Studied for Home Ec. 30 in eve.

Thursday, June 10, 1926

Took Home Ec. 30 exam in morning. Fooled around all aft. Did some sewing. In eve. had a date with Wilton Wright. Went out to Willow Grove Park. Had the best time. Took in 4 roller coasters, crazy house, Venice and some other things. My first time there. Lois, Barb, George Proctor[164], Bobby Dare, and Bob Swift were along. Miss Dorsey had given us all 12:00 permissions to go to the theatre.

Friday, June 11, 1926

Last day of school this year. Passed Chem. and English, and I am so glad. Studied Bacteriology all morning, took the exam in aft. Not so good. Had a date with Jack Roberts in eve. Dot Oakes and Bill went with us. Went out to Willow Grove Park again and danced. Saw Al Mathers who went to school here last year.

Saturday, June 12, 1926

Wrote Marjorie and C. Reece. Wrote Mama. Fooled around, packed some books in morning. Went to Tea Rose for lunch. Jane and I went down town in aft. John Joseph called me while I was at dinner to say good-bye. Only wish I had been here. (First he had called since February.) Finished Memory Book.

Sunday, June 13, 1926

Got up for breakfast. Packed my trunk all morn. After dinner went for a ride with Ruth Stout and her Mother and Father. Fooled around all eve. Did some sewing.

Monday, June 14, 1926

Jane left on the 10:30 train. Went down to see her off. Had lunch at the drug store at the station. Wrote letters all aft. Went down to the Cathay to dinner with the Knobs and Ida Bromley and her Mother. Went down to the Sesqui[165] in eve. Rode on one of the big busses. Took a ride (Went in Electric House.) all around the grounds. Hardly anything was finished. Saw some fireworks.

---

[164] Phi Kappa Beta '26

[165] In 1926, Philadelphia hosted a celebration commemorating the 150th anniversary of the founding of the United States. This Sesquicentennial Exposition drew exhibitors from around the world and featured speeches, sporting events, a military camp, and an 80 foot tall replica of the Liberty Bell covered in 26,000 light bulbs. Another feature was the Electric Fountains and presumably a house that was all electric. Unfortunately, the diarist was spot on. The exposition was delayed and wasn't completed by the opening date. In addition to the delays, the weather was unusually wet, with rain most of the summer. It was a dismal failure.

In the 1926 yearbook, *Lexerd*, the following words well described the then Sophomore Class as special in that it had just finished its second year at Drexel (Class photo on page 100 of the *Lexerd 1926*):

> "We returned last September all pepped up and rarin' to go, and we have being going ever since. We have to make organizations around Drexel just a little more active than they were before."

From this point some Home Economics majors were finished with a two-year program and some were absorbed into the full program, with Mary Alice among them, for a four-year degree.

Tuesday, June 15, 1926

Kathleen came back last night. She went down town in morning. I mailed my laundry. Had lunch at the Tea Rose. Uncle Charley, Aunt Grace, Aunt Mary, Dick and Cecil all came in. They stayed a while with me. Kathleen and I left for Bay Head, N.J. about 3:00. Took ferry to Camden. Got train there. Had an awful dirty ride down. Got here about 7:00. Had dinner. Took a walk on the boardwalk, my first time to see the ocean. Came back to our room, unpacked, and wrote letters.

"Down the Shore......"

Wednesday, June 16, 1926

Slept in the front room. Didn't like it. It's awfully windy and the bed was so hard. Going to sleep with Kathleen. Got all unpacked today. Baked two cakes, one doz. dropped cakes (cupcakes) and iced them after breakfast. Fooled around in the gift shop. Sold a handbag and some fudge. After lunch I took a walk along boardwalk to the end. Went up to the post office. Helped make salads for dinner and helped with whatever needed to be done. Took bath and wrote letters in eve. Wrote to Jane.

Thursday, June 17, 1926

Baked 3 cakes and 1 doz. drop cakes this morning. Helped with lunch, made salads. We took a walk after lunch, took some pictures, pressed some dresses. Helped with dinner. Took a walk along the beach after dinner.

Friday, June 18, 1926

Wrote K. Smith. Did a lot of baking this morning. Made salads and helped with lunch. Mama & Papa came during dinner, went out and talked to them awhile, then went back and helped. We ate dinner together. They took us for a ride in our new Franklin Sedan. Took a short walk on the beach and came in.

Saturday, June 19, 1926

Wrote Bubby. Baked more cakes than ever this morning. Four large layer, 2 small and 1 doz. drop cakes. Had a large crowd for lunch, had to finish icing cakes after lunch. After dinner went down to the movies. Sydney Chaplain in "On Top of the Box." It was real funny. The movie house isn't so bad; had music[166] and everything. Took a short walk along the ocean. It was beautiful out, the moon was shining. Stopped in the drugstore and ate some ice cream.

Sunday, June 20, 1926

Wrote to Grace Johns and baked a few cakes in the morning. Didn't go to church. Had a big crowd for dinner. The best looking and nicest boy came in for a cake and I got it for him. If only I would meet someone to help pass the time. We took a short walk in the aft. Stayed in most of eve. Just went down to the post office.

Mon, June 21, 1926

Baked a few cakes and fooled around all morning. No mail. Mama had a white coat sent out to me, but it was too large. Sent it back for a smaller size. Went to movies in eve. Real good. "The Winding Stair."[167] These cruisers are all getting on my nerves. If we would only meet someone worthwhile.

Tuesday, June 22, 1926

Wrote Alice, J.S., Alice Kay, Jessie, M. Hill. Baked cakes and worked around all morning. We put on our bathing suits and went down on the beach. Started to write letters and it began to rain. Got real wet. Too cold to go in the water. Rained all eve. Stayed in and finished letters.

Wednesday, June 23, 1926

Didn't feel very good all day. Helped to make some sandwiches after lunch. We walked up to the post office and right back.

Thursday, June 24, 1926

Was finished with the cakes early today. Pasted all my pictures in my memory book. Made an appointment to have my hair curled. Didn't get out in eve.

Friday, July 25, 1926

Baked and iced a lot of cakes today, but got through early. Had my hair washed and curled. Curl came out, almost all of it in one eve. After dinner took a walk on the beach and then went to the movies. An exciting evening for the beach.

Saturday, June 26, 1926

Awful rainy day; didn't clear off until dinnertime. Bobby Cruise, who is 6, has been here all week. His father, Dr. Cruise, came this eve. Got a new dress down at "The Wool Shop." Kathleen and I walked the whole length of the boardwalk after dinner. Tired.

---

166 By music, Mary Alice is saying that the silent films are accompanied by music, likely a piano, which was surprising to her to find at the seashore.

167 "The Winding Stair" is a 1925 American silent drama film directed by John Griffith Wray and is based on the 1923 novel of the same name.

Sunday, June 27, 1926

Didn't get to church, was busy baking cakes. Wore my new pink dress. Like it a lot. Sat on the porch most of the afternoon. Walked up and down the boardwalk after supper, then came back and sat in the porch. Was all undressed and ready for bed when Miller Preston from school and another fellow came to see us. They live not so far from here. We have a date with them Thursday night.

Monday, June 28, 1926

Had a letter from Jack Roberts. Took my first swim in the ocean this aft. The water was so cold and salty. It was low tide and the waves were not so big. Took a long walk on the boardwalk after dinner. Saw a real nice fellow, hope to see him again. When we got back Miller Preston and some other fellow were here in a Ford coupe. We can't be bothered with them the whole summer!

Tuesday, June 29, 1926

Last day of baking for 2 weeks. Got through lunch early, not much business. Went swimming in aft. The water was cold. Took a walk after dinner.

Wednesday, June 30, 1926

Last day of June. I started taking care of "Grandma" today. Brought up her orange juice, breakfast and gave her a bath. Read to her awhile downstairs on the porch. Got her lunch. After we had ours we went swimming. The sun and sand were boiling hot but the water was ice cold at 60°. Didn't stay in long. Took a walk after dinner.

Thursday, July 1, 1926

Wrote Jack. Had a big day. A lot of people in. Gave Mrs. Cruise another bath today. Went down to the beach after lunch, but didn't go swimming. Kathleen and I had dates in eve. Miller Preston and Jay Miller. I wonder if they noticed the name similarities….. [168] They had an old 1924 Model Ford Touring Car and took us up as far as Asbury Park. Danced there once. Stopped at another place and danced. The country is fine on the way up. Went through Point Pleasant. Got home at 12:30.

1924 Model Ford

Friday, July 2, 1926

Sewed on curtains all morning besides dressing Grandma. Took Grandma for a nice ride in her wheel chair. Stayed in our room all eve. Wrote to Jane.

Saturday, July 3, 1926

Wrote Alice. Gave Grandma another bath this morning. Did some dusting around. Helped with some of the cakes. Went swimming after lunch. The water was wonderful. Didn't stay long. Took Mrs. Cruise for a ride in her wheelchair.

[168] I wonder if anyone commented on the name similarities…..ed.

Sunday, the Fourth of July, 1926

Spent a quiet 4th. The people who live across the street were having a big time. Two of the men came over and bought some fudge from me. Took a short walk in evening. Read awhile.

Monday, July 5, 1926

Not much doing today. Took a short walk in afternoon and evening. The ocean was awfully rough; heard that someone was drowned today.

Tuesday, July 6, 1926

Wrote Kate, Howd, Mama. Went up to see Mr. Strickland about a cottage for Mama and Papa, but couldn't get one. After lunch went to "Bluffs" and "Grenville Arms" to find out the price of room and board. Took Mrs. Cruise out for a ride. Went to movie in evening. Tom Moore played in "Money Talks." Miller and Preston and another fellow were here to take us for a ride and we missed seeing them. I should worry; I can't be bothered with him.

Wednesday, July 7, 1926

Wrote Alice. K. gave Grandma another bath. Guess who gets one every day now? Not a bit busy in the Tea Room today. Had a grand swim. Too hot. Didn't do a thing in the evening. Went down to Post Office for the mail. Ate onion sandwiches and smoked a cigarette before going to bed.

Thursday, July 8, 1926

Did the same old thing every day. Went swimming in aft. The water was grand. Great big waves. Stayed in all evening.

Friday, July 9, 1926

Wrote Hugh, K., Howd. Same old thing today. Too tired to go swimming. Did a little ironing. Took a short walk on the beach after dinner.

Saturday, July 10, 1926

Terribly hot. Rained very hard in the evening. Had quite a few here today. Waited on tables in eve. Got my 1st tip. 25¢. My white coat came today. Took it over to the tailor's to be shortened.

Sunday, July 11, 1926

Was busy all morning. Did a lot of serving at noon. We each made $1.05 in tips. Doing pretty good. Johnson left this morning. Took Grandma for a ride in her buggy. Took a long walk after supper. Went to bed earlier than usual.

Monday, July 12, 1926

Didn't get swimming. Too busy here. Did some more serving. Took a short walk in eve. after dinner.

Tuesday, July 13, 1926

My last day of Grandma. Have two weeks off, thank goodness. Went down to the beach but didn't go in the water. Too cold. Took a short walk after dinner.

Wednesday, July 14, 1926

Started smocks after breakfast. Had several tables for lunch. New waiter today. Miss Alice also came back. She is the world's worst. Sewed on smocks all aft. Took short walk after dinner.

Thursday, July 15, 1926

Got a special from Blair Mann in morning. Letters from Jane C. and Miller Preston. Wrote letters all aft. including Marjorie and P. Kirk. Played bridge with Miss Margaret and Miss May after dinner. It rained all day.

Friday, July 16, 1926

Got paid from the 1st month today. Got $50. Letter from Alice. Baked cakes all morning and finished icing after lunch. Made a big mistake in some of my cakes. Didn't spoil so many, but Miss Alice had to come up and say something to us about it. She makes me sick. Bawled us out about the old smocks that we don't even need. Went down town a couple minutes in afternoon. I took a short walk on the boardwalk after dinner and wrote to Al Murray.

Saturday, July 17, 1926

Had a card from Mama. They are at Atlantic City and coming to see me. Was busy nearly all day. Went to movies in eve., "Hellbent from Heaven."[169]

Sunday, July 18, 1926

Didn't get to church again today. Not many in for dinner. Went down to go swimming but the tide was too high. Had a big crowd here for supper; worked until late. Had a terrible thunderstorm. Never saw one like it.

Monday, July 19, 1926

Got all ready to go swimming after lunch when a big crowd came in. We helped get their orders. Just then Mama, Papa, Philip, Katy, Richlens and Witmers came. We went down to the beach and went swimming. Had a grand time. Came up to the house and they left for Atlantic City right away, are staying there for a week. In eve. I went to the movies with Margaret and saw "The Runaway."[170]

Tuesday, July 20, 1926

Wrote to Blair. Helped Margaret fix the flowers. Wrote some letters. Went swimming after lunch. Went to movies in eve. Saw Douglas Fairbanks in "The Black Pirate."[171]

---

[169] The play "Hell-Bent for Heaven" won the Pulitzer Prize for Drama in 1924. It was rewritten for the movie.

[170] In one of her first Paramount vehicles, Clara Bow stars as Cynthia Meade, a movie actress on location in the hills of Tennessee. This film may have been lost.

[171] "The Black Pirate" is a 1926 silent adventure film shot entirely in two-color Technicolor. It stars Douglas Fairbanks, Donald Crisp, Sam De Grasse, and Billie Dove.

Wednesday, July 21, 1926

Didn't feel well all day. Went to the post office after dinner.

Thursday, July 22, 1926

Had 24 at a bridge party in the afternoon. I helped serve ice cream. It was awful hot all day. In the evening we had dates with Miller Preston and a friend. Got home at 12:00. Miller took my class ring, only hope I see him again soon.

Friday, July 23, 1926

Baked a lot of cakes today. Lizzie and Daniel had a little (**big**) fight at dinnertime. I never saw or heard anyone rave like she did. Margaret and I went to the movies in eve. Saw Marion Davies in "Beverly of Graustark"[172] It was real good.

Saturday, July 24, 1926

Had a big storm in the morning. It hit Manorman just a short distance from here. Baked a lot of cakes. Took a walk on the boardwalk in evening.

Sunday, July 25, 1926

Had a lot of people here today. Took a long walk on the boardwalk. The moon came up red. It was beautiful on the water.

Monday, July 26, 1926

Alice and her mother came today. We were busy at lunch and dinner time. Took a walk along the ocean in the evening. The waves were large and high and rolled in under the boardwalk.

Tuesday, July 27, 1926

Went swimming after lunch. Went to movies in eve. Saw "Stella Dallas."[173]

Wednesday, July 28, 1926

Started in my two weeks off from Grandma. Daniel left today and Alice came home with a new Jones dishwasher. Had a big crowd in at dinner time. Took a walk on boardwalk after dinner.

Thursday, July 29, 1926

It was dark and gloomy all day. It rained about dinnertime. Went down to post office. Letter from Jack.

Friday, July 30, 1926

Got 4 letters today from Bubby, Aunt Grace, C. Reece and J. Kirk. Went swimming in aft. Water was very rough. Miss Margaret and I went to see "The Blonde Goddess" with Jack Holt.[174]

---

[172] "Beverly of Graustark" (1926) is a silent film starring Marion Davies.

[173] With Ronald Colman and Jean Hersholt. This was a silent movie in 1926, not to be confused with the very popular movie of the same name in 1937.

[174] "The Blind Goddess" is a lost 1926 American silent mystery film directed by Victor Fleming. The film is based on the novel by Arthur Cheney Train.

121

Saturday, July 31, 1926

Worked hard all day. Went down at 12:30 to help Kathleen and stayed until way after 8:00. Had about 34 for lunch and about the same for dinner. Worked all afternoon, shelled peas, etc. Was not out all day.

Sunday, August 1, 1926

Big crowd here today. 93 in all. I waited on tables on the porch. Took short walk along the beach in the evening. Worked nearly all day. Wrote K. Smith.

Monday, August 2, 1926

Helped downstairs awhile in morning. Went down to go swimming, but the water was too dirty for me to go in. Went to movies in eve. Saw Jack Holt in "Sea Horses."[175]

Tuesday, August 3, 1926

A nice, hot day, but didn't get cooled off all day. Planned to go swimming, but the life guard wouldn't let anyone go in because of the undercurrent.

Wednesday, August 4, 1926

Mailed laundry myself this morning. Card from Mama at Niagara Falls. John Wandall came to see Kathleen after lunch. We went down to the beach, but couldn't go in as the water was too high and rough again. Helped serve at dinner. Went to movies in eve with Miss Margaret. Saw "Brown of Harvard."[176]

Thursday, August 5, 1926

Helped in the morning. Took John down to the train at 3:18. Set up the tables for dinner and had 25. Made some money. Took walk on boardwalk.

Friday, August 6, 1926

Kathleen's birthday. Gave her a pair of beads. Miss Margaret fixed a cake with candles and gave her a pretty handkerchief. Stayed in in evening.

Monday, August 9, 1926

Went swimming after lunch. Had the grandest swim. The life guard helped us in the boat and we took a little ride. The tide was low so we went way out. After dinner went up to Carson's to see Kitty Plotts. Spent the whole eve. up there.

Tuesday, August 10, 1926

Just 3 weeks from today I will be going home. Can hardly wait. Had the grandest swim after lunch. Have learned to float. The tide was low and we went way out. Some lady came in to eat with her husband and little boy. She was so drunk and sick.

---

[175] "Sea Horses" is a 1926 American drama silent film with William Powell. Released by Paramount Pictures, it is considered a lost film.

[176] "Brown of Harvard" (1926) is a silent film released by Metro-Goldwyn-Mayer and starring William Haines. The film is the best known of the three Brown of Harvard films, having been film legend John Wayne's screen debut. Uncredited, Wayne played a "Yale Football Player".

Wednesday, August 11, 1926

Had another grand swim in aft. Met a cute boy, one of the two who had us out in the boat the other day. He came and talked to me. Must find out his name. He lives in Philadelphia and goes to Haverford.

Thursday, August 12, 1926

Card party of 20 in aft. Went swimming, water is still fine. Didn't go out in eve.

Saturday, August 14, 1926

Had date with Jack Roberts in eve. He came down to see me. He stayed until 1:30 and it was twenty of 2:00 when I got in. They had locked me out so I called Miss Margaret. Sat on ironwork swing waiting. Rained all the time.

Sunday, August 15, 1926

Jack came up. Took a short walk on boardwalk and went swimming in aft., then we came up and I had supper with him. Went to train and he kissed me. Gave me his high school fraternity pin to keep for him.

Monday, August 16, 1926

Just at lunch time Kathleen cut her finger and fainted in the kitchen. Lizzie was scared to death and started running out the back door.

Tuesday, August 17, 1926

In eve we went to movies with Margaret and saw Rudolph Valentino in "Son of the Sheik."[177] It was real good. Wrote to Blair.

Wednesday, August 18, 1926

Kathleen got a telegram in morning from John who came in aft. with his roommate. Sat in Tea Room in aft and talked to him. He took us to the movie in eve. Real good. Bebe Daniels in "The Palm Beach Girl."[178]

Thursday, August 19, 1926

Richard, our waiter, left today. K. and I waited on tables in eve. Went to movies. Saw Mary Pickford in "Sparrows."[179]

Friday, August 20, 1926

Worked hard all day. Didn't finish until late. K. broke the news to them about leaving the last of this month. They are so cross. Can't help that though.

---

[177] "Son of the Sheik," Rudolph Valentino's last film, may well be his best. It was a sequel to Valentino's 1922 blockbuster "The Sheik." It also starred Vilma Banky.

[178] "The Palm Beach Girl" is a lost 1926 silent film romantic comedy starring Bebe Daniels and directed by Erle C. Kenton. It is based upon the short-lived Broadway play, "Please Help Emily," written by H. M. Harwood.

[179] "Sparrows" is a 1926 American silent film about a young woman who rescues a baby from kidnappers. Originally titled "Scraps," it starred and was produced by Mary Pickford, the most powerful woman in Hollywood at the time.

Sunday, August 22, 1926

Took short walk in eve. This is the first we were outside since Thursday night.

Monday, August 23, 1926

Miss Alice went to Phila. in morn to get a new waiter. She didn't get one so stayed in the city. Went to movies in eve. Lon Chaney in "The Road to Mandalay."[180] Rudolph Valentine died today.

Tuesday, August 24, 1926

I must be telling Miss Alice when I am going. Baked 2 times today with three devil's food. Went down to go swimming in aft. Ocean was full of dirty seaweed and real low tide. Went for mail in evening and took a walk and stopped at Iceman's awhile.

Wednesday, August 25, 1926

Only 2 weeks from today and I will be home. It rained again nearly all day. Didn't go anywhere.

Saturday, August 28, 1926

Helped K. in the morning. Didn't get through until rather late. Went swimming. It was grand. Helped serve at dinner. Jack Roberts called me from Asbury Park just before dinner. Came down in eve. Had his Mother & Father along. We drove back to Asbury. Danced down on the boardwalk at a place. Best orchestra and floor. First I had danced for ages. Had the best time. Liked his parents a whole lot. Got back here at 1:00. Stopped at a drug store and got some ice cream at Belmar, N.J. Went over and sat on Iceman's porch. Jack was real nice tonight. Stayed out until 2:00.

Sunday, August 29, 1926

Hot all day and didn't cool off much in eve. Helped downstairs all morning. Had a wonderful swim in the afternoon. Kathleen packed her trunk this evening. Went up and bought her ticket.

Monday, August 30, 1926

Wrote to C. Reese. Went down and said good-by to Mrs. Carson after going to the post office. Met Miller Preston on the way home. He gave me back my ring. Went down to Priests and had some ice cream. A boy working down there is going to Drexel this year. Must go see him again. We were sitting out front in the car when my Haverford boyfriend I met in bathing went by. He spoke so sweetly. Only hope to see him again before I leave. Would love to know his name.

---

[180] Lon Chaney is regarded as one of the most versatile and powerful actors of early cinema, renowned for his characterizations of tortured, often grotesque and afflicted characters, and his groundbreaking artistry with makeup. His make-up and performance were/are fascinating to watch.

Tuesday, August 31, 1926

Got awake at 6:15 and called Kathleen. Got dressed and went down and got Miss Margaret and her some breakfast. Went to train with K. Came back and ate my breakfast. Went to see Rudolph Valentino again in "The Son of the Sheik." He was just buried yesterday. It hardly seems possible that he is dead. Wrote Kathleen.

Friday, September 3, 1926

Had a big crowd in for lunch. Washed all of those dishes. After lunch I went over to the Yacht Club and watched the tennis tournaments. Went with Miss May. She showed me all around the place. After dinner Miss Margaret and I went to the movies. Saw "The Midnight Sunday."[181]

Sunday, September 5, 1926

Big fire last night down on the corner. I never even got up to see it. Jack called from Ocean City. Worked hard today. Went down to the station and bought my ticket and saw about my trunk.

Monday, September 6, Labor Day

Labor Day and wouldn't I just love to be home. Baked cakes all morning for the last time, thank goodness. Was dead tired in the morning when I began. Got a special from Cecil and then wrote saying I would meet him tomorrow. He leaves for Florida Thursday. Went down to post office and mailed letter. Washed dishes at noon and in eve. Marian came in eve. for dinner. Got paid off. Had a bunch of people here today. Rained all eve. Here's hoping it stops before morning.

Tuesday, September 7, 1926

Henry called me at 6:00. Got dressed and went down and got a little breakfast for myself. Said goodbye to the family. Jack met me at Camden; we taxied up to Broad St. Was supposed to meet Cecil, but didn't. Had long trip home. Met Patty Kirk at Tyrone. Alice, Jessie, Bubby and the family met me at the train.

"Back Home from the Shore"

Wednesday, September 8, 1926

Went down to Aunt Grace's and up to Mama Spencer's. Had my hair washed. Alice and Jessie were over in morn. and aft. Up at Alice's awhile. Hugh drove me up. Had date with George in evening. Had Walls' car. Chased around. Went down to Clearfield and saw Blair Mann. Drove up to Groff Acres.

---

[181] "The Midnight Sun" is a 1926 American silent drama film set in pre-Revolutionary Tsarist Russia.

125

Thursday, September 9, 1926

Supposed to go to Bellefonte, but didn't. Went to Clearfield in morning and was home nearly all afternoon. Patty Kirk was up awhile. Had a date with Blair Mann in eve. He certainly is a nice fellow and I like him a whole lot, but he is so bashful. Went to the dance down at the Driving Park at Clearfield. Got home after 1 o'clock.

Friday, September 10, 1926

Went to stores for Mama. Cleaned upstairs. Patty was up. In afternoon went to bank. Alice drove our car to Clearfield. Made date at dentist. Got a new fountain pen at Kurtz. Saw Johnny Leitzinger. Took Patty and Jessie along. Decided to go on a picnic. Alice, Hugh, George and I. Hugh's mother took sick and he couldn't go, so the 3 of us went. Ate down by Irvin's camp. Went up to Norrises and talked to Hugh for a while. Drove to Clearfield.

Saturday, September 11, 1926

Left early in morning for Bellefonte. Mama Spencer went along. Stopped at Unionville to see Julia Bullock. Went up to a peach farm. Got a new dress up at Katz. Mrs. Heverly is clerking up there. Had dinner at the Brockerhoff House. Went up to Kitty Reese's in aft. Went up to Millers. She and Eddie built a little house up by the football field. She and Ida Fisher spent the aft. painting the kitchen. Went down to the Richlieu.[182] We stayed to see the movies. Ate dinner. Marjorie drove Kitty and me up to Snow Shoe. Saw Mariella Redding. Didn't see Harmie. Went to dance in eve. with Joe Parrish, Kitty and Dick Noll, Porter and Magdeline Sunday, Ty and some girl. Went to Yeagers Park at Mill Hall.[183] Dave Harmons played. Had the best time.

Sunday, September 12, 1926

Marjorie came up to see Heverlys (Bellefonte) about 10 o'clock. Had breakfast and went up to Millers. Left for home about 12 o'clock. Ate dinner at Philipsburg, then went up to Custers. Came on home. Met Alice and George and went out to Greenwood. Marjorie and Eddie drove me home. With John Wright. Had our supper out. Mama and all were there. Went up top of the beacon light. Drove to Clearfield and stopped at The Pig and Whistle.

Monday, September 13, 1926

Went to Clearfield in aft. with Alice. Took things to the cleaner. Chased around with Jessie, Kate, Al, and Edith in eve. Went down to see Libby. Mama and I went up to Jimmies for a sandwich.

Tuesday, September 14, 1926

Went down to the dentist in morning. Came up on 12:30 bus. Went up to see Audrey Hyde and saw Maude Ann. Bought a pin at O'Brien's Jewelry from Bob Daughtery. Had date with J. S. over at Jessie's in eve. I don't like him much anymore. Only hope Blair doesn't find out I was with J., for I like Blair a whole lot.

---

182 Movie Theatre in Bellefonte, owned by H.J.
183 In or around Clinton County, likely not too far from Bellefonte.

Wednesday, September 15, 1926

This is the day we were supposed to leave Bay Head.[184] Took Philip down to the dentist. Made some fudge. Had a date with Blair in eve. I like him so much. He is so nice. Alice had the Franklin and a date with George. We drove as far as Houtzdale.

Thursday, September 16, 1926

Sewed and worked all morning and afternoon. The rest went to the Fair, but I didn't have time. Had a date with George in eve. Went up to Alice's awhile. Miss Harper from school (Beaver[185]) is visiting her. Went up to Jimmies. Couldn't get George to go home.

Friday, September 17, 1926

Sewed all morning. Went to Clearfield in afternoon with Alice and Miss Harper. Sent my trunk to school. Stayed up late fooling around. Was up the street to say good-bye to Mama Spencer, Libby King, and Aunt Frances. Was up at Jimmies. Saw George, John, J.S. to say goodbye as well.

Saturday, September 18, 1926

Got up at 5:30 and got ready to leave for Philadelphia. Took Alice and Miss Harper along. Saw George as we passed the bus; he was on his way to Clearfield, or rather, Hyde City. Alice drove part of the way. Stopped at Parksburg[186] awhile. Papa had a meeting. Alice and I stayed at 216 all night. Papa and Mama stayed up on 34th Street. Went down to movies in eve. Was dead tired.

Sunday, September 19, 1926

Got up at 9 o'clock and had breakfast with Mama at the Tea Rose. Got the car and drove down on South Street, and looked at coats. Then went down to the Sesquicentennial Exposition. Was in Fine Arts building, Treasure Island. Saw Matt Storey there and was surprised. Morris and Mable came down today. We had supper at Tea Rose. Called Jack, but couldn't get him.

Monday, September 20, 1926

Alice and I went over to the house for breakfast. Went to see Mama and Papa. I went down to school to register. Alice went to the Sesqui with them. Saw all the kids. Jane didn't come back. E. Newton is rooming with me this year. Met Alice at Wanamaker's at 2 o'clock. She got her lunch. Then went to movies and saw Gloria Swanson. In eve, talked to Jack. Alice and I went down to Stanley. Saw Gimbel's Fashion Show and "You Never Know Women."[187]

---

184 Location of the NJ shore tearoom. Both Mary Alice and Kathleen left before their contract stated, Kathleen sooner than did Mary Alice.

185 The name and college that replaced Beechwood. See November 15, 1924 entry.

186 Chester County.

187 A 1926 American silent romantic drama film from director William Wellman who made "a rousing comeback" with this film produced by Famous Players.

Tuesday, September 21, 1926

Went over to see Mama & Papa after breakfast. Alice went out to school in morning. Had classes until 5 o'clock, but had 4 hrs. off. Finished unpacking in eve when Jack called.

Wednesday, September 22, 1926

Had classes all morning and then assembly. Talked to Jack awhile. Met Mama and Papa downtown. Got a new coat, gloves, and umbrella. Wrote J. Clark and Blair.

Thursday, September 23, 1926

Was dead tired all day. Had classes till 5 o'clock. Talked to Stetina for quite a while. Then Jack walked up to the house with me. Took some books over and put them in the car after dinner. Went down and met Mama at Broad Street Market Station. Mable and Erma and Mrs. Norris, Mrs. Kittelberger and a lady and a little girl from Bellefonte were along. Saw "Gay Paree"[188] at Chestnut St. Theatre. Wonderful dancing. Initiated the Freshmen at 12 o'clock. Chased them all over the house blindfolded.

Friday, September 24, 1926

Mama and Papa left in morning. Went over and said good-bye. Saw Jack and Stetina to talk a couple of minutes. There are some good looking Freshmen I would like to meet. Had a date with Jack Roberts in eve. Went to Devon Park Hotel[189] to dance. It is a wonderful place. A bunch of Society people there.

Saturday, September 25, 1926

Had a 2 hr. class in morning. Was dead tired. In eve. went to Methodist Reception. Came home about 11 o'clock. Nothing exciting.

Sunday, September 26, 1926

Gained an hr. today. Didn't go to breakfast. June and I met Stanley Harris and Carl Gregory on our way to church. They went with us and then took us for a ride through the Park in their "good" Ford. I was afraid it would fall apart. Had a date in eve. with Carl Gregory.

Monday, September 27, 1926

Letters from Mama and J. Billock. Had classes all day. Saw Jack just to speak to. Had my first date with John Joseph since last fall. Was so surprised that he came over. He is so sweet. I only wish he liked me better. I wonder if he ever will?

Tuesday, September 28, 1926

Letters from Arthur Wall, G. Johns, Mama. Kathleen and I went downtown at 11 o'clock. Went to Agency and paid out $12.50 for commission. Had lunch at the Cathay. Chased around at the stores. Didn't get to talk to Jack all day. The lights were out most of the eve. The Freshmen gave a stunt at 9:45 and then we had some sandwiches and I went up in Kathleen's room and had some cake and candy Ruth Ransom brought.

[188] A musical review with music and lyrics by J. Fred Coots.
[189] The Philadelphia Devon in Wayne is situated on the Main Line of PA, minutes away from the Devon Horse Show Fairgrounds, Villanova University, and Valley Forge Military Academy.

Wednesday, September 29, 1926

I wonder what is wrong with Jack; he must be cross or something. I cannot understand. Had lunch at Waffle Shop. Kate and I went down to Broad Street Theatre and saw Glenn Hunter in the stage play, "Young Woodley" by John Van Druten. It was so good. Studied in eve.

Thursday, September 30, 1926

Wrote to J. Bullock. Had 2 hrs., then came up to house. Had lunch at Tea Rose with Ann Robinson. Got a letter from Blair. Talked to Jack after class. Have a date with him tomorrow night. Alice called. She is coming in tomorrow.

Friday, October 1, 1926

Alice came about 4:30. We talked and fooled around. Went over to Tea Rose for dinner. She went out to Robinsons and I had a date with Jack Roberts. Went down to the Fox. Had an hr. Came up to drug store by station and had some ice cream. Parked up here in the alley. Was almost late.

Saturday, October 2, 1926

Saw Jack at school in morning. Had classes until 12:00. Rode downtown with Kay Smith and a girl friend who has a Packard sedan and colored chauffer. They took me to Wanamaker's.

Packard Sedan

Met Alice and Mrs. Robinson. Had lunch there. Was supposed to meet Marjorie, but missed her. She called the house. Shopped all aft. with Alice. I didn't get a thing. Had a sundae at Whitman's. Then went to the movies and saw Thomas Meighan in "Tin Gods." Had dinner at the Cathay. Stayed in all eve. to meet Bubby (who had sent a telegram) and Arthur tomorrow.

Sunday, October 3, 1926

Got up at 7:30. Had breakfast at Childs. Got a "taxi" and rode down to the Sesquicentennial Exposition. Met Bubby, Arthur, and Edgar Benson at Mt. Vernon building.[190] Fooled around all day in the buildings. Alice and I came up to the house at 2 o'clock. Was dead tired. She went out to school (Beaver). Did some work. Wrote to L. King and M. Wall.

Monday, October 4, 1926

Wrote to Mama and J. Clark. Had classes all day until 5 o'clock. Didn't even see Jack. It was so hot all day. Studied in eve.

Tuesday, October 5, 1926

Wrote to D. Oakes. Stayed down at school all day and studied in the library. Talked to Jack a couple of minutes. Had classes until 5 o'clock. Studied in evening.

---

[190] A cousin of the Walls worked at Mount Vernon as assistant superintendent. (In 1929 Cecil Wall would accept this position, replacing the cousin who had died in a drowning accident.) Two years later he became the Resident Director, a position he held for 39 years.

Wednesday, October 6, 1926

Had classes all morn. Saw Jack at a distance to speak to. Kay Smith and I went downtown. Got some tickets for "The Miracle" on Saturday night. Had lunch at the Cathay. Went to movies at Stanley. Saw Dick Barthlemess in "The Amateur Gentleman." It was real good. Studied in eve. Wrote Mama.

Thursday, October 7, 1926

Wrote to Arthur Wall. Had my hair washed and curled in the morning. Had classes until 5 o'clock. Was dead tired. Wrote some letters and studied in eve.

Friday, October 8, 1926

Had only 2 hrs. of class today. Stayed down for the court dance after school. Had the best time. Danced with Stetina and Amos Kilesy, two boys I have always wanted to dance with. Also danced with Jack (Roberts). Had a date with him in evening. Went out to 69th Street to movies. Then stopped someplace and had some ice cream. I asked Jack to the House Dance on the 30th. Fun day.

Saturday, October 9, 1926

Didn't get to see Jack at school in the morning. After lunch I went down town and met Julia Bullock, Elizabeth Hoag and Hazel McMann. We brought their suitcases to West Philadelphia Station and then went to the Drexel football game. We lost 21-0 to Susquehanna. We were just ready to go to the Tea Rose for dinner when Marjorie Wall came in. She went on out to Norristown and the rest of us went to see "The Miracle." It was pretty good, but a Catholic play all the way through. Had a feed when we came home.

Sunday, October 10, 1926

Had breakfast at the Tea Rose. The girls left at 10:30. Alice Murray left on the same train. Saw Dottie Ake Clymer. Went to church with June. Carl Gregory and Stanley Harris brought me home. In aft. we took a ride. Were supposed to go to the Sesqui. Had dates with them again in eve. Miss Dorsey is raving because we did. She makes me sick.

Monday, October 11, 1926

Had classes from 10:00 straight through. Saw Jack at a distance, but not to talk to. Why doesn't he call me up at night once in a while? Got my bookrack today that Mama sent me. Studied in eve. Wrote to Cecil.

Tuesday, October 12, 1926

Was down at school all day. Saw Jack a couple of minutes at noon and then again after school. There was a Tea Dance, but I didn't go. Jack is coming into the house tonight to a fraternity meeting. Hope he calls me up. John Deitz (Jessie's good friend from Clarion) called me tonight.

Wednesday, October 13, 1926

Wrote Marjorie and Jessie. Saw Jack just in Assembly today. He has my roster card. Stayed down in Library and wrote up my Chem experiments.

Thursday, October 14, 1926

Wrote Alice. Came up to school at noon and mailed my laundry. Had classes until 5 o'clock. Talked to Jack and he walked up to the House with me. Wish I could have a date with him tomorrow night, but I have to go to the old House Warming. Edith had a Proctors Meeting to bring June and me up about Sunday. For my part, I cannot see that we did one thing wrong. They all make me sick. You can't trust girls with anything and I am through. Edith might at least have told me what I was to say instead of springing it on me as she did. I got 3 demerits and will probably be getting 2 weeks restriction soon. All over my "sweet" roommate's doing.

Friday, October 15, 1926

Wrote Mama. Had classes until 2 o'clock. Was supposed to see Jack, but didn't. Wonder if he had a date tonight? We had the House Warming in eve. for the Freshmen. I wanted to go out so badly, but thought it best not to.

Saturday, October 16, 1926

Got things ready for camp. We left about 2:15. Miss Dalton chaperoned. Went out to Drexel-Paul. 19 of the girls went from our house. Helped get dinner and fooled around. Walked into Wayne in eve. with K. Hand, E. Newton Rosenbury, and Pat Latimer. Chased around and came back and played some bridge and toasted marshmallows. Reminded me of Greenwood. Smoked and smoked. Was dead tired. Slept with Edith. In Wayne I called up Jack. His Dad answered and then I talked with his Mother. Bet they thought I was awful. Jack wasn't at home.

Sunday, October 17, 1926

The kids got up at 8 o'clock and awakened us. It rained nearly all morning. Took a walk up to a little store before dinner. Cleaned up and started to walk to Wayne about 3:00. Came up to house and got cleaned up. Didn't go to Tea. Wasn't hungry. Had a date with John Joseph in eve. I can't like Joe as much as I used to, but he is so sweet anyway.

Monday, October 18, 1926

Went up to Waffle House. Kay Wrigley called. Didn't even get to talk to Jack today. Saw him twice. He couldn't call me up in the eve. either. Guess I will have to tell him a few things. Had classes every hour until 5:00.

Tuesday, October 19, 1926

Was down at school all day. Studied in library. Saw Jack for a few minutes at noon, then talked to him at 5 o'clock. He walked up to the house along. It was almost dark and the moon was beautiful. Wonder what he really thinks of me. I am always doing something I shouldn't. Have a date Friday night.

Wednesday, October 20, 1926

Didn't see Jack to talk to. Got the camp picture. Had a big surprise. John Sidener called me. Some crazy boy I went with when I was a Freshman. I can't possibly give him a date. Wrote to J. Clark.

Thursday, October 21, 1926

Didn't get to talk to Jack. I think he tries not to see me at school. I was on campus until 5 o'clock.[191] Studied in eve. Wrote K. Smith.

Friday, October 22, 1926

Had classes until 2 o'clock. Went downtown and had check cashed. Did some shopping. Had a date in eve. with Jack. Went out to 69th St. to the movies. Saw "Marriage License?"[192] Had some more good banana ice cream. The moon was wonderful. When I was ready for bed I put on my arm what I thought was glycerin and rose water, but it must have been pure carbolic acid. It began to burn awfully about 1 o'clock so Betty Biddle, Evelyn Rosenberg, and Frances Light went up to see Miss Chellis with me. She put something on it, but I couldn't sleep much.

Saturday, October 23, 1926

Had to go see Dr. Arnette after breakfast. Had my arm all bandaged up. It hurt all day. Saw Alice and her Father and Mother up at the Tea Rose after breakfast. Saw them a few minutes after dinner. Also Marguerite Reichenbaugh. Saw Jack at school in the morning. He brought me up to the house in the car. June and I chased around town all aft. Went down to the "Barn Dance" at school in the evening in the gymnasium. Had the best time. Piggie and Al Mathis were there. Jack brought me home.

Sunday, October 24, 1926

Had breakfast up at the Tea Rose with Walls. Went out to Robinsons for awhile. Then drove out to Beaver. Had a terrible time finding the way out. Had dinner at Jenkintown. Went over to the school. Had a date with John Joseph in eve. He was so sweet tonight; I can't get over it. He is also very changeable.

Monday, October 25, 1926

Wrote Mama. Had classes all day. Didn't even see Jack. Did a lot of work in eve. Was so tired.

Tuesday, October 26, 1926

Studied in the library for 4 hrs. today. Got out of History early and went to the Fashion Show in the Auditorium. It was real good. Stetina. Had House Meeting at 9:45 and was elected House Treasurer.

---

[191]   Just a reminder that the dorms were close to the campus.
[192]   Released in September 1926, the cast included Walter Pidgeon.

Wednesday, October 27, 1926

Didn't talk to Jack today. Took Chem quiz and didn't pass. Took long walk after school with June. Had bandages taken off my arm. John Joseph called in the evening and I went out with him until 10:30. He is so sweet lately; of course, it is better if we are no more than friends, but I can't help but like him.

Thursday, October 28, 1926

Wrote Mama, Alice, and Tony. Took Home Nursing exam today. Talked to Jack and he walked up to the House with me. Fooled around most of eve. Had a feed on 4th floor. Onions and all. Alice called me.

Friday, October 29, 1926

Worked in the library for a while. Served at Freshmen Tea at 4:00. Jack and Stetina were there helping Rider introduce the Freshmen. Jane, Kathleen and Alice and I went down to Jack Hart's in evening. Had the best time. Carl Gregory brought me home.

Saturday, October 30, 1926

Had breakfast at the Tea Rose. Went to class at 10:00. Alice went along. After lunch we bought the supplies for the food. Kate, Alice, and I made cookies down at school all afternoon. Was dead tired before dinner. Had to dress for the formal dinner. Had our Halloween House Dance in evening. Had the best time. I had Jack Roberts and Alice had Bill Brown. John Wandall sure was feeling good. Penn lost to Illinois, 3-0.

Sunday, October 31, 1926

Got up about 10:00 and got something to eat and went back to bed! Carl Gregory called me just about dinner time; he wondered why I wasn't at church. Studied some history in afternoon. Alice and I went down to Broad Street Station at 5 o'clock and saw Bubby and Catherine. They were down on an excursion from Bellefonte. Also saw John Bower. Wrote letter in evening. Wrote to Clair and K. Smith.

Monday, November 1, 1926

Wrote H. Kohrer. Saw Jack, but not to talk to. Had classes all day.

Tuesday, November 2, 1926

Election Day. Didn't get to talk to Jack today, just to speak to across the hall. Ann Robinson and I took a tutoring lesson from Dr. Hanson today. Don't know if it did much good or not. John Joseph called me about 5:45. He just wanted to talk to me. He is so sweet, if only he would ask me for a good date soon. Studied Chem in evening.

Wednesday, November 3, 1926

Jack told me he got the tickets for the game Saturday. Went downtown alone. Went to the Stanley and saw Richard Dix[193] in "The Quarterback" and also "Waring's Pennsylvanians"[194] played. Saw John Deitz. Read some English in the evening.

---

[193] Popular lead in movies.
[194] Generally known as Fred Waring and His Pennsylvanians, formed years before at Penn State.

Thursday, November 4, 1926

Wrote Marjorie and Alice. Didn't get to talk to Jack all day. Didn't feel so good. John Joseph called in eve. Asked me to go to the Penn-Penn State game on Saturday and I am going with Jack. I only wish he would ask me for a date. Studied Chem all eve.

Friday, November 5, 1926

Got permission in morning from Miss Dorsey to go to the Phi Kappa Beta dance tomorrow night. Talked to Jack today for the first since Saturday night. Was through classes at 2:00. Started to work on Memory Book after dinner. William Spundle and John Joseph called and came over and took Edith and me out. Had the most wonderful time. Went down to El Patio at Benjamin Franklin. Ate and danced. Joe[195] is so sweet. I am scared to death I won't get out tomorrow night to the fraternity dance as I took my privilege tonight. Here's hoping and praying I can work it.

Saturday, November 6, 1926

Met Jack down at school at 1:30. The football game was wonderful. Penn beat Penn State 3 – 0. Saw Zetler on our way back from the game. Marjorie was up here at the house. Kay Wrigley dropped in about 5 o'clock. He took me over to the Tea Rose for dinner. I only wish he wouldn't come to see me. Marjorie and Zetler went downtown. I went over to the Phi Kappa Beta House to the dance with Jack. Had the best time. Danced with Joe Foley. He surely is a wonderful dancer. I am only hoping no one finds out I was out both Friday and Saturday nights.

Sunday, November 7, 1926

Marjorie went to Sesqui in the morning with Zetler. Didn't see them again. June and I went to church. Met Stanley Harris and Carl Gregory. They walked home with us. Joe called after ten and came over. I like him so much. Oh, if I only didn't. He was so sweet tonight. If only I could have had a date somewhere else tonight besides in the parlor.

Monday, November 8, 1926

Wrote to Alice and J. Clark. Saw Jack in the Court today, but not to talk to. I don't think he likes me much. Piggie was down at school awhile today. He is sure a peculiar boy.

Tuesday, November 9, 1926

No mail today. Was down at school all day. Didn't talk to Jack. I do believe he doesn't want to see me during the week, so I am going to help him out. I like John Joseph better than him anyway. Edith and I went downtown and got our curtain material; did it in one hour. Got one curtain made up. Here's hoping Joe calls tomorrow night. Alice left for Florida. Talked to Mrs. Harper.

Wednesday, November 10, 1926

Went down to Sesqui with Lois Hamilton and 2 other kids. It was so cold down there I about froze. Went in a lot of the buildings. John Joseph and Min Spardle came over in eve. We had house dates. I only wish I knew just how much Joe likes me. I must find out.

134

[195] More reason to believe that John Joseph and Joe Joseph are one in the same.

Thursday, November 11, 1926, Armistice Day

No vacation today. Classes until 5 o'clock. Talked to Jack a second. Penn didn't have school all day. Whistles blew a long time at 11 o'clock. Went to Newman Club Tea Dance. Danced with Stetina.

Friday, November 12, 1926

Wrote Mama. Came up to house at 2:00. Fooled around. Took laundry up. Had a date in eve. with Jack Roberts. Went out to 69th St., but sat in the car and didn't go to the movies. I'll bet he thinks I am awful. I like Jack alright, but not so much as Joe. I hope Joe has a nice time at the game and tomorrow night, only I wish I was going to be with him. I wonder if he likes me a little and if it will ever be any more? I know it is best not to, but I think so much of him.

Saturday, November 13, 1926

Stayed in all afternoon for a change. Sewed on cushions and curtains and fooled around. Also stayed in in eve. At 10:45 Edith, Pat, June and I went up to the Waffle Shop. Had a good time. Got all our curtains done, thank goodness. Jack Roberts was down at school to the dance and he never said anything about it to me. Guess he had a girl from Lansdown. I know one thing he is not getting is a date next weekend. I am getting rather tired of him. Went to bed late.

Sunday, November 14, 1926

Wrote Miss Dashiell. Got up for Sunday breakfast. First time this year. Had waffles. Went to Church with June. Carl was there. Talked to him a few min. and had a date with Neville ("Bugs") Smith from Cleveland at 5 o'clock and Pat Latimer was with Sam Somebody. Kay Wrigley called. I went out in a Studebaker car until 7:15. Stopped and got some junk to eat; parked and ate in the car and smoked. While I was gone John Joseph called and was to call again at 7:15, but didn't. I was so disappointed. I wonder now when he will ever call.

Monday, November 15, 1926

Had classes all day. Saw Jack, but didn't let him see me. I don't want to see him. John Joseph called in eve. He is sweet.

Tuesday, November 16, 1926

Classes all day. Worked in library. Was dead tired in eve.

Wednesday, November 17, 1926

Cut Chem and Child Care in morning. Went down to campus at 11:00. After Assembly Edith and I went down town. Did a lot of shopping. Got some new shoes. Had lunch at the Italian restaurant by the Adelphia Hotel.[196] Not so good. Had date with John Joseph in eve. and Edith with John Spentel. We decided they were the last house dates we were going to

---

[196] The Adelphia Hotel was completed in 1914 at the intersection of 13th and Chestnut Street in Downtown Philadelphia and was designed by the famous architect Horace Trumbauer. The Adelphia was advertised (during this era) as one of the best hotels in Philly. It would have remained so at least through the era herein.

give these boys. I like Joe alright, but he is not going to always have a house date with me and take his other girl friends out to some high hat place. I have done it long enough. I am through.

Thursday, November 18, 1926

Classes until 5:00. Met Jack. Talked to him in the Library. He is alright, but nothing exciting. Walked up to house with me. Wonder if he is going to their fraternity dance Saturday night? Kay Wrigley called me up. Bill Kittelberger was there. Talked to him and have a date with him tomorrow night. How exciting.

Friday, November 19, 1926

Stayed down at school for the Court Dance. It was a bum one. I can't stand him. Jack didn't go. Had a date with Bill Kittelberger and June was with Kay Wrigley. Had a real nice time. Went down to the Earle and then to Child's. I thought I would die laughing at Kay. We never left there until 12. Kay ate his toast on the way out. We had the whole place laughing. Went down to an El and missed one. Flew up and got a taxi and got here just in time.

Mama sent a box for my birthday. Had a big feed up in Kathleen's room. Everything was so good. Potato buns, meat loaf, cheese, pickles, chow chow, cake and cookies.

Saturday, November 20, 1926

Jack was down at school at noon. They got a new car. Took me for a ride through the Park. Stayed in all afternoon. Sewed and cleaned up. Got 2 birthday presents. Edith a cigarette case. Kathleen a jewel case.

Sunday, November 21, 1926

I am 21 today. Wonder when I will ever be married. Didn't go to church, studied a little. Jack called after lunch, Took me for the grandest ride out to Valley Forge and all around. His mother and father were along. I didn't know what to say.

Monday, November 22, 1926

Wrote Bubby. No mail today.

Tuesday, November 23, 1926

Went downtown with Edith. Got tickets for a show. Had lunch at Strawbridge's. Cut psychology class. Had classes until 5:00. Studied for Chem quiz all eve.

Wednesday, November 24, 1926

Fooled around all aft. up at house. Mailed my laundry.[197] Most of the kids went home for vacation today. In eve. Edith and I went down to the Lyric and saw "Abbie's Irish Rose."[198] I sure got a good laugh out of it.

---

[197] There were no laundry facilities for the students.
[198] This legendary 1922 comedy by Anne Nichols had one of Broadway's longest runs — 2,327 performances. And also played in other cities.

Thursday, November 25, 1926

Thanksgiving. Didn't get up until about 11:00. Had a turkey dinner over at the dining room at 12 o'clock. Went down to the Stanley with Mim Rodrick. Saw Adolph Menjou in "The Ace of Cads."[199] Jack came for me at 4:00. Went out to Hoodners and had another Thanksgiving dinner. His Mother and Dad were there. Had the best dinner, felt so dumb, didn't know what to say. Helped with the dishes afterwards. Jack and I went to the movies somewhere, then came in here to the fraternity house.

Friday, November 26, 1926

Got up at 10:00. Went to the Tea Rose at 12:00 for lunch. Walked up Lancaster Ave. Wrote to Mama. Went out to dinner at Miss Worrell's tonight. Had a good dinner, but what a dead crowd. Edith was along. We left and then chased around and went over to the Waffle Shop.

Saturday, November 27, 1926

Didn't do anything all morning. Jack called about 12:00 and asked me to wear the red evening dress I looked so pretty in. Met Mrs. Robinson at Wanamaker's at 1:30. Went shopping with her all aft. Came out to the house for dinner. Jack came at 7:30. Took Mrs. Robinson out home and then went to the party. It was a surprise for someone who had just turned 21. A bunch of us met at another house. All had sheets on when he (the honoree) came in. Danced and carried on all eve. Had a good time. Had some ginger ale cocktails. Parked out front of Robinson's until almost 2:30. Had left about 1:00. Mrs. Robinson didn't say a thing.

Monday, November 29, 1926

Wrote to J. Clark and Blair. Saw Jack just to speak to. Had classes until 5:00. Kay Wrigley called. Went down to Cathay to dinner with him, but never again if I can help it. Went to the Cinderella dancing place on Market Street. Good food and good music, but a tough crowd and Kay is a terrible dancer. Went to bed early.

Tuesday, November 30, 1926

Studied in Library for hrs. Got my train reservation to go home on the 18th for Christmas vacation. Saw Jack at 5 o'clock. He walked up to the house with me. John Wandall called and asked me to get Kathleen's ring size for an engagement ring for Christmas. John Joseph called and wanted a date, but I didn't give him one. I don't like him much anymore. Worked on my Child Care Charts.

Wednesday, December 1, 1926

Came up to house at noon. Fooled around. Kathleen, Emma Hess, and I had lunch in Kathleen's room. I went down to Saxony's with Emma. Saw May Crider. I am to be invited to a shower for Edie Walker next week. Had headache all eve. John Joseph called again. Had an "onion" feed up in Kathleen's room.

---

[199] "The Ace of Cads" is a 1926 American silent romantic drama film directed by Luther Reed and stars Adolphe Menjou and Alice Joyce.

Thursday, December 2, 1926

Haven't seen Jack for 2 days. Had my hair washed and curled. It was awful cold out today. John Joseph called again. I can't understand him. 3 nights straight. I do like him, but I won't give in as he doesn't care enough for me to take me anywhere.

Friday, December 3, 1926

Talked to Jack a couple of minutes. Letter from Mama. Sent me $15.00. Went down town and got a new hat and a couple Xmas presents. Worked on handkerchief for Jack in eve. Wrote to Mama.

Saturday, December 4, 1926

Stayed in all afternoon. Finished the silk pongee handkerchief for Jack. Went to a fraternity dance with him in eve. Had a real good time. He has my black onyx ring that Jimmy gave me.

Sunday, December 5, 1926

Was so cold last night. Snowing hard when I got up. Went to breakfast. Didn't go to church. Studied some in afternoon. My throat got so sore. Went to bed early.

Monday, December 6, 1926

Wrote to Mama and to J. Joseph. Went over to see Dr. Arnette in the morning. He painted my throat with iodine. Had breakfast at the Tea Rose. Stayed at the house all day. Studied Chem and fooled around. Also had lunch at the Tea Rose. Edith was here all aft. Had letter from Bill Kittelberger. John Joseph called in eve. I could hardly talk to him as my voice is almost gone.

Tuesday, December 7, 1926

Went to class first 2 hrs. Went downtown with Kathleen. Shopped all day and didn't get much. John Joseph called again and expects to call tomorrow night. Wrote Joe another letter, my last until I hear from him.

Wednesday, December 8, 1926

Didn't see Jack today. **Played basketball on the junior team.** We beat the Freshmen 24-7. Went downtown with Kate and Howd. The stores were all packed. John Joseph didn't call and he was supposed to. Wonder what happened?

Thursday, December 9, 1926

Mailed laundry today. Had classes until 5 o'clock. Talked to Jack a couple of minutes. Joe called after I left for the shower for Edie Walker. Had the best time. May Crider was there and also Edna Kilpatrick. Played bridge. She got some cute gifts.

Friday, December 10, 1926

Didn't have psychology class. Dr. Taft forgot to come! Talked to Jack at 2 o'clock, then went out down town with June. Got a new dress. Had a date in eve. with John Joseph. He is

Guys showing off their raccoon coats

so sweet. He was wearing a good raccoon coat and looked so cute.[200]

I went down to the Stanley and then up to John Wandall's apartment. He wasn't home so we made ourselves at home and stayed awhile. Saw Helen Kephart at Wanamaker's. I was certainly surprised.

Saturday, December 11, 1926

Wrote to Mama and Bill K. Studied and worked all afternoon. Marjorie called up from 69th St. Didn't go out this evening. Studied Chemistry instead.

Sunday, December 12, 1926

Spent a good day in studying. Got up for breakfast, studying Chem in morning, Ed. in afternoon, and English in the evening. Stayed up until 2:00 and got up in the morning at 6:00. Drank a Coke to keep awake.[201]

Monday, December 13, 1926

Got up early and studied Ed. Took the exam in the morning and English in the afternoon. Both were terrible. Had a letter from Mama, then studied for Chem and Sociology.[202] Then went to bed at 1:45 and got up about 5:00. Am just dead. I can only hope I know something. I even drank another Coke to stay awake!

Tuesday, December 14, 1926

Took chem exam in the morning and sociology in the afternoon; hope I didn't mix them up in my head. Am scared to death I didn't pass either exam. Came home and slept before dinner. Fooled around all evening and didn't study anything. Just wanted to clear my head. No exams tomorrow, thank heavens.

Wednesday, December 15, 1926

Had a letter from Blair Mann and wrote to Alice. Went down town with June and had lunch at the Cathay. Decided to shop all afternoon and got a lot done. John Joseph called to say good-bye. Also John Spentel. Joe is leaving tomorrow afternoon. Wish I were as well. Instead, I studied Child Care and Home Nursing all evening.

---

[200] In the early to mid-1920 American Ivy leaguers and other college undergrads began sporting heavy, full-length raccoon coats, which set the trend in later 1920s & 30s men's fashion and sparked a voracious demand across the country. If a man could afford a fur coat, he had one; bankers, salesmen and students alike used the style to signify or improve their social status. **And if you were a Ivy League undergrad in the 1920s with a reputation to keep, you wouldn't have been seen at the homecoming game without one...** (https://www.messynessychic.com)

[201] Dr. John S. Pemberton invented Coca Cola on 8th May 1886 in Atlanta, Georgia. It was particularly popular during Prohibition and earlier as a "soft" drink for those who preferred not to imbibe.

[202] The study of sociology was new to most college students during the first half of the 20th Century, originated by French philosopher Auguste Comte in 1838, who believed that science could be used to study the social world.

Thursday, December 16, 1926

Got up at 5:00 to study, then took the exam mid-morning, finishing it in just an hour. Went to Assembly, then went down town, my last trek until I come back after Christmas.

Got my Chem grade; I flunked. Made only 52 in the final exam. Disappointing, but not surprising. Jack called and I had a date with him this evening. We went over to the fraternity house. There were so darn many boys chasing around that I don't like him much anymore. Went home and studied Psychology until late into the night.

Friday, December 17, 1926

Got up at 4:30 and studied psych and then went and took the exam in the morning. Only hope I passed it. I said goodbye to Jack, then came up to the house. Packed and mailed packages; bought a coat. Studied History the rest of the day and evening.

Saturday, December 18, 1926

Got up at 5:00. Kate and I studied History. Got all ready to go home later. Got an 85 in English exam, such a surprise, but a welcomed one. Came up to the house after the history exam. Took luggage down to the station, then went up and had my hair washed and curled. Went on to the station and left on the 3:33. It was 20 min. late leaving Philadelphia and an hour late arriving at Tyrone. Met Abe Baker, a friend of Jane Clark, on the train. Papa and Papa Spencer met me at Tyrone. Bill Kittelberger was on the same train and he came home along with us. Talked to Mama and then went to bed.

Sunday, December 19, 1926

Had some good buckwheat cakes for breakfast. Went to church with Mama and saw Raymond, J. Holten, George and Bill K. They were all there. Went around to see everyone, then went up to Alice's. Raymond came up and we went up to Jimmies. J. S. was in there. He hardly looked at me. Walked home with Alice.

Monday, December 20, 1926

Worked around all morning. Wrapped Xmas presents. Did some laundry. Papa decided to give a dance next week! I started making out a list of people to invite. Was over at Strickland's in the afternoon. Saw "Jackie." He is so cute. Had a date with Raymond in the eve. I like him a whole lot.

Tuesday, December 21, 1926

Wrote all my Christmas cards in the morning. Went to Clearfield with Alice. Saw Bob Daughtery and Bub King. Chased around to the stores. Saw John Leitzinger but not to talk to. J. Holten came up awhile in the eve.

Wednesday, December 22, 1926

Chased around all morning. Alice came up about 12:00 and we drove out to DuBois to meet Hugh, but his family were all there so we didn't stay. Came back, did some chores and wrapped some presents. Had a date with Kirk Hile in the evening and Kate Smith was with

Dave. Went to a dance at the Royal Gardens. Had the best time. Saw Steve Mc Kenzie and a bunch of Clearfield boys I know—Blair, Bill Brown, Karl Rowles, John or Eddie Howes.

Thursday, December 23, 1926
Fooled around all morning. Up at Mama Spencer's and down to Aunt Grace's. Hugh was here in the afternoon during Orlie Norris's mother's funeral. Alice was here. Went downtown. Had a date with Raymond in the evening. His grandfather was buried today. Too many deaths for a holiday.

Friday, December 24, 1926, Christmas Eve
Cleaned upstairs in morn. Marjorie came home and I went down to see her. She didn't feel very well. I delivered Xmas presents in the afternoon. Was chasing around downtown and saw Blair Mann. He and Dave Bowes and Kate Smith came up and helped trim our Xmas tree. Went down to the Catholic Church to late Mass.

Saturday, December 25, 1926, Christmas Day
Finished Bubby's handkerchief in the morning. Met Winfield's wife. Got my grades from school. Flunked Chem and had a Condition[203] in History. Fourteen of us were here for dinner. Got a lot of nice presents. Chased around all afternoon. Was down to visit Kings, Walls, Alice and Jessie. Had a date in evening with Kirk Hile.

Kirk and I drove out to Dubois Area and picked up 5 fellows from Dubois standing along the road on their way to the dance at Clearfield. Had more fun up there. The boys had had something to drink and it was so crazy. It snowed and hailed. The windshield got covered with ice. Had some time coming home. Kirk came in and stayed until 1:00. I like him a whole lot.

Sunday, December 26, 1926
Went to church with Mama. Wrote out invitations to the dance on Wednesday night. Was down to see Marjorie and up to Alice's. Had a date with Raymond. He came up to Alice's. Stayed there awhile and he came and stayed until 11:30. Mama called.

Monday, December 27, 1926
Didn't feel good this morning. Slept awhile. Went down to Legion Room in afternoon and decorated for the dance on Wednesday. Raymond, Alice, and Hugh helped. Aunt Maude came from Buffalo in the afternoon. In the evening I went down to the Strand[204] (movie theatre) with Mama and Aunt Maude and Papa and Philip. Went up to Jimmies[205] afterwards.

---

[203] Typically an indicator that the student can produce additional assignments and be awarded a passing grade if the work is satisfactory.
[204] Owned by H. J. (and possible Francis) Thompson; Francis operated the "Chocolate Shop" adjacent to (or part of) the Strand Theatre.
[205] A popular hangout and restaurant. May have been owned by Jim Booth.

141

Tuesday, December 28, 1926

Went to Clearfield with Papa. Bought some stuff for our dance. Went down to Uncle Fred's for dinner. I was down at the Legion Room awhile. Marjorie and Philip and I were at Mama Spencer's for supper. I felt so sick I could hardly eat a thing. Went to the doctor's afterwards. Had a temperature of 102 ¾. Came home and went to bed.

Wednesday, December 29, 1926

Stayed in bed until lunch time. Fooled around all afternoon. Alice was up awhile. Felt rotten all day. Letters from Edith. Went down to the Legion Room about 8:00. Frances Custer came over. Am going over there Saturday afternoon. I danced with Leonard Kantar, Kay Quigley, Scott Ammerman, Jerry McNaul, Bub King, Blair Mann, Kirk Hile, Ted Bowes, Ken Robinson, Bob Wolf.

Had a good time. Hope everyone else did. I hope Raymond isn't cross because I didn't dance with him when I was supposed to. Why didn't Kirk ask me for a date? I like him a lot. That's always the way when you like anyone. We had punch, ice cream and sandwiches. Had confetti. Frances stayed all night with Marjorie. Kirk and Blair brought us up.

Thursday, December 30, 1926

Was supposed to go to Bellefonte in morning, but I was in bed all day. My throat was so sore. I had a letter from Jack Roberts. Wrote to him. The girls stopped in for a little while. I then read before going to bed.

Friday, December 31, 1926, New Year's Eve

Still didn't feel so well this morning. Fooled around a little, then did some work. I had to go to Clearfield on the bus for a dentist appointment. I talked to John Leitzinger after the appointment, then Karl Rowles took me to the Pig and Whistle. I came back up home by bus and went up to Alice's for a while. After supper Marjorie, Kate, Jessie, Edith, and I went to Clearfield in Kate's car. Dempsey from Philipsburg went down along. He got us a quart of wine. I drank some and I felt so good.

Went to the dance at the Royal Garden. Had the best time. Had not stagged it to a dance at Clearfield before. Blair was there. Danced with him. He was with a girl. Danced with J. S., Jimmy Johnson, John Wright, and John Howe. Everybody was celebrating. Got home at 1:30 and I wasn't even supposed to go! Quite an evening.

1927

Saturday, January 1, 1927

Worked around and helped Mama in the morning. Marjorie, Alice, and I went over to Frances Custer's to a bridge party in the afternoon in Marjorie's car. Had a good time and wonderful eats. Had a date with Raymond in the evening. He was so nice. I liked him better than I ever did.

Sunday, January 2, 1927

Dusted in front rooms after breakfast. Packed and got dressed. Went down to Marjorie's. Went up to Aunt Mary's and Mama Spencer's. Said good-bye to everyone. Left at one o'clock. Bubby drove us over to Altoona thinking we could get a chair.[206] Arthur, Catherine, and Raymond came along. Raymond kissed me goodbye. The train was packed and one hour late. Was dead tired.

Marjorie went on out to Norristown. Three other girls and Mrs. Scott were here at our campus house. Unpacked and went to bed about 12:00.

Monday, January 3, 1927

Went down to school at 12:00 and registered. Came up to the house with Kathleen. She had some food. Had lunch in her room. Wrote to Mama. After dinner went to the movies with June and Janet. Saw "The Scarlet Letter."[207] Alice was here when I came home. Stayed all night.

Tuesday, January 4, 1927

Had a letter from Blair. Wrote to Raymond. Had a 9:00 class. Alice went out to school. Came up to house for 3 hours. Had lunch in Kathleen's room, then had classes until 5:00. I talked to Jack as he walked up to the house with me. John Joseph called me.

Wednesday, January 5, 1927

Wrote to Bubby and Blair. I had classes all morning; then I came up to the house and had lunch in Kathleen's room again. I went downtown for the rest of the afternoon.

Thursday, January 6, 1927

I got up for breakfast for the first time since my return. Had classes every hour until 5:00. Talked to Miller Preston a couple of minutes. Did some sewing during the evening.

Friday, January 7, 1927

Wrote to Mama. Was down at school all day. It's terrible to try and study in the court; we can't use the library.[208] I didn't talk to Jack and I don't even care a thing for him. John Joseph

---

206 Rather than the usual bench seating.
207 Based on the classic American novel by Nathaniel Hawthorne, this silent film was put together by star Lillian Gish, who was forced by Louis B. Mayer to assure religious groups that the still-controversial material would not offend their sensibilities.
208 The library was being renovated.

called in the evening and I told him to come over. He brought me a box of candy and I about passed out; it was Whitman's Sampler! He was really nice. We have a date for Sunday night.

Saturday, January 8, 1927

I stayed in all afternoon. Had a date with Jack Roberts in the evening. We went out to Swarthmore-Drexel basketball game and Drexel lost 40-13. Danced after the game. I don't like Jack much anymore.

Sunday, January 9, 1927

Went to church in the morning, then wrote to Mama and Mrs. Heverly. Spent the afternoon studying. This evening I had a date with John Joseph. He was so sweet tonight, but I wonder when I will see him again.

Monday, January 10, 1927

Wrote to Marjorie and J. Clark. I was at school until 5:00, except for a break for lunch at Hyler's all by myself. Stayed for basketball practice, then wrote letters and studied.

Tuesday, January 11, 1927

Today is John Joseph's birthday; I sent him a card. Had a letter from Raymond and I wrote to Blair and to Papa and Mama Spencer. It was awfully cold today and I had classes until 5:00. Alice called this evening.[209]

Wednesday, January 12, 1927

Had classes again all morning. I then did some reference work before coming home. Took laundry up and went to the Waffle Shop with Edith, Kate, and Nellie Coleman.

Thursday, January 13, 1927

Wrote to Mama and Raymond. Then I put in a big day at school and played basketball from 5–6. I am tired tonight. Nellie went home today to stay. I guess she was homesick.

Friday, January 14, 1927

Didn't have class the first hour today. Later I went downtown with Kathleen from 2 to 4, came back for history class. Alice met me on my way up from school and we went down to the Cathay for dinner. Came back and Jack Roberts was waiting for me. We took Alice out to Robinsons at Drexel Hill and then went to see "The Waning Sex"[210] at 69th St. Then we had some good banana ice cream. I don't even want Jack to kiss me anymore… .

Saturday, January 15, 1927

Had a class at 9:00 so I didn't go to breakfast. Met Alice, Marguerite Reichenbach and 2 other girls, had lunch at the Cathay, and then went to the movies at the Stanley. Saw Colleen Moore in "Twinkletoes."

---

209 The girls did not have private telephones in their rooms. There was only a house telephone and whoever answered was expected to take a message if the girl being called was not in.

210 Directed by Robert Z. Leonard, with Norma Shearer, Conrad Nagel, George K. Arthur.

Went to see one of the girls sister's apartment. Had some tea and cake. Came up to the house for dinner, then went down to the basketball game where Drexel lost to Haverford, 38-39.

Sunday, January 16, 1927

Wrote to Mama. Got up for breakfast and went to Church with June. Carl Gregory walked up with me and Stanley H. with June. Read the play for English.

Monday, January 17, 1927

Wrote Jessie. Was down at school all day. Basketball practice at 4:00. Studied in the evening.

Tuesday, January 18, 1927

Wrote to Alice Wall and C. Reese. Had my hair washed and curled in the morning. Classes until 5:00. Studied all evening.

Wednesday, January 19, 1927

Wrote to Mama. Came up to the house about 3:00 and took a short nap. Worked on millinery paper in the evening, then went over to the drugstore with Edith and dragged a lot of stuff back. John Joseph called for the first time in over a week. Heard that he had a new girl; they don't last long. I have a date with him on the 29th. Wonder if I will? You never can tell.

Thursday, January 20, 1927

Classes again until 5:00. Haven't talked to Jack since last Friday night and I don't want to see him. John Joseph called before dinner and wanted to come over tonight, but I am not allowed to have house dates. It makes me cross to think that it will be the same next year. Had some house meeting after dinner. We are not having a formal house dance this term. The kids make me tired.

Friday, January 21, 1927

June and I went over to the U. of Penn Library to do some reference work for history. Had quite a house meeting after dinner. Big fight about the house dance. Went down to Jack Hart's and had the best time. Bob Drake and Harry Bixler walked up with me. Have a date with Harry two weeks from tomorrow. Had some good dances.

Saturday, January 22, 1927

Didn't get up for breakfast. Started for Norristown[211] right after lunch. Marjorie met me at the trolley. Went up to her room. It is the nicest place. Met her roommate, Lucy Nichols. Talked awhile. Lucy has a Ford roadster so we chased around. Went downtown, saw their school. There was a dance in the evening of Practice Teachers and we decided to go. Called up John Joseph and he and Min Spandle came out. We had the best time. Joe was so sweet. Made another date with him. Had the best supper. Came in about 1:00.

---

[211] This would be Marjorie's Wall's room (or apartment) in Norristown where she was teaching.

Sunday, January 23, 1927

Never got up until about noon when we got some breakfast. Met another girl who also lives there. Had some good cinnamon toast. Had dinner at 1:30. Fooled around and read the paper. Made some wonderful fudge; it got so creamy. Left about 5:00. Didn't get in on time for Tea. Wrote Mama. John Deitz called.

Monday, January 24, 1927

Wrote to Jessie. It's getting to be funny now that I don't see Jack any more. Guess he doesn't want to see me. I am not going to wear his pin again until I talk to him. Why should I? Had basketball practice at 4:00. Rather tired.

Tuesday, January 25, 1927

Wrote to Alice. At school from 9:00 to 5:00. Wrote up a history paper on Napoleon. Talked to Jack a minute before history class. He wants to see me again, but I don't want to see him. Sewed some in the evening. Mrs. K. called me. John Joseph called.

Wednesday, January 26, 1927

Wrote to Aunt Grace. Played basketball game with Juniors vs. Seniors after Assembly. We won, Juniors 11-14. Did some reference work afterwards. Came up to house, fooled around and packed my laundry. Alice called; she won't be in for the formal dinner. John Deitz called for a date, but I couldn't give him one, thank goodness.

Thursday, January 27, 1927

Talked to Jack a long time today. Was at school until 5:00. Alice (Wall) called after dinner and then I called the Preceptress of Beaver College. Studied in evening.

Friday, January 28, 1927

Took Ed. exam in morning. It was terrible, only hope I passed in it. Came up to house at 1:00. Took dress up to Cleaners. Had lunch up at Lintons, a new restaurant on Market Street. Pretty good. Met Alice at school at 4:00. Went to History Class. In evening I got a special from Mrs. Dorsey and went down to the Stanley and saw "Valencia" with Mae Murray.[212] Had a big onion feed up in Kathleen's room after we came home.

Saturday, January 29, 1927

We got up for breakfast. Betty Biddle has charge of the dining room this weekend. Alice went down to Sociology class alone, then met Thelma Sykes downtown. At 12:30 I met them and also Marjorie Wall. Went to Cathay for lunch. Marjorie got what I got, shoes. Chased around most all afternoon. Came up to the house and got dressed for the formal dinner. Alice (Wall) and Thelma went down to the movies. Had a date with John Joseph; we went over to John Wandall's apartment, also Kathleen was there. Had some hot time. Joe was so sweet. I am curious to know if it will ever mean anything more than good friends between us. I hardly think so.

---

[212] "Valencia" is also known as "The Love Song." It is a 1926 American silent film directed by Dimitri Buchowetzki, who came from Paramount to direct. The film stars Mae Murray and features Boris Karloff in an uncredited role. The film was a box office hit and the title song, "Valencia," was the top song in the U.S. for the year.

Sunday, January 30, 1927

John took Kathleen, Alice, Thelma and me down to church in a taxi. Went over to the Tea Rose for dinner. Talked most of the afternoon. John Joseph called just before I went to Tea. He and John Wandall came over. Joe is ----. I am falling in love with him; I know it. He is so wonderful. I am afraid I hurt his feelings, but I hope not. I said I supposed he would forget me if he went up to New York this week. If he would only write a letter. I wonder? Wrote to Mama.

Monday, January 31, 1927

Down at school all day. Had basketball practice until 5:00. Just spoke to Jack. Joe wrote me a letter last night. It was the sweetest letter I ever got. I only hope he means what he said. He called me after dinner and is going to call tomorrow at 5:30 and tell me about his finals.

Tuesday, February 1, 1927

Wrote to J. Bullock and Ethel B. Had Psych exam in morning. Had a paper for History to write and Education reports to write up. Classes until 5:00. Was dead tired. Wrote letters and studied in the evening.

John Joseph called. He is coming down to school tomorrow at 1:00 and take me out for lunch. I am so happy. He flunked 2 subjects and unless he gets the one brought up to 70 he will have to go home. I only hope he makes his grade all right.

Had a big house meeting over in June's room. Miss Dorsey talked to us. We are having a house dance February 19. Hurray! Big feed in Kathleen's room afterwards.

Wednesday, February 2, 1927

Wrote to Alice and Marjorie. Classes until 1:00. John Joseph came down to school for me and we went down to Club Madrid for lunch, then to the Fox, and dinner at an Italian Restaurant, Ferriae's on Market Street. I had the most wonderful time. I am only wondering how long Joe is going to like me and if he really and truly does, it is hard to believe; then he is so changeable I can hardly believe it. Anyway, I am not going to think of him seriously. I am just going to love him. I am hoping and praying he doesn't flunk out of school, but if he does that he will work here in the city. Why do I like him? I really shouldn't, but he is the sweetest, cleanest boy I know or have ever gone with.

Thursday, February 3, 1927

Wrote to Jessie. Classes until 5:00. Was dead tired. Looked for telephone call from Joe all eve. Wonder why he didn't call, where he is and what he is doing and if he has changed his mind about me and won't call again. I cannot understand him.

Friday, February 4, 1927

Wrote to Frances Custer. June and I had lunch at Linton's today, then went over to the University and worked on our History papers. Went to boys' basketball game after History class. We beat Susquehanna 34-13. I had a call from Harry Bixler before dinner, but I wasn't

147

back yet and then he didn't call again and I hope he doesn't call at all. I decided I was going to ask Joe to go to the dance tonight and called only to find he had gone up to New York. I am really cross that he didn't call last night. I think he should have.

Saturday, February 5, 1927

Edith and I met Alice and Eleanor Steinbauch at Wanamaker's at noon and had lunch with them at The Golden Dragon. Harold Knight from Clearfield plays in the orchestra there. Alice and I sent our cards up and he came back and talked to us. Just as I was about to get on a 38th Street bus I saw Mahlon Robb to speak to. Had a date with John Joseph in eve. He said I would have to change my religion to Catholic if I married him, but I could never be a Catholic at heart.

Sunday, February 6, 1927

Wrote to Mama and Cecil. I got up for breakfast. Didn't go to church. Wrote some letters and studied in the afternoon. Had a date with Joe in the evening. Edith had a date with Min Spardle. Sat up in Kathleen's room until 1:00 talking.

Monday, February 7, 1927

Took pictures at basketball today. School until 5:00. Got a 94 in an Ed. quiz. Too much. Haven't seen Jack for ages. Am going to ask him for my ring the next time I see him to talk to. The kids sort of think Joe called Selma Shanabe up tonight. If I only find out he did things won't be so smooth for him. I wonder if he would do that. I hardly think so as that would be just too much for me.

Tuesday, February 8, 1927

Wrote Alice. Went down town with Kathleen in the morning. Had lunch at Hylers, the best toasted cheese sandwich. Did some shopping. Came up to house and mailed laundry. After school went to girls' basketball game. Played Ursinus and it was a tie 23-23, a very exciting game. John Joseph called before dinner and then again about 10:00. I have a date to go to lunch with him tomorrow at 1:00. I am anxious to see him.

Wednesday, February 9, 1927

Joe met me in the Court today after assembly. Went down to Club Madrid for lunch. Then up to the "Fox" and then to the Tea Rose for dinner. I had the most wonderful time. I always do with him. I do love him and I think he loves me some at least. We got into some good conversation. He believes in birth control, etc. and is going to get me some papers explaining it, from all fields. Joe certainly has high ideals and also some good ideas, and I love him for them.

I found out that his father is President of Cincinnati Rubber Co. They must have plenty of money. I wonder if it would make any difference to Joe if he saw our home and family, how we live and the past life we have had, so different from his I know. That is something I would find out before I ever had any serious intentions with him. He would have to visit me in Curwensville. Of course we would probably live under different conditions after we were married, but all the same he should know everything. I wonder if anything such as marriage will ever occur for Joe and me to be together the rest of our lives. We both have several years before us, before we ever do such a thing. I want to make some good use of my education and he must find out what he wants to do in life. Studied in the evening after I came in.

Thursday, February 10, 1927

Wrote to Catherine Pifer. Had classes until 5:00. Got out of here early and went to girls basketball game with Pitt and we lost 31-11. Boys also lost 38-22 to Juniata. Talked to Bill Hirschman at school today. Karl Rowles called me up and talked to June and came over to see her; then in the evening he and Bill Brown went out with Bill and Carl. Joe called twice before dinner and wanted me to have dinner with him. He came over afterward and showed me the proofs of his pictures. Have a date Saturday.

Friday, February 11, 1927

Had breakfast at the Tea Rose and lunch at Linton's[213] with June and Ann. Went to a Fashion Show of Strawbridge's in the afternoon. Joe called right after I got in from my 5:00 class. Had dinner over at the Tea Rose with him. Evelyn and Frances came in and sat with us. Joe had another date at 8:00, so I went to "Cap and Bells" at school with June. It was real good. Jack was there with another girl, thank goodness. Now he can take his extra energy out on her. Danced two dances in the Court, then June, Peg Bean and I dropped in at Jack Hart's. Harry Bixler and Bob Drake brought me home. Harry asked me to a basketball game on Wednesday night, but I can't do that.

Saturday, February 12, 1927

Had my hair washed and curled at 4:00. Joe came over at 6:00 and we had dinner at Harris Café up near 40th Street. Then went over to John's apt. Joe was so wonderful and I really think he does like me. I mailed him a Valentine today.

Sunday, February 13, 1927

Got up for breakfast and did some washing. Went to church with June. Wrote to Kirk Hile. I was so surprised in the afternoon when Winfield Sykes and Mable & Tom Forcey dropped in on me. It seemed so good to see them. We talked a blue streak. Miss Dorsey thinks I am having too many dates, but she cannot do much as I have not broken any rules. Had a date with John Joseph in the evening. We had a regular rough house in the parlor tonight. Miss Dorsey and Mrs. Scott were both out.

Monday, February 14, 1927, Valentine's Day

Did a lot of studying at school. Came up to the house at 4:00. Joe called and then called the station for me and told me Mama and Papa's train got in at 6:30. He was going to take me to dinner, but then decided he had better not. He was so sweet. I met the train and went up

213 Founded in 1890 Linton's had 26 locations in the Philadelphia area. It was the all-night restaurant rival to Horn & Hardart, "where the coffee was always fresh and the specials - apple brown betty, baked apple with vanilla sauce, the fish fry and the breakfast platters - clattered out of the kitchen on conveyor belts."

to the Benjamin Hotel with them. John Wright came down. Went and had dinner. Went to the first meeting of the Convention[214] up in the Ballroom. Danced after a few speeches. John brought me home.

Tuesday, February 15, 1927

Classes until 5:00. Mama called at 6:30 and I went down and went to the Forrest Theatre with Mama, Papa, Mrs. Gates and John Wright. Joe called after I had gone. He is such a dear. Saw "Collette"[215] which was real good. Miss Dorsey had a fit that I am going out so much. Have an appointment with her in the morning.

Wednesday, February 16, 1927

Miss Dorsey gave me a good bawling out in the morning. I have to report myself to Student Government. I met Mama at 9:30, but didn't say anything to her about this. We looked for an evening dress, but didn't find any that I liked. Came up to the house at 1:00 and had lunch at the Tea Rose. I called Joe in the morning and he returned my call about 2:00. I wonder when I will be seeing him. I hope real soon. Karl Rowles called in the evening. He has a date with Alice Wall on Friday night. I was brought up before Student Government and got a week's campus restriction and cannot go to the House dance. Studied and talked to Alice in eve.

Thursday, February 17, 1927

Cut classes all except Millinery. Kathleen and I went down town. Got a new evening dress. Had lunch at Venture Inn with Edith, Evelyn, and Selma. Went down to Dennisons and helped with decorations for the House Dance Saturday night. Went over to the room at the Hotel, but Mama and Papa were not there. Joe called in the evening. He is sore that I was campused. Is coming over tomorrow afternoon.

Friday, February 18, 1927

Came up to the House about 1:30. Talked to Mama after breakfast. Had a date with John Joseph from 2:00 till 5:30. Alice came in with Karl Rowles. She had a date with him in the evening. Worked on decorations for House dance all evening. Talked to Jack Roberts down at school today, first for a couple weeks. Got the written notice from Student Government saying I am campused and cannot go to the House dance. Joe is so cross.

Saturday, February 19, 1927

Didn't get up for breakfast. Alice went out to Phoenixville to see Marguerite Reichenbaugh. Met Mama, Papa, and Marjorie at 12:15 and had lunch at Wanamaker's. Went to the Stanton and saw Lon Cheney in "Tell it To the Marines."[216] It was real good.

---

[214] A political convention; H. J. was active in the Democrat Party, later running for the State Senate.

[215] 1927 was the last year before the talkies took over, and so this is silent film drama ("Collette") at its most sophisticated. A great film for its time.

[216] Released in 1927 "Tell It to the Marines" is one of Lon Chaney's most famous roles. The movie was received well at the box office. Because of this movie Chaney was the only civilian to be made an Honorary member of the US Marine Corp.

Came up to the House and helped to finish decorating and got dressed for the formal dinner. Marjorie had dinner with Papa and went to the show with him. Mama went to the dinner with me. Played bridge in the evening with Mrs. Scott, the House Mother, and Mrs. Phillips while the House Dance was going on. I had one dance with John Wandall. Joe called me before and after dinner.

Sunday, February 20, 1927

Never got up until 11:15. Went over to 34th Street where Mama and Papa are staying. The weather is terrible. Marjorie had dinner with us. Had the best dinner down at Green's Hotel. Mama and Papa went on out to Robinsons. I had a date with John Joseph and Kathleen with John Wandall. Had Mrs. Scott's room. We all went to the Tea Rose with them. Had more fun. (I wasn't supposed to be there being campused.) Studied history all evening.

Monday, February 21, 1927

Took my final in Hygiene. Only hope I passed it. Was over to see Mama and Papa after breakfast. Played basketball. Joe called before dinner. I could have had a 12:00 date with him, but he had made a date beforehand. Oh, if I only had him. Mama and Mrs. Kittelberger were over at the room after dinner. Went into the Tea Rose with them and had a sandwich and coffee. Stayed in this evening. Wrote to Alice Wall and Jessie.

Tuesday, February 22, 1927

Papa and Orlie (Norris) went up to Springfield in the morning. Mama came over to the house and sewed on my evening dress. Had lunch at the Tea Rose. Mama went out to Norrises in the afternoon. I stayed in and sewed. John Joseph called. I was supposed to have a date with him and he forgot it. He is in for a good bawling out. I fear I have been seeing too much of him. I am going to see just what he thinks about it. I think he had a girl up to John's apt. last night and if he did I am not going up there with him anymore.

Wednesday, February 23, 1927

Went over to see Mama after breakfast. She spent the day with Mrs. Kittelberger. Stayed down at school in the afternoon and wrote a paper for millinery. Studied in the eve. Alice called. Then Joe called. He had been talking with his Mother and Father over the phone and felt pretty bad. Guess they bawled him out. I feel so sorry for him, but I can't do anything.

Thursday, February 24, 1927

Wrote to Libby King. Had classes all day. Over to see Mama after breakfast and before dinner. Papa came back late in the evening at Orlie's. Alice was with Mama all day. She called me in the eve. Joe called again and he has a date tomorrow night. I fear he is having too many dates.

Friday, February 25, 1927

Saw Mama and Papa after breakfast. Classes until one o'clock. Met them and also Orlie, Mrs. Kittelberger, and Mr. & Mrs. Jim Norris at Wanamaker's. Went shopping and then they left and went to the movies and I finished my shopping; cut History Class. Met them again at Broad Street Station at 7:30. Joe came down also and met them. I felt so dumb. Went to the show at the Adelphia; saw "The Girl Friend."[217] It was real good. Joe didn't go along as he had a date. Norrises brought us up in their car.

Saturday, February 26, 1927

Mama and Papa left on the 10:30 train. Stayed in all afternoon and fooled around getting ready for the dance. Had the best time at the Junior Prom. Joe was so sweet. The dance floor down at school is terrible. Got the most wonderful Angel Food cake from Aunt Mary (Mae, wife of Verner Wall).

Sunday, February 27, 1927

Wrote to Alice. Got up for breakfast but didn't go to church. Got a lot of work done. Studied history for Conditional exam all afternoon and evening. Joe didn't call; I am disappointed, only I guess I can't expect him to call every night.

Monday, February 28, 1927

Wrote a thank-you to Aunt Mary. Worked on hat in Millinery in the morning. Studied for History Conditional all afternoon. Took it from 4 until 6. It was terrible; am scared to death I didn't pass it. Had dinner at the Tea Rose. Harry Bixler called and wanted me to go to a basketball game with him Saturday night. Also John Deitz called just to talk.

Tuesday, March 1, 1927

Felt terrible in the morning when I got up, my throat was so sore. Went over to the infirmary and stayed all day. Didn't do much work. Wrote a couple of letters.

Wednesday, March 2, 1927

Had to stay in bed all day today. Joe didn't even call last night. He called in afternoon over at the house and then over here at the Infirmary. Throat felt some better in eve. Elizabeth Koosier, Dot Wing and Constance Doriwarkle were in also. We got up and had a short game of bridge in the evening.

Thursday, March 3, 1927

Got up and went downstairs for breakfast. Went to school all day. Rather tired in eve. Joe hasn't called yet and it is 8:00. There may yet be hope. I am greatly disappointed Joe didn't call. I think he might have at least to see if I was still sick in the infirmary. Only wish I had given Harry that date for Saturday night. I am such a fool.

Friday, March 4, 1927

Went down town with June for lunch. Ate at the Golden Dragon and talked to Harold Knight for a long time. He is real nice. Went down to Gimbels and saw part of the Fashion

---

[217] "The Girl Friend" is a musical comedy with music by Richard Rodgers, lyrics by Lorenz Hart and book by Herbert Fields. This was the longest running show to date for the trio. Later filmed and shown as a silent film with a full orchestra in the pit.

Show. Talked to Dottie Clymer. She gave me a couple of tickets for the show tonight. June and Edith went. I didn't want to go as I want to go out tomorrow night. Did some shopping. Joe called just before dinner. He is getting too funny. Didn't even ask for a date for tomorrow night. Guess he is going to give me a chance to go with someone else. I could just shoot myself for refusing Harry Bixler to go to the game. Joe makes me so cross. Guess it will be best if we would quit altogether; it would be best for both of us. There will never be anything more between us; it would just cause a lot of trouble on both sides. Talked to Jack Roberts a couple minutes today. Wants his pin and is going to give me my ring. I am going to ask him what all the changing in him is about. These boys, soon I will be off all of them. They drive me crazy. I cannot understand any of them.

Saturday, March 5, 1927
Went to the girls' basketball game in the afternoon. Lost to William and Mary, 10-34. It was a punk game. Our team is terrible. Miss Dasheill called and I had dinner with her at the Woman's City Club. Had the nicest time. Went down to school for some of the Dramatic Plays. Villanova got first place and Drexel second. They were both pretty good. Miss Dashiell couldn't stay until it was over. We danced afterwards. Carl Gregory[218] danced about a min. with me. He is a wonderful dancer.

Sunday, March 6, 1927
Didn't go to church. Wrote letters and did some work. Studied in the afternoon and evening. John Joseph called and I was foolish enough to give him a date, but it is better to have it with him than not to have a date at all and I don't know anyone else I would want a date with. Oh, if I would only meet someone new and different.

Monday, March 7, 1927
Wrote to Alice. Down at school until 5:00. Went to basketball practice. Talked to Phyllis Weinburg; she had a date with John Joseph last week. Studied in evening.

Tuesday, March 8, 1927
Wrote to Jessie. Down to school all day. Didn't see Jack to give him his pin. John Joseph called after dinner. I had a good conversation with him. I think he will be coming around again, but never will I be as much in love with him again. I don't want to.

Wednesday, March 9, 1927
Wrote to Miss Dashielle, Jane Clark, Cecil, and J. Joseph. Finished my hat in Millinery and handed it in today. It doesn't look so awful; I have seen worse. John Joseph called up before dinner. We had one grand conversation. I love to talk to him like that and I can now see that it won't hurt me so much if he does get cross and I don't think he will anyway. I just don't care so much for him anymore, I guess.

---

[218] Phi Kappa Beta '27

Thursday, March 10, 1927

Classes all day and a gym meet from 4 to 5. It was pretty good. Went to a fraternity Tea Dance afterwards. John Joseph called in eve. He received my letter and was not a bit cross, but took it as I wanted him to. He said that all I said was true, that it was a Masterpiece. I am only hoping and looking for an answer tomorrow. Talked to Jack Roberts today and gave him back his pin. No hard feelings on either side I guess. I hope not. Fooled around all evening and didn't do a thing and here I have finals to study for.

Friday, March 11, 1927

Wrote to C. Pifer and W. Hill. Had my hair washed and curled in afternoon. Called Alice up. She came in and got my evening dress to wear to their dance tonight out there. Had a sweet letter from John Joseph. Then he called in the evening. Studied for final in Physiology.

Saturday, March 12, 1927

Wrote to Mama. Had a letter from Mama in the morning. Had classes and then took my final in Physiology in the afternoon. I am glad it is over. Went down town and got a new hat. Had a date with John Joseph in the evening. Went to Fox and saw John Gilbert in "The Count of Monte Crisco." We stood in line for about an hour and a half. It was so funny to be with John again. I just didn't know what to say or do.

Sunday, March 13, 1927

Did some washing and fooled around and studied Millinery in the morning. In the afternoon I studied English. It was the most wonderful day. Studied English in the evening. Joe called and also Alice. Expect to see them both Friday at the 3:33 train.

Monday, March 14, 1927

Wrote to Mama. Took 2 finals today. Millinery in the morning and English in the afternoon. English was rather hard. Fooled around most of the evening, but studied some Psychology.

Tuesday, March 15, 1927

Wrote to J. Clark, M. Hill and Alice. Studied Psychology all morning and took an exam in the afternoon. Joe called in the evening. Studied Education in eve.

Wednesday, March 16, 1927

Studied for Ed. all morning. Had lunch at Tea Rose. Went down town and had check cashed. Studied Sociology all evening.

Thursday, March 17, 1927

St. Patrick's Day. Had a letter from Kirk. Studied all morning. Had lunch up in Lois' room with her and June. Took Sociology exam in the afternoon. It was terrible. Wrote until 4:15. Called Marjorie out at Norristown. Sounded so good to hear her. Talked to Jack at school and he came up in the evening and we went down to St. Agnes Hospital to see Walter Harm. Came back at 9:30. Studied history until 1:00. Slept up in Kathleen's room. Joe called, leaving a message for me, and is going to call in the morning.

Friday, March 18, 1927

Stayed up late studying History. June and I studied up in Kathleen's room and slept up there. Got up at 6:00 and studied all morning. Took exam at 12:00. It was awful. Am scared I didn't pass. Joe came down to school at 2:30 and so did Alice. Went down to the station. Joe went over to Newark, New Jersey since I wouldn't let him come with me. I don't even care. Had a grand time coming up on the train. There were 8 of us. Papa, Mama, and Philip met me at Tyrone.

Saturday, March 19, 1927

Slept until 9:00. Helped Mama all morning. Katy is away. Did some shopping. Went down to Aunt Grace's. Called Marjory Hill at Bellefonte and told her I couldn't come over. They are to come over here tomorrow. Went to Clearfield in the afternoon with Mama. Got a new coat and scarf. Had a date with Kirk Hile in the evening. Went down to Clearfield to the movies and to the Chatterbox for something to eat.

Sunday, March 20, 1927

Mama and I went to church. Marjory, H. Miller, Eddie, Catherine Reese, and J. Clark were to come over today, but it rained all day. Made some fudge. Jessie and Kate[219] came over. Went downtown and Kate took us for a little ride. Had a date with Kirk Hile in the evening. Went up to McGees Mills and had a chicken and waffle dinner. Had the best time. The six of us danced and played cards.

Monday, March 21, 1927

Helped Mama in the morning. Fooled around, sewed a little. Made some croquettes for dinner. In the afternoon I went calling. First, up to D.P. Wall's house. Saw Libby King. Went to the store. Kept house in the evening and put Philip to bed. Had a date with Raymond; it was some date. He was real nice, though. Wrote a letter to Alice after he left. Talked to J.S. quite a while in the afternoon.

Tuesday, March 22, 1927

Got a lot of stuff ready to take back to school. Had a date with Kirk in the evening. Aunt Grace was in and I went to Jessie and Kate's to say good-bye. Kirk is so sweet. I wonder if he likes me much? He didn't kiss me all the time I was with him and he left early.

Wednesday, March 23, 1927

Got up at 4:00 a.m. and had breakfast and started for Philadelphia with Papa driving. Got here about 1:30, 285 miles. Had our lunch with us. Stopped at Harrisburg for about half an hour. Frances Light drove part of the way. Went down to school and registered.

Got grades. Passed everything, thank goodness. Frances and I had dinner at Green's Hotel then went and saw "Flesh and the Devil."[220] It was real good. I was dead tired. Went

---

[219] Likely she is referring to Catherine, Jessie's sister, whose nickname was Kate.

[220] *Flesh and the Devil* is the movie that made Greta Garbo a legend. She had appeared in a few movies for MGM but hadn't really caught the public's attention until she played the vamp opposite John Gilbert in the silent movie adaptation of the novel "The Undying Past."

to bed early. John Joseph had called in the morn. I was supposed to have a date with him, but went with Papa. Joe had theatre tickets also. Gee, he was cross.

Thursday, March 24, 1927

Called Joe after breakfast. He was so sleepy. Had classes all day. Joe called before dinner and came over in the evening. Went over to his apartment. Joe was so wonderful. I believe he "loves" me again, really more than I do him. Took a 12:00 permission.

Friday, March 25, 1927

This was a wonderful day. Got ready for dance in the afternoon. Joe came at 6:45. We had our evening clothes and taxied down to Club Madrid and had dinner. They had a show on down there. Went over to the Lyric Theatre and saw "My Maryland."[221] It was wonderful. I enjoyed it so much. From there we went to the Inter-Fraternity dance. I had only a 2 o'clock permission. Gee, we had to come home just as the fun was beginning. Joe was so sweet all eve. I liked him so much.

Saturday, March 26, 1927

Had classes in morning. Fooled around in afternoon. Wrote to Kirk, Mama, J. Clark. Joe called and wanted to come over, but I couldn't have a date[222] so I wrote to him.

Sunday, March 27, 1927

Wrote to Arthur Wall and M. Hill. Went to church in the morning with June. Did some studying in the afternoon and evening. Wrote letters.

Monday, March 28, 1927

Wrote to Mama. Had lunch at the Waffle Shop. Did a lot of reference work at school. John Joseph called before dinner and again after dinner. I just don't like the way he acts. I know he doesn't love me, and why does he say he does. Never will I do as I did Thursday night up at the apartment. Not that it was anything awful, but I just won't.

Tuesday, March 29, 1927

Had breakfast at the Tea Rose at 10:00 with Evelyn, Frances, and Sara Bennett. Went down to the library and worked until 1 o'clock. Went on field trip to the Commercial Museum. Am dead tired. John Joseph called before dinner. Had a crazy conversation with him. Said he wrote me a letter today in class and was going to send it special, but I haven't seen it yet. Maybe it will come in the morning.

Wednesday, March 30, 1927

Wrote to Mama. Had a sweet letter from John Joseph. He called me before dinner. Was down town in the afternoon. Had lunch at Hylers. Didn't do much shopping. Had a class at 3 o'clock, Fooled around and studied in eve.

---

[221] *My Maryland* was staged by J. C. Huffman. Produced by Lee Shubert and J. J. Shubert, the Broadway production opened on September 12, 1927 at Jolson's 59th Street Theatre.

[222] Likely a house rule of some kind.

Thursday, March 31, 1927

Took my first observation trip this morning. Visited the Holmes Junior High School. Had more fun. Had classes until 5:00. Studied in the evening. Letter from Kirk. Joe called in the evening.

Friday, April 1, 1927

Met Alice at Wanamaker's. Had lunch at the Golden Dragon with her and the other girls. She left for home on the 3:30 train. Gee, only wish I could have gone along. Did some shopping. Joe came over and we had dinner at the Tea Rose after much fooling around. Went over to John's apartment, but he had some date. It surely was rather warm! Haven't asked him to the dance yet.

Saturday, April 2, 1927

Kathleen went up to Allentown with John today. Stayed in all afternoon and evening. It was awful cold and rainy out. Did some sewing and washing. Marjorie called about her coat. Joe called. He was so sweet.

Sunday, April 3, 1927

Went to breakfast. Went to church with June. Took some pictures after dinner. Studied all afternoon. Had a date with John Joseph in eve. He was so nice. I only hope he keeps it up for a while.

Monday, April 4, 1927

Had lunch at Linton's with June. Through with classes at 4:00. Joe called after school. Studied in eve.

Tuesday, April 5, 1927

Didn't have classes all morning, so went down to work in the library. Went on a field trip to McCallum Hosiery Mill. Didn't any more than get there until I had to leave for History class. Joe called again before dinner. He acts so simple over the phone. John Wandall bawled me out for asking Joe to the dance on Friday night, but I thought I really should. I probably won't see him again for a long time, but for some reason I don't seem to care…Tonight anyway.

Wednesday, April 6, 1927

Went downtown after assembly. Got some shoes. Did some more shopping. **Got a letter from Mrs. Jackson and she invited me out to dinner next Thursday to meet William.** I am anxious to meet him. Wrote to her. Joe called before dinner. He was going to come over and take me out for dinner, but I had a meeting afterwards and thought it best not to go. I wonder what he thought about that.

Thursday, April 7, 1927

Wrote to Mama. Went out to Overbrook High School and observed in the morning. Saw a sewing class and a boys' cooking class. Had a lot of fun. Talked to Miss Godfrey and I am still on probation. Made arrangements about summer school. Joe called before dinner; he

157

doesn't know yet if he is going home for Easter. Went to a lecture at the M. E. Church given by Mrs. Gilbreth.[223] Home Ec. Club had her here. She was very interesting.

Friday, April 8, 1927

Had my hair washed and curled in the afternoon. Had classes until 5:00. Fooled around before dinner. Went to the Sophomore Hop at the Bellevue. Took John Joseph. Had the best time. Had a 1:00 p.m. permission.

Saturday, April 9, 1927

Practiced some tennis up in the gym in the morning. Met June and Kathleen downtown after lunch. Went shopping all afternoon. Was dead tired in the evening. Janet and Doug had tickets and didn't use them so they gave them to June and me. We saw "Trelawney of the Wells" with John Drew.[224] It was real good.

Sunday, April 10, 1927

Today is Bubby's birthday, also Betty Biddle's. Went to church in the morning with June. Carl Gregory walked up with me and Stanley Harris was with June. Studied and fooled around all afternoon. Joe called about 5:45 and came over. We had tea over at the Tea Rose. John and Kathleen were there also. Had a real nice time. Had a date with him in the evening.

Monday, April 11, 1927

Wrote to A. Murray. I was down at school all day. Studied in the library. Joe called me in the evening. He was so nice. Was down talking to Miss Dorsey. I had a House Meeting in the evening. Took Edith's place as House Chairman.

Tuesday, April 12, 1927

I was up at the house all morning. Had lunch all alone over at the Tea Rose. Had a quiz in History. Didn't know much. Studied in the evening. John Joseph called. He is going home tomorrow. Gee, I surely am going to miss him a whole lot. Even if I don't see him much, I talked to him on the phone.

Wednesday, April 13, 1927

Had assembly up at Asbury Church. It rained all morning. June and I went down to the B.&O. station to see John Joseph off. He went home for his Easter vacation. He kissed me goodbye. I only hope I hear from him while he is gone. Went on down town, and went to the movies.

Thursday, April 14, 1927

Went down and worked in the library in the morning. Classes until 5:00 . Got dressed. Bill Jackson called me before he came. He took me out to his house for dinner. Mr. and Mrs. Jim

---

[223] Lillian Gilbreth was the mother of modern management. Together with her husband Frank, she pioneered industrial management techniques still in use today. She was one of the first "superwomen" to combine a career with her home ... Of course, Mary Alice could not have known this at the time . . . .

[224] "Trelawny of the Wells" is a 1916 British silent romance film.

Norris also were there.[225] I had the best time. I am crazy about Bill; he is the sweetest thing and so good looking and curly hair. He looked wonderful and their car is real cute looking. It is blue. It was so funny when I went downstairs to meet him. I had heard so much about him. He is a Delta Upsilon at State and a Junior. Had the best dinner. I sat beside him. Jane Shaw and Bill Horn came over in a 7 passenger Lincoln car. We chased around and stopped for ice cream, then went back to Jackson's and played bridge. I just wonder what he thinks of me. We have a date on Saturday night.

Friday, April 15, 1927
Wrote Mama and K. Smith. Fooled around all morning. Had lunch at the Tea Rose. Went downtown with Kate. Chased all around. Got a new red dress. Just had Mama's fountain pen fixed and mine was with it and I lost them both. I am just sick about it. I hate to tell Mama about it. Stayed in all evening. Bill Jackson was supposed to call, but he didn't. I am going to find out why, too.

Saturday, April 16, 1927
Had the sweetest letter from Joe, written on the train going home. Bill Jackson called this morning. Had breakfast at the Tea Rose. Studied in afternoon. Bill came about 7:30. Went down to the Penn Athletic Club to dinner and dance. There were two other girls and boys along. We drove around awhile until 12 o'clock. Had the best time. I am crazy about Bill. Have a date Tuesday for dinner.

Sunday, April 17, 1927
Easter Sunday. Got up and went to breakfast. Went to Asbury Church with Kate. Was in all afternoon and evening. Had tea at the Tea Rose. Some of the kids came back.

Monday, April 18, 1927
At school all day and put in a good day's job. I thought maybe Bill Jackson would call tonight, but he didn't. I am so anxious to see him tomorrow. I only hope he continues to like me and same here.

Tuesday, April 19, 1927
Saw Miss Dorsey after breakfast. Got a special for dinner tonight. Was down town all morning. Got a hat and gloves. Went through Stetson Hat factory in the afternoon. Bill Jackson came down to school for me at 4:15. Kathleen met him. Went out to the house. Saw Mr. and Mrs. Norris, but they didn't stay. Played some bridge before dinner and until 8:30 and had to rush to be in at 9:00. Just to think I won't see Bill until June. I know I am in love with him and I wonder what he thinks of me. Probably just as a good friend, but I am only hoping it turns out to mean something more. I wrote to Mama.

---

[225] Mrs. Jackson was a Norris, likely a sister to Mr. Norris mentioned here.

Wednesday, April 20, 1927

School all morning. It got awful warm today. Bill went back to school today. I just can't wait to hear from him. I hope it is real soon. Wrote to Alice E. Barklew.

Thursday, April 21, 1927

Went over to breakfast early. Met Almeta at West Phil. at 8:15. Went down to Kensington H.S. to observe. Had classes until 5:00. Dressed for dinner. Studied in the evening up in Kathleen's room. We had a terrible thunderstorm.

Friday, April 22, 1927

John Joseph came back this morning. He called me after breakfast. I asked him to go to the Freshmen-Senior Dance with me. It rained nearly all day. Got real cold. Alice came in and down to school at 5:00 for me. Had dinner at the Tea Rose. Kathleen went to the Architectural Ball. I went to the dance at Green Hill Farms.[226] Went out on the train. Had more fun. It was a real nice place for a dance. Alice had a date with Karl Rowles.

Saturday, April 23, 1927

Got up for breakfast. Alice stayed up at the house. Had lunch in the dining room. Went down at Stanley and saw "Knockout Reilly."[227] Waring's Pennsylvanians played. They were wonderful.[228] Alice had a date with Karl Rowles in the evening. I stayed in.

Sunday, April 24, 1927

Lost an hour today. Clocks were turned ahead. Went to church with Alice and June. Studied and fooled around all afternoon. Alice went out to school about 4:30. I had the nicest date with John Joseph in the evening. He told me how much he loved me and that he wished it was 5 years from now and he still felt the same then about me then as he does now. He wanted to know if I would marry him. It is so far ahead to hardly even think of. It would never do for us to get married any way.

Monday, April 25, 1927

Down at school all day. Had social committee meeting in evening. Collected House Dues the rest of the time. Joe didn't call and I am disappointed. Roller skated after dinner.

Tuesday, April 26, 1927

Had a letter from Mama. Called Mrs. Heverly. She is over in Camden. Am going to have her over next week. Went out to 46th Street and learned something about archery in the morning. Had lunch at the Tea Rose. Had a House Meeting after dinner about the many things which have been stolen from the House. Wrote to Mama.

---

[226] Approximately five miles from Drexel.

[227] "Knockout Reilly" is a lost 1927 American silent drama film based upon a story by Albert Payson Terhune.

[228] Waring's Pennsylvanians was a dance band that was founded by Fred Waring. First named the Collegians, the group was formed in 1918 at Penn State by the brothers Fred and Tom Waring.

Wednesday, April 27, 1927

Joe called. Wrote to Cora and Kirk. Classes all morning. Lunch at Linton's. Studied in the library in the afternoon. Joe called about 5:00. He and John came over and took Kathleen and me over to the Tea Rose for dinner. Had more fun. They stayed until 8:00.

Thursday, April 28, 1927

Was supposed to go to Roxbury High School today, but missed my train in the morning. Did some shopping. Came up to school and worked in the library. Talked to Stetina for a while. Had a sweet letter from Bill Jackson and one from Kirk. After dinner, Kathleen and I walked over to John's apartment. Joe had an appointment downtown and couldn't be there. He didn't even have time to talk to me. Just wait until tomorrow night.

Friday, April 29, 1927

Classes until 5:00. Had a date in the evening with John Joseph. Went over to John's apartment. He was so sweet. I love him a whole lot, but I could never love him enough to marry him.

Saturday, April 30, 1927

It rained all day until after dinner. We went to camp (Drexel-Paul) after lunch. There were 12 of us. Leah Siberon chaperoned us. Had more fun down at the station. In the evening after dinner we went into Wayne. Called John Joseph up. He and John came out on the 9:15 train and Kathleen and I met them at the station. Walked out to camp and had a date over at the Church. They only stayed until 10:30. We were afraid to have them stay any longer. Kate and Edith never came in until 12:00. Kathleen and I slept downstairs with Pat Wotimer and Ann Robinson. Had more fun.

Sunday, May 1, 1927

Wrote to Alice. It was a beautiful day. Didn't get up until about 10:00. Our old oil stove wouldn't work so we had to cook our breakfast over the fire in the fireplace. We had some time. Didn't even get it fired before dinner and then cooked our steaks over the fire. Chased around all day. Picked some flowers. Came in about 5:15. Got dressed for tea. Am dead tired.

Monday, May 2, 1927

Wrote to Bill Jackson. Down at school all day. Felt bum all morning. Was dead tired. Studied in evening and went to bed early. Joe didn't call tonight or last night.

Tuesday, May 3, 1927

Wrote to Marjorie and Mama. Didn't have any classes until 4 o'clock. Went down and worked in the library. Joe called in the evening. He has 3 exams tomorrow. I hope he gets through them all right.

Wednesday, May 4, 1927

Wrote to Alice and Kirk. Cut Psych class the first hr. Was so sick last night and felt terrible in the morning. Jane and I observed a Kindergarten today. It was real interesting. Met Mrs.

Heverly at 2:00. Went to the Fox and was coming up to the house for dinner, but it was pouring rain. Waited until it stopped. She went over to Camden and I had dinner at the Tea Rose. Went to a committee meeting.

Thursday, May 5, 1927
Went to William Penn High School in the morning to observe. Went to one of Alice Cursic's classes. She was rather surprised to see me walk in her classroom. Had my hair waved at 12:30, then I was down at school until 5:00. Had the Court decorated real pretty. Joe and John came over about 9:30. Had a nice time at the dance, but nothing exciting. We had 2:30 permissions. For favors we got boxes with sachet in them. Seniors only. Bill and Joe can't come to the dinner tomorrow night, how sad.

Friday, May 6, 1927
Had classes until 12:00. Had a musical concert in the court at noon. Came up to the house, fooled around and went down town and got Miss Dorsey and Mrs. Scotts' corsages and flowers for decorations. Had our formal dinner.

Saturday, May 7, 1927
Didn't have any classes today, but had charge of an exhibit at school from 10:30 to 12:00. Marjorie came after lunch. We went down to school to the May Pageant and we met Alice down there. Jack Roberts was there with Marian Haim. Talked to her a long time. Crowned Ellen Johnson as the May Queen. The Pageant was real good. Came up to the house. Alice met Karl Rowles at 6:00. After dinner fooled around, Marjorie slept. We went down to school at 10:00. Met Joe and Min Spardle. I had a dance with a cute Drexel boy. We danced awhile and when Marjorie and I went to get our coats, Min and Joe left; I never heard of anything so dumb in my life. I cannot imagine any boys doing such a thing. Met Alice at Reading Terminal and we both went out to school with her. Was dead tired.

Sunday, May 8, 1927
Got up and went to church in the morning. Chased around after dinner and came in about 3:00. Fixed my room up. Edith is over in the Practice House. Joe called after Tea. Wanted to see me and apologized and I said he could tell me what he wanted to over the phone. He is real sorry now it all happened, but I am so cross about it I am not going to see him all week or this weekend. I can't be bothered with anyone who would do such a thing.

Monday, May 9, 1927
At school all day. Nothing exciting happened. Studied and worked on budgets in the eve.

Tuesday, May 10, 1927
Worked in library all morn. Classes until 5:00 Went through a Dry Cleaning plant in afternoon. Studied in the evening. Joe has not called again and I hope he doesn't for a long time.

Wednesday, May 11, 1927

Worked in library awhile in afternoon. Came up to house, mailed laundry and pressed some dresses. Went over to the practice house for dinner. Edith was the cook. Had a fine dinner. Studied in the eve.

Thursday, May 12, 1927

Observed at the Jones Junior High School this morning. It was real nice. June took a letter down and put it in the box for me and someone took it. I never got it.

Friday, May 13, 1927

School until 5:00. Went to Jack Hart's in evening with Jane, Lois, and Edith. Had a real good time. Bob Drake came home with me. Carl Gregory and Harry Bixler were there.

Saturday, May 14, 1927

Talked to Jack Roberts in the morning at school. Have a date with him tomorrow night. June and I went down town in the afternoon. Did a lot of shopping. Ate at Wanamaker's. Didn't go to dinner. Went over to John's apartment about 6:00. Fooled around and got dressed by 8:00. Went to the Kappa Sigma Spring Formal with Harold Clark. However, he never came until 10:30. I had about given him up. Had a grand time. Took my good old time getting home. It was held out at the Merion Tribute, a beautiful place. Went over to the fraternity house afterwards and sat around. Got in at 3:00. Hal stayed awhile. Went to bed at 3:30.

Merion Tribute

Sunday, May 15, 1927

Slept until 11:45. Got up and went down to the Broad Street Station and called June. We had dinner down at Green's Hotel. Had a grand dinner. Went to see a friend of hers. Went over to the apartment; made fudge and coffee. Ted, her boyfriend, came over. She came back to the house at 8:30. Jack Roberts came up for me. Went down to the hospital to see Walter Haim. Drove around and didn't come in until 12:30. It was a beautiful moonlit night. Kathleen came about 1:00. She was with John at his roommate's home over the weekend. The boys went over and slept at the dorms.

Monday, May 16, 1927

Got up at 8:00. Wrote to Alice. Fixed things up. Went down to school at 9:00. Classes until 4:00. Lost the key to my suitcase and can't get it opened. Had house meeting in the evening and was elected House President for next year. Some job.

Tuesday, May 17, 1927

Wrote to Mama and Marjorie Wall. Stayed up at the house most of the morning. Took a trip through Wanamaker's store in the afternoon. Talked to Jack and have a date Saturday night. Joe called and I gave him a date to go to dinner tomorrow night. I really shouldn't, but what's the difference.

Wednesday, May 18, 1927

Classes all morning. Went down town and had suitcase opened at Snellenburg's and got a key for it. Got dressed and met Kathleen and we went up to John's apartment and met him and Joe. Had dinner at Harry's. Came back to apartment and stayed until 12:00. They went to the movies and came up later. Just got in on time and was saved.

Photo of the Benjamin Franklin Hotel by Kenneth Zirkel

Dining Room, Ben Franklin Hotel

Thursday, May 19, 1927

Observed at a Junior High School all morning. Classes until 5:00. Was studying in the evening when Mama walked in. Was so surprised to see her. Papa was out in the car. They drove from home today and are staying at the Benjamin Franklin. John Wandall dropped in on Kathleen. Joe was out in the car and didn't come in. Yes, he loves me—tell me another and I will believe it. Anyway, I don't want him to.

Friday, May 20, 1927

Mama called about 9:00; then I called Alice at 9:30. Cut afternoon classes and met Mama and Papa at 1:15. Had lunch at Wanamaker's. Papa left us. We did some shopping, then went to the movies. Went down to the hotel a couple of minutes. Then Alice and I left them. Chased around awhile, then ate over at the Tea Rose.

Alice had a date with Karl Rowles in the evening. Mama and Papa went out to Jackson's. Too bad Bill wasn't home. I went down to Jack Hart's with Kathleen. Had more fun. George Stevens, a boy from California, brought me home. We took a taxi ride. He is a freshman and a Phi Gamma Delta. He is real sweet. Joe came in while I was there and was he cross! Couldn't blame him, but he didn't understand the reasons. He brought Kathleen home. He didn't like it so much that I was with this other boy.

164

Saturday, May 21, 1927

Mama, Papa, and Alice drove over in N.J. today. Didn't get back until 4:00. Went to class all morning and fooled around in the apartment. Got things ready to go home. Alice and I had dinner with them in the evening. Went to the Fox and came home early. Alice had a date with Karl. Leah went to bed and I took her place being on duty.

Sunday, May 22, 1927

Got up at 8:30. We had breakfast at Tea Rose with Mama and Papa. They left right afterwards for Harrisburg and home. Went to church. Alice had a date with Karl in the afternoon. I studied. Also studied in the evening. Joe didn't call all day; guess he is ready to call it quits; well, it is up to him, but I guess we will both be better off if we do stop.

Monday, May 23, 1927

Down at school all day. Studied in the library. Joe called before dinner. He said he just got my letter of May 12 this afternoon. I can't imagine what happened to it. Studied in the evening.

Tuesday, May 24, 1927

Wrote to Kirk and C. Reese. No classes until 4:00. Was in the library studying. Wrote psy. term paper. Did budget in the evening. Joe didn't call. I didn't expect him to.

Wednesday, May 25, 1927

Classes all morn. Went down town all afternoon; got a hat and shoes. Joe has a final tonight, hope he gets through OK. Wish he had called. Studied in the evening. Wrote to Bill Jackson and Aunt Grace. Joe called after his exam.

Thursday, May 26, 1927

Went to the Friends School to observe in the morning. Had lunch at King Joy with Alveta and Marie Sloan. Classes until 5:00. Talked to Bill Hirschman in the library. Joe called before dinner and came over at 8:00. Walked over to John's apartment. Joe was never so nice. I wonder if he will still like me so much tomorrow.

Friday, May 27, 1927

Wrote to Grace Johns. Had my last class in Ed. 10 this morning. Cut Home Ec. 18. Went out to Robinsons and saw Alice and Elizabeth. They are going home tomorrow. Studied some in the evening. Joe called and he was so sweet. It never lasts long though.

Saturday, May 28, 1927

Talked to Jack a minute in the morning at school. They had their Phi Kappa Beta spring formal last night and he took another girl. See if I care. Was down town most of the afternoon chasing around. Bought a few things. Had date with Jack Roberts in the evening.

Went down to Aldine and saw "The Better 'Ole."[229] (Syd Chaplain); it was real funny. Heard a vitaphone[230] for the first time.

Sunday, May 29, 1927

Got up about 8:00. Went to breakfast, dusted, and did some washing. Marjorie Miller and Eddie, Neema Clarentine and Charles Stern came. Their car broke a bearing out in Downingtown and they had to leave it there and come in on the trolley. Carl Gregory and Stan Norris and another boy came and took June, Selma and me to church. Stan has a cute roadster. Took a ride after church. The kids went downtown and Eddie went to see about the car. They came back and had tea at the Tea Rose. Went to bed early. Joe had called in the afternoon.

Monday, May 30, 1927

Got up and went to breakfast. Went out and spent most of the morning at the zoo. The boys went to the baseball game. Went to the Golden Dragon for lunch. Talked to Harold Knight.

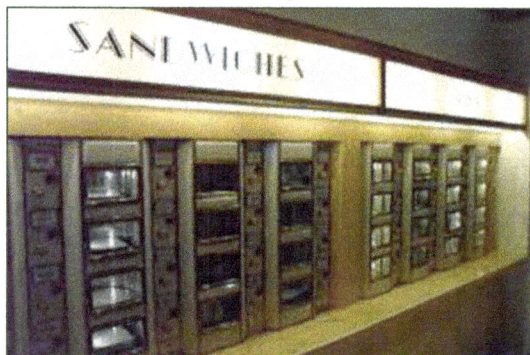

Met the boys Nelva went with to the ball game in afternoon. Marjorie and I chased around. Went to the Stanley to see "Rookies.[231]" Then met the others and ate at Horn and Hardart.[232]

Horn and Hardart Automat

Nelma and Charles went back to Bellefonte on the train. Eddie and Marjorie went out to Carsons all night. Came back to the house and Mrs. Dorsey bawled me out for having June sign me out. I called Joe from the dormitory and he was not in and he had told me he had two finals on Tuesday. I will never be able to take his word for anything. Grace Johns came up for a few minutes to chat.

Tuesday, May 31, 1927

Worked up in the Art Gallery all morning. Had classes until 8:00. Joe called after dinner. I told him I couldn't have a date until Saturday night. Went to bed early.

Wednesday, June 1, 1927

Institute Day. Classes in the morning. Had assembly first time for this term. Came up to the house and then went down town awhile and chased around. Came here and Joe called. Got changed and he took me out to dinner at Tea Rose. He was so nice tonight. Took a walk;

229 A sergeant (Syd Chaplin) in the British army during World War I becomes suspicious of his commander's (Theodore Lorch) off-duty activities and discovers that he and a local villager are working together as spies for the Germans.

230 Vitaphone was a sound film system used for feature films and nearly 1,000 short subjects made by Warner Bros. and its sister studio First National from 1926 to 1931. Vitaphone was the last major analog sound-on-disc system and the only one which was widely used and commercially successful. The soundtrack was not printed on the film itself, but issued separately on phonograph records.

231 "Rookies" (aka "Red, White and Blue") is a 1927 American silent comedy film directed by Sam Wood.

232 Horn & Hardart was a food services company in the United States noted for operating the **first food service automats** in Philadelphia and New York City.

it was so wonderful out. Went over and called on Al Fisk while Joe stayed awhile after we came over to the house. Had House Meeting about House Chairman for next year. I wanted to resign and they didn't want me to. Miss Dorsey came to the meeting. We finally elected Dot King for first half and me for the last half, but I am hoping she will have it the whole year. Collected some house dues.

Thursday, June 2, 1927

Wrote to Alice. Didn't have any classes all morning. Worked on my term paper, finished it in evening. Studied in evening.

Friday, June 3, 1927

Class at 11:00. Did some work at school in afternoon. Class until 5:00. Edith moved back from the Practice House today. John and Joe dropped in after dinner and stayed until 8:30. Joe was so crazy.

Saturday, June 4, 1927

Studied Soc. until time for History class. Had lunch at Fintons. Took Soc. final in afternoon. It was terrible. Had date with John Joseph in eve. Went to Stanton, saw the John Barrymore movie, "When a Man Loves."[233] Went over to the old apartment at 223 S. 36th Street. Joe was so sweet. Gave me his Penn ring just before he left.

Sunday, June 5, 1927

Got up for breakfast. June and I went to Church. Didn't study in afternoon. Wrote to Alice and Miss Dashiell and F. Custer. Studied History in eve. Joe didn't call all day. I think he must have had a date, but I should worry as I don't like him as much as I should anyway and he seems to like me more.

Monday, June 6, 1927

Studied Ed. 5 in the morning. Had lunch at Tea Rose. Took Ed. 5 exam in afternoon and wrote almost 4 hrs. on it. Studied History in eve. Joe didn't call again; wonder what's wrong. He needn't bother if he doesn't want to. It would be just as well if something would happen.

Tuesday, June 7, 1927

Went downtown and then down to school to study. Took Home Ec. 19 in afternoon. Don't think I made much in it. Studied Home Ec. 18 and History in the eve. Joe didn't call again. I really cannot understand it at all. Guess he has found someone else. Hope so, only hope he takes me to the train tomorrow night.

---

[233] 1927 American silent historical drama film directed by Alan Crosland and produced by Warner Bros. The picture stars John Barrymore and features Dolores Costello. The film was the third feature from Warners to have a pre-recorded Vitaphone soundtrack.

Wednesday, June 8, 1927

Got up at 5:00 and studied History. Took exam in morning. It was hard. Took Home Ec. 18 exam in the afternoon. Went down town and got my white shoes. Joe called before dinner. I dressed and packed. Joe came over at 7:30, left about 8:00. Dorney kissed me goodbye. Went over to John's apartment and stayed until my train left at 12:50. Took the sleeper at W. Philadelphia.

Thursday, June 9, 1927

Got up at Huntingdon. Slept some, I think. Got off at Tyrone. Mary Parish from Bellefonte was on the train. We had breakfast together at the Ward House. Went home on the 10:44 train. Alice and Jessie and Dick met me. Fooled around all afternoon. Went out with the girls in the evening. Saw Bub King. Hope to have a date with him.

Friday, June 10, 1927

Did a lot of baking in the morning. Made a pie, salad and salmon. Libby King came up in the afternoon and we went over to the Park and went swimming. Had a date with Kirk Hile in the evening. Went down to Bill Betts and played bridge. Got home about 1:00.

Saturday, June 11, 1927

Went to stores in the morning. Libby and I went swimming again in the afternoon. It was great. Alice came down in the evening. Stayed and kept Philip until after 10 o'clock. Went up to the Sweet Shop. Took Alice home and stopped at Kings on the way home. Met some boys from Clarion; they were real nice.

Sunday, June 12, 1927

Went to church with Mama and Papa Spencer. Went to Greenwood in afternoon. Walls went out too. Had supper up at Holtens' new place.[234] It is real nice. Went down for Libby and she had a date, so Bub King asked to take me for a ride. Went up around Bloomington Hill and parked. I really like him a lot. Never came home until 12:30.

Monday, June 13, 1927

Got some material for a dress and a pattern. Saw Bubby in the morning. Last I saw him. Alice came up in the eve. Saw Dave Bowes and Tom Betts up at the Sweet Shop.

Tuesday, June 14, 1927

Got up early and went with Alice, Elizabeth, and Mrs. Wall. Drove the Franklin and met Hugh. Got back about 5:00. Alice and Hugh came down in the evening. Stayed in.

Wednesday, June 15, 1927

Sewed all morning and most of the afternoon. Made a white dress. Was down street a minute. Alice was down awhile in the evening. Kirk Hile came up and Alice and Hugh. Took a ride to DuBois; were looking for some "Cheer" but didn't find any. Came back to Holten's and ate and danced.

[234] See J. Holten in Cast of Characters.

Thursday, June 16, 1927

Wrote to Joe. Wrote Kathleen. Did some sewing and pressing. Went up to Aunt Mary's in the evening. Drove over to a dance at the Park with Mama and Papa and Alice. Didn't stay long. Wanted to, but there wasn't anyone to stay with.

Friday, June 17, 1927

Got dinner, fooled around all afternoon. Drove out to Sykesville and the farm to see Katy. I drove the car out. Got back late.

Saturday, June 18, 1927

Went shopping in the morning with Mama. Alice went to Hugh's Commencement today. Fooled around all afternoon. Kay Wrigley came up before supper and wanted a date, but I told him I had one when I didn't. After supper I drove up to Mahaffey.

Sunday, June 19, 1927

Went to church with Mama. It was Children's Day and Philip gave a speech. Mama and I got dinner. Mrs. Erbert went out. It rained nearly all day. Stayed in. Made some fudge.

Monday, June 20, 1927

Fussed around all morning. Wrapped up Catherine's wedding presents and took them over. She and Bubby were married at Clearfield about 11:15 at Presbyterian minister's home. Mama, Phil and Mrs. Pifer and I were there. Had dinner at the Dimeling. Came up and they (Catherine and Bubby) started out in their car for Harrisburg, Philadelphia, and Gettysburg.[235] (The bride wore a peach-colored, silk-pongee, street-length dress.)

Went to Philipsburg in the afternoon with Papa. Was up at Custers. Saw Francis. Went to the Strand with Kate Smith and saw "The Fire Brigade."[236] Talked to J. S. a long time.

Tuesday, June 21, 1927

Went to Bellefonte with Papa and Philip. Drove over and back. Saw Marjory, K. Reese, Marie Bower and baby, Louise Taylor and baby, Grace Cohen, Lisa Foreant, and a bunch of others. Chased around all day. Got back about 9:00. Alice and Hugh were up, went down to the Sweet Shop. Wrote some letters.

Wednesday, June 22, 1927

Got up early and went to Commencement at Huntingdon. Saw Betty Biddle. Cora and Mary Wolf went along. Got home about 8:30. Alice came up and we chased around. Came home and went to bed early.

---

235 This is as my mother told us. She said that Howard very much wanted to see the Gettysburg Battle Field and thought this a good idea to include on their wedding trip beyond Harrisburg, the state capital, and on to historic places in and around Philadelphia.

236 A forgotten silent film, "The Fire Brigade" starring Lionel Barrymore and Charles Ray. The producers of the film contributed 25 per cent of the film's receipts toward a college for the instruction of fire-fighting officers.

hursday, June 23, 1927

Wrote to Joe. Served at the S.S. Convention at noon and in the eve. Had a lot of fun. In the eve I also had a date with Raymond. Went up to Holten's with John Wright and a girl from DuBois as well as Alice and Hugh. Marjorie came home and Marge Irvin came up along.

Friday, June 24, 1927

Wrote to Kathleen, Bill J, Jessie. Went down to see Marjorie (Wall) and Marge (Irvin). Did some sewing in afternoon. Went for a ride after supper, then went to the movies.

Saturday, June 25, 1927

Baked a shortcake and also one for Marjorie. In the afternoon Philip went swimming. Hugh, Kenny, and Bubby (being home from his honeymoon) played tennis. In eve I had a date with George Wrigley, Hugh & Alice, and Rose Bloom and Bob Wright. Went out in the country and drank some beer then went up to Holten's.

Sunday, June 26, 1927

Got a picnic dinner and went out to Greenwood. Had more fun. Marjorie & Marge Irvin, Bubby and Catherine, Alice and Papa and Mama and Philip. Stayed for dinner and supper. Alice and Hugh took us for a ride and to the Sweet Shop.

Monday, June 27, 1927

Went to Clearfield in afternoon with Alice. Saw Bob Daugherty and John Leitzinger. In the evening a group of us serenaded Bubby and Catherine. Had more fun. Went over to the Pifers for them. Took the trunk and put a board across, had cow bells and tin cans. There were Alice, Marjorie, May, Joe and Joseph Hipps, Brownie, Guerry, George Wrigley. Drove all around town and then went out to Holten's and ate and danced. Bubby had to pay the bill.

Tuesday, June 28, 1927

Sewed in the morning and afternoon. Didn't dress until late. Had date with Billie McClure in eve. Alice was with George someone from Altoona. We went out to Holten's.

Wednesday, June 29, 1927

Sewed in the morning and afternoon. Went downtown with Alice and Bob Humphreys. He is here from the West for a while. Had a date with George Wrigley in eve. Went to a dance at the Park. Not many there. He bores me so.

Thursday, June 30, 1927

Did some work in the morning. Went to Dubois in the afternoon with Marge and Marjorie. Went over to the Park swimming after supper. Took Philip. Had a date with Ray. Hugh was with Peg Hayes. We went up to Holten's.

Friday, July 1, 1927

Katherine Thorn and Audrey Hyde came for me. Katherine is going to school with me.[237] Went down to the station to see about the train. Audrey is engaged and her boyfriend is home with her. In evening had a date with Billie McClure.

Saturday, July 2, 1927

Alice didn't get home yet so I went with Hugh. Got Becky Causie and June Ellis from Clearfield for Bill Wessel and Jim from Pittsburgh. Stopped at Philipsburg and went to Candyland. They had ginger ale and mixed it with gin. Not so good. I felt sort of dizzy. Went over to Fairview; some tough dance.

Sunday, July 3, 1927

Went to Church with Mama in the morning. Marjorie, Marge and Libby were there in the apartment. Took some pictures. Went up to Holten's for our supper. In evening I stayed home. Was up at Alice's for a while. Hugh and Bill and Jim came up. I didn't want a date. George Biddle wanted one for tomorrow. Went to bed early.

Monday, July 4, 1927

Packed my trunk. Went to Clearfield to the parade in the morning. In the afternoon I went over to the Park. Danced. In the evening I had a date with George. Went to the dance at the Park. Talked to Kirk. Stopped at deluxe diner on the way home. Stayed all night with Kathryn Thorn[238] and went to bed at 2:00.

To Philadelphia

Tuesday, July 5, 1927

Got up before 5:00. Not much sleep. Drove over to Tyrone with Mr. Thorn. Got in to Philadelphia at 2:30. Joe met us. We went to the school to register. Joe then came over and took us to the Tea Rose for dinner. Had awful greens which gave me a pain. Wrote to Mama and went to bed early.

Wednesday, July 6, 1927

Got up at 6:45 and had breakfast at 7:15 and to school at 8:00. Came up to the house at noon and had lunch at the Tea Rose with Tat. Classes until 3:00. Had a House Meeting after dinner. Am on the Social Committee. Later S. Bennett and Kathleen and I went to the Stanley. Saw Rod La Roche in "Resurrection."[239]

---

237 Mary Alice would be attending summer school to make up courses in order to be graduated in the spring of 1928. Katherine Thorn, known as "Tat," was also attending Drexel in the Home Ec. Program.

238 Note correction in the spelling of her first name. Kathryn Thorn had been graduated from Clearfield High School in 1922, making her also a classmate of Mary Alice's brother. Her nickname was "Tat." She had a sister Marjory and brother Ken. She may have been attending only in the summers or there may have been a special program for Home Economics teachers.

239 A lost 1927 Hollywood adaptation of the Leo Tolstoy novel, "Resurrection" was adapted to a feature-length silent production starring Dolores del Río.

Thursday, July 7, 1927

Got up for breakfast. Had an 8:00 class until 12:00. Had lunch in the cafeteria. Slept in the afternoon and fooled around. Called Bill Jackson and asked him to come over tomorrow night, but he can't come. Have a date for Saturday night. Joe hasn't called yet and I don't even care. Took a long walk over near the University after dinner. Was up to Karl Rowles' apartment. Wrote to Alice.

Friday, July 8, 1927

Classes until 12:00, then went down to Dr. Stone, the dentist. He took an X-ray of my tooth. Have an impacted wisdom tooth. Have to have it out on Monday.

Shopped all afternoon. In the evening we had a reception (Kenny Wall was over) and dance. Karl Rowles was with June and he brought Bill Green over for me. Had a real nice time. Bill has a Dodge Roadster; took a ride and was over to their apartment. Never signed out. Came back at 11:30 and the boys could stay until 12:00. It certainly doesn't seem like Drexel at all. Fewer rules.

Saturday, July 9, 1927

Got up at 9:15 and got dressed and went down to the dentist. Saw my X-ray picture and my wisdom tooth is coming up sideways instead of straight and on the wrong side of my tooth. It is impacted. I have to have it out on Monday.

Ate a little breakfast and came back to the house. Bill Jackson came about 5:30. We went out to his home and they wanted another girl. Came back in and got Tat (Kathryn) for Herb Horn. Had a wonderful dinner. Took a ride and then came back to the house. Mr. and Mrs. Jackson went to bed. We danced and played the radio and sat out on the sunporch. Bill is wonderful; I am crazy about him. Only wonder how much he likes me. Was ten minutes late getting back to the House.

Sunday, July 10, 1927

Didn't get up until 12:00. Joe Lainer and Jerry Miller came down from Allentown to see June and took us for a ride. Went over the Camden Bridge for the 1st time. Was bored to death. Wrote letters and studied in the evening. Wrote to Mama and Alice.

Monday, July 11, 1927

Class at 8:00. Went down to the dentist at 3:00 and had my wisdom tooth pulled. It began to hurt awfully in the evening. I went to bed after dinner. Ate at Tea Rose, just liquids. Wrote to Mama.

Tuesday, July 12, 1927

My tooth hurt all day. Didn't go to school at all. Got up about 10:00, fooled around and went down to the dentist. Went to the movies and saw Ronald Coleman in "The Night of Love."[240] It was real good. Didn't do much in the evening. Wrote Alice.

[240] Ronald Coleman, Vilma Bánky, Montagu Love, and Natalie Kingston. A duke kidnaps the gypsy Montero's young bride, intending to exercise a nobleman's then-presumed right to make love to her.

Dodge Roadster

Wednesday, July 13, 1927

Had classes all morning and went down to the dentist at 11:00. Came back to the house and slept awhile and studied some. Took a bath and dressed before dinner. Bill and Herb came about 7:00. Bill had called about 4:00. They looked so nice in white knickers, hats and shirts. The four of us had an exciting evening. Stopped and talked to Bill Horn and Jane Shaw. Started out to where they were going swimming. We were going along not so fast, and I was looking at Bill and never saw the car coming and neither did Bill. Herb yelled and Bill turned out, but hit a Ford Coupe.

No one was hurt, but the Ford fell apart and the wheels were knocked out of line in Bill's car and the mud guard smashed in. I am so sorry for Bill it happened. Went out and Bill, Herb, and Tat went swimming. We drove back to Jacksons and explained the accident.

Bill is so wonderful and I love him so much. If only he would say if he likes me or not and how much. I can hardly wait until Saturday.

Thursday, July 14, 1927

Wrote to E. Newton, M. Wall, J. Clark, C. Pifer[241], and C. Reese. Classes from 8-12. Had lunch at Tea Rose and came over to the house. Took a walk after dinner. It is awfully hot. Only wish I could be with Bill. I like him so much and only wish I knew he liked me as much as I do him.

Friday, July 15, 1927

Had classes all morning. Went down to the dentist. Went over to Wightman Hall and danced. We about passed out it was so hot. I was so bored all the time. No boy seems to interest me anymore but Bill.

Saturday, July 16, 1927

Didn't get up until 10:00. Tat and I went down to the Golden Dragon for lunch. Saw Harold Knight. We were so crazy, stopped at a place on Market Street and had one picture taken for 25¢ and got 8 different pictures. Most of mine were awful. Got dressed before dinner. Karl Rowles came over for a letter from Alice. Tat and I had dates with Bill and Herb. Went out to Devon Park Hotel and danced. It rained and we couldn't dance outside. Had a wonderful time. Was supposed to be in at 12:30 and never got here until 1:15.

Sunday, July 17, 1927

Got up and went to breakfast. Couldn't sleep. Went to church. Cecil was over for a while. Kenny had a date with Pearl Todhunter in the evening. Jack Roberts was over in the apartment. Took a ride; I was sort of bored. All boys except Bill bore me right now. Carl Gregory asked me for a date last night.

---

[241] Evidently forgetting that Catherine's last name was now Thompson and not Pifer.

Monday, July 18, 1927

At school from 8 to 4. Studied in the library. Tat and I went down town. Got organdy for a dress. Joe dropped in after dinner. I wasn't even thrilled; guess I don't care much for him anymore. He had a cute boy along from Puerto Rico. Don't expect to see him for a while. Am going to give Bill all the dates he wants.

Tuesday, July 19, 1927

Rained nearly all day. Came home at 3:00. Slept until dinner time. Studied Chem in the evening. Am so disappointed Bill didn't call; guess he won't ask me for a date tomorrow night. I feel so funny about it.

Wednesday, July 20, 1927

Had Chemistry quiz in the morning and I got the highest grade in the class!! 94. Too much for me. Went down to the dentist after school. Tat went to see "Yes, Yes, Yevette"[242] with Herb. Bill hasn't even called since Saturday. I can't understand. Guess he thought he was seeing too much of me. I only wish he would call.

Thursday, July 21, 1927

Wrote to J. Bullocks. Classes until 12:00. Studied in the library awhile. Came up to the house and slept. Bill finally called after dinner. It sounded so good to hear his voice. I wonder why he waited so long to call. Guess he doesn't like me as much as I do him. Haven't a date until Sunday. It will be over a week that I didn't see him. I wonder if anything beyond friendship will ever happen. I guess not; there must be someone else for him.

Friday, July 22, 1927

Classes all morning. Came up to the house in the afternoon. Slept awhile. In the evening a bunch of us took a boat ride to Wilmington. Tat, Kathleen, Fran and Selina/Sylvia Solomon were along. We acted so simple, sent post cards. We were disappointed as there was no music on the boat.

Saturday, July 23, 1927

It rained very hard all day. Sewed on my organdy dress all afternoon. Joe called first before dinner. Had a date in the evening with him. Went over to the apartment. It was one awful mess. We agreed not to go over there again. It's best all around that we don't.

Sunday, July 24, 1927

Wrote to Alice. Did some washing. Packed picnic lunch. Joe came over about 12:30. Talked awhile, then had dinner at the Tea Rose. Had fried chicken. He stayed until 3:30 and Bill came soon after Joe left. I was scared for fear they would meet.

Tat was with Herb Horn and Kathleen with Jimmy Hall. Had more fun. Took some pictures and roamed around. Never laughed so much. Ate and went back into the Jacksons.

---

[242] "Yes, Yes, Yvette" (Original, Musical, Comedy) opened in New York City Oct 3, 1927 and played through Nov 5, 1927. Then went on the road, with Philadelphia on the list.

Cleaned up. Played the radio and Bill the piano. Went to Tendrills and I had some ice cream. Came back to house and parked in an alley. I love Bill so much.

Monday, July 25, 1927

Wrote to Mama and J. Roberts. Classes until 3 o'clock. Had a board meeting at school about May who stayed out until 3:00 the other night. She told several stories about it, but told us the truth today. She was out with Mr. Beck from the drugstore. She has her 12:00s taken away for two weeks but keeps her 10:30s. Studied in the evening.

Tuesday, July 26, 1927

Wrote M. Wall and M. Hill. Classes until 2 o'clock. Studied. Tat had a date with Herb.

Wednesday, July 27, 1927

Gave my Education report today. It was awful. Had Chem lab in the afternoon. Sewed on dress in afternoon when I came home. Studied Nutrition in the evening. Herb came over and brought the pictures.

Thursday, July 28, 1927

Wrote to Alice. Got up early and studied Nutrition. Didn't do so well in the quiz. Was dead tired. Got dressed before dinner. Tat and I had dates in eve with Carl Gregory and Sam Jones. Went out to Woodside and danced. Had the best time.

Friday, July 29, 1927

Took Ed. quiz in morning and got 80 in it so I heard. Got organdy dress hemstitched in the afternoon. Fooled around. Alice Dorsett came up to the house for overnight. Wrote to Mama. Had a date with Bill in the morning and Tat with Herb. Went out to Jackson's. Played bridge and fooled around. Bill and I went out for ice cream and took it back to the house. Bill was so sweet tonight, rather different from usual. I liked him so much.

Ocean City

Saturday July 30, 1927

Wrote to Jessie. Got things ready to go to Ocean City. Mr. and Mrs. Roberts came for me about 3:30. Met Jack at West Philadelphia. Got there about 6:00. Walked on the boardwalk after dinner. Jack and I left his Mother and Father. Took the car and parked and drank some sherry wine. Went up on the boardwalk and danced. Took a ride afterwards and didn't come in until 1:30 and they were waiting up for us. It poured rain.

Sunday, July 31, 1927

Got up about 8:30. Sat on the porch awhile. Three girls from Drexel were waiting on tables at the hotel where we stayed. The Strand. Went in bathing about 11:00 and came out at 4:00. Just Jack and I. Played ball and walked away up the beach. Had a good time. Started back about 6:00 and Jack made the 9:00 train to New York. I got a terrible sun burn. Am as red as can be. Put some stuff on it.

Monday, August 1, 1927

Wrote to D. Mallory. Cut Chem lab. Came up to the house and finished my organdy dress. Studied in the evening and was dead tired.

Tuesday, August 2, 1927

Through at 2:00. Tat had a date with Herb in the evening. Bill had other arrangements. It makes me feel funny when I think of him having a date with someone else. I only wish he liked me as much as Herb does Tat. I like Bill more than I do anyone else.

Wednesday, August 3, 1927

Had classes until 3:00. Came up to the house, did some ironing. Got dressed for dinner. Bill and Herb came about 8:30. Went out to Devon Park Hotel. Saw McDonald twins from Dubois out there. John Wandall came and surprised Kathleen. Stayed over at Mrs. Irlish's. Came in at 2:00. Signed out to Dot Arkis. Had more fun. Kathleen stayed there, too. Bill was real nice, but I can't quite understand him as he sort of annoys me by his ways, but I can't help but like him.

Thursday, August 4, 1927

Wrote to Mama and E. Barkling. Came down to school at 7:30. Went out the back gate. Bill was to call at 1:00 and he didn't. I can never depend on what he says. Had lunch at the Tea Rose. Heard something about Joe today and I am never going with him again. He has lowered himself in my estimation after all the high ideals I thought he had and now he has broken them. Went out to Mrs. Kittelberger's for dinner. Her sister, Mrs. Thompson, was there and her husband. Played bridge afterwards and had some beer and cheese and crackers. Came home at 11:00.

Friday, August 5, 1927

Didn't have a class until 10:00 and came home at 1:00. Slept most of the afternoon. Bill called after dinner. Have a date on Sunday and am going out there for dinner. I only wish I knew if he liked me much or not. Tat had a date with Herb. Joe called for a date and I didn't give him one. I have lost my good opinion of him. Studied Chem.

Saturday, August 6, 1927

Studied Chem most of the morning and took quiz Saturday morning. Got 97 on it. Too much. After dinner Tat and I played tennis with Henry Miller and Carl Gregory. Had more fun. It is Kathleen's birthday. We were going to have a party, waited until 12:30 when the kids would come in and we went to sleep and forgot the party. When the girls came in, they thought it was all over!

Sunday, August 7, 1927

Studied some more chemistry and took the quiz. Got ready to have a date with Bill. He came at 3:10 and we went out home for dinner. Listened to the radio. Heard the Prince of

Wales speak over the radio.[243] Had the best time. A girl friend of Bill's, Florence Green, called him to take her out to help her mother and father who were stuck with a flat tire. We took her out. She is real cute. Can't blame Bill for liking her. Took some ice cream back to Jacksons and talked. Later Dot Dimeling and Margie Thorn joined us. Had Kathleen's Birthday Party and made more noise.

Monday, August 8, 1927

Classes until 3:00. Worked in the library. Wrote Ed. report. Poured rain. In the evening Tat, Dot Dimeling, Margie Thorn, Sara Bennett and Kathleen and I went over to Phi Kappa Beta house and danced. Had a nice time.

Tuesday, August 9, 1927

Gave a report in Ed. class. Worked on term paper. Had a date with Bill in the Eve. We were going to go swimming, but didn't. He was so dear. He wore his fraternity pin for the first time this summer. Went out to Herb's—Tat, Dot, Margie, Jimmy Hall and Harry Wilson. Had some refreshments, played the Victrola and danced. Had dinner at Tea Rose.

Wednesday, August 10, 1927

Finished term paper. Mrs. Robinson called; also talked to Cecil and Kenneth. Studied Chem. Wrote to Mama.

Thursday, August 11, 1927

Got up early and studied Chem. Cut 1st hour of Nutrition to prepare oral study report for Ed. Gave it. Went off pretty good. Took Chem quiz at 2:00. Got a 95 in the final and a 93 average, the highest in the class. Went down town. Florence Kreutzer came over to the house for dinner. Cecil and Kenneth were over a while. Cecil took my trunk. He goes to Chicago on Saturday.[244] Studied Nutrition in the evening.

Friday, August 12, 1927

Took Ed. and Nutrition exam in the morning. Packed some. Got dressed and Tat and I went out to Jackson's and went over to Horne's to dinner with Bill. Played bridge all evening. Herb's sister Ruth and brother Fredrick are so nice.

Saturday, August 13, 1927

Got up for breakfast and packed. Went and got ticket. Took everything up to the 3rd floor bathroom and dressed. Tat and Margie went to the show. Dot went to New York. Bill came about 5:00. We went to his home for dinner. Margie and Jimmy came out. Stayed there all evening. I love Bill so much. I just can't quite make him out. He kissed me good night up in his room. I slept in his room with his Mother.

[243] From a Buffalo newspaper: On August 7th, 1927 Prince Edward of Wales, Prince George the Duke of Kent, Prime Minister of Great Britain Stanley Baldwin, Prime Minister of Canada William Lyon Mackenzie King, Premier of Ontario Howard Ferguson, U.S. Vice President Charles Dawes, U.S. Secretary of State Frank Kellogg, New York State Al Smith, and over 100,000 North Americans flocked to Buffalo's Peace Bridge for a dedication ceremony "uniting the two nations across the mighty Niagara."

[244] His address is given as Chicago in one of Echo yearbooks of the time. He presumably was going to Curwensville before heading to Chicago.

Sunday, August 14, 1927
Got up at 10:00. Had breakfast at 11:00. Talked and then Bill drove me into W. Phila. Got me a magazine. Gee, but I hated to leave him. Met Helen Cruse and Peg Alexander on the train, also Buddy Bilger.

Williamsport

Got into Williamsport at 7:00. Got off at wrong station. I missed Kate (Thorne). Went out to Kellers all night. Bobby was in Bellefonte but I stayed anyway. Tried to get Kate on the phone, but couldn't.

Wellsboro

Monday, August 15, 1927
Got up and took 7:00 train to Wellsboro. Played tennis with Bill Haud in afternoon. In evening went to movie and then out to the Park and roller skated.

Tuesday, August 16, 1927
Didn't get up till late. Washed my hair and had it curled. Fooled around downtown. Went up to the "Lookout" on a steak roast in the evening. Ben Edwards was with his Greek friend Gus. Kate and John Marvin and I were with Jimmy someone. Didn't like him much.

Coudersport

Wednesday, August 17, 1927
After lunch Bill and Kate and I drove up to Coudersport and met Edith Newton. In the evening I went out to Putnam Park and danced. Had a good time, only Bill Haud is so queer.

Thursday, August 18, 1927
Chased around all morning. In the afternoon Kate had three tables of bridge for Edie and me. In the evening I was with Jimmy again and Edith with his brother Ned; I don't like either one much. Went out to some camp and was bored all evening.

Williamsport

Friday, August 19, 1927
Packed in the morning. After lunch Kate, Edith and Ben drove me down to Williamsport. Bobby and I went to the movies and Ellis kept Ann.

Back Home

Saturday, August 20, 1927
Fooled around at Bobby's all morning. Left for home at 1:05 and never got to Clearfield until 6:30 on the NYC train. Called Mama and Bubby came down for me. Went down shopping with Mama.

Sunday, August 21, 1927

Unpacked some. Went out to Greenwood after dinner. Picked huckleberries. Went down to Beaver Dam with Papa and saw 2 beavers. Went to Bubby's awhile and to Aunt Grace's.

Monday, August 22, 1927

Helped Mama. After lunch I went out to Anchor Inn where the girls were camping. Olive and Eliz and Marjorie Wall, Al Murray, Edith Sawtelle and Kate Smith and Jessie. Ate so much and got sick. Felt punk all eve. Marge and I didn't have dates. Waited until 1:45 and came in home that night with the boys.

Tuesday, August 23, 1927

Was sick all day. Helped up at the church, set tables in the afternoon and served the Rotarians in the evening. They stayed so long.

Wednesday, August 24, 1927

Did a lot of washing. Went to Clearfield at 4:00. Alice drove our car down. Saw Tat. Was over to Thorns. In the evening we chased around with Alice and Hugh. Billie McClure was up awhile.

Thursday, August 25, 1927

Ironed in the morning and did some shopping. After lunch I went up to Mahaffey and helped take inventory at M and N store.[245] Marjorie drove our car up in the evening. Had a date with Billie McClure. Was up at Walls. Elizabeth was with Bob Daughery.

Bellefonte

Friday, August 26, 1927

Got up at 7:00 and went over to Bellefonte with Cousin Dema and Lew and Papa Spencer. Chased all around and saw the kids. Was up at Heverlys for dinner. Came back about 2:30. Julia Bullock came back along. Saw Cousin Anna at Unionville. In eve. had date with Kirk Hile and Alice and Hugh. We had some moonshine and gin but we all felt good. Went up to Groffe Acres and acted perfectly terrible. Never got home until after 1:00.

Curwensville

Saturday, August 27, 1927

Did the cleaning downstairs in the morning and iced the cake. Helen Bromie was here awhile in the afternoon. Julia, Alice, Marjorie and I chased around. Did some shopping. In the evening. Alice and Marjorie had dates. Bubby drove Julia and me to Clearfield. Saw John Leitzinger, Billie McClure, and Ray. Got a sundae at the Pig and Whistle.

---

[245] Likely a "company store" near the mines owned by her father.

Sunday, August 28, 1927

Didn't go to church. Richlens stopped on their way to Pittsburgh. Julia and Marjorie were here for dinner. Fooled around all afternoon. Took Julia over to Philipsburg about 5:00. In the evening had a date with Billie. Edith Shaw from Clearfield was up to see me. She is going to Drexel this year.

Monday, August 29, 1927

Cleaned downstairs, did some washing. Didn't get dressed until late. In the evening went to the movies by myself.

Tuesday, August 30, 1927

Ironed some in morning, addressed a lot of envelopes for Papa in the afternoon. In the evening went to the movies with David McKinley.

Wednesday, August 31, 1927

Helped bill letters in the morning and clipped grass. Drove to DuBois in the afternoon and got a new dress. In the evening Marjorie drove to Clearfield. Saw Blair and he came up along, first I have seen him this summer.

Thursday, September 1, 1927

Went down to Thorns for dinner in the evening. Went over to see Edith Shaw. Then chased around. Went over to see Dot and she went along with us to the carnival. Saw Blair, and Rayonner, Tat and Margie; a guest of Margie drove me home.

Friday, September 2, 1927

Tat, Margie and I drove to Punxsutawney. Had lunch at Holten's. Saw Fran Light, Alice Dorsett, Pauline Synder, and Mary Estricker and some more kids. Left about 5:30 and ate supper at Groffe Acres. Alice stayed all night with me. Went to bed at 9:30.

Saturday, September 3, 1927

Worked and shopped all morn, then Alice and I went to Clearfield and chased around. Had a date with Ray Maurey in evening.

Sunday, September 4, 1927

Fooled around all morning and afternoon. Had a picnic at Riff Raffs in the evening. Marjorie and John Wright, Alice and Hugh, Eileen King and Bob Wright and George Wrigley and me. Had ham and eggs. The boys went swimming.

Monday, September 5, 1927, Labor Day

Alice was here for dinner. Went over to the Park after dinner with Mama and Papa. Chased around. Went in and danced most of the afternoon. Came home and slept awhile. Was going to the movies, but went over to Park with Bob Wright. Had more fun. John Leitzinger was there.

Tuesday, September 6, 1927

Worked all morning. Got dinner. Ironed in the afternoon. Went to DuBois at 3:00 with Alice, Marjorie, Libby and Margaret Sharp. Went to Chatterbox at Clearfield for dinner. Came up and went to the movies and saw "Lovers."[246]

Wednesday, September 7, 1927

Sewed all morning and afternoon. Went to Clearfield at 4:00. Saw Tat. Was in and saw Dot Dimeling's gifts. Went to the movies in the evening with Mama.

Thursday, September 8, 1927

Did some shopping and went to Clearfield in the morning with Marjorie. Saw Tat and chased around. In afternoon I did a lot of mending and some packing. In eve I had my 1st date with John Leitzinger. Drove out to Greenwood and parked. Gee, but he is nice. Got home at 1 o'clock and got the devil.

Friday, September 9, 1927

Alice and I took our car to Clearfield. Went over and observed Tat teaching. Drove to Tyrone and met Bill. Went to Ramey for Hugh. Bill and I were at Thorns for dinner. Just the four of us. Hugh and Tat went down to Dot Dimeling's. She and Wess Sauter and Kenny Thorn and Gene someone all went up to the Country Club. Came home at 11:45 and waited until 2:00 for Mama to come in from Greenwood. I love Bill so much and he was so dear and sweet.

Saturday, September 10, 1927

Got up at 7:00. Couldn't sleep. Helped get breakfast, got Arthur's knickers for Bill. Went shopping. Orlie took us down to the Wilie mine. Was going to play tennis. Got dressed, helped get dinner. Went to Clearfield at 12:30. Went to luncheon (40 girls) and bridge at Audrey Hyde's at 1:00. Bill came back at 4:30 and Marjorie and I drove him over to Tyrone and came back. I then dropped him a note.

Sunday, September 11, 1927

Mama and I went to church. Miss Bill so much. Went out to Avelon Inn for dinner with Dot Dimeling and a crowd, 22 in all. Was with Kenny Thorn. Went swimming at 5:30. Got home about 8:00. Had a grand time.

Monday, September 12, 1927

Got up about 6:00 and went to Clearfield with Bubby in the truck. Went to Thorns and then down to school. Had enrolling room and 4 different sections of sewing. Herb and Tat took me to dinner at the Dimeling at noon. After school went and got dressed for the wedding. Sat with Herb. It was beautiful. Had a grand reception afterwards. We had more fun in throwing rice and fixing their car up. They left about 9:30. Joe Rhinehart, Jack Thompson,

---

[246] 1927 silent film romance drama produced and distributed by MGM. It stars Ramon Novarro and Alice Terry. It is a remake of a 1920 silent of the same name from Paramount. *Lovers* is a lost film.

Margie and John somebody and I got Nate Smith and went up to the Country Club. Had more fun. Nate brought me up then in his car. We stopped and he played his banjo for me. I like him a lot.

Tuesday, September 13, 1927
Worked all morning. Went to Clearfield with Alice and went to dentist. Drove to Tyrone with Tat and Margie. Took Herb back to meet his train. Had to call Alice to come down for me. Was rather cross at Tat for not bringing me home.

Wednesday, September 14, 1927
Worked all day and got things ready. For Mama's birthday we went to Anchor Inn.

Bellefonte

Thursday, September 15, 1927
Got up early and left on the 8:00 train for Bellefonte. Bill came on the 4:00 bus. Marjorie and Eddie took us up to their house for dinner. Had the best time. Then went down to Hecla Park to dance to "Whitey Kauffman." Their new dance pavilion is grand. Saw a bunch of people I knew. Bill stayed in Bellefonte all night. He told me a lot tonight.

Friday, September 16, 1927
Bill went up to State on early bus and I went on a later one. Met him at 10:00. Went up to Delta Upsilon, then to Mar Hall to see Jane Clark. Walked around campus up to the creamery and had some ice cream. Had lunch with Bill. He had a class at 1:00. Hated to leave him. Met fraternity brother of Herb's. Got home at 7:30. Went to bed early.

Curwensville

Saturday, September 17, 1927
Parked and fooled around all day. Alice drove me to Clearfield in the evening. Went to the dentist and said good-bye to the Thorns. Went to bed early.

Philadelphia

Sunday, September 18, 1927
Back to school today. Hardly seems as if I have been home. Catherine and Bubby were up for dinner. Edith Shaw came up for me and the Orcutt boy drove us to Tyrone. Got in here at 10:30 daylight. Edith slept with me all night.

Monday, September 19, 1927
Got up for breakfast, a gang of new girls here. Went down and we were through registration by 12:00. Had lunch at the Golden Dragon. Shopped. Got a pair of shoes. In evening John Joseph came over.

Tuesday, September 20, 1927

Classes all day. Fixed room up some. Wrote some letters in the eve.

Wednesday, September 21, 1927

Went down town a couple hours. Got a sweater. Came home at 3:00 and fooled around. Wrote Bill and studied.

Thursday, September 22, 1927

Class at 9:00. Had lunch at Tea Rose. Classes until 5 o'clock. Wrote Mama. Listened to Jack Dempsey – Gene Tunney fight over the radio. It was so exciting.

Friday, September 23, 1927

Went down to the fashion show at Strawbridge and also got a new tan hat. Classes until 5:00. In eve June, Edith Shaw and I went to the Aldine and saw "The Way of All Flesh."[247] It was real sad.

Saturday, September 24, 1927

Class from 10:00 to 11:00. Went down to the Cathay with Edith Shaw, Joe Ellis and Betty York. Did some shopping. Fooled around all evening.

Sunday, September 25, 1927

Went to church. Gained an hour today. Read some in the afternoon. Wrote to Mama. In the evening had a date with Ark (Noah) Belding, a Drexel Phi Kappa Beta. I liked him a lot. Haven't had a word from Bill. I only wish I knew what is wrong.

Monday, September 26, 1927

Six hours of class. Board meeting after dinner. Studied some.

Tuesday, September 27, 1927

Classes until 5:00. Letter from Bill. I feel much better now. It was such a sweet letter too. Kenny called in the evening. Wrote some letters.

Wednesday, September 28, 1927

Wrote to Alice and Mama. Was through classes at 3:00 today. Talked to Ark Belding down at school and had a date with him in the evening. Carl Gregory called for a date too.

Thursday, September 29, 1927

Went downtown with Alameta and looked at sampler patterns. Had lunch at new place: too much garlic. Edith Newton was here. Had dinner at the Tea Rose. Stayed in this evening.

Friday, September 30, 1927

Had hair washed and curled. Classes until 5:00. Carl Gregory took me up to Alpha Sigma Alpha Tea Dance. Had more fun. In the evening I went to Phi Kappa Beta House dance with Ark Belding. Had the best time.

---

[247] A 1927 American silent drama film directed by Victor Fleming.

Saturday, October 1, 1927

Edith Newton and I had breakfast over at the Tea Rose. Evelyn told us that John Joseph had been there last evening just after we left. Had a class at 10:00. Did not have class at Penn. Went up to Eblings to see Margie Thorn; she wasn't in. Went up to John Wandalls. Saw Kenny. We met John, and Joe passed in a car. Ran into Margie. Came over to house and Edith had gone. Fooled around all afternoon. Virginia Ebling called and I am going over there tomorrow night. Her brother is coming over for me. Went down to Methodist Reception, then over to Jack Hart's. Carl Gregory came home with me.

Sunday, October 2, 1927

Went to church and Carl walked home with me. Kate Howd was here awhile. Wrote Mama. Slept in afternoon. In the evening I went over to Virginia Ebling's and played bridge. Her brother Ward came over for me. She also has a cute brother Snowden Ebling (Malvern, PA). Had punch and cakes. Stayed all night.

Monday, October 3, 1927

Came to school from Eblings at 9:00. Went downtown and got dress material. Wrote Tat and Catherine. Studied some.

Tuesday, October 4, 1927

Classes until 5:00. Talked to Ark at school. Margie was to come to dinner, but didn't. Had date with Ark. Wrote Mama and Alice.

Wednesday, October 5, 1927

Came home at 3:00. Mailed laundry and took dresses to cleaners. Wrote a couple of letters. After dinner went over to 216. Piggy Burr called and had a date with him in the evening. Met Ark and Carl Gregory at the corner. They came over for a while.

Thursday, October 6, 1927

Had lunch at the Waffle Shop with Kathleen. Classes until 5:00. Stayed and danced with Ark Belding. He came up with me. Had dinner at the Practice House. June is the cook. She had Stanley Harris and Carl Gregory here. We went for a ride afterwards, came home early.

Friday, October 7, 1927

Classes until 5:00. Think Ark had a date tonight. Had dinner at Practice House. John and Kathleen were over awhile. Sewed in the evening.

Saturday, October 8, 1927

Had class over at Penn until 1:00. Rushed over to the House for lunch. Went shopping in the aft. Got a new dress. In evening I had a date with Ark. Went over to fraternity house.

Sunday, October 9, 1927

Wrote to Mama. Had breakfast at Tea Rose. Fooled around all afternoon. Sewed some. Alice went out to school at 4:30. Went to bed early.

Monday, October 10, 1927

Wrote Mama and Bill. Classes until 4:00. Wrote letters before dinner. Studied some in the evening. Girls in our group gave us a party tonight!

Tuesday, October 11, 1927

School until 5:00. Didn't talk to Ark again today. Hope to see him tomorrow night; he had better come over. Margie Thorn was over for dinner. Paul Gregory was over awhile. He is so crazy. John Joseph called tonight. Am going out with him Thursday evening.

Wednesday, October 12, 1927

Had quiz in Ed. today. Didn't know much. House meeting after dinner. Telegram from Haimie; she has a date for me for the game and dance. Had date with Ark. We got along fine. I wonder what he thinks of me? I like him a lot, but it could never be anything more.

Thursday, October 13, 1927

June and I went down town after 9:00 class. Shopped. Went to a movie. Saw John Gilbert in "Twelve Miles Out."[248] Had lunch at "King Joy." On way up from school I met Ark and he came over awhile. He is so nice. In evening I had a date with John Joseph. He doesn't mean a thing to me anymore. Went down to the movies. Came home at 11:00.

Friday, October 14, 1927

Saw Ark at 10:00. Talked to him. He went home for the weekend. Cliff called in the morning and wanted me to go to his fraternity dance. Jane Clark came down for the game. I went to call Mrs. Jackson and much to my surprise Bill answered the phone. I almost passed out and he didn't even intend calling me tonight. I had thought he liked me some, but have now changed my mind entirely.

Saturday, October 15, 1927

Went over to see about a room after breakfast. Said good-bye to Janie. Didn't go to class until 11:00. John and Kathleen walked up to the Hotel Pennsylvania with me. Met Haimie, her Bill Tice, Charley someone, Sally Schaffer, and Timmy (Ralph) Tompkins. Went to Penn-Penn State game. It was wonderful. State won 20-0. After the game I got Charley's car. Went down to YWCA and the girls got their suitcases. Went up to Mrs. Irlisher's. We got dressed. Had dinner at the Lamb Tavern. Went on to Norristown and got back about 12:00. Went to eat at Child's and went into the Belvedere Statler, surely was celebrating. **Bill Jackson** passed me 3 times and looked past me. I will never again think he cares much for me. Just merely a friend. Drove part way to Atlantic City. Got back about 3:00.

Sunday, October 16, 1927

Got up about 9:15. Came over to the house. Bill and Herb came about 11:00. I just can't make Bill out. Never will I let myself like someone so much anymore after what he did this weekend. I couldn't if I wanted to; some of my regard for him is lost. Went over to Mrs.

---

248 John Gilbert was one of MGM's top stars when he appeared in this melodrama. Playing against his usual early matinee idol type, Gilbert played a tough and restless wanderer.

Irlisher's and went to dinner with Marnie, LaRue and Bill. Wrote letters in the afternoon. Wrote Mama. In evening had a date with Ark.

Monday, October 17, 1927

Classes until 4:00. Ark met me and came up along. It was raining so we came up in a taxi. Sewed and worked in evening. Laura Reed and Sara Parshall gave a party in the evening. Had more fun.

Tuesday, October 18, 1927

Rained hard nearly all day. Classes until 5:00. Went to Drexel Tea Dance with Ark. Studied in the evening. Wrote to Alice.

Wednesday, October 19, 1927

Went over to Kathleen's after school and had some cheese and crackers. Mailed laundry. In the evening had date with Ark. Had more fun. Jack Moore, Asst. Coach, was here for dinner with Laura Reed and Dutch Waite and Sara Parshall. We danced downstairs.

Thursday, October 20, 1927

Worked on H. Ec. 20 term paper. Classes until 5:00. Ark was over awhile before dinner. Studied in the evening. Wrote to Mama.

Friday, October 21, 1927

Had lunch at Tea Rose with Almeda Tembovitz. Cut 2 hrs. of chemistry. Had hair washed and curled. In the evening went to Phi Kappa Beta Fraternity dance with Ark. Had the best time.

Saturday, October 22, 1927

Classes till 1 o'clock. Ark came about 2 o'clock. Went out to Drexel-Haverford game at Haverford with Wilton Wright and his wife. We lost 26-0. In eve. we went to see "King of Kings" at Aldine with Ark and stayed over at Mrs. Irlisher's all night.

Sunday, October 23, 1927

Got up at 9:00 and went out to Jenkintown. Slept with Katie Howd. Fooled around all day. Went in to Jack's and had some breakfast. Came back in after Tea.

Monday, October 24, 1927

Out at 4:00. Saw Ark after school. Sewed some after school. Worked on House Plans in evening.

Tuesday, October 25, 1927

June and I had our pictures taken for the yearbook at Kubey Rembrandt Studios[249] in the morning. Classes until 5:00. Ark met me at the fraternity house. In the evening June and I gave our party to the Practice House. Ark and Paul Gregory came over and painted the pantry. They never finished until 12:30.

249 Official Photographers for Class of June 1927.

Wednesday, October 26, 1927

Wrote Mama. Through classes at 3:00. Seniors had their class picture taken today. Was dead tired. In eve. had date with Ark. Went over to the fraternity house.

Thursday, October 27, 1927

Had lunch at Waffle Shop with a gang. Classes until 5:00. Ark was over awhile before dinner. In the evening I worked on house plans. Marjorie and Kenny both called. Emil was over helping June and me with our plan.

Friday, October 28, 1927

Classes until 5:00. There was a court dance, was there with Ark. Took a Chem quiz and didn't know a thing. Talked to Kenny and also Alice. Studied in the evening.

Saturday, October 29, 1927

Anna Raisim, Kathleen's cousin, slept here all night. In the afternoon we went out to the Drexel game. We beat Upsula 43-0. In the evening #216 had their formal dinner and a Halloween dance. Had the best time. Took Carl Gregory. Asked Ark, but Ann Gross was down this weekend and he had planned a long time ago to be with her. They went to the dance at '05 and '07.[250] Paul and I chased around to the other dances. Went over to #214. Saw Ark several times. Kenny, Min Spardle, Speed Bland, John Wandall, John Wells were there. The kids from the other dances came over to #216. Danced with Cobbly Mascal. He is so sweet I could just kiss him. Coach Morro came in late, and I danced the last dance with him.

Sunday, October 30, 1927

Eleanor Steinbauch and Alice were here all night. Had breakfast at Tea Rose. They went out to school about 3:00. Wrote to Mama and also Bill. Am wondering how he will like the letter I wrote. Studied in eve.

Monday, October 31, 1927

At 10:00 all the boys walked out of class celebrating our victory Saturday. Dr. Taft wouldn't let us out. They cheered and yelled in the court. Dr. Matheson called them down. Next hour we were all out front cheering, but were sent back to class. We will get a holiday if we beat St. Joe's. Ark walked up with me from school. Had Student Board meeting after dinner. Party in Practice House in eve.

Tuesday, November 1, 1927

Classes until 5:00. Ark was over awhile before dinner. Studied for Home Ec. 30 exam.

Wednesday, November 2, 1927

Took final in Home Economics 31 this morning. Only hope I made a good grade. Finished dress in sewing. Went downtown after Assembly. Mr. Curtis was there and we had a special. Made an appointment to have pictures taken. In evening I had a date with Ark. Went over to fraternity house.

---

[250] These are house number addresses.

Thursday, November 3, 1927

Didn't have class until 1:00. Went down at Bachrachs in the morning. Class until 5:00 p.m. Ark was over awhile before dinner. House meeting after dinner. Studied in the evening. Talked to Marjorie.

Friday, November 4, 1927

Ark went home at noon for the weekend. Saw him at school before he left. Had a sewing quiz. In evening went down to Jack Hart's. Until 10:30 with Ethel York.

Saturday, November 5, 1927

Letter from Bill this morning inviting me up to a House Party this coming weekend. Here's hoping I get there. Wrote him and also Mama for permission. Class at Penn from 11:00–1:00. Met Marjorie at Wanamaker's at 1:00. Had lunch at Cathay. Went to see "Criss Cross."[251] It was wonderful. In the evening Carl Gregory took me down to the Purple Spot at school and Jack Moore took Marjorie. **Had the best time I ever had down at school.** We just carried on awful. Had tables set up all around and danced and ate.

Sunday, November 6, 1927

Got up for breakfast. June and Marjorie and I went to church. Fooled around all afternoon. Wrote letters. Wrote Bill and asked about the chaperones. Kenny and his roommate came over for a while. Went up to Waffle Shop for tea. John Schiemer came for Marjorie in the evening. Studied some. Ark called about 9:45.

Monday, November 7, 1927

Talked to Ark at school. He was over awhile at 4:00. Told him I might go to State this weekend. He was so sweet about it. Studied in evening. Had party at 9:45.

Tuesday, November 8, 1927

Met Almeda at 9:30. Shopped and got material for a dress at school. Ark was waiting for me, came over for a while. Studied in the evening. If I don't get that permission soon—. Wrote to Mama.

Wednesday, November 9, 1927

Received permission last night, special from Mama. Feel much relieved now. Went over to see Miss Dorsey after breakfast and got permission. Went down town, got a hat and galoshes.[252] Met Ark at 3:00. He came over for a while. Had proofs of my pictures. Had a date with Ark in the evening. Went over to the House awhile and then went over to the Waffle Shop. Called Margie.

Thursday, November 10, 1927

Had hair washed and curled in morning. Picked up permission. Class until 5:00. Talked to Mrs. Jackson. Ark came at 10:15 and put me on the sleeper. Fooled around all evening.

---

[251] The musical ran for 210 performances, closing on April 9, 1927 in NYC.

[252] A new trend, supposedly the origin for the term "flapper" from the sound & action of wearing the galoshes unbuckled.

Bellefonte

Friday, November 11, Armistice Day, 1927

Got off at Tyrone at 7:05. A girl who was going up to the House Party was on the train. We talked awhile. Went down the street and had breakfast. Took train to Bellefonte. Went up to Richlens. Left my suitcase there. Saw Harmie. Went up to Heverlys. They were not home. Marjorie Hill and Eddie came for me. Had lunch up there.

In the afternoon I was to meet Bill at 2:00. He called and couldn't get down until 4:30. So Marjorie and Eddie took me up and I got there at 5:15; first saw movies at Richlens and then went up to the football game. B. H.S. beat Lewistown. My roommate was awfully sweet. "Berdie" Phillips from Pittsburgh. She was with Harold Keifer. We sat around, had dinner, then went down to the movies. Saw Jane Smith and Tommy Mensch, also Dave McKinley.[253] Ann Ulrich was at the D. U. House also.

Came back and dressed for the formal dance. Got there about 10:00. Had a good orchestra, Ross Smith from Johnstown. Danced till 2:00, then took a ride with Bill and Caroline. Went and parked on top of Center Hall Mountain. Got in at 3:30 and to bed about 4:00. Bill was the nicest tonight.

State College

Saturday, November 12, 1927

Penn Day. Got up about 10:30. Bill came about 11:30. A bunch of us went down to the Fenway on East College Avenue. I had breakfast and lunch together. Got through about 1:00. Saw Janie Clark. Went back to the House,

Penn State football, mid-1920s

then went to the football game. It was so exciting, 13-13 with New York University. A bunch of NYU's were at the house. Some of them had been in an accident. Met Mama and Papa after the game. Went up to the House and showed them my pictures. They didn't stay long.

Got dressed for dinner. Went down to the auditorium and heard the Revelers; they were real good. They record records. Came back to the house and danced till 12:00. Got a telegram from Ark saying we (Drexel) lost the game.

I can't understand Bill, though, and am going to give up trying. I can't make out why he asked me. He isn't nearly as attentive as he should be and I know he likes me, but that is all. After the dance we went out and sat in Bill's car. The sweetest boy was with us. Skip Skinner or something. He plays football. Roeke, the captain, is a D.U.

I came in and went to bed about 2:30. Bill is so indifferent. Florence Green, Bud's sister, had to come up and spoil things. She was always Bill's House Party date before.

---

[253] High school classmate of Mary Alice's one day to be a top administrator at Penn State.

Sunday, November 13, 1927

Got up about 9:30 and Bill came about 10:30. Went down and had breakfast at the Corner Room. Got back to house about time for dinner. Sat around and talked after dinner, then got ready to go. Florence Green appeared on the scene. I drove to Harrisburg[254] and got the train with two other girls and 3 boys. Bill didn't come. There was hardly room and then again he really didn't want to go. The sooner he left me the better, I think. I couldn't get pepped up a bit all weekend. Everyone was so dead-like. I don't know what was wrong. Maybe it was me. Anyway, Bill made me feel the way I did. We had a picture taken Saturday morning.[255] Got in at 9:30. Went to bed early. Ark called.

Philadelphia

Monday, November 14, 1927

Class at 10:00. Saw Ark, then he came up to the house awhile. Studied and wrote letters in the evening. Wrote to Bill.

Tuesday, November 15, 1927

Did some work up at the house and went downtown. Took pictures to Bachrach's and got 1½ dozen. Went to school. Worked in library for 2 hours. Classes till 5:00. Ark was over awhile. In evening we made sandwiches. Practice House had a sale. Had Student Government Board meeting at 10:00. Brought 2 girls up.

Wednesday, November 16, 1927

Fooled around up at the house until nearly 12:00. Redding up after the sale. Made $5.60 clear. Mailed laundry. Had a date with Ark in the evening.

Thursday, November 17, 1927

Wrote to Mama. Went down to school. Sewed some ribbon together for "Smitty" for their fraternity orchestra. Ark walked home with me. Studied in the evening.

Friday, November 18, 1927

Worked in the library awhile. Saw Ark. Went out to dinner after class. In the evening we went to a dance at Mount St. Joseph's College with some boy. I could hardly stand him. Jack Stock was his name.

Saturday, November 19, 1927

Got up about 9:30. Had class at 11:00. In the afternoon I went to the Drexel game. We beat Washington College 20 – 6. In the evening I went to the Phi Kappa Beta fraternity dance with Ark. Had a real good time.

---

254   What did she do with the car? Hmmm.

255   Note that Bill and Mary Alice could not have been farther apart in this group photo taken at the house party shown on the cover of this book.

Sunday, November 20, 1927

Got up for breakfast. Went to church with June. Cliff walked up with us. Studied and wrote letters in the afternoon and evening. Called Alice.

Monday, November 21, 1927

Am 22 years old today. Got a bottle of perfume from June, 2 handkerchiefs from Kathleen, and a Penn handkerchief from E. Newton. Class until 4:00. Ark walked home with me. He is acting peculiar. Guess he doesn't like me anymore. Had a blind date in the evening with Jane Heath. Bob Suley was the boy. He was real nice.

Tuesday, November 22, 1927

Went down to school early and worked in the library. Saw Ark, but didn't talk to him all day. He is acting so funny lately. Will have to call him down tomorrow, IF I get the chance. In the evening Lois Hamilton and I went down to the Stanley and saw Dick Barthelmess in "The Drop Kick."[256] We also heard Fred Waring's Pennsylvanians play. Was at the drug store afterwards and was talking to Cobby Mascal. He is a dear boy.

Wednesday, November 23, 1927

Went to school early and worked in the library. Saw Ark and said "good-bye" to Mim. They got their new fraternity pins. Fooled around after school; Mama called about 5:00. Went down to J.F. and had dinner. Went to the Fox, then left there at 9:30 and went over to Broad Street. Got there in time to meet Tat. Herb, Margie and Jimmy Hall were there. Herb brought me up. Played bridge for a while, then went over and stayed at 213 all night with Kathleen.

Thursday, November 24, 1927, Thanksgiving

Got up about 8:30 and came over to the house and dressed. Went over and saw Margie and Tat. Met Mama and Papa at the hotel and had dinner at 12:00. Came out to the Penn-Cornell game. Penn won, 35-0. State lost today, 30-0. Came over to the house after the game. Then went downtown and went to the movies at the Karlton. Came home and went to bed early. Didn't feel so good. Bill had called.

Friday, November 25, 1927

Bill called at 8:00 in the morning and got me out of bed. Went and had breakfast at the Tea Rose. Went down to the bank with Miss Parker. Went over and met Tat and Margie Thorn. Went down town and chased around. Had lunch at the Pirate Ship, a cute place on Camac Street. Came up to the house and talked. Mary Lou Wainer and Ruth McCullough came over. Had a date with Bill in the evening. Had Herb, Jim Hall, and Tat and Margie. Went out to Jacksons awhile then went to a dance at the 20th Century Club at Lansdown.[257] Stayed

---

256 *The Drop Kick* is a 1927 silent film about a college football player (Richard Barthelmess) who finds his reputation on the line when he pays an innocent visit to a woman whose husband kills himself.

257 The Twentieth Century Club of Lansdowne was organized in 1897 by a small group of women whose objective was to create an organized center for the promotion of science, literature and art. After the Borough acquired the building in 1979, the Club became Lansdowne's community center.

all night with the girls. Got in about 1:30. After they left we went up to the Marlyn Hotel and saw a boy, Charley Kennedy, a Delta Epsilon Delta fraternity brother of Cliff Gregory. Got to bed about 3:00.

Saturday, November 26, 1927

Got up about 8:00. Came over to the house and dressed. Met Mama at Wanamaker's at 10:00. Chased around. Met Marjorie and Papa and Mrs. Kittelberger. Had lunch and went to the movies. Mama came up to the house along and Marjorie went out to Norristown. Bill came in at 5:30 and we went out to the Jacksons for dinner. Had a big turkey dinner. Bill Horn was there. Mr. and Mrs. Norris came over. Bill and I went out with Bill Horn and Jane Shaw in Bill's La Salle. Drove out to the movies at Bryn Mawr. Had something to eat at Betty's. Stayed with Tat and Margie. Wish I hadn't, as I didn't get a minute alone with Bill.

Sunday, November 27, 1927

Got up at 8:30. Came over and dressed. Tat and Margie came over. Had breakfast at the Tea Rose. Marjorie came in. Margie got a room at Mrs. Ilrisher's. Met Mama at the hotel. Kenny and Mrs. Kittelberger came down for dinner. Went out to Mrs. K's and played bridge. Fred (Kittelberger) was there. Came back to the house at 6:30. Redd up and fooled around. Bill called about 10:00 before he left to take the train. He was so sweet. I wonder if he doesn't like me a little. Am so glad he called.

Monday, November 28, 1927

Classes from 10:00 till 3:00. Met Mama. Shopped. Met Kathleen, then Mr. and Mrs. Jackson. Had dinner at the hotel. Papa was at some doctor's all evening and night and couldn't be with us. He had some X-rays taken. Met Mr. and Mrs. Jim Norris. Saw "Broadway" at the Lyric. Went to Hylers and ate. Norrises brought us home.

Tuesday, November 29, 1927

Got up and had breakfast with Mama. Went shopping. Got some shoes. Met Papa. Mama and I went to lunch at Cathay. I left them. They went home on the 3:30 train. Went to school. Saw Ark for a minute. Had Margie over to dinner. Talked to Alice. Wrote Mama and Bill.

Wednesday, November 30, 1927

Went down and got pictures. Gave Ark one. Classes till 3:00. Stayed down for the basketball game. Beat Philadelphia Textile 57-21. Ark went to the game with me. Studied in the evening.

Thursday, December 1, 1927

Worked in the library a couple of hours. Talked to Ark at school. He met me at 5:00 and came over to the house awhile. Kenny Thorn came down and he and Margie took me to dinner at the Tea Rose. Studied in the evening.

Friday, December 2, 1927

Went down to school at 9:00. Worked on a poster for two hours. Had class until 5:00. Had a combined Student Board and Executive Meeting. Betty McDowell resigned presidency of Student Government. We don't know just what to do. I thought Ark would ask me for a date in the evening, but for some reason or another he didn't. Wrote up a book report.

Saturday, December 3, 1927

Finished book report in the morning. Had Voc. Ed. at Penn. Met Eleanor Steinbauch at 1:00. Had lunch at Wanamaker's. Went up to movies at Fox. Came out here to dinner, then the girls went down to the movies again. Wrote letters. Wrote to Mama.

Sunday, December 4, 1927

Got up for breakfast. Went to church with Helen Nace and Bob Eichelburger. In the afternoon I went out to the Arthur Robinsons. It sleeted terribly all day. Came in at 7:45. Studied in the evening. Ark called about 5:00 and I wasn't here. He never called again in the evening. Guess he is tired of me. I will give him a chance this week to miss me. I won't be around when he is. He had better ask me to the Junior Prom. If only Cobby Mascal would ask me for a date.

Monday, December 5, 1927

Ark walked up with me after school Talked quite a while. Guess he isn't going to ask me to the Junior Prom. Had Student Gov. meeting after dinner. Lasted quite late. Hope I hear from Bill tomorrow.

Tuesday, December 6, 1927

Went shopping in the morning. Bought some Xmas presents. Went up to basketball game at 5:00. Then Ark walked up with me. He asked me to the Junior Prom Friday night. Studied in eve. Wrote report.

Wednesday, December 7, 1927

No letter from Bill again today. Why doesn't he write? Mailed laundry after school. Didn't talk to Ark all day. Studied and sewed in the evening.

Thursday, December 8, 1927

No letter again today. This is getting serious. I cannot imagine what happened. He surely got my letter. If I don't hear, I am going to write to him on Sunday. Went shopping in the morning and had hair washed and curled. Class till 5:00. Wrote Mama.

Friday, December 9, 1927

Our Practice Home group met Miss Parker at 10:00. Worked out our schedule. Went down town. Had a check cashed. Took negative to Kubey-Rembrandt and had ½ doz. prints finished. Classes till 5:00. Met Ark. In evening I went to the Junior Prom with him at the Bellevue. Had a grand time. Went up to the Waffle Shop afterwards. Had a 1:30 permission. Got gold snake bracelets for favors.

Saturday, December 10, 1927

Breakfast at Tea Rose. June and I went shopping after Ed. Class. Chased all around. Had Xmas dinner at the dining room in the evening, then wrote letters.

Sunday, December 11, 1927

Got up about 10:00. Almeda came in and we sewed on our dresses all morning and aft. Am almost finished. Saw Margie Thorn after dinner. In the evening studied for English final with Kathleen. I am worried about Bill. If he would only write. I just don't know what to think.

Monday, December 12, 1927

Wrote to Mama. Studied Chem. and English in the morning. Ate at the drug store. Took English final in the afternoon. Talked to Ark a couple of minutes. Finished dress in evening and studied for Chem. Saw Piggie Burr.

Tuesday, December 13, 1927

Took Physiology final in the morning. Didn't know a thing. Had lunch at Tea Rose. Had Home Ec. exam in the afternoon. Saw Ark for a few minutes. Went over to see Margie. Haven't heard from Bill yet. Two weeks ago today I wrote to him.

Wednesday, December 14, 1927

At last a real nice letter from Bill and he is forgiven. I just can't help it. Have a date Saturday night. Went down shopping in the morning. Went to the Fox and saw "Seventh Heaven."[258] In the evening I had a date with Ark. My last one for a while. Went to the Stanley and saw "The Fair Co-Ed."[259]

Thursday, December 15, 1927

Had early breakfast at 7:15. Went down to school at 9:00. Cooked and set tables for Founders' Day luncheon. Helped serve. Made $1.05. Came up to the House, then went shopping. Got the other pictures at Rembrandt's. Not so bad. Went over to 216 after dinner. Studied Ed. with Kathleen. Miss Dorsey had a party. Studied until 2:30. Wrote to Mama.

Friday, December 16, 1927

Studied all morning for Ed. final. Took it in afternoon. It was terrible; I hope I at least pass the course. Fooled around all evening and went to bed at 9:00.

Saturday, December 17, 1927

Breakfast at dining room, class at Penn and up to house to lunch. Went downtown and got a pin. Came home. Bill called after lunch and again about 5:00. Jane Shaw and Bill Horn came with Bill. Chased around. Had a sundae first, was going to the ice hockey game, then went to see "Wings."[260] I love Bill so much, but it is all one-sided. He likes me, that is all; maybe someday—and I am waiting.

---

[258] A street cleaner saves a young woman's life, and the pair fall in love until war intervenes.
[259] A 1927 American silent film comedy starring Marion Davies and produced by William Randolph Hearst.
[260] American silent war film set during the First World War starring Clara Bow, Charles "Buddy" Rogers and Richard Arlen.

Sunday, December 18, 1927

Got up about 8:00. Had breakfast at the Tea Rose with Dot Orwig. Took the train for home at 10:30. Not a soul that I knew at Tyrone. Bubby, Kenny, and Philip met me at the train at home. Ate some and talked. Didn't go out. Alice and Billie McClure were up for a while.

Monday, December 19, 1927

Fooled around all morning. Went to Aunt Grace's and up to Bubby's. Mama and I shopped all day in Clearfield. Papa went to Bellefonte and took us that far. Came up on the bus. Stayed in all evening and wrote Christmas cards.

Tuesday, December 20, 1927

Slept with Mama. Got up early and mailed some packages. Wrote more cards and wrapped presents. Did some ironing. Baked a pie. In the evening I went to the movies with Jessie and Libby and Alice. Haven't heard a word from Johnny yet. Hope to soon. Wonder if I will hear from Bill?

Wednesday, December 21, 1927

Fooled around all morning. Went to Clearfield right after lunch. Met Tat, Margie, and Mrs. Thorn. Talked to John Leitzinger. Have a date Friday night. Kirk Hile passed by and hardly recognized me. Alice and I were downtown awhile in the evening. Came home early.

Thursday, December 22, 1927

Made fudge in the morning and cooked dinner. Made candy all afternoon. Went up to Mama Spencer's awhile. In the evening Cora and Mary Wolf were here and we played cards.

Friday, December 23, 1927

Fooled around all day. In the evening I had a date with John Leitzinger. He asked me to go to the Christmas Dance at the Dimeling Tuesday night, but Leonard Kantar had already asked me this afternoon. I would much rather go with Johnny. We went up to Holtens in the evening. Was at Clearfield with Hugh Norris in the afternoon. Got Alice's Christmas present. Had more fun. Saw Billie.

Saturday, December 24, 1927, Christmas Eve

Put up the Christmas tree in the morning. Did some shopping. Delivered presents in the afternoon. Went to Dubois with Walls. Had supper up there. Marjorie came home last night. Trimmed the tree in the evening. Didn't have a date.

Sunday, December 25, 1927, Christmas Day

Got things ready for dinner at Aunt Grace's. There were 14 of us. Cecil wasn't home. Nothing doing all day. Had date with Billie McClure in the evening.

Monday, December 26, 1927

Uncle Fred's kids came up. Went to the movies with them in the afternoon and then got their supper. Mama and Papa went to Dubois with Uncle Charley. Everything was closed up today. In the evening I went to N. O. S. Club Dance at DuBois with Billie McClure. It was at the Elks. Joe Ellis was with Bob Daugherty and John Wright had Kate Sayers. Had a good time. Ate at St. James afterwards. Got in at 3:45.

Tuesday, December 27, 1927

Slept until 11:00. After dinner went down to Marjorie's. Did some pressing. Went to Clearfield and saw John Leitzinger and Billie. In the evening I went to the Charity Ball with Leonard Kantar. Had the best time. Saw a lot of kids I haven't seen for a long time. Got home at 2:00.

Wednesday, December 28, 1927

Got up at 11:00. Went to Grampian with Marjorie, Kenny, Jessie, and Phil. Edith Shaw, Joe Ellis and Becky Carine were up awhile. Mr. and Mrs. Haim were up to see the house. Mama and Papa came home for supper. Went up to Wolfs awhile in the evening. Went to a party up at Hugh's. Mostly Helen's friends. George, John Wright, Alice, Marjorie, Gordon Herrington, and Jennie Mitchel, too. Home at 1:30.

Thursday, December 29, 1927

In the afternoon Mama, Marjorie, and I went to Clearfield. Shopped and went to Thorns and Hydes. In the evening we went to the Charity Ball at Dubois with Billie. Had a good time. It was awful foggy. In at 3:00. Alice and Hugh; John and Edith Shaw; Bob Daugherty and Lib Wall were there.

Friday, December 30, 1927

Went to Clearfield in the afternoon with Papa. Went to the dentist. Up at Uncle Fred's awhile. Up to Thorns. Saw Dot Dimeling. Up at Amelia Butler's. Had date with John Leitzinger in the evening. Eddie Hile was with Louise Kittelberger. Went up to Huttons. I like Johnny a whole lot.

Saturday, December 31, 1927

Did some shopping. Mama and I went over to Custers awhile in the afternoon. Cold out in the evening. Marjorie and I chased around. Went up to Libby's. Went to bed early.

1928

Sunday, January 1, 1928

Mama and I went to church. It was awfully cold. Marjorie went back at noon. Made fudge. Billy came about 9:00. Went down to Sheridan's Sweet Shop.[261] Leonard Kantar came for us about 11:45; he was with Rose Bloom, Bob Daugherty was with Lib Wall. Went to Junior Board of Trade dance at the Royal Gardens. Had the best time. Got home at 5:00. Ate at Jordan's before coming home.

---

[261] Catherine Plfer worked there during this time.

Philadelphia

Monday, January 2, 1928

Said goodbye to Mama Spencer and Bubby and Catherine. Had dinner and went to Clearfield with Papa. Tat took Marjorie and me to Tyrone. Had trouble with the car, just made the train, and it was late. Got in at 9:50. A friend of Margie's met us.

Tuesday, January 3, 1928

Had breakfast at the Tea Rose. Went down to school and made out roster. Taking only Chem. (in addition to the Home Economics Classes, including living in the Practice House.). Had first meal in Practice House tonight. Wrote letters in aft. Wrote to Mama and J. Leitzinger.

Wednesday, January 4, 1928

Had breakfast in Practice House at 7:30. Worked nearly all morning. Cleaned the front room. Had Chem at 11:00. Didn't do much in the afternoon. In the evening I went to the basketball game at school; we beat Schuylkill 39-23. Met Carl Gregory after the game. Went up to the Waffle Shop.

Thursday, January 5, 1928

Breakfast at 7:30. Cleaned front room, shined the brass. Went shopping after lunch. Looked at coats. Studied some in evening. Wrote Tat.

Friday, January 6, 1928

Last day as hostess. Letter from Bill in morning. Called Mrs. Norris to come in tomorrow and help get my coat. Went downtown. Got an evening dress and also a sports dress. Sewed in evening. Marjorie called.

Saturday, January 7, 1928

Chem Class at 9:00. Class at Penn till 1:00. In afternoon met Marjorie and Mrs. J. Norris. Went down on South Street and got a good looking coat. Stayed in this evening. Wrote Mama and Bill.

Sunday, January 8, 1928

Breakfast in Practice House at 8:30. June and I went to Asbury Church. Helped with noon dishes. Sewed and ironed in the afternoon. In evening I had a date with George Wrigley, went over to the Waffle Shop.

Monday, January 9, 1928

Did my work after breakfast. Took care of Charlotte[262] until 3:45. Gave her lunch and a bath. Had Chem from 4 to 5. Had dinner late. Studied and wrote letters.

---

[262] Charlotte was the (actual, living) foundling who was in the care of the Home Economics Department! Evidently, this practice in child care is authentic. Among the reasons given to add real infants to the Home Economics program is that child welfare ranked it high as did the experience for the students. The benefits to the child included good development and positive spiritual benefits since the babies would receive more attention than they received in boarding homes or orphanages. Students would better appreciate the responsibilities of motherhood, learn child training in a "normal" way, and realize (it was hoped) how much they would enjoy children of their own.

Tuesday, January 10, 1928

Nurse here today to check on Charlotte. I had nothing to do but clean my room. Had Chem lab and class until 4:00. Mrs. Kittelberger was here for dinner. Stayed until 9:30. Wrote to Alice. Called Mrs. Jackson.

Wednesday, January 11, 1928

Got Charlotte at 9:00 and had her every minute until 5:00. She is more bother. Studied Chem. in evening.

Thursday, January 12, 1928

Had Charlotte all day. She at least took a nap. Had Chem. class from 3:00 – 4:00. Helped wash dishes. Made out menus in the evening.

Friday, January 13, 1928

Went shopping with Annette. Went up to 40th Street Market. Prepared big dinner party in the evening. Seven boys were here. Ella Radford invited a boy for me, Enos Derham. We cooked all afternoon getting ready. Made salad dressing, set the table, had dinner at 7:00. The boys helped to serve. Had more fun. Had permission for the boys to stay here till 12:00. Played the radio and fooled around. 14 of us. Went out back and smoked. Was dead tired.

Saturday, January 14, 1928

Got up at 6:00 and helped Annette get breakfast. Served it. Class from 9:00 to 1:00. Dr. Ash excused us early. Got lunch. Miss Dashiell was here. Cooked and got dinner. Cleaned the dining room in the afternoon. Didn't get through all the dishes until 8:30. Had a date with George Wrigley. Went over to Penn-Penn State basketball game. State lost 21-23. Danced after. Was so tired I could hardly dance.

Sunday, January 15, 1928

The Lobby of The Erlanger Theatre

Got up at 7:00 and got breakfast. Cooked dinner and got ready for Tea. Took short nap after dinner. Had 14 for Tea, including some of the girls' parents. I invited Mr. and Mrs. Jackson, but they couldn't come. Helped serve. Carl Gregory came over awhile in the evening.

Monday, January 16, 1928

Got up at 6:00 and helped to get breakfast. Cleaned up the dining room. Did a big wash. Am now Laundress! Used the washing machine and mangle today. E. Newton came down from home. We went to see "Honeymoon Lane"[263] in the evening at the Erlanger Theatre.[264]

---

[263] Honeymoon Lane (Original, Musical, Comedy, Broadway) opened in New York City Sep 20, 1926 and played through Jul 23, 1927. The movie by this name did not appear until 1931.

[264] The Erlanger Theatre at 21st and Market Street was Philadelphia's most elaborate legitimate theatre ever and it was said to be one of the most magnificent ever built in the United States. The exterior was Georgian. The elegant interior was furnished in Napoleonic French.

Tuesday, January 17, 1928

Didn't have to get up so early this morning. Had a big wash. Washed the nursery and kitchen curtains. Then had Chemistry class. Had a sweet letter from Bill. Marjorie was here for a couple of minutes. Washed up the laundry floor, then in the evening I ironed the curtains, pressed a dress and mended.

Wednesday, January 18, 1928

Washed and ironed all morning. Did the living room curtains and also the big tablecloth. Took time and went up and had my hair washed and curled. Ironed and mended again in the evening. Then wrote to Mama.

Thursday, January 19, 1928

Did laundry in the morning. Not so much to do. Miss Richardson, some big Home Ec. teacher, was here in the morning. Had to clean everything up. Wrote to Bill after lunch then shopped and came back and prepared dinner for 11. Carl Gregory was over. He helped to mash the potatoes, carved the meat, and then even helped with the dishes. Went over to the fraternity for an hour afterwards. Alice called.

Friday, January 20, 1928

Got up at 6:15. Got breakfast. Washed dishes and fussed around the kitchen nearly all morning. After I washed the lunch dishes I went shopping up to 40th Street. Came back and prepared dinner. Washed the dishes and the floor, and made salad dressing. Then I worked on menus and counted money. Ate an onion sandwich. Miss Parker[265] hosted the party.

Saturday, January 21, 1928

Arose at 6:30 and prepared breakfast. Made a lima bean loaf before 9:00 a.m. Had Chem. at 9:00. Went up to 40th Street. Kathleen went with me while I shopped. Then went over to John's. Joe was there. We cut Ed. 61 and stayed there with the boys. Had more fun. Joe mixed me something to drink. I clipped off a cute curl of his head of hair. Went to dental school with Kathleen and saw someone with "pink" hair. Came home and got lunch. Cooked all afternoon. Jane and Kathleen and Lillian were here for dinner.

Went down to the basketball game; we lost to Seton Hall,[266] 23-25. Had a date with Carl Gregory. Henry Stetina (Kappa Sigma Delta) had asked me to go to the Kappa dance with him also.

Sunday, January 22, 1928

My last day of the Practice House, thank goodness! Had breakfast at 8:30. Cooked all morning getting dinner, after I got things ready for Tea. Finished at 7:00. Scrubbed the kitchen floor.

---

[265] Miss Emily D. Parker, B.S., an Instructor in Home Economics.
[266] The yearbook mentioned by name only the four (of the six played) games that were won by Drexel women.

199

Monday, January 23, 1928

A great relief not to have to get up and get breakfast. Got up at 9:00. Cleaned up the room, fooled around all morning. Had lunch at Tea Rose. Fixed out accounts in the afternoon and slept two hours. Walked down to the school after dinner. Had a home meeting.

Tuesday, January 24, 1928

Wrote to Mama in the morning. Class at 11:00. Was supposed to have a date with Carl Gregory but they had a basketball game. Chem class until 4:00. Sewed and slept in the evening and wrote letters.

Wednesday, January 25, 1928

Fooled around all morning again, then wrote a report. Shopped for a couple of hours, then went out to Beaver to see Alice about 2:00. Went over to the Wyncote in the afternoon and ate. Went to a Tea, then over to Chapel after dinner. Read some in the evening. Ate an onion sandwich after lights out at 10:00 and talked.

Thursday, January 26, 1928

Got up about 8:45. Went over to Wyncote and ate. Came in about 10:00. Came up to the house and went to school and served at a luncheon for 8. The Dean of Cornell was the guest of honor. Had Chem from 3 to 4. Made out the report of food for Miss Parker.

Friday, January 27, 1928

Got up about 9:30. Finished the report for Miss Parker. Read Vocational Ed book. Wrote to Johnny Leitzinger.[267] Slept awhile in the afternoon, then met Margie Thorn after dinner. Studied for Ed. final in the evening.

Saturday, January 28, 1928

Had Chem. class at 9:00. Took final in Vocational Education over at Penn from 11:00 to 1:00. Professor Ash. It was terrible. Only hope I passed it. Fooled around all afternoon. Had formal dinner at D. R. It snowed a lot, about a foot or more. Had a date in the evening—a blind date with Jack Wetherhold, a friend of Otto's, June's friend. Went over to his fraternity, Sigma Kappa Kappa (not at Drexel). It is a medical fraternity. I had something to drink. Not so good.[268]

Sunday, January 29, 1928

Wrote to Mama. Got up for breakfast. June and I went to church. Cliff Gregory walked up along. Took some pictures. In the afternoon I wrote letters and baked drop cakes to sell tomorrow. In the evening I had a blind date. Went down to some boys' apartment. Jane and Lois were along.

---

[267] Just had to note that as soon as I saw this nickname I immediately recalled that this is the name I had always heard when adults (when I was a child) mentioned him.

[268] The reader is reminded that this was during Prohibition.

Monday, January 30, 1928

Had the sweetest letter from Bill. I wrote back to him. Went down to school about 11:00. We had a cake sale in the Court. Made enough money to get ¼ cord of wood. Came home and went down to the movie. Saw "Love," with John Gilbert and Greta Garbo.[269]

Tuesday, January 31, 1928

Had an appointment with Miss Ebersole at 10:00. Studied Chem. Took a quiz in the afternoon and made an 85. Talked to Alice; she is coming in Saturday.

Wednesday, February 1, 1928

Went down to school at 10:00. Worked on Protein paper. Walked up to 40th Street with Kathleen and went to the Stanley in the afternoon to see "Sorrell and Son."[270] Wrote Bill again.

Thursday, February 2, 1928

Chem class today. Went down and ate lunch at the Cafeteria. Worked on the Protein paper. After dinner Miss Parker, June and Lois and I played bridge.

Friday, February 3, 1928

Read in the morning. Had lunch at the Tea Rose with June. Went to the basketball game at school at 4:00. We lost to Western Maryland 25-33. In the evening I had a date with Carl Gregory. Went to the Fox and saw "The Sharpshooters." Went up to the Waffle Shop. Saw Margie and Charley Kennedy.

Saturday, February 4, 1928

Class from 9 to 1. Met Alice at Wanamaker's and had lunch at the Golden Dragon. Saw Kate Howd and E. Newton. Shopped all afternoon. Alice went out to Robinsons. Had date with Carl G. after the basketball game. We beat Albright 39-24. David and I went to eat.

Sunday, February 5, 1928

Went out to Robinsons. Had dinner and came in about 4:30. Had a date with Carl Gregory. Had dinner at the "Golden Dragon." Came up to the fraternity house and played the Victrola. Wrote to Mama.

Monday, February 6, 1928

Went out to Wayne observing today for the first; left at 8:30. Had lunch out there and came in at 1:27. Had check cashed, got a new blue dress. Sewed in the evening and wrote to Mama.

Tuesday, February 7, 1928

Had Chem lab at 11:00. Conference with Miss Ebersole at 4:00. Studied, sewed, and ironed in the evening.

---

[269] Still a silent film, except that it was filmed with an audience, which was distracting to the actors being filmed and later to those watching the film. The process was not repeated.

[270] "Sorrell and Son" is a 1927 American silent drama film and nominated for the Academy Award for Best Director in the 1st Academy Awards the following year.

Wednesday, February 8, 1928

Observed again today. Came in and went downtown and got a hat. Went to the basketball game. We beat Washington College 27–22. Studied in the evening.

Thursday, February 9, 1928

Observed at Rosemont today. Came in at noon. Lunch at Tea Rose. Had Chem. class. Also another conference with Miss Ebersole. Talked to Carl. Alice called in the evening.

Friday, February 10, 1928

Went out to Wayne 2nd period and came in at 2:27. Had my hair washed and curled. Alice came in and stayed all night. She and June went out. I went to the Military Ball with Carl Gregory. Had a grand time. Had our pictures taken. Came home at 2:00. Had dinner at the fraternity house and went to Child's after the dance.

Friday, February 11, 1928

Had Chem at 9:00. Went out to Norristown right afterwards. Marjorie met me at the station. Went out to Boyd's where she lives. Went to see Mary Pickford in "My Best Girl"[271] in the afternoon. Fooled around, then played bridge in the evening.

Sunday, February 12, 1928

Got up about 9:30. Went to church. Had dinner about 2:00. Marge Irvin came over. Met Clate. Came into house about 6:00. Carl stopped a few minutes on his way over to the house. They lost to Gettysburg last night. Stayed in and worked.

Monday, February 13, 1928

Taught for the first time today. Had a conference 2nd period. Not so bad, but could be much better. Jack Roberts met me at 3:00. Drove out to Valley Forge. Stopped and he told me he loves me. I was so surprised and I didn't know what to say. Sorry that I couldn't return his love. Had the sweetest letter from Bill. Called Mrs. Jackson up and am going out there to dinner on Sunday. Jack called up from West Philadelphia before he left for New York.

Tuesday, February 14, 1928, Valentine's Day

Didn't go to Chem lab. Stayed in bed until 9:30. Have a terrible cold. Went down to school about 2:30. Stayed at the Court Dance awhile. Talked to Carl.

Wednesday, February 15, 1928

Got up early and went out to Wayne. Came in on the 1:27. Went to a basketball game. We beat St. Joe's 27-22. A wonderful game. Studied in the evening.

Thursday, February 16, 1928

Taught at Rosemont today.[272] Had a grand time. Went down town for a few minutes. Had Chem Class and a Conference. Made out lesson plans in the evening and wrote to Mama.

---

[271] Best Actress of 1927-28, Mary Pickford was the most popular actress of the Silent Era, earning the nickname "America's Sweetheart" with a series of winning performances as the plucky girl who overcomes long odds.

[272] This marks her first day of student teaching; evidently it was not fulltime but only an assignment of a few days.

Friday, February 17, 1928

Had early class at Wayne. Came in on the 3:27 train. Conference with Miss Ebersole at 4:00. E. Newton came before dinner and Alice after. We all went down to Jack Hart's after dinner in the evening. Had a pretty good time. Harold Clark brought me home.

Saturday, February 18, 1928

Class at 9:00. Had lunch with Edith downtown. Went to see "The Love Call"[273] in the afternoon. It was real good. Went to bed early.

Sunday, February 19, 1928

Went out to Jacksons for dinner. I miss Bill so much. They brought me back to the Drexel house. In the evening I had a date with Carl Gregory.

Monday, February 20, 1928

Classes at Wayne. Came in on the 3:27. Studied for the Chem quiz in evening.

Tuesday, February 21, 1928

Worked on lesson plans till 11:00. Had Chem lab. Had quiz in Chem, but didn't take it. I had a terrible earache. Came up to the Infirmary all afternoon. In the evening I went to see "The Patent Leather Kid"[274] at the Erlanger with Carl. Liked it a lot.

Wednesday, February 22, 1928, Washington's Birthday

Vacation day. Stayed in bed all morning. Had dinner at Practice House. In the evening I went over to the fraternity house with Carl.

Thursday, February 23, 1928

Got up early, went out to Rosemont. Came in at noon and went over to the infirmary and went to bed. My cold was awful.

Friday, February 24, 1928

In bed all day. The kids were in to see me. Two other girls were in also, so I had some company.

Saturday, February 25, 1928

Came over to the house and dressed for the formal dinner. 216 had a House Dance. I had asked Carl Gregory, but broke the date when I knew Hazel Thompson would be here. Didn't feel well. Went over awhile and danced a couple of dances.

Sunday, February 26, 1928

Had breakfast at the Tea Rose with June. In afternoon went out to Mrs. Kittelberger's. Talked a lot. Had dinner at 5:00. Fredrick brought me home. Wrote Mama.

---

[273] "The Love Call" (Original, Musical, Broadway) opened in New York City Oct 24, 1927. Music by the Shuberts. It likely played Philadelphia after its NY opening.

[274] A silent drama film with Richard Barthelmess (who won an Oscar nomination for best actor) who scoffs at fighting outside the ring... particularly for the United States once it enters World War I.

Monday, February 27, 1928
Went on field trip through Van Scivers and Budget Homes. Worked in the evening.

Tuesday, February 28, 1928
Studied Chemistry all morning. Took quiz in the afternoon. Made a 73. Talked to Carl a few minutes. Wrote up lesson plans in the evening. Moved some of my junk back to 216.

Wednesday, February 29, 1928
Got up early, went out to Wayne. Came in on the 1:57, ate lunch with Mr. Croyle. Saw Ebersole and she had a fit because I forgot my Conference with her on Monday. Came up to the house and finished moving. Mama called. She and Papa arrived this afternoon. Papa went down to John Brown's. I went down and met Mama. We went to see "The Student Prince."[275] Slept in 216 tonight.

Thursday, March 1, 1928
Went out to Rosemont today. Miss Ebersole was there most of the morning. Came in and went down town and got some material for the kids. Had a conference and Chemistry from 3 to 4. After Mama called I worked the rest of the evening.

Friday, March 2, 1928
Went out to Wayne early. Had a textile class to teach today and they were terrible. Think I lost $5.00. Makes me so mad.

Saturday, March 3, 1928
Chem lecture and lab. Met Mama, Alice, and Marjorie at Wanamaker's. Mrs. K. and Mrs. Robinson were there, too. Had lunch at the Cathay. Got a dress. Went to the movies and saw Pola Negri in "Hotel Imperial." Met Papa at hotel at 5:00. Had dinner there. Left them and came out to the house. Went to the basketball game. John Trumpy brought us home. He is real nice.

Sunday, March 4, 1928
Worked all morning. Made out lesson plans in afternoon and evening. Margie was over.

Monday, March 5, 1928
Had conference in morning. Ebersole is terrible. If she flunks me I'll die. Had 2 classes. Stayed and kept some girls in after school.

Tuesday, March 6, 1928
Chem lab & class. Saw Carl, but didn't talk much. Talked to Bill Hirschman. Wrote Bill, but not much of a letter. I just can't. He is too indifferent with me. Hope to hear from him.

Wednesday, March 7, 1928
Came in from Wayne about 3:00. Slept for an hour and a half before dinner. Worked in the evening.

275 1927 Metro-Goldwyn-Mayer silent drama film starring Norma Shearer.

Thursday, March 8, 1928

Went out to Rosemont today. Only once more to go out there. Had Chem. at 4:00. Was to have a conference at 4:00 and Miss Ebersole wasn't there. There was a court dance.

Friday, March 9, 1928

Went out to school early. Ebersole was out there. Classes until 3:00. Went down to Jack Hart's in the evening. Bill Brown and Karl Rowles were there. Left and went up to Karl's apartment. Bud Ganlin was there, also Bill Green. Bud walked me home.

Saturday, March 10, 1928

Chem lecture at 9:00. Alice and Eleanor came down to school. Showed Eleanor around. Went downtown and shopped. Had lunch at the Golden Dragon. Then went to the movies at Fox. In the evening we went to the basketball game at school. We lost. It was Carl's last game to play. Danced afterwards, but Carl didn't dance with me. Sammy Jones took me home. Went over to the fraternity house.

Sunday, March 11, 1928

Didn't get up until 11:00. Wrote to Mama. Studied and wrote lesson plans in the afternoon and evening. Wrote J. Roberts and Ark.

Monday, March 12, 1928

Conference down at school before I went to Wayne. Letter from Johnny Leitzinger. I wonder if Bill is ever going to write to me again. Studied Chem. till late.

Tuesday, March 13, 1928

Letter from Mama, but none from Bill again. Wrote to him again. The last until I receive a nice letter from him. Wrote Mama. Wrote to Johnny Leitzinger. Studied Chem all morning. Took final in the afternoon. Didn't do so well. Hope to pass the course.

Wednesday, March 14, 1928

Went downtown from Wayne. Bought material for the kids. Went out to school for a few minutes. Worked some in the evening. Heard I passed Chem.

Thursday, March 15, 1928

My last day at Rosemont. One big sigh of relief. If only this were next Thursday. Miss Burdick had a Tea for us after school, so I went out to Wayne. Dot Williams, Ella Radford, and Peg Leitzinger. Ebersole was out there. I'll die if she comes out tomorrow. Worked in the evening.

Friday, March 16, 1928

Thank heavens today is over. Miss Ebersole was out at Wayne nearly all day, but not to my textile class or I would have been lost. Had a conference at 4:00. My last one. Got 70 in Chemistry. Most everyone has gone home. In the evening I went to the movies with Jane

Heath and Ruth Miller. Saw "I am Doomsday."[276] Then went up to Jack Hart's. Had a pretty good time. Karl Rowles came home with me.

Saturday, March 17, 1928

Got up for breakfast. Cleaned all morning, and went downtown right after lunch. Got shoes and fooled around. Looked at coats. Received a special from Bill when I got home. Was so surprised that I didn't know what to do. Was dead tired in the evening.

Sunday, March 18, 1928

Wrote Mama, Alice, and Bill. Went to breakfast and church. Fooled around all afternoon and evening.

Monday, March 19, 1928

My last day of practice teaching. What a great relief. Didn't go out until the 11:15 train. Came in on the 3:27. The girls had a party in the evening. I didn't invite anyone, so I didn't go.

Tuesday, March 20, 1928

Wrote J. Stamp. Ironed and fussed around most of the morning, then went down town. Got material and a pattern. Went up to school and sewed all afternoon. Sewed some in the evening.

Wednesday, March 21, 1928

Dusted room. Went to school about 10:30. Never finished making out my roster till after 1:00. Sewed all afternoon. The kids all came back. Sewed in the evening. Didn't even see or hear from Ark. Guess he doesn't want to see me. I don't care much though.

Thursday, March 22, 1928

Wrote Mama and Alice. First day of class. Chem Lab, 9-12. Went downtown with June and Kathleen. Got a red hat and had Phy. from 4 to 5. Talked to Ark a couple minutes. If he doesn't soon ask me for a date.......

Friday, March 23, 1928

Sewed all morning on a dress and finished it. Had 2 hours of class. Came up to the house and fooled around. Read in the evening.

Saturday, March 24 , 1928

Chem. class at 9:00. Came up to the house, then went down town. Was to meet Marjorie at 11:30 and she never arrived. Saw Alice and Eleanor, George Wrigley and Karl Rowles. Karl then took me to the Golden Dragon for lunch and up to his apartment. Came over to the house. Ark called and asked for a date. Have one tomorrow night. Had dinner at the Women's City Club with Miss Dashiell. Came back to the house and went to a bridge party of three tables. Dot Wing and Mable Ellsworth gave it. Had more fun. Talked till late.

---

[276] "Doomsday" is a 1928 American romance drama silent film directed by Rowland V. Lee and starring Florence Vidor and Gary Cooper.

Sunday, March 25, 1928

Went to church with the girls. Fooled around all afternoon. After dinner Mr. Byington took a bunch of us for a wonderful ride. Drove down to Valley Green. Had date with Ark in the evening. He is most peculiar, can't say either if I like him much, just someone to go with. Have an idea he is having Ann Gross down soon to a dance and if he does, it's all off. There is a house fraternity dance this Saturday night and as yet he has not mentioned it.

Monday, March 26, 1928

Class over at the dining room in Quantity Cookery; didn't have to cook today, 3 hrs. off. Class at school till 3:00. Saw Ark, but not to talk to. Studied in the evening.

Tuesday, March 27, 1928

Cooking in the Cafeteria all morning. Chem Lab in the afternoon. This made 7 hours of class today. I then went in the evening to the Stanley and saw Greta Garbo in "The Divine Woman,"[277] with Lillian Moxie and Mable Ellsworth. Had a house meeting about a house dance. Saw Ark at the drug store; he asked me to their dance Saturday night. Wrote to Mama, Marjorie, and Alice.

Wednesday, March 28, 1928

Went down town and got a new spring coat and dress. Can't decide if I like my dress. Class till 1:00. Had student assembly here for the first time in ages. New pipe organ is almost finished.

Thursday, March 29, 1928

Chem lab in the morning. Went down town, got shoes and a dress and gloves. Fooled around in the evening. Hope I hear from Bill tomorrow.

Friday, March 30, 1928

Stayed up at house all morning and washed and sewed. Went to school awhile and went down to the Kent Day Nursery all afternoon and observed. Had a sweet letter from Bill, also a letter from J. Roberts.

Saturday, March 31, 1928

Chem class at 9:00 to 10:00. Met Alice at 10:30. Got a hat and she got shoes. Met "Shorty" from Beaver and had lunch at "King Joy." Shopped and went up to Karlton to the movies. Alice had a date with Karl Rowles. I went to Phi Kappa Beta fraternity dance with Ark Belding. Had a real good time.

Sunday, April 1, 1928

Had breakfast at the Tea Rose. Went to church. Had vespers at 5:15. In evening had a date with Ark. Went over to the fraternity house.

Monday, April 2, 1928

Cooked in the cafeteria all morning. Classes to 3:00. Came up to house and slept awhile. Worked in evening. Home meeting after dinner.

[277] 1928 silent film with only nine minutes still intact.

Tuesday, April 3, 1928

Cooked in cafeteria all morning. Chem lab in the afternoon. Classes till 5:00. Letter from Mama.

Wednesday, April 4, 1928

Class from 9 – 10. Went to Dr. Matherson's luncheon for the Seniors. In the evening had a date with Ark. Went to the Stanley and saw Colleen Moore[278] and heard Waring's orchestra.

Thursday, April 5, 1928

Chem lab. in the morning. Went downtown and got Philip's Easter egg. Met Alice at the train at 12:25. She went home. Also got a tie for Bubby's birthday. Had a class from 4 to 5. June and Kathleen went home today. Expected Bill to call and he didn't. If he doesn't call tomorrow------- Have decided to go home next Wednesday if Dorsey says "Yes."

Friday, April 6, 1928

Got up late. Did some washing and ironing. Slept awhile in the afternoon. Bill called right after dinner and came in at 8:00. Met Professor Harris, went out to Jackson's home. Bill and I sat out on the porch. He was so sweet tonight. I wonder if he does love me a little –until Sunday.

Saturday, April 7, 1928

Got up for breakfast. Fooled around all morn. Studied some. Went shopping in the afternoon. Jack Roberts called. Had a date with him in the evening. Can't even see him (no time). Wish he didn't like me. He had a friend with him; got Jane Heath for this Mr. Clancy. Went out to Devon Park Hotel and who should we run into but Herb Horn.

Sunday, April 8, 1928, Easter Day

Easter Sunday. Only wish Bill had sent me some flowers. Went to church with Lillian Forcey. Bill called about 3:30. Wrote Mama. Slept awhile. Had a date with Bill. Kathleen gave us the key for John's apartment. If only I didn't have to come in at 10:15; I was five minutes late, but it was worth that and more.

Monday, April 9, 1928

Classes all day. June came back in the evening. Expected Bill to call—but he didn't. Didn't talk to Ark today. Studied some in the evening. Hope to get my permission to go home tomorrow.

Tuesday, April 10, 1928

Bubby is 24 today. Wrote Mama. Class from 9 to 5. Had date with Bill in the evening. Went to Adelphia and saw "The Road to Rome."[279] Jane Cowl played in it. I liked it a lot. Bill leaves for State in the morning. He is so wonderful and I love him so.

[278] Likely saw "Lilac Time," a 1928 American silent romantic war film directed by George Fitzmaurice and starring Colleen Moore and Gary Cooper.

[279] "The Road to Rome" is a play by American author Robert Sherwood. The plot revolves around Hannibal's attempt to capture Rome during the Second Punic War.

Wednesday, April 11, 1928

Wrote Bill a real nice letter. Only wish I knew what he would think of it. Hope he likes it and writes me a still even nicer one. Think he does like me a little more than he used to. Went over to dance in the evening. Saw Ark. He asked me to the Sophomore Hop and I asked him to our house dance. Wrote to Tat.[280]

Thursday, April 12, 1928

Was up at house awhile in the afternoon. Met Ark after school. Took my white coat up to the cleaners. Worked in the evening.

Friday, April 13, 1928

Slept late. Lunch at Tea Rose. Went down to school about 12:30. Went to a lecture of the Dairy Council for Home Ec. 28. In the evening I went to the Sophomore Hop with Ark. Had a grand time and was over at the fraternity house before and after the dance. 1:30 permission.

Saturday, April 14, 1928

Chem quiz unexpected the first thing in the morning after the dance. Didn't know a thing. Then after lunch went to the Stanley with Ruth Ransom. Heard Fred Waring and saw a Norma Shearer play. Had date with Ark in the evening.

Sunday, April 15, 1928

Didn't go to breakfast or church. Wrote to Mama. Studied some and read in the evening.

Monday, April 16, 1928

Class from 9 to 3. Saw Ark in the court, but didn't talk to him. He was also over at the drug store in the evening. Had a Board Meeting after dinner. Brought a lot up. Had House Proctor meeting at 10:30 and meeting of girls on probation and also a meeting of the dance chairmen. Wrote Bill and had a letter from Mama.

Tuesday, April 17, 1928

Observed the cafeteria at the Overbrook High School all morning. Classes till 5:00. House Board meeting after dinner. Brought Peggy Lou up. Had a letter from Mr. Zerfoss saying I have been given the job at Clearfield at $1,350 salary. Am so glad. Wrote Mama, Bill, Alice, and Marjorie.

Wednesday, April 18, 1928

Went down town and had a check cashed. Got a new cook book at Leary's.[281] Classes till 4:00. Had a meeting about May Fete and dinner. Worked some in eve.

---

[280] By that time, Tat was teaching Home Economics in the Clearfield Schools. She had attended Drexel's Home Economics program but likely it was in a program of shorter duration. During the mid-1920s the length of the program changed several times.

[281] Leary's Book Store was a landmark in downtown Philadelphia, Pennsylvania, for nearly one hundred years.

209

Thursday, April 19, 1928

Chem lab in the morning. Up at the house awhile in the afternoon. Talked to Ark at school and saw him at 5:00. Studied and read in the evening.

Friday, April 20, 1928

Went over to Camden and observed in 2nd and 3rd grades. A lady from the Dairy Council told the children a story. Copied recipe cards most of the afternoon. In the evening Jewel and I went down to Jack Hart's. Donald (someone) came home with me.

Saturday, April 21, 1928

Met Alice at 11:00. Had lunch at the Roundhaven. Went to the movies, bought flowers for house dance, and came up to the house and helped decorate. Alice had a date with Karl Rowles and didn't go to the dance. I had a grand time. Miss Dorsey wasn't here.

Sunday, April 22, 1928

Had breakfast at Tea Rose. Went to church. I was at Dr. Foster's last Sunday at Asbury. Alice left at 3:00. Wrote Mama and Bill. Wrote a note to Ark.

Monday, April 23, 1928

Worked in the cafeteria all morning. Helped prepare menus for camp next weekend. Studied.

Tuesday, April 24, 1928

Was dead tired after dinner. Last day in the Cafeteria. Chem lab in the afternoon. Ark met me at 5:00. Came over awhile. Miss Dorsey had a few of us down for cucumbers and strawberries at 9:45, as a thank-you to those who had helped her at some parties. Ark sent the Sophomore Hop favor over from the drug store for me to review.

Wednesday, April 25, 1928

Was up at the house a couple of hours. Met Ark at 4:00 and saw him again at the drugstore in the evening.

Thursday, April 26, 1928

Had a real sweet letter from Bill. Went down town after Chem lab. Met Kathleen and went down on 4th Street. Met Ark after school. Went to a birthday party in Mary Frances' room.

Friday, April 27, 1928

Wrote to Bill. Class in the afternoon. Ark came home with me. For the last time if I can help it. He is a big pain. He had a date tonight and he must think I am an awful fool in his taking Ann to the Senior Ball.

Saturday, April 28, 1928

Terrible weather. We are not going to camp. Had Chem. in the morning. Went to the Stanley Theatre in the afternoon. Saw Clara Bow in "Red Hair."[282] It was real good.

---

[282] "Red Hair" is a 1928 silent film starring Clara Bow and Lane Chandler, based on a novel by Elinor Glyn, and released by Paramount Pictures. The film had one sequence filmed in Technicolor, and is now considered a lost film except for the color sequence at the UCLA Film and Television Archive.

Sunday, April 29, 1928

Didn't get up till late. Lost an hour's sleep. Daylight Saving time started today. Studied and read in afternoon and evening.

Monday, April 30, 1928

Cooked at Dining Room all morning. Fried 50 lbs. of Swiss steaks. Class till 3:00. Over at the Practice House for a while. Board Meeting after dinner.

Tuesday, May 1, 1928

Didn't go to Quantity Cooking. Had my hair washed and curled. Class till 5:00. Ark passed me in the court today and didn't see me. I wrote to Bill.

Wednesday, May 2, 1928

Sat down in the court area quite a while today. Got a date for the Senior Ball. John Trumpy. Alice called and wanted me to come out. Went out on the 5:32 train. Freshmen gave a party in the evening. Wrote to Bill.

Thursday, May 3, 1928

Came in this morning from Alice's for a 9:00. Started to decorate. Went down to 311 Juniper for the material for Home Ec. Exhibit. Talked to Ark at school and also to John Trumpy. Went to school in the evening. Wilton Wright and his wife brought me home.

Friday, May 4, 1928

I only wish Bill could be here for the dance tonight. No classes all day. Fooled around all morning. Lunch at the Tea Rose. Went down town, got a new pocketbook. Went to school, stayed to see part of the Beau Brummel presentation. Came up to the house with John and Kathleen. Made a date for tomorrow night with Carl Gregory. Got dressed for the reception which was held here. Before the May Festival dinner at the Dining Hall 20 of us had a formal dinner at the Tea Rose. I had John Trumpy with me. Had a grand time at the dance. John has a Chrysler Roadster. We got charms for favors at the Senior Ball. Took Miss Parker and Miss Agar (Instructors in the Home Economics program) to the dance as guests.

Saturday, May 5, 1928

Had breakfast at the Tea Rose. Met Mrs. Robinson at 10:30. Showed her the exhibits here, then went to the organ recital in the auditorium. Went out to the field at 46th Street and had lunch. It was too hot to stay for the (college) races. Mrs. Robinson went shopping and I came back and slept. Carl couldn't come over as he had to go for a car they had stranded last night. Went down to school and saw "A Midsummer Night's Dream" and the crowning of the May Queen. No dance. George Custer walked up along with me.

Sunday, May 6, 1928

Marjorie came in at 12:00 last night and stayed with me. Ate over at the drugstore in the morning. Carl came over at 5:30 and took me to dinner at the Tea Rose. Spent the rest of the evening on the Practice House porch talking to Miss Parker.

211

Monday, May 7, 1928

Started the Carnegie exams at 9:00. June and I ate lunch at the Fenton. The exams were terrible. Everything I didn't know. Took more in the afternoon. Talked to Carl. John Joseph called and came over and took me over to the Tea Rose for dinner. His roommate, Paul Ryan, took Isabel Earhart. They were both feeling good, especially Joe.

It seemed so good to see him again. Talked to Helen, his girl, and I know she is cross at him. He had a date with her in the evening. Karl Rowles took me down to the Stanley. Was over at his apartment first. Am crazy about him.

Tuesday, May 8, 1928

Talked to Karl and Ark a minute. Letter from Bill. Took exams today again. All finished now. Wrote to Bill. Student Government Board meeting after dinner. The Board had to suspend Ruth Powell for the rest of this term. Studied some Chem. I only hope Trumpy asks me to their spring formal on the 25th, but it is doubtful.

Wednesday, May 9, 1928

Class at 9:00. Chem quiz today and I didn't know a thing. Another board meeting after dinner, then a house board meeting. Wrote to Mama.

Thursday, May 10, 1928

Wrote to Alice. Chem lab in the morning. Worked on Home Ec. 25 term paper all afternoon in the library. Studied and wrote letters in the evening.

Friday, May 11, 1928

Got up early and went down to the Children's Hospital for an hour. Worked on term paper. Talked to Trumpy a minute. Came up to the house about 1:30. Found a note saying that Bill Jackson was home and wanted me to come out to dinner. Could hardly believe it. He tried to call, but I finally called him at 5:15. He came in about 6:30. Went out to his house for dinner. Herb and Jimmy Hall came over until 10:30. Then Mr. and Mrs. Jackson went to bed. I love Bill more every time I see him.

Saturday, May 12, 1928

Class at 9:00. Sewed some. A bunch of us got Mrs. Scott flowers for Mother's Day—tomorrow. Got onions and cheese and had a little feed up in my room.

Sunday, May 13, 1928

Wrote to Mama and Bill. Didn't go to church, Mother's Day, too. Looked for Bill or a call from him, but was very much disappointed. Finished Home Ec. 25 term paper. Alice was here for a few minutes on her way out to school.

Monday, May 14, 1928

Cooked over at Dining Room (D.R.) of the Home Economics classrooms all morning. Just spoke to Trumpy, Carl G. and Ark. Karl Rowles called in the evening. Worked some.

Tuesday, May 15, 1928

Worked at D. R. again all morning. Quiz in Home Ec. 25. Not so good. Talked to Carl awhile. Trumpy looks at me so queerly; I only wish he would talk. Ark highhats me mostly. All 3 are a pain mostly. Hope to hear from Bill, "dear" man. Wrote to Alice.

Wednesday, May 16, 1928

Morning classes were cut short because of a longer assembly, a play, "The Robbery." Nice letter from Bill. Wonder if he likes me better than he used to. Am hoping he asks me up for June House Party. Wrote him in the evening over at the Penn Library.

Thursday, May 17, 1928

Worked in the library for a couple of hours. Carl came in and talked a couple of minutes. Heard that Ark and Ann Gross were "practically" engaged since the Senior Ball.

Friday, May 18, 1928

Went down to school and got a special from Miss Dorsey. Cut Home Ec. 28. Went out to Beaver College, meeting Marjorie Wall on the train. Had May Day Pageant in the afternoon. Went to the movies at Jenkintown in the evening. Wrote Mama.

Saturday, May 19, 1928

Had lunch at Cathay. Called June. Went to the movies and saw "The Shephard of the Hills." Went to Karl Rowles' apartment. He took Alice and M. and me to dinner at Fay's. Lester Long from DuBois was along. Went back out to Beaver on the 10:30 train.

Sunday, May 20, 1928

Went out on a date with Jane Heath and Warren Steel from School. Had dinner at Brynwood Manor.[283] Drove all around all afternoon. Had a close call with a cop… .

Monday, May 21, 1928

Wrote Mama and Bill. Worked in the cafeteria all morning. Passed Ark twice and he didn't speak. Never saw such ignorance before. It rather hurts me to have anyone act that way, especially when I didn't do a thing to him. Went over to Gertrude McMasters with Al Dorsett after dinner.

Tuesday, May 22, 1928

Letter from Bill inviting me up to the June House Party—am so excited! Letter from Mama. Wrote and asked for permission—if I only get it now real soon, I can hardly wait. Asked Jimmy Hall to the Freshman-Senior dance; he is coming. Talked to Mrs. Jackson. Wrote to Bill and Alice Wall. Studied some.

Wednesday, May 23, 1928

Went down town for a couple of hrs. before Assembly. Karl Rowles called in the evening. <u>Wanted a date,</u> but I couldn't stand one with him.

---

[283] At the time (beginning in 1926) this area in Narbeth was being developed with upscale family homes, one of the early developments of the areas around Philadelphia.

Thursday, May 24, 1928

Class at 9:00. Went shopping. Got white shoes. Met June and tried to get a hat. Alice called after dinner. Went over to John's apartment with Kathleen.

Friday, May 25, 1928

Have the letter saying I can go to the House Party! Wrote to Mama and Bill. Didn't have any classes today. Lunch at the Tea Rose. Worked on Home Ec. 25 cards in the afternoon. Talked to Ark – half a minute. Phi Kappa Beta Spring Formal—rather wish I was there, but don't know who with.

Saturday, May 26, 1928

Chem at 9:00. In the evening Carl Gregory called. We were going to the movies but went too late, came back to the fraternity house—drank gin and ginger ale. Did I feel queer when I came in—not much. He kissed me for the 1st time.

Sunday, May 27, 1928

Met Bud Smith at Childs on 15th. Went down to Navy Yards, Independence Hall, and all around the Park. Went out to Robinsons awhile. Went to tea at Practice House. Kathleen and John are the cooks this week. Had a fire in the fireplace and sat there all evening. Enjoyed it so much. Bud said he wanted to see me again—I wonder.

Monday, May 28, 1928

Class all day. Worked in the library till after 5:00. Got Bill's lighter today. Hope it is all right; am worried about it.

Tuesday, May 29, 1928

Classes till 5:00. Fixed evening dress. Went to Freshman-Senior dance at Bala Cynwyd Country Club. Took Jimmy Hall. Had a real nice time.

Wednesday, May 30, 1928, Memorial Day

No School today. Wrote to Mama and Bill. Wrote letters after dinner. Went down to Edith Shaw and Edna Chasen's apt. at 1626 Spruce Street. The cutest place. Had tea there. Studied in the evening.

Thursday, May 31, 1928

Chem. lab all morning. Wrote Alice. She is coming in tomorrow. Went down town, got a hat. Hat dinner at the Practice House. Had more fun, no teacher was there. Studied in the evening.

Friday, June 1, 1928

Got my written permission to go to the House party and stay until Monday night. Went down to Kent Day Nursery in the afternoon and helped teach a Nutritional Class. Alice was at house when I got home. She stayed all night with E. Shaw. Went to the Freshman Frolic with Carl Gregory. Had a good time, but the music wasn't so hot. It was, however, a hot night.

Saturday, June 2, 1928

Took Chem final at 9:00. It wasn't so bad. I hope the Foods part isn't much worse. Had lunch at King Joy. Ran into Margie Thorn. Got a pair of green shoes.

Sunday, June 3, 1928

Got up for breakfast. Studied in the morning. Had dinner at Practice House. Took walk with John Wandall in the afternoon. Studied for Home Ec. 28 final.

Monday, June 4, 1928

Took Nutrition final in the morning. Not so bad. Checked out my Chemistry apparatus. Studied Chemistry in the evening. Can hardly wait till Friday. Got train ticket today.

Tuesday, June 5, 1928

Studied all morning for the Chem quiz. Didn't know much, but I hope enough for a 65. Wrote to Bill. Studied Home Ec. 25 in the evening. Had House Meeting after dinner.

Wednesday, June 6, 1928

Took Quantity Cooking exam in the morning. It was not so good. Had assembly today, awarded the honors. My last assembly. Met Alice Wall downtown. She had her Commencement this morning and went home this afternoon. Karl Rowles brought Alice's present to me.

Thursday, June 7, 1928

No classes today. Went down to school for a few minutes. Had hair curled. E. Shaw and Edna Chasen came up for dinner. Fooled around in the evening. Wrote to Alice.

State College

Friday, June 8, 1928

Did a dumb trick this morning. Looked at the clock wrong and got up an hour early. Was already to go to breakfast at 6:45. Was in a fog. Dressed and packed. Took 10:30 train for Tyrone. Bill met me. A gang of girls got off for the house parties. Took our time driving to State. Had dinner. Then went down to the apartment and got Prof. Harris and went up to a musical at an auditorium. (Note: This is Schwab Auditorium[284]) It rained hard all night. Went back to the house and got into evening dress. Dance till 2:00. Went to Phi K. Sigma and Kappa Sigma and Sigma Chi. Saw Mary Lou Warner on Saturday night at Kapa Sigma House. Sat out in car in front of house until 4:00 a.m. It was daylight when I went to bed. Had a grand time. Bill told me he loved me—the first time. I love him so much.

Saturday, June 9, 1928

Got up and went downstairs about 11:00. Bill came in about 12:00. It rained all morning and afternoon. Had lunch at the house. Went to the movies in the afternoon. Mr. and Mrs. Jackson and Bill's aunt came about 5:00. Had dinner then went up to the apartment and

---

[284] Schwab Auditorium was the first Penn State building financed by a private gift from Bethlehem Steel Corporation founder Charles M. Schwab. Completed in 1903, Schwab houses a proscenium stage and a 900-seat seating area, and is the home of the Penn State Thespians of which this author is a member.

talked. Went up to the house and got dressed. Had a wonderful time. Informal dance. Went to S.A.E. house and P.K. Sigma. Mrs. Jackson was at the DU House for a while. I went down to the COOP[285] and ate. Parked in front of the house again till 4:00. When we went in almost everyone was still up and the chaperones were in bed—thank goodness.

Sunday, June 10, 1928
Bill called on phone—then Mr. and Mrs. Jackson came and got me. Went downtown and had breakfast at Blue Moon. Went to Baccalaureate Service. Met Bill afterwards. Went up to the House. Had dinner, then went calling over to Phi Kappa Sigma and to Jones' home. At 4:30 met Bill Prichard and his girl. Drove over to Water Street for dinner. Went over to the house where Jacksons are staying and talked awhile.

Came back to the fraternity house. Sat in front of the place till 3 o'clock, alone for 2 hrs. It was wonderful. **Had my first, last, and only proposal.** It was too wonderful to understand. I love Bill. If anything should now happen between us, I don't know what I would do.

Monday, June 11, 1928
Never got awake until Bill came for me at 10:30. Went down to the Co-Op and had breakfast. Met the Jacksons at the house and had lunch there. Parked to come back. Then went up to the Ball Game and Bill and I went up to the apartment. Intended to go to the game—but just didn't. He was so sweet. Never said goodbye to anyone. Never left State till 3:20. Made the 4:20 train at Tyrone. I hated to leave after such a wonderful time.

Philadelphia

Tuesday, June 12, 1928
Went down to school after breakfast. Studied Chem all morning. Made 85 on the last quiz. Took final in the afternoon. If only I pass it. Studied for Physics Final in evening with Ruth Miller. Mrs. Kittelberger called. Only wish Bill would call—but tomorrow—I can hardly wait. Did some packing.

Wednesday, June 13, 1928
Passed Chem with a 65. Am so glad. Took Phy final in the morning. My last exam in Drexel. Not at all sorry. Had lunch at Tea Rose. Packed trunk. Bill didn't call, so at 8:15 I called him, as I was worried sick. They never left till this morning. I had just been home a short time and he was going to call me. Am not going to see him tonight; he is calling at noon tomorrow. June had a big party up in our room—the whole house.

Thursday, June 14, 1928
Bill called about 12:30. Mama and Papa came about 1:00. Went down to Friends Hotel for lunch. Papa went down to Bromes in New Jersey. Mama and I shopped. Saw Mrs. K. at Stukes. She gave me a cute bracelet. Met Mama and came out to house for dinner. Bill came about 8:30. Took Kathleen over to John's; we stayed awhile; it was so awful hot.

[285] Preceded the HUB

Went down to Edith Shaw's and stayed all night. Kathleen and I both stayed. Kenny was down there and so tight. We all drank beer. Bill left about 2:00.

Friday, June 15, 1928

Came up to the house about 9:00, dressed and went down to school to practice for our Commencement. Mama came up at 12:00 and we went up to the hairdressers. Had lunch at a little tea room. Went down town and got her dress, got white gloves. Got my Commencement gift, a beautiful diamond ring. I just love it. Ran into Bill and his Mother in Wanamaker's.

I wonder—will he give me a fraternity pin?? Wish he would, for I love him so much. Mama and I came out to school for the President's reception for the seniors. Papa came out later. They had dinner with Mr. and Mrs. Jim Norris.

Saturday, June 16, 1928

The Home Economics faculty gave a breakfast at the cafeteria for 4-year Senior Home Ec. girls. It was so nice. Came up to the house and finished packing and sent my trunk off. Went over to Edith Shaw's, then met E. Newton and Milly Larkin and had dinner at the Golden Dragon. Went out to Mrs. Green's with June who got 2 diamonds, one from her Mother and one from her Father. Ironed gown later in the evening.

Sunday, June 17, 1928

Got up about 8:00. Went to breakfast. Had Baccalaureate at the M.E. Church at 33rd and Chestnut-Asbury. The President of Beaver College delivered the message. Mama and Papa were there. Afterwards had dinner at Tea Rose. Drove down to John Browne's and stayed till late. Saw Helen. Bill called about 4:00. Marjorie Wall and E. Shaw were both here and I wasn't home. Came in at 10:00. Talked to Mrs. Jackson.

Monday, June 18, 1928

GRADUATION DAY. Had breakfast at Home Ec. D. R. Last meal there. Went down to school about 9:30. Saw Mama and Papa and Bill and Mrs. Jackson. Got hood and put on cap and gown. Had Commencement. Over at 11:50. Jacksons went on home. Mama and I had lunch with Mrs. K. and Papa went to New York. Had dinner in the eve. with Bill at the Arcadia. Saw movie at the Stanley. Went over to E. Shaw's apartment. Kathleen and John were there, but John left early. Bill stayed till about 1:00. I hated to say good-bye. He was so sweet tonight.

Tuesday, June 19, 1928

Got up about 8:00. Went out to the house and finished packing. Papa, Mama and Kenny came about 9:00. Stopped at Harrisburg, went up to the Capitol. Got into Huntingdon about 6:00. Had dinner and went to the movies in the evening. Was dead tired.

Wednesday, June 20, 1928

Went to Commencement exercises at the Reformatory. Ate a lot. Left for home about 5:30. Went up to Mama Spencer's house and down to Aunt Grace's. Went to bed early.

Within a week, Mary Alice and a friend from Drexel were on their way west. Her son later recalled his mother's cross-country adventure that summer of 1928, "This was still a pretty wild country west of the Mississipppi River when she graduated in 1928, yet she and a roommate hopped in her little Chevrolet coupe and drove cross country to California, part of the way on two lane dirt roads—not something usually undertaken by the sweet young ladies of the day."

Even-tempered as Mary Alice was, it is likely that once she began teaching, the classroom became her main focus for the first several months as she became accustomed to a regimented school schedule. Years later when I was old enough to notice, Mary Alice's practicality and level-headedness remained the core of who she was, and pragmatism with kindness remained her trademark throughout her life.

Even her Dairy writing style never changed during the four years of college and her basic grounded foundation remained with her, although the entries expectedly became longer in length after her Freshman year, moving with a confident stride as she matured.

However, something did change with her 1929 Diary: The entries are shorter, maybe because the new 1929 Diary notebook is greatly reduced in size—less than half the size of her earlier notebooks with only five lines given for each entry. More importantly, and what I find very puzzling is that when I began to read this 1929 Diary—beginning with January 1, I sensed a completely different "tone." Most striking was its lack of joy and light-heartedness that had been the hallmark of the college diary entries. Even though many of her phrases are similar to the delight expressed in the first four years of diary entries, these newer ones have far less emotion than the entries during the college years—a change that suggests more than just being a year older and no longer a college co-ed. In fact, this diary is more an appointment book than anything else.

And even more startling is that Bill Jackson does not appear to be a primary player in the first several months of entries.

In the fall of 1928 Mary Alice began teaching Home Economics at the Clearfield Junior High. She knew many of the faculty, in particular Katherine "Tat" Thorne and they shared many interests and friends in common.

As Mary Alice indicated, she did not keep a diary for the remainder of the calendar year, maintaining only a shadow version of her exuberant Drexel Diaries.

1929

Curwensville

Tuesday January 1, 1929
Slept till 12:30. Was in bed at 6:00 a.m. Took Mama to Clearfield. Talked to Ted. He doesn't feel well. Is not coming down.

Wednesday, January 2, 1929
School again. Saw Eddie at the "Pig" after school. Date with Ted in the evening.

Thursday, January 3, 1929
Eddie after school. Had a little fuss. Brought Papa home. Bed at 9:30.

Friday, January 4, 1929
Saw Eddie after school. Up home for dinner. Basketball game with Tat. Eddie played cards at Kurtz. Bill F. and Tat. Ride to Philipsburg. Pete Barney.

Saturday, January 5, 1929
Up late and home all morning. Said Goodbye to Cora. Mama to Clearfield. Good-bye to Eddie. Ted didn't come down. Roads are terrible.

Sunday, January 6, 1929, 1929
Didn't go to church. Home all day. Ted came at 4:00. Up to Snyder's to Barnesboro. Left at 1:00. Wonderful time.

Monday, January 7, 1929
Eddie still here. Went to see him after school; has bronchitis. Home and bed early.

Tuesday, January 8, 1929

Eddie's for dinner. Movies with Vilma Banky in "The Awakening." Tat and Bill came up here along. Stayed till 1:00.

Wednesday, January 9, 1929

Lost ring at school today. Hope to find it. Home right after school. Wonderful date with Ted. Movies in Clearfield.

Thursday, January 10, 1929

Baked cake after school. Got great. Ted called after school and he was so sweet. I can never talk right when he calls.

Friday, January 11, 1929

Car washed. Worked on it in the eve. Tat's for lunch. Talked to Ted on phone at noon. Home in evening. Ted called in eve.

Saturday, January 12, 1929

Papa's birthday. Baked him a cake. Up to Ann and Bob O'Grady's at Glen Campbell with Ted. Indiana in the evening. In bed at 3:00. Letter from Eddie.

Sunday, January 13, 1929

Awake about 8:00. Breakfast at 10. Dressed and helped get dinner. Made biscuits. Ted was wonderful. Date till 2:45.

Monday, January 14, 1929

Overslept till 7:30. Shoes at Lytle's. Ted dear called. Mama in not so good humor. Phil to bed. Wrote to Ted, Eddie and Alice.

Tuesday, January 15, 1929

2nd letter from Eddie. Talked to Ted at noon. Baked cake in eve and wrote Eddie.

Wednesday, January 16, 1929

Tat's for dinner. Gave one bridge party. 3 tables, Junior High School teachers. Was dead tired. It went off fine.

Thursday, January 17, 1929

Date with Ted. Movies at Clearfield. Tom, Don, Lib Wall and King. Stayed late.

Friday, January 18, 1929

Dinner and bridge at Park House with Lib Wall's bridge club. Could hardly stay awake.

Saturday, January 19, 1929

Baked a cake and muffins. Date with Ted. DuBois to the movies. Stayed late. 6 of us.

Sunday, January 20, 1929

No church. Lib Wall's for dinner, 6 of us. Moved fridge. Drove to Clearfield in afternoon. All here awhile.

Monday, January 21, 1929

Ted called. Talked to Orlie Norris about Bill Jackson—I am all upset about everything. Wish this was three years from now.

Tuesday, January 22, 1929

No classes all day. Fooled around. Home early. Ted called; couldn't come down, snow and sleet; roads bad.

Wednesday, January 23, 1929

Intended to go to Bellefonte and couldn't. Movies in afternoon. Date with Ted. Lib Wall and Don here all eve. Played bridge.

Thursday, January 24, 1929

School all day. Took things to donate to poor people. Movies alone at the Strand. "The Love Mart."[286]

Friday, January 25, 1929

Home right after school. Back (to Clearfield) for Papa. Alice [Wall] home yesterday. Played bridge. Lib, Alice and Hugh.

Saturday, January 26, 1929

Home all day. Date with Ted. Movie at Clearfield. Went to Walls for a while.

Sunday, January 27, 1929

Didn't go to church. Phil and I up to Mama Spencer's for dinner. Ted, Don, Tom and Lib Wall down in the apartment. Lib King's for big turkey dinner. Alice went back. She wasn't invited to this.

Monday, January 28, 1929

Called Ted at noon. Talked to Ann. Wrote letters in evening.

Tuesday, January 29, 1929

Saw Frances Custer after school. Got a new coat. To bed early. Up the street after school.

Wednesday, January 30, 1929

Date with Ted. Movies at Clearfield. Saw Kay Custer.

Thursday, January 31, 1929

A sled load. Everett Davis went along. Went to Mrs. Jenson's (McFerson's) camp. Date at Tats and stayed all night.

---

[286] "The Love Mart" is a 1927 American silent drama film featuring Boris Karloff with Billie Dove and Gilbert Roland.

Friday, February 1, 1929

Took Johnny Leitzinger for a ride. Talked to Everett. Movies with Phil in the evening. Bed early. Letter from Bill Jackson.

Saturday, February 2, 1929

Went upstreet in the morning, Clearfield in the afternoon with Mama. Date with Ted. Don and Elizabeth Wall were down and played bridge.

Sunday, February 3, 1929

Home all day. Talked to Ted, was going up, but didn't. Wrote letters and did school work.

Monday, February 4, 1929

Freshmen Dinner every day this week. Dead tired. Home all evening.

Tuesday, February 5 , 1929

Talked to Ted at noon. Fixed draperies. Home all evening. Up at Walls after school.

Wednesday, February 6, 1929

Shopped for food for Freshmen Party. Saw Eddie Hile up the street on way home from Ann Arbor. Date with Ted up at Walls. Cake for Don. Had a long talk with Eddie[287] after school.

Thursday, February 7, 1929

Home late. Made candy for Alice. Was dead tired.

Friday, February 8, 1929

Freshman Class Party. Came up home and back down to school. Had a real good time Danced with some Freshmen boys.

Saturday, February 9, 1929

Up late. Hair washed in afternoon. Went to see Mama Spencer and Aunt Grace. Date Ted. Home all evening.

Sunday, February 10, 1929

Home all morning. Elizabeth Wall and I went up to Burnside and Barnesboro. Home at 9:00.

Monday, February 11, 1929

Eddie after school. Made candy for Marjorie. Eddie up unexpectedly. Stayed till 1:30.

Tuesday, February 12, , 1929

J.B.T.[288] dance at the Dimeling with Ted. Best time. Home 1:30. Mailed Valentines.

Wednesday, February 13, , 1929

Shopped for 7th grade party. Home all evening. Wrote letters.

287 Based on the wording, this Eddie may be Eddie Hile.
288 Junior Board of Trade.

Thursday, February 14, 1929

Flowers from Ted. Valentine. Ellis Keller up for dinner. Took him home later. Played bridge.

Friday, February 15, 1929

Home late after school. 7th grade party. Down in evening.

Saturday, February 16, 1929

Intended on going to Bellefonte, but didn't. Clearfield in afternoon. New dress and hat. Date with Ted in evening.

Sunday, February 17, 1929

Mama and Papa went to Pittsburgh. Ted, Don, Tom, Lib Wall and Lib King here for dinner. Ride to Mahaffey in afternoon. Back here all evening.

Monday, February 18, 1929

Hard day at school. Up to Mama Spencer's home all evening. Corrected papers.

Tuesday, February 19, 1929

Things for 8th grade party. Clearfield movies. "Abbey's Irish Rose" with Lib Wall.

Wednesday, February 20, 1929

Brought Junior High School Boys up for the basketball game. Mr. Beggs for dinner. Date with Ted. Made up again about last Sunday.

Thursday, February 21, 1929

School was late. 8th grade Home Economics served the 8th grade lunch. Home all evening. Phil's lessons. Went to bed early.

Friday, February 22, 1929

Audrey Hyde's wedding today. Was not invited. Made sandwiches after school. 8th grade party this evening. Home, 11:30.

Saturday, February 23, 1929

Clearfield in the afternoon. Up street. Date with Ted. Movies at Clearfield.

Sunday, February 24, 1929

Home all day. Jessie and Kate were down. Naomi is home. Helped get dinner. Served. Later wrote letters.

Monday, February 25, 1929

Came home right after school. Corrected papers.

Tuesday, February 26, 1929

Mama and Papa went to Bellefonte. Helped Philip with his lessons. Went to bed early.

Wednesday, February 27, 1929

Date with Ted. Played bridge up at Wall's. (Thompsons had moved into their newly built home at 517 Lower State Street in 1927.)

Thursday, February 28, 1929

Basketball game at Jr. H. S. Clearfield vs. Curwensville.

Friday, March 1, 1929

Basketball game in the evening. Curwensville & Indiana. C-ville lost. Box of candy from Ted. Bet on Sharky winning the fight.[289]

Saturday, March 2, 1929

Up late. Date with Ted. Went up to Walls. Alice came home.

Sunday, March 3, 1929

Mama and Papa left for Philadelphia at 7:00. Ted here for dinner. Got "Freddie" Brooks for Kenny Wall.

Monday, March 4, 1929

School all day. Phil is sick. Hoover inaugurated today.

Tuesday, March 5, 1929

Came home right after school. Basketball game. Clearfield Jr. High School and Curwensville. Cur. won. Tat here for dinner.

Wednesday, March 6, 1929

Went to see Lenore after school. Date with Ted. He was elected cashier of the Glen Campbell Bank.

Thursday, March 7, 192

To see Lenore after school. Went up street. She leaves tonight. Have all evening appropriated to Mama Spencer.

Friday, March 8, 1929

To Mama Spencer's after school. Movies at Clearfield with Tat.

Saturday, March 9, 1929

Baked cakes. Shopped in Bellefonte and did banking. Ted, Don and Lib Wall. Stayed late there. Mama and Papa came home.

Sunday, March 10, 1929

Ted called at noon. Up to Glen Campbell[290] in the afternoon and to Barnesboro. Dinner at Snyders.

---

[289] Rickard died unexpectedly and all preparations ceased.
[290] A very small borough in Indiana County.

Monday, March 11, 1929

In school late. Waited for Papa. Home all eve. In bed early.

Tuesday, March 12, 1929

Brought Evelyn Ogden up. She was hired for Papa and at Mama Spencer's all night. Went to the movies.

Wednesday, March 13, 1929

Home late after school. Date with Ted. Home all evening. Am going to stop Friday afternoon.

Thursday, March 14, 1929

Hair fixed. Dot Wolf. Mr. and Mrs. Rice here in the evening and played cards.

Friday, March 15, 1929

Went to Pittsburgh after school. Stopped at Indiana. Sam M. Gates there. Date with J. Martin, Penn Alto. Had dinner and danced.

Saturday, March 16, 1929

Saw E. Newton, Al Dorsett and the Karstetters. Went to Flotilla Club.[291] Danced and socialized. To bed at 3:45.

Sunday, March 17, 1929

Ate lunch in East Liberty. Saw Joe before leaving at 3:30. Home at 8:30. Stopped in Indiana for late dinner at Bruner's.

Monday, March 18, 1929

No classes in the afternoon. 8th grade play. Home at 4:30.

Tuesday, March 19, 1929

Movies after school. Took Tat and Margie down to school in the evening for the play. Home early.

Wednesday, March 20, 1929

Home late from school. Date with Ted. Basketball game and dance at Mahaffey. Not so good.

Thursday, March 21, 1929

Teachers Meeting. Worked on Basketball dinner. Movies in evening at Clearfield with Lib Wall. "Battle of the Sexes."[292]

Friday, March 22, 1929

At school nearly all day. Served Jr. High School Basketball Team Banquet. Was dead tired. Glad it is all over.

---

291 Built in 1924 on what is now Monongahela Wharf. The Club no longer exists.
292 1928 American comedy film directed by D. W. Griffith, starring Jean Hersholt.

Saturday, March 23, 1929

Up late. Baked a cake. Went to Margie's announcement party. It was so nice. Date Ted. Rode to Clearfield. Saw Tat and Margie for a while.

Sunday, March 24, 1929

Kenny, Lib Wall and I rode up to Ted's, then to Barnesboro. Saw Harry and Al at Snyders, also Tat and Margie. Ate at Chatterbox in Clearfield.

Monday, March 25, 1929

Mid-semester exams at school. Big teachers' dinner. Trostle, Spencer, Breth, Ross, Mitchell[293] and Tat and I. Went to a movie after.

Tuesday, March 26, 1929

Out of school early. Called Ted at noon. He called in evening.

Wednesday, March 27, 1929

Home all day. Got lunch, baked a cake. Pressed. House cleaning my room. Date with Ted in evening. Got along great.

Thursday, March 28, 1929

Sent Eddie Hile a birthday card. Talked to John Leitzinger. Clearfield in the afternoon with Tat. In evening home. Flowers for Mama Spencer.

Friday, March 29, 1929

Up street shopping. Worked around home. Went to Tyrone for Marjorie. Lib King went along. Date with Eddie, home unexpected. Marjorie with Zetler.

Saturday, March 30, 1929

Colored Easter eggs. Iced cake. Clearfield in afternoon. Saw Eddie. He wanted a date. I had a date with Ted. With Alice and Hugh.

Sunday, March 31, 1929

Easter Sunday. Church. Groff Acres for a lunch with Ted. Stopped at Alice's and down to Tat's. Ted down in afternoon–evening and home early.

Monday, April 1, 1929

Didn't get fooled once. Went to Easter Dance at DuBois. Had a nice time, although nearly everyone was wearing formal except our crowd.

Tuesday, April 2, 1929

Up late. Last long morning for a while. Went to Clearfield in the afternoon and movies in the evening with Marjorie and Tat.

---

293 Speculation by the author based on the names found in this diary is that many young men taught a year or so, then moved into businesses.

Wednesday, April 3, 1929

First day after vacation. Didn't feel so good all day. Ride in the evening with Marjorie and Clyde Pifer. Talked to Ted on the phone.

Thursday, April 4, 1929

Talked to Ted on the phone at noon. Dead tired. Marjorie and Viola visited school in the afternoon. Movies in the evening.

Friday, April 5, 1929

Didn't feel so good. Took medicine. Marjorie had a bridge party in the eve. Ted, Dan, Tom, Lib W., Lib King, Tat, Viola, B. Shaw, Ann Clark, Marjorie and I.

Saturday, April 6, 1929

Up street in morning. Drove to Bellefonte with Aunt Grace and Uncle Charley, Marjorie and Viola. Movies in eve with Lib Wall and Louise Decker.

Sunday, April 7, 1929

Talked to Eddie. Mama/Papa in Bellefonte. Home alone. Lunch at Aunt Grace's. Ted down in aft. Tat, Bill, Kenny and Mauvis. Groff Acres for dinner.

Monday, April 8, 1929

School till late. Talked to Eddie quite a while. Home all eve. Mama in bad humor — I must find out.

Tuesday, April 9, 1929

Movies after school with Tat. Talked to Eddie a minute. Home all evening. Put initials on handkerchiefs for Bubby.

Wednesday, April 10, 1929

Bubby's birthday. 25 years. Home late from school. Wrote letters in evening. Home all evening.

Thursday, April 11, 1929

Up to Lib Wall's awhile. Called Eddie in evening and said good-bye. Date with Ted. Down to Tat's. Played bridge and danced.

Friday, April 12, 1929

Ellis called. Bobby's father had a stroke. Can't visit them. Left after school. Stayed at Lycoming Hotel.[294] Up to Williamsport (Muncy) Normal School.

Saturday, April 13, 1929

Ted's 26th birthday. Home Ec. Meeting in Williamsport. Breakfast. Lunch. Speeches. Saw Libby Wilson. Lost car key. In Bellefonte at 12:00.

---

[294] The Genetti Hotel was built in 1921 in the midst of Williamsport's huge logging boom. The hotel opened in 1922 as the Lycoming Hotel.

227

Sunday, April 14, 1929

Met Bill Jackson 2 years ago on this date. Home at 11:30. Up to Ted's for his birthday dinner. A real nice time all day. Up at Walls in the evening.

Monday, April 15, 1929

Up to see Margaret Fowler. Worked at home all evening. Tired.

Tuesday, April 16, 1929

Mama Spencer's birthday. Got her some flowers. Date with Ted.

Wednesday, April 17, 1929

Home right after school. Did dishes. Home in evening.

Thursday, April 18, 1929

Movies after school. Wrote letters in evening.

Friday, April 19, 1929

Home after school. Lib Wall and I went out in the woods for arbutus.[295] Movies at the Strand, "Street Angel."[296]

Saturday, April 20, 1929

Baked two angel food cakes in the morning. Took Mama to Clearfield in the afternoon. No Ted. Weather is bad. Had date with Hugh. Up to Holtens.

Sunday, April 21, 1929

Ted down in the afternoon. Here for supper. Also Don and Lib Wall. Mrs. Jim Norris came up from Philadelphia. Ritz Theatre in the evening.

Monday, April 22, 1929

Home right after school. Phil dressed to go to Clearfield opening of the new Ritz.[297] Date with Everett Davis. All right with Tat.

Tuesday, April 23, 1929

Home all evening. Put Philip to bed. Wrote letters.

Wednesday, April 24, 1929

Up to Aunt Grace's. Lib Wall and I to movies at the Ritz. "The Bellamy Trial." Ted called at 11:00. Will be down on Saturday.

Thursday, April 25, 1929

Home after school. Hard rain. Wrote letters in the evening.

---

[295] Shrubs and trees of the heath family with white or pink flowers and red or orange berries.
[296] One of three movies for which Janet Gaynor received an Academy Award for Best Actress in 1929.
[297] Owned by H. J. Thompson. This was the premiere.

Friday, April 26, 1929

No school in the afternoon. County Debates in the auditorium all morning. Movies in the afternoon. "Redskin."[298] Then, at home in the evening.

Saturday, April 27, 1929

Hair washed and curled. Up street shopping with Mrs. Norris. Clearfield in the afternoon. Date with Ted in the evening, but not many more, I fear.

Sunday, April 28, 1929

Home all morning. Went to Burnside in the afternoon, then to Ebensburg for dinner. Big fuss with Ted.

Monday, April 29, 1929

Ted called for a date tomorrow night. Billie McClure and Ray Wiley from Altoona came up and got Lib Wall and me.

Tuesday, April 30, 1929

Big day at school. Lunch with Ray Wiley. Not so good. Date in eve with Ted to see Mary Pickford in "Coquette"[299] and up to Tat's for a birthday party.

Wednesday, May 1, 1929

Tat's Birthday. Busy all day getting ready to leave at 4:05 and in Lititz at 10:30. Saw Kenny. Stayed with Alice (Wall).

Thursday, May 2, 1929

In Philly about noon. Lost an hour. Shopped all afternoon. Saw Miss Dorsey and some of the girls at Tea Rose. At the new Mastbaum in the evening.

Friday, May 3, 1929

Breakfast and dinner at the Tea Rose. Lunch at Whitman's. Saw Lucinda Clark. Senior Ball with Harry Gardner, then out till 4:00 with June and Lois.

Saturday, May 4, 1929

Shopped. Met Marjorie (now living in Norristown). Earlanger Theatre in afternoon. Met Alice. Marjorie and I to Jacksons for dinner. Mrs. Norris there. Tower Theatre.[300]

Sunday, May 5, 1929

Over to Park and out to Marguerite Thorpe's to see Cecil. Dinner at Golden Tea. Alice to Lititz, 5:30. Home at 12:00. Tire trouble.

Monday, May 6, 1929

School all day. Not out at noon. Home all evening. Ted called.

---

[298] A 1929 American film with a synchronized score and sound effects, partially in Technicolor. Its final six minutes were shown in Magnascope, an enlarged-screen projection novelty.

[299] Pickford's first "talkie."

[300] Built new in 1927 near 69th Street.

Tuesday, May 7, 1929

Up to Mama Spencer's and Aunt Grace's. Movie date with Ted.

Wednesday, May 8, 1929

Home late. Went down to movies. Took Phil and Mama.

Thursday, May 9, 1929

Up street after school. Awful tired. Home all eve. Wrote letters.

Friday, May 10, 1929

Home for lunch. Took nap after school. Dance at Punxsutawney with Ted, Tat, and Bill Horne. Home at 3:30.

Saturday, May 11, 1929

Took Mama Spencer to Clearfield. Did shopping. Planted and fixed flowers. Home all eve. Pressed and mended.

Sunday, May 12, 1929

Mother's Day. Mama and Papa Spencer down for dinner. Date with Ted. Kenny with H. Weaver. Up to Barnesboro. Another battle.

Monday, May 13, 1929

Tired all day. Stayed after school until 8:00 and helped girls sew. Movies alone.

Tuesday, May 14, 1929

Papa Spencer's birthday. Got him a box of candy. Up to the Walls awhile in the evening.

Wednesday, May 15, 1929

Talked to Ellis Keller. May get me a new job. No school in afternoon because of practice for May Day. Lib Wall to movies in evening.

Thursday, May 16, 1929

Rain nearly all day. Jr. High teachers went up to Groff Acres for dinner. Date Ted. Went up for him. Ellis here.

Friday, May 17, 1929

No school. Practice in the morning. May Day at the Park in the afternoon. Walked over with kids. Drove Naomi to Westover in the evening.

Saturday, May 18, 1929

Took Mama to Clearfield. Baked cake and got lunch. Date with Ted in the evening. Up to Holtens. Jimmy was home and married. Alice was home.

Sunday, May 19, 1929

Helped get noon dinner. Ted called. Came down about 5:00. Got Alice and had dinner at the Chatterbox.

Monday, May 20, 1929

Home right at 5:00. Hair trimmed and permanent, 4 hrs.

Tuesday, May 21, 1929

Home late. Ted called. Home all eve. Dead tired.

Wednesday, May 22 , 1929

Wave reset. Home late for supper. Date with Ted. Movies. In bed rather late.

Thursday, May 23, 1929

Busy at school all day. Freshman Tea. Home all evening. Dead tired.

Friday, May 24, 1929

Another Tea. 8th grade. Cleaned up and went to movies.

Saturday, May 25, 1929

Out to camp in the afternoon and for supper to see the girls: Alice, Kate, Lib, Helen, F. Decker. Date with Ted out to camp until 1:30.

Sunday, May 26, 1929

Helped get dinner. Helen Weaver and I up to the Country Club near Barnesboro. Met Ted and had dinner there. Home early.

Monday, May 27, 1929

Up to Mama Spencer's after supper. Wrote letters and worked.

Tuesday, May 28, 1929

Hair waved in eve. Went to "The Singing Fool"[301] at the Ritz.

Wednesday, May 29, 1929

Worked on costumes. Aunt Maude and Mr. Stamp came. Ted called 3 times about the dance.

Thursday, May 30, 1929, Decoration Day

Worked with flowers in the morning. Baked a cake. Uncle Fred's kids here. Dance at Sunset in the evening with Ted. Home at 3:30.

Friday, May 31, 1929

School in the morning. Exams, wrote cards. Track meet in the afternoon. Movies with Mr. Stamp in the evening. Saw "The Broadway Melody."[302]

Saturday, June 1, 1929

Up late. Fooled around the house all day. Aunt Maude went back at noon. Date with Ted for Clearfield and up to Holtens.

---

[301] 1928 American musical drama Part-Talkie motion picture starring Al Jolson, a follow-up to "The Jazz Singer." It helped cement the popularity of American films of both sound and the musical genre.

[302] "The Broadway Melody" (1928-29), released in February of 1929, was billed as the first all-talking, all-singing, all-dancing motion picture.

Sunday, June 2, 1929

Up to Chetremon Country Club in Cherry Tree, Indiana County near Lookout Mountain. Took Rebecca Ardary with us. Met Hugh and Ted. Dinner at the Brandon Hotel in Spangler. Home early.

Monday, June 3, 1929

Exams in the morning. No classes in the afternoon. Freshmen are in the dress rehearsal this evening for their play. I got home late.

Tuesday, June 4, 1929

At School with Classes. Worked on continuous pressing of costumes. The play was this evening. Glad it's over. Got home late.

Wednesday, June 5, 1929

Classes and nothing for them to do. Rooms are a wreck after the play. Date with Ted in the evening for movies at the Ritz.

Thursday, June 6, 1929

Up late. Junior High School picnic at the park in Clearfield. Worked in the garden all evening. TIRED.

Friday, June 7, 1929

Last day of school. Just awhile in the morning. Teachers meeting in the afternoon. Tat and I chaperoned 14 girls to Goshen. They about drove us crazy.

Saturday, June 8, 1929

In from camp at 1:30. Date with Ted. Drove to Clearfield and to Park.

Sunday, June 9, 1929

Church in the morning. Rode to Clearfield in afternoon alone. Dave Franklin out to Kurtz and back. In bed early.

Monday, June 10, 1929

Worked around all day. Cleaned car. In evening Lib Wall and Helen and Louise Decker and I went to Mahaffey. Met Ted.

Tuesday, June 11, 1929

Letter today. Got job at Cape May. Clearfield all afternoon with Tat and Dot Dimeling. Over to the Park in the evening. Listened to music.

Wednesday, June 12, 1929

Tat, Dot Dimeling, and I drove to Philipsburg in the afternoon. Stayed all night with Tat. Date with Ted.

Thursday, June 13, 1929

Home late in the morning. Baby Clinic in afternoon. Mama and Papa at Bellefonte. Eddie (Miller) here awhile. Movies in evening with Lib Wall.

Friday, June 14, 1929

Clearfield in the afternoon. Met Eddie. He was here for supper. Dance at Triangle in the eve.

Saturday, June 15, 1929

Shopped in the morning. Wrote letters and sewed in the afternoon. Elizabeth, Alice and I went to the Ritz. Ted hasn't called since I last saw him.

Sunday, June 16, 1929

No word from Ted. Wonder what's wrong? Up at Alice's, went to Tyrone along. Home and in bed early.

Monday, June 17, 1929

One year ago tonight—my last date with Bill Jackson. Commencement at school. Clearfield in Jointure. "The Jazz Singer"[303] in the evening.

Tuesday, June 18, 1929

Dentist in the morning. Ted called, but didn't come down.

Wednesday, June 19, 1929

Left for Pittsburgh at 9:00. Stopped to see Ted. Arrived at 1:30. Wrote Ted. Margie, Tat and I saw "The Follies" at the Aldine (Pittsburgh's trailblazing theatre, ed.). Joe called.

Thursday, June 20, 1929

Shopped all morning with Tat. Hair waved. Met Margie and went to Penn to the movies and shopped. Date for Joe in evening. Went to the Willows and danced. In at 3:30.

Friday, June 21, 1929

Up late. Lunch and Breakfast together. Out to see Helen Kocher in the afternoon. Date with Joe in the evening. Out to Rogers Flying Field.

Saturday, June 22, 1929

Left at 9:00 for home. Home at 12:20. Went to see Ted. Crystal Springs all night. Ted, Jessie, Doc Hawes[304], Lib Wall, Hugh and Kate Sayers.

Sunday, June 23, 1929

Up late. Fooled around all day, rained hard. Home early. Dead tired.

---

[303] The first feature-length motion picture with not only a synchronized recorded music score but also lip-synchronous singing and speech in several isolated sequences. Its release ended the silent film era.
[304] The man Jessie would marry—for a short time.

Monday, June 24, 1929

Washed and ironed all day. Talked to Ted twice, but he didn't come down. Was disappointed. Packed trunk and sent it.

Tuesday, June 25, 1929

Julia and Bob Keeler. Over to Bellefonte in afternoon. Eddie Hile, Dick Langell, and Marjorie. Went to J. Bullocks wedding.

Wednesday, June 26, 1929

Left home at 10:45 heading to the shore. Got in Lititz at 4:30. Stayed all night with Alice.[305] Went into Lancaster in the evening.

Thursday, June 27, 1929

Up early, in Philadelphia by 10:30. Went shopping. Lunch at Golden Gate. Out to Jacksons for dinner and overnight.

Friday, June 28, 1929

J. Frankenfield's birthday. Shopping with Mrs. Jackson in morn. Drove to Cape May; arrived at 5:30. Down and danced in the evening.

Saturday, June 29, 1929

Up at 7:00. Work at 8:00. 2 hrs. off in afternoon. Unpacked trunk. Worked late. Down to pier in evening. Nothing exciting.

Sunday, June 30, 1929

Work at 8:00 a.m. Karl Rowles dropped in about nine. Took a ride. Also a ride in the evening with Ann, Millie, and some boys.

Monday, July 1, 1929

Worked all day, 8:00 till 9:00. No mail. Ted makes me tired.

Tuesday, July 2, 1929

Swimming in the afternoon for the first time. All alone—not so good. Went down on the pier for a while.

Wednesday, July 3, 1929

Down on the beach but not in the water. On pier again in the evening. Drove up to Wildwood and stopped for dinner.

Thursday, July 4, 1929

Busy today. Dead tired in the evening, but went down to the movies with Millie.

Friday, July 5, 1929

Getting tired of the place. Was dead tired today. Down on the boardwalk for a while in the evening.

234   [305] She was working in Lititz, but came home frequently.

Saturday, July 6, 1929

Worked 12 hours today. Went down on the pier awhile, but not a thing doing.

Sunday, July 7, 1929

Not so busy today. Slept in the afternoon and in bed early.

Monday, July 8, 1929

I am bothered about a letter from Mama. Down on the pier awhile in the evening.

Tuesday, July 9, 1929

In bathing; didn't get real wet as water was too cold. Home all evening. Received laundry from home.

Wednesday, July 10, 1929

Mailed laundry and washed things here. Not so busy. Ann and Millie had dates. Stayed here and went to bed early.

Thursday, July 11, 1929

Hair washed and waved. Very little business today. Chased 2 boys in their car. Drank beer at Merion.

Friday, July 12, 1929

Busier than usual. Went down on the pier and then went to the Merion and drank some more beer.

Saturday, July 13, 1929

Letter from Mama. Ted is going with someone else—he can go to the dickens now. Down on the pier awhile in the evenings. Paid again.

Sunday, July 14, 1929

Busy today. Up at the house on my time off. Had some beer. Down to a concert in the evening on the pier. Took gang for a ride down to McAdams.

Monday, July 15, 1929

Down on beach but not in. Cold today. Date with Jack, the singer. He gives me a pain.

Tuesday, July 16, 1929

In bathing today. Not so warm. Not very busy. Down on pier awhile. Millie and I went to a movie starring John Gilbert.

Wednesday, July 17, 1929

Left for Ocean City at 10:00. Met Tat and family on way down here. Spent the day at Atlantic City. Went up to Ocean City and danced.

Thursday, July 18, 1929

Arrived in Cape May at 9:15. Tat came along. Went fishing. Her family came up for dinner and all went home. Down at the pier in evening.

Friday, July 19, 1929

Up on the roof on my time off. Rather bored. On pier awhile.

Saturday, July 20, 1929

Letter from Mama telling me that Ted was married to Charlotte on Wednesday—some surprise! Wrote to him.

Sunday, July 21, 1929

Awful busy all day. Took a while off in the afternoon. Saw Jane Murray. Down on the pier in the evening.

Monday, July 22, 1929

Fixed up things after moving my room. Down on the pier late in the evening for a while.

Tuesday, July 23, 1929

Over at home during time off. Up to Ocean City in the evening to see Tat. Went down on the Boardwalk awhile. Saw Mrs. J. Norris.

Wednesday, July 24, 1929

Talked to Jane and Betty Murray. Late getting up at Tat's. Here by 9:00. Arthur Robison arrived. Date with a Mr. Hare who was 34-years-old. Not so hot.

Thursday, July 25, 1929

Bathing with the Robison kids. Home and in bed at 8:30.

Friday, July 26, 1929

Up at house all morning. Went on a beach party. Was with Dave Conner. He is real nice. More fun. Tom Murray from Clearfield was there.

Saturday, July 27, 1929

Slept awhile on time off. Date with Dave in evening. Saw Jane Kirk at pier. Went to the Merion. In bed late.

Sunday, July 28, 1929

Still tired. Not so awful busy today. Home and in bed early.

Monday, July 29, 1929

Up at house with time off. Slept until nearly 10:00. Dressed and went over to the Tea Room and met Ann and Millie at pics at the Marion.

Tuesday, July 30, 1929

Went swimming. The water was grand. Home right after work.

Wednesday, July 31, 1929

Had a date in eve with Jack Reynolds—works at the American Store. Ann with Milton Blume. Out to Cliff House.

Thursday, August 1, 1929

Went to Hydrangea Show at pier. Saw Tom Murray.

Friday, August 2, 1929

In swimming. It was rather cool. Busy today. Didn't go out.

Saturday, August 3, 1929

Very busy today. Worked hard. Not even out after coming home.

Sunday, August 4, 1929

Very busy all day. Down on pier to concert and up to Merion.

Monday, August 5, 1929

Felt punk all day. Wrote letters on time off. Down to the Pier in evening. Talked to Tom Dolan and Roy Taylor.

Tuesday, August 6, 1929

K. Hill's birthday. Biggest sunrise. Bill Jackson and his family came down. I love Bill so much. Stayed four hours. Down to the pier for a while.

Wednesday, August 7, 1929

Fooled around at House; didn't even go down to the pier.

Thursday, August 8, 1929

Jane Kirk in to see me. Hair washed and waved. Went down to the pier. Took Carl Vilsack for a ride along with another girl and boy.

Friday, August 9, 1929

Bill was supposed to be here today. Sent a telegram saying he couldn't come. I was disappointed. Went down on the pier for a while.

Saturday, August 10, 1929

Busy all day. Took only a half hour off. Worked late as well. Dressed and went down to the pier. Nothing exciting.

Sunday, August 11, 1929

Terribly busy. Worked every minute all day. Dead tired, but went down to a concert.

Monday, August 12, 1929

Jane Kirk in to see me in the morning. Went to Wildwood in the evening. Walked up and down the boardwalk. Didn't see Dave C.

Tuesday, August 13, 1929

Talked to Jane Kirk awhile on the boardwalk. Date with Clarke Bauer. Too dumb. Down to Merion.

Wednesday, August 14, 1929

In swimming. Met Carl and Jane Murray and talked. Down on pier awhile. Millie's family here.

Thursday, August 15, 1929

In swimming with Carl Valsack, Nelson Harris, and Clyde Pifer. My family and Alice came, staying at Miss Morrow's. Down to pier; Alice and I danced.

Friday, August 16, 1929

Bathing with Phil. Talked to Tom Murray. Worked late. Alice and I danced.

Saturday, August 17, 1929

Short time off. Alice helped me at the restaurant. Date Tom Murray—up to Cliff's house. Parked car and drank gin.

Sunday, August 18, 1929

Very busy. Mama and Papa went up to Ocean City. Date with Tom Murray in afternoon and evening. Home early.

Monday, August 19, 1929

Alice helped all day. Down on the pier with Mama and Papa at noon. With them in the evening as well. Alice and I danced. Saw Tom Murray and Karl Rowles.

Tuesday, August 20, 1929

Mama and Papa left this morning. Up at the house with time off. Alice stayed with me. Down on the pier and up to Wildwood. Saw Tom Murray.

Wednesday, August 21, 1929

Didn't go out in the eve. Wrote letters and slept. Supposed to have a date, but didn't.

Thursday, August 22, 1929

Went down on the beach, but not in the water. Didn't see anyone. Millie, Alice and I went up to Ocean City. Didn't see Mr. Norris.

Friday, August 23, 1929

Didn't do much on time off. Met Carl at Wildwood at 9:00. Took walk on the boardwalk and back to Cape May. Saw Tom M.

Saturday, August 24, 1929

Went bathing. Alice and Carl didn't. There was a beach party—Ann and Millie went. Al hosted it. I stayed home all evening.

Sunday, August 25, 1929

Busy all day. Went down to the pier in the evening. Listened to concert. Up to Kobe. Alice, Milly, and Carl came back to apartment.

Monday, August 26, 1929

Card from Marjorie from Ocean City. Drove up, walked boardwalk, but couldn't find her.

Tuesday, August 27, 1929

Went bathing. Water was cold and so was the air. Down on the pier in the evening. Danced with Harold, Millie's boyfriend.

Wednesday, August 28, 1929

Didn't go bathing, rather cool. Took some pictures. Drove to Ocean City in the evening and was with Marjorie.

Thursday, August 29, 1929

Through work. Slept till late and on beach all afternoon. Afternoon with Harold. Down on pier in the evening. Ate at Concord Tea Room.

Friday, August 30, 1929

Rained all morning. Couldn't go bathing. Baby parade in the afternoon. Said goodbye to Carl and Nelson and everyone left at 7:15. Two and a half hours to Philadelphia. All night with Mrs. Kittelberger.

Saturday, August 31, 1929

Shopped in the morning. Lunch at the Golden Gate with Mrs. K. Date with John Joseph all afternoon. Jacksons for dinner. In all evening. Listened to the radio and wished for Bill.

Sunday, September 1, 1929

Up early. Left Philadelphia at 9:00. Met Marjorie at the Thorps. Got here at 7:00. Carl Gregory, Ed Clark here late. Got Marjorie. Down to Tats.

Monday, September 2, 1929

Chased around all morning. Called Eddie. Up here for supper. Teachers meeting in afternoon. Date with Eddie. Dance at the Country Club. He left for Pittsburgh at 12:30.

Tuesday, September 3, 1929

1st day of school. Not so bad. Out early. Talked to Mr. Boggs and Taylor. Date with Blair and Don Robison with Alice. Down to movies.

Wednesday, September 4, 1929

School all day. Out early. Up to Bilger's Rocks. Got Blair. Took ride, took Alice and Don. Home all evening. Unpacked trunk.

Thursday, September 5, 1929

School all day. Picnic with Alice, Don and Blair Robison, Don and Lib Wall over to the park to dance in eve. Real nice time. Practice for pageant.

Friday, September 6, 1929

No school in afternoon. Teachers' Meeting. Slept for a couple of hours. Pageant practice at the park. Date Billie Mc. after. Goodbye to Bill Fister.

Saturday, September 7, 1929

Up at 9:00. Did shopping. Saw Hugh. Clearfield in afternoon. Hair washed. Saw Pete Barney. Down to Clearfield in the evening. Date with Johnny T. Alice with Billie Mc, out to farm.

Sunday, September 8, 1929

Alice stayed all night with me. Iced cake in morning. Did some work in the afternoon. Out to Greenwood for supper. Home in evening.

Monday, September 9, 1929

School all day. Pageant practice in evening. Went terrible. Lights went out.

Tuesday, September 10, 1929

School all day. Dead tired. Pageant in even. J.B.T. Dance and no one to go with. Stayed all night with Tat.

Wednesday, September 11, 1929

School only in morning. Marched to the park with the kids. Home in the afternoon and slept. Dinner at Walls. Pageant in evening. Home early.

Thursday, September 12, 1929

No school in the afternoon. Home—pressed, etc. Pageant in evening. Dead over town. Came home early.

Friday, September 13, 1929

Car all done over. It looks great. Movies after school. Home all evening. Phil to bed. Alice was down.

Saturday, September 14, 1929

Baked cake for Aunt Grace. Saw Bub King in afternoon. Alice and I went to Clearfield in the evening.

Sunday, September 15, 1929

Helped with dinner. Took car to Clearfield and drove the family to Holtens in the evening. Alice and Tat and I went up to Dot D.'s.

Monday, September 16, 1929

My first cooking classes. No letter from Bill. Alice and I to movies at Clearfield. Called on Lib K. and Bub and Barbara in the afternoon.

Tuesday, September 17, 1929

Cleaned car some after school. Put Phil to bed. Over to dance at the park with Alice. Real good time.

Wednesday, September 18, 1929

Teachers Meeting until 5:15. Libby Wilson's wedding at noon. Home in evening. Wrote some letters. Bed by 9:30.

Thursday, September 19, 1929

Didn't feel so good all day. My cold is worse. Went to bed at 6:30. Julia Bullock came. Bob went to a meeting.

Friday, September 20, 1929

Aunt Maude came today. Went to Walls for dinner. 8 of us there. Fooled around all even.

Saturday, September 21, 1929

Baked a cake in the morning. Clearfield awhile in the afternoon. Date this evening; Cy Boggs and his wife brought Howard Chapman.

Sunday, September 22, 1929

Clearfield in the morning. Took Aunt Maude. Jacksons here in the afternoon. Up to Walls for supper. Drove to Clearfield to Pig and Whistle.

Monday, September 23, 1929

Alice here for supper. Down to movies in evening. In Pig and Whistle – nothing exciting.

Tuesday, September 24, 1929

Letter from Bill. Home late from Clearfield. Went over to the Park late in the eve. Didn't dance any.[306]

Wednesday, September 25, 1929

Up to Alice's and up street after school. Home all evening. Wrote Bill and sewed some.

Thursday, September 26, 1929

Up to Miss Bloom's after school to get a dress fixed. To Fashion Show in evening with Alice. Didn't stay for bridge.

Friday, September 27, 1929

Home early. Up street with Alice. Home all evening. Went over old clothes.

Saturday, September 28, 1929

Up late. Did shopping. Aunt Maude and Mama and I up to DuBois in afternoon. Looked for coats. To Clearfield in the evening. Lib Wall and Louise Decker.

---

[306] It is very curious that there is no mention of the Wall Street crash of 1929 which was occurring at the time, particularly since Mary Alice's father was a founder of a local bank, established in 1925.

Sunday, September 29, 1929

Fooled around all morning and afternoon. Made some fudge. Alice and I went to Clearfield. Kirk Hile took us for a ride.

Monday, September 30, 1929

Out of school early. Home and dressed for the teachers' party at the Country Club. Had a real nice time. Home at 10:45.

Tuesday, October 1, 1929

Home after school. Aunt Grace and Uncle Charley here for dinner. Home all evening.

Wednesday, October 2, 1929

Brought a raccoon coat home from the store today. Can't decide on it. Down to see "Desert Song" with Alice.

Thursday, October 3, 1929

Teachers meeting after school. Home late. In all evening. Lib and Alice over for a while.

Friday, October 4, 1929

Out to Ogdens Farm for Mama Spencer after school. In evening, Alice and I down to see the Pageant.

Saturday, October 5, 1929

Met Tat at 10:30. Went to Altoona. Got 2 dresses. Out to Highland Hall. Ate at Allegheny Furnace (in Blair County). Date Everett (Davis).

Sunday, October 6, 1929

Up at 9:00. Helped get dinner and do the dishes. Home all day. Walked up street at 8:00 to mail some letters.

Monday, October 7, 1929

Hair fixed after school. Movies at Clearfield with Alice. "The Single Standard." Real good. Greta Garbo.

Tuesday, October 8, 1929

Home after school. Up to Bubby's. Home all eve. Sewed and pressed. Cold out.

Wednesday, October 9, 1929

To Mama Spencer's home after school. Tat's for a waffle supper. Dot Dimeling. Up to see Alice. Home early.

Thursday, October 10, 1929

Out of school early. Took Alice to Tyrone. Tat and I ate at the Triangle. Went to the Heverlys. Drove up to State in the evening.

Friday, October 11, 1929

Up at 9:00. Hurried to Lock Haven. Late for meeting. Thru at 4:00. Met M. Jane Mundy at hotel. Big dinner. Called in eve.

Saturday, October 12, 1929

Shopped till noon. Met M. Jane after work. To basketball, Washington & Jefferson game. Ate at Sunbury. Met boys. Jim McNulty from Dickinson, Lambda Chi house.

Sunday, October 13, 1929

Up at 10:00. Down to see Williamsport YWCA. Girls came as far as Bellefonte. Ate. Home 7:30. Bed early. Tired.

Monday, October 14, 1929

Hated to start in again. To stores awhile after school. Home all evening. Made out grades.

Tuesday, October 15, 1929

Car to garage after school. Up to see Lib Wall. She spent a night with Ted and Charlotte. To movies at Clearfield with Mama and Papa.

Wednesday, October 16, 1929

Home after school. Up street and shopped. Home all evening. Mended and wrote some letters.

Thursday, October 17, 1929

Home after school. Shopped for Mama. Date with Kenny Gearhart. Tat with Dave Kephart. Played bridge up here. Had a lunch.

Friday, October 18, 1929

Fooled around at Clearfield after school. Home all evening. Made Marjorie and Blair Robinson some fudge. Up street with Jessie.

Saturday, October 19, 1929

Fooled around all morning and afternoon. Iced cake and cleaned the car. Date in evening with Al Colegrove from Smethport. Goes to West Point. Awful nice.

Sunday, October 20, 1929

Philip's birthday. 10 years old. Just his friend Harold Thompson for dinner. At Tat's all night. Eddie Hile home. With him till 7:00. Date with Al till 2:15. He's sweet.

Monday, October 21, 1929

Meeting about Halloween Party. Up to Mama Spencer's after school. Home all evening. Bed early. Wrote some letters.

Tuesday, October 22, 1929

Up street after school about Halloween Party and down to Aunt Grace's awhile. Home all evening.

Wednesday, October 23, 1929

Ordered some things for the Freshman Party. Talked to Pete Chase. Home all evening. Wrote letters and cleaned bureau drawers.

Thursday, October 24, 1929

Home after school, out late. Down to movies with Helen Decker, Louise Satelle, and Lib Wall.

Friday, October 25, 1929

Tested places for Freshman Halloween Party after school. Over to the H.S. party for a while. Home at 12:00.

Saturday, October 26 and Sunday, October 27, 1929

Mama and Papa over to State. Met Mr./Mrs. Stiles and Bill and Mrs. Stiles' father. Here all night. Date with Eddie. He came in late from Pitt. Movies first. (He) slept with Phil. The Stiles left after dinner. Eddie came for me. We went for a drive and at Hiles for dinner. Eddie left for Pitt at 7:30.

Monday, October 28, 1929

Movies after school . Saw "Madonna of Avenue A."[307] Date with Kenny Johnston in eve. Halloween Dance, Punxsutawney. Grand time. Home at 3:30.

Tuesday, October 29, 1929

Up to J. Bullocks at Luthersburg. Talked all night. Bob Euler was at a meeting. Was dead tired and sleepy.

Wednesday, October 30, 1929

Home after school. Down to Bob McCloud's Gift Shop. Home all evening. Wrote a couple of letters.

Thursday, October 31, 1929

Home after school. Teachers' bridge party with Miss Weber and Miss Wertz. Met Al Colegrove after. Stayed with Tat. Over to flower show.

Friday, November 1, 1929

Car washed after school. Lunch with Al. Hair washed after school. Date Al. Bill and Tat to movies. Up to Tat's. Crazy about Al.

Saturday, November 2, 1929

Up late. Did some ironing. Clearfield and Flower Show. M. Wall; Marge Evans. Date Al. Home most all evening.

Sunday, November 3, 1929

Al up in afternoon about 3:00. Took a ride. Up past Glen Campbell, passed Ted's, later at Tat's awhile. Al left at 11:30.

---

[307] "Madonna of Avenue A" is a 1929 talking drama film starring Dolores Costello in one of her last silent films... reportedly another lost film.

Monday, November 4, 1929

Saw Al at noon. Left then for home. Home right after school and all eve. Up to Mama Spencer's.

Tuesday, November 5, 1929

Shopped some after school. Invitation to Fall House Party from Bill Stiles. Home all evening with Philip.

Wednesday, November 6, 1929

Up street after school. Walls awhile. Home all evening.

Thursday, November 7, 1929

Shopped after school. Got a new hat. Down to Second Show with Mama and Papa. Billie Dove.[308] Real good.

Friday, November 8, 1929

Dentist after school. Evening date with Johnny Leitzinger, came up unexpectedly. Not so good.

Saturday, November 9, 1929

Up late. Baked cake. Picture taken at Shull's. Card party in evening over at Tillie Robinson's.

Sunday, November 10, 1929

Up late. Helped get dinner. Naomi away. Slept in afternoon. Date in evening with Hugh Norris. Down to late show. Don and Lib Wall.

Monday, November 11, 1929

No school in afternoon. Sewed some and slept. Dance at Sunset with Kenny Johnston. Saw Ted and Charlotte, first since June 28.

Tuesday, November 12, 1929

Home after school. Washed stockings. Home all evening. Finished skirt and pressed.

Wednesday, November 13, 1929

Stores after school. Up at Lib Walls. To Home Talent Play in evening. Took Mama Spencer. It was real good.

Thursday, November 14, 1929

Dentist after school. Hair fixed in eve. Picture taken again. In bed late. Packed, etc.

Friday, November 15, 1929

Up early. Left 3:30. H. Decker and Thelma Kephart over to State House Party at Phi Kappa Sigma. Formal dance. In bed 4:30. Good orchestra.

---

[308] One of the most popular actresses of the 1920s.

Saturday, November 16, 1929

Up at 11:00. Lunch at House. Mama and Papa and Mr. and Mrs. Stiles came for the game: Bucknell 27-6. State lost. Dinner. Long ride to Co-Op twice. Bed at 5:00.

Sunday, November 17, 1929

Up at 11:30. Dressed for dinner at the House. Sat around all afternoon. Cutest boy George Shoutz from Scranton. Mary Gongler came along.

Monday, November 18, 1929

Took Section 9[309] to Clearfield Dairy in morning. Home after school. In all evening; wrote letters.

Tuesday, November 19, 1929

Dentist after school. Took Section 12 to Dairy. Got a couple Xmas gifts. Down to movies in evening. Fanny Brice in "My Man."[310]

Wednesday, November 20, 1929

Wish I would hear from Bill J. Stores at noon. Up at Mama Spencer's after school. Home all evening. Corrected papers.

Thursday, November 21, 1929

I am 24 today. Present from June. Home after school. Mama came up along. Home all evening. Sewed.

Friday, November 22, 1929

Up to Aunt Grace's home after school. In the evening to a bridge party at Tat's for Dot Dimeling.

Saturday, November 23, 1929

Up late. Sewed and ironed in the afternoon. Upstreet awhile. Clearfield in eve. alone. Went to movie.

Sunday, November 24, 1929

Up late. Home nearly all day. Jessie came down. Took ride to Clearfield to the Pig Whistle and Manor Grill.

Monday, November 25, 1929

Busy in school today. Home after school. In all evening; sewed and made out grades.

Tuesday, November 26, 1929

Terribly busy at school today. Bobby Stevenson dropped in. Made out grades. Home in the evening. Wrote letters.

[309] Classes in schools were sometimes identified by the group of peers by which they were placed. Some schools divided students alphabetically, others by the choice of curriculum and still others by the students' grades.

[310] "My Man" is a 1928 black and white part-talkie American comedy-drama musical film directed by Archie Mayo starring Fanny Brice. This was Brice's feature film debut at the age of 37. She was a star in the Ziegfeld Follies before she started acting in motion pictures.

Wednesday, November 27, 1929

No classes in afternoon. Home early. Nothing much to do. Movies in the evening with Tat.

Thursday, November 28, 1929

Up late. Got things ready for Thanksgiving dinner. Mama and Papa Spencer here. Curwensville and Clearfield football game. We lost 14-0.[311] Movies in the evening with Lib Wall.

Friday, November 29, 1929

Left for Bellefonte at 10:00. Took Dick Wall and Dick Kirk over along. Met Bubby. Drove up to State to see Porter. Dot M. spent the evening. M. Hill there.

Saturday, November 30, 1929

Shopped all morning. At Beverly's all night. Up to Haines, S. Taylors and Hugh Quigleys. Movies at Clearfield. In bed early.

Sunday, December 1, 1929

Helped get dinner. Fooled around all afternoon. Wrote letters. In all evening. Called Tat.

Monday, December 2, 1929

Terribly busy at school. Tat sick in bed. I went up to see her. Home all evening. Ironed and corrected papers.

Tuesday, December 3, 1929

Tat not in school today. I took her sewing class and also Miss Mook's homeroom. Hair fixed after school. Up to see Tat. Home all evening.

Wednesday, December 4, 1929

Up to see Tat after school. Letter from Bill Stiles. Not coming this weekend. And I am going to Pittsburgh. Movies in evening at Clearfield.

Thursday, December 5, 1929

Home after school and up to Jessie's to plan for the trip to Pittsburgh. Teachers and School Board Banquet in the evening. Home and packed.

Friday, December 6, 1929

Tat here for Pittsburgh at 4:20. In there (by train) at 8:30. Kate and Jessie. Met Joe Nichols. Stayed at the William Penn. $14.07.

---

[311] From the 1930 *Echo* regarding the previous fall's football games: "Our Thanksgiving Day game with Clearfield was played on one of the coldest days we had. It was nearly two o'clock before the snow was removed from the field. Finally with the aid of old Dobbin the task was accomplished. Both teams played wonderful football but Clearfield went home at the long end of a 13-0 score. Had it not been so cold, it would have been the best game of the season to watch." (Dick Martin, Manager) This author remembers similar games two decades later and she also remembers the handsome Dick Martin......

Saturday, December 7, 1929

Up early. Too hot in room to sleep. Got new dress. Out to Homestead in apartment with Joe. Date in evening. Danced with Jessie's date. Dave Bowers with Kate. Boys stayed late.

Sunday, December 8, 1929

Up late. Ate breakfast and packed. Started about 2:30. Had dinner in Indiana. In bed early. Dead tired.

Monday, December 9, 1929

Did some shopping after school. Mama and Papa in Clearfield for supper. Home all evening. Did pressing.

Tuesday, December 10, 1929

Shopped after school. Down to movies and fashion show in evening with Mama and Papa.

Wednesday, December 11, 1929

At stores awhile after school with Tat. Up to Mama Spencer's, Walls, and Aunt Grace. Home all evening.

Thursday, December 12, 1929

To Methodist Church Supper. Real good. Went to movies before coming home. Fooled around all evening.

Friday, December 13, 1929

Out of school early for the Junior Class Play this evening. Shopped some, Date in the evening with Kenny Johnston to movies at Philipsburg. Tat and Bill along over to "Rio Rita."[312]

Saturday, December 14, 1929

Up late. Baked cake. Shopped. Home all afternoon. In Clearfield in the evening with Lib Wall. To the movies.

Sunday, December 15, 1929

Wrote to Mrs. Jackson about Bill. Up late. Home all day. Wrote some other letters and sewed.

Monday, December 16, 1929

Home after school. Made things in school for Jr. High Exhibit. Won first prize.

Tuesday, December 17, 1929

Gene McKenzie's birthday. Home after school. Up the street. In the house all evening. Pressed and sewed. Worked on Christmas presents.

---

[312] Radio Pictures "RIO RITA" is almost a copy of Flo Ziegfeld's stage success by the same name. The film was a great success in its day.

Wednesday, December 18, 1929

Up to Walls for a while after school. Sent some Christmas cards. Movies in the evening. Lyric Theatre with Jessie.

Thursday, December 19, 1929

Didn't feel so well today. Home after school. Date in the evening. Pete Martin. Movies and up to Holtens.

Friday, December 20, 1929

Took all the girls to the Ritz after school. Felt punk all day. In bed early. Hair fixed today.

Saturday, December 21, 1929

Got up today at noon. Sick all day. Sore throat. Marjorie came home. Down in the evening with Clyde Pifer.

Sunday, December 22, 1929

Home all day. Didn't do much. Did some sewing and read. Jessie, Kate, and Helen Decker came down.

Monday, December 23, 1929

Outside for the first time in two days. Took the car down to have the battery charged. Up to Mama Spencer and Aunt Grace's for supper. Finished Christmas gifts in the evening.

Tuesday, December 24, 1929

Made candy all morning. Clearfield in the afternoon with Marjorie. Delivered gifts. Trimmed the tree in the evening.

Wednesday, December 25, 1929

CHRISTMAS DAY

Baked a cake in the morning. Christmas dinner at Aunt Grace's. I was there nearly all day. Up to Alice's later. Date in the evening with Tom Murray.

Thursday, December 26, 1929

Up late. Helped get meals and wash dishes. Chased around all afternoon. Had a date in the evening with John Martin.

Friday, December 27, 1929

Clearfield in the afternoon to the stores. Marjorie and Alice. Went to Tat's. Movies in evening with Mama and Papa. Early to bed.

Saturday, December 28, 1929

Bill Jackson's Birthday. I wish I could have been with him. Went to Clearfield in the afternoon with Marjorie, Cecil, Marguerite, and Mama. Date in the evening with Mr. Burton.[313] Up to Alice's. Karl was there.

---

[313] Cannot find any information on this gentleman. No family listing in any of the 1920s directories I have.

Sunday, December 29, 1929

Up late. Drove to Tyrone with Mr. Burton and Bob Wolf. He stayed in the evening. And is so sweet. I like him so much.

Monday, December 30, 1929

Cleaned upstairs in the morning. Clearfield in the afternoon with Cora. Over to Rowles. Bridge at Wolfs in the evening. Mr. Burton party.

Tuesday, December 31, 1929

Last day of the year. Finished up Memory Book. Went to Clearfield with Marjorie. Up to Tat's awhile. Date in evening with Mr. Burton.

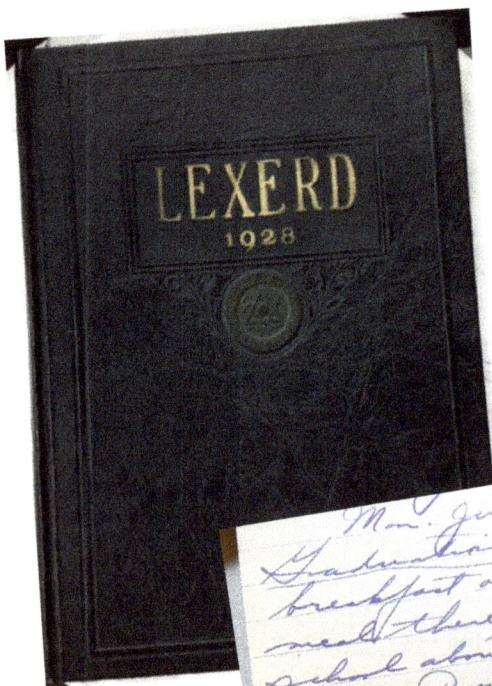

Mary Alice finished the school term and likely taught the 1929–1930 and the 1930–1931 school terms. In the summer of 1931 she and Tat Thorn traveled by car to the West Coast and back, June 16–August 26. They attended the National Home Economic Teachers Convention as their destination, but this was a major sight-seeing tour of more than two months, unusual at the time for two young women to take such a trip.

Cast of Characters

The following names are of those persons mentioned in the Diary, with a description accompanying the name (to the extent possible given the setting in which they are mentioned). The names have been alphabetized by first name, as Mary Alice wrote them in her Diary entries. Some of these more than 600 persons appear only once in the story and others are noted multiple times throughout the Diary. There is a variation in the spelling of some of the names, written in some cases as Mary Alice has spelled them.

Abe Baker, *simply a friend of Jane Clark (identified under her own name).*

Adeline Barber, *one of a large group of friends in Curwensvile/Clearfield who participated in many social events together.*

Al Colegrove *from Smethport, a West Pointer who dated Mary Alice several times.*

Al Fisk, *friend of John Joseph, who offered to provide printed information on birth control for John to share with Mary Alice in his quest to win her love. (There is no evidence that the information was forthcoming! This was not a typical topic of conversation, but followed a reference to the possibility of marriage.)*

Albert Mathers, *one of the Drexel group of friends.*

Alice Dorsett, *one of Mary Alice's friends from Curwensville at Drexel.*

Alice Kay, *Drexel classmate; VP of Home Economics Club in 1925-26.*

Alice Murray, *Class of 1919, Curwensville High School. "Al" is part of the group of Curwensville friends of which Mary Alice was a member. Her family lived at 233 Ridge Avenue. Alice attended the gatherings at Greenwood Lodge, located outside of Curwensville, and other recreational and social events with "the gang." Alice is one of 8 children in her family; one of whom is Louise, also a friend of Mary Alice.*

Alice Wall, *Class of 1924, is part of the social group of friends in Curwensville and a particularly good friend of Mary Alice. She frequently visited Drexel. Mary Alice kept up a close friendship with her. Alice's parents are Dillwyn Parrish Wall (brother of Charles Wall) and Bessie Wall; thus, Alice is Marjorie Wall's first cousin on her father's side. (Mary Alice and Marjorie Wall are first cousins through their mothers who were sisters.)*

Allan Gilbert, *Mary Alice's date at a Drexel Phi Kappa Beta dance; Editor-in-Chief of* Drexerd, *Drexel's nascent humor magazine. Mary Alice noted in her diary that she was not fond of Allan.*

Allen Petace, *an acquaintance from Clearfield/Curwensville.*

Almeda Tembovitz, *an acquaintance at Drexel; Mary Alice noted that she had met Almeda for lunch.*

Almelia Butler, *friend in Clearfield.*

Alton Mathis, *friend at Drexel.*

Alveta Sloan, *friend at Drexel; Alveta had a sister Marie.*

Amos Kilesy, *Drexel; Mary Alice danced with him at one of the Court Dances.*

Angeline Rubie, *Curwensville, Class of 1926; paramour of and, in later life, married to H. J. Thompson, Mary Alice's father.*

Ann and Bob O'Grady, *friends of Ted, whom Mary Alice dated regularly after finishing at Drexel and returning home; these friends of Mary Alice all lived in Glen Campbell.*

Ann Clark, *played bridge with the group in Clearfield/Curwensville.*

Ann Gross, *close friend of Noah (see "Ark" below). Ann and Noah likely were later engaged.*

Ann Pritchard, *friend at Drexel.*

Ann Robinson, *from Virginia, was Mary Alice's tennis mate and lived in the same dorm (house)[1] as Mary Alice.*

Ann Ulrich *(likely a Clearfield High School graduate) attended the same House Party at Penn State as attended by Mary Alice and Bill Jackson.*

Anna Raisim, *Kathleen Hill's[2] cousin who attended a fraternity party at Drexel. (Kathleen was among Mary Alice's best friends at Drexel.)*

Annette, *a Drexel dorm (house) mate.*

Ark (Noah) Belding *was an important person in the college life of Mary Alice. They were firstly friends and dated occasionally. He was Circulation Manager for the start-up of the* Drexel Triangle, *launched in the fall of 1926; on the* Drexerd *staff; and an officer in Phi Kappa Beta fraternity.*

Arthur Robison, *related to the Jacksons in Philadelphia and the Curwensville Robisons.*

Arthur Wall, *third of the four sons of Charles Wall; cousin to Mary Alice; President of Curwensville High School's Class of 1928.*

Audrey Hyde, *Curwensville/Clearfield friend of Mary Alice.*

Aunt Grace Wall, *Mary Alice's aunt and sister to Mary Alice's mother. Grace, married to Charles; Grace was the mother of Cecil, Kenneth, Arthur, Richard, and Marjorie Wall.*

Aunt Mary, *married to Vern Wall who was a brother to Charles Miles and D.P. Wall.*

Aunt Maude (Maud Thompson Davidson), *Mary Alice's father's only sister.*

Becky Causie, *Clearfield area friend of Mary Alice.*

Ben Edwards, *acquaintance from Wellsboro.*

Berdie Phillips, *a young woman whom Mary Alice met at a house party at Penn State.*

Bernice Anderson, *Clearfield acquaintance who married Bill (William) Betts.*

---

[1] Those in the Home Economics program referred to their houses as such. From all indications, there were not typical dormitories for women.

[2] See Kathleen Hill.

Beth and Catherine McKendrick, *Clearfield sisters and part of the group of young people who frequently gathered at Greenwood Lodge.*

Betty and Jane Murray, *friends Mary Alice ran into at the shore.*

Betty Bell, *friend at Drexel.*

Betty Biddle, *friend at Drexel, mentioned multiple times.*

Betty Boyd, *Drexel, mentioned only once.*

Betty York, *friend at Drexel.*

Bill Beam, *a friend who rode the same train home with Alice Wall.*

Bill (William) I. Betts, Jr., *part of the Clearfield bridge-playing crowd.*

Bill Brown, *Clearfield; attended Drexel; popular; mentioned often in the diaries.*

Bill Daugherty, *Clearfield friend.*

Bill Fister, *CHS, brother of Barbara and JoAnn; "dropped" by Mary Alice.*

Bill Green, *Drexel; drove a Dodge Roadster.*

Bill Haud, *a casual date.*

Bill Hirschman, *Drexel acquaintance.*

Bill Horn, *Drexel; a high roller, popular, drove a 7-passenger Lincoln car.*

Bill Hutchens, *popular; from Schenectady, New York; dated Mary Alice.*

Bill (William K.) Jackson, *the man Mary Alice would marry.*

Bill Kern, *a freshman at Penn when Mary Alice was a frosh at Drexel.*

Bill (William) Kittelberger, *friend of Mary Alice, Editor of the 1923 Yearbook,* The Echo. *Curwensville; son of Harry Kittelberger; his sisters were Louise, Class of '25 and Elizabeth, Class of '26.*

Bill Meade, *a Phi Delta whom Mary Alice met at the Drexel Sophomore Hop in 1926.*

Bill Patterson, *invited and escorted Mary Alice to the Junior Prom at West Chester.*

Bill Seig, *a fellow Mary Alice dated on a visit to Bellefonte.*

Bill Simmons, *Alpha Tau Omega at Penn State; acquaintance of Mary Alice's crowd.*

Bill Stiles, *invited Mary Alice to the Fall House Party, 1929.*

Bill Thorpe '20, *Clearfield; member of Mary Alice's circle of friends; friend of Cecil Wall and brother to Marguerite whom Cecil Wall would marry.*

Bill Tice, *friend of Kathleen Hill (Mary Alice's best friend at Drexel).*

Bill Wessel, *one of the fellows who dated a friend of Mary Alice.*

Bill(ly) McClure, *part of the Curwensville/Clearfield Greenwood Lodge crowd. Mary Alice dated him a number of times.*

Blair Mann, *Clearfield H.S., 1922, identified at most of the gatherings of the Clearfield group in 1925-26.*

Blair Robinson, *at a picnic with the group on September 5, 1929; also dated Marjorie Wall.*

Bob Daugherty, *dated Alice Murray the summer of 1925.*

Bob Fox, Phi Kappa Beta, *dated friends of Mary Alice at Drexel.*

Bob Hartman, *dated Alice Wall in Philadelphia.*

Bob Humphreys, *Curwensville, dated Alice Murray the summer of 1927.*

Bob Suley *had a blind date with Mary Alice, the fall of 1927.*

Bob Swift, *part of the group who went to Willow Grove Park with the Home Economic majors.*

Bob Way, *Mary Alice danced with him at the Legion Party in Curwensville, December 29, 1926.*

Bob Wright, *brother of John; Curwensville, part of the gang who held socials at Greenwood Lodge and frequented other area attractions during the summer of 1927.*

Bobby Dare, *part of the group at Willow Grove Park, 1926.*

Brownie (Harry Brown), *Curwensville Fire Company; part of the group of friends celebrating the marriage of Katherine (Catherine) Pifer and Howard V. Thompson.*

Bruce Norris, *Mary Alice's date at the riff raffs, the summer of 1925.*

Bub King, *Clearfield, dated Mary Alice a number of times.*

Bubby (Howard) Thompson, *Clearfield High School, Class of 1922; Mary Alice's older brother.*

Bud Ganlin and **Bud Green,** *part of the social group, 1928.*

Bud Minner, *part of above group.*

Bud Smith *dated Mary Alice; they went to Childs Restaurant.*[3]

Burch, *a friend at Drexel.*

Burt King, *Mary Alice's friend (and occasional date), Curwensville, 1925.*

Byron McDowell, *one of the crew of friends, Curwensville, 1925.*

Carl Gray, *one of the friends mentioned at a dance at Drexel, possibly from the Bellefonte area.*

Carl Gregory, *Drexel; President of Phi Kappa Beta; Basketball Team Captain; Member of Blue Key (Honorary Fraternity); Chair of Military Ball; ROTC Officer.*

Carl Hoffman, *Drexel; Mary Alice's date for a dinner dance at the Pelham Club in Germantown.*

Carl Valsack/Vilsack, *Mary Alice met him at Cape May, 1929.*

Carson family *who lived at 235 E. Ave. near Drexel campus; may have rented to students.*

Catherine Allison, *friend from Bellefonte.*

Catherine McKendrick, *Clearfield friend.*

Catherine Reese, *Bellefonte, friend of Mary Alice.*

Catherine/Katherine Pifer,[4] *Curwensville; sister to Jessie; married Bubby (Howard) Thompson, brother to Mary Alice.*

---

[3] Childs was one of the first national dining chains in the United States and Canada, having peaked in popularity in the 1920s and 1930s.

[4] Mother of the author of this book.

Cathryn Reese, *Clearfield friend of Mary Alice.*

Cecil Walker, *Clearfield friend.*

Cecil Wall, *Cousin of Mary Alice; oldest of the four Wall brothers; Curwensville H.S. '21; University of Pennsylvania '25. (Later became highly respected Resident Director of Mt. Vernon, historic home of President George Washington.)*

Charles Albright, *Drexel likely.*

Charles Cutler ("Cutt") Coolbroth, *Curwensville High School Class of 1930, but unmarried so occasionally joined the social group of young people. (The author remembers him, among many others listed here).*

Charles Stern, *Drexel.*

Charles Miles Wall, *married to Grace Spencer and is uncle of Mary Alice. His brothers were Wilbur, Verner, and D. P. Wall; sister, Hannah Mary.*

Charley Halfred, *Clearfield.*

Charlotte Starken, *Drexel.*

Chester Snively, *Drexel, Sigma Alpha Rho.*

Clarence, *Drexel.*

Clark Blair, aka **J. Clark Blair;** *Drexel.*

Clate, *Clearfield friend of Marge Irvin.*

Clyde Pifer *(Clearfield), friend of Marjorie Wall. (possibly a distant cousin of Jessie.)*

Cobbly Mascal, *Drexel; real name is likely* **Charles Mashcal,** *identified as a freshman in Drexel's 1927 yearbook,* Lexerd

Constance Dalrymple (Doriwarkle), *Drexel, a transfer student from California; her parents occasionally sent her a crate of oranges.*[5]

Cora Swoope Wolf, *Curwensville High School 1922, Assistant Editor of the yearbook and Vice President of her class; sister to Mary Wolf; Mary Alice knew both and ran into Cora at Wanamaker's in Philadelphia.*[6]

Cornelia Smith, *likely a classmate from Highland Hall, a private girls' school that Mary Alice had attended 1921–1922.*

Cousin Anna Robinson,[7] *a possible 2nd cousin of Marjorie Wall.*

Cousin Dema Robinson Spencer, *Bloomington Avenue, Curwensville; her father is Harry; siblings are Florence and Avanell; related to Mary Alice through her mother Elizabeth Spencer Thompson and her Aunt Grace Spencer Wall.*

Cousin Lew Spencer, *likely as above, married to Dema.*

---

[5]   This is included as a reminder of what a specialty this was. I recall my mother telling us how very singular it was to find an orange under the tree on Christmas morning or at any other time!

[6]   Trains made it possible to easily get from Curwensville to Philadelphia. Today, this would not be possible.

[7]   Father was Harry Robinson, Bloomington Avenue, Curwensville. Children: Dema, Florence, Avenell. Dema married Lew Spencer who operated Spencer's dry goods store.

Cousin Susie, *actually a cousin of Kathleen Hill, Mary Alice's best friend.*

D. Mallory, *likely a friend of Mary Alice in Clearfield.*

D. P. Wall[8] **(Dillwyn Parrish)** and **Bessie Wall** *are the parents of Elizabeth M. Wall and Alice Wall who was born in 1906 and was graduated in 1922. (See special genealogy section.)*

D. Strickland, *attended New Year's party 1925.*

Dan Hennery, *Drexel, dated June Frankenfield; there is mention of a party they attended.*

Daniel, *worked with Mary Alice at a tea room at the Jersey shore.*

Dave Bowers, *Clearfield; dated Kate Smith.*

Dave Conner, *one of a group at a beach party at Cape May.*

Dave Franklin, *friend in Clearfield.*

Dave Harmon Band, *played at Mill Hall.*

Dave Kephart *was Tat Thorn's date for a game of bridge and lunch in Clearfield.*

Dave McKinley, *Curwensville classmate, lifelong friend, later Dean of Admissions at Penn State.*

Dick (Richard) Wall, *the youngest of the four Wall brothers.*

Dick Kirk, *Curwensville family member and acquaintance of Mary Alice.*

Dick Langell, *Bellefonte friend.*

Dick Leopold, *Drexel, native of Clearfield.*

Dick Neil/Noll, *attended dance at Bellefonte.*

Doc Hawes, *married Jessie Pifer, but the marriage was short-lived. Hawes appears in* All the Gentlemen Callers *and* Jebbie, Vamp to Victim, *both by the author of* It's the Berries.

Don Dunsmore, *one of the guests at a weekend gathering at Greenwood Lodge.*

Don Rexroad, *name on a short list of men Mary Alice dated, 1924-25.*

Don Robinson *dated Alice, Clearfield/Curwensville, 1929.*

Don Rowe, *Drexel.*

Dorney, *Drexel student.*

Dorothy (Dot) Dimeling '21, *Clearfield and Highland Hall friend of Mary Alice. Dot appears to have attended Highland Hall after graduation from high school.*

Dorothy (Dottie) Ake (married name is Clymer), *Class of '20; Curwensville; attended Drexel; father was a local physician and on the board of directors of the Curwensville State Bank.*

Dorothy Wing, *Mary Alice's "little sister" in the dorm/house at Drexel; Student Government; Van Rensselaer Medal winner; Home Economics House president.*

Dot King, *shared House Chairmanship with Mary Alice at Drexel.*

Dot Orwig, *acquaintance at Drexel.*

Dot Williams, *Drexel classmate; they both observed or student taught at Rosemont.*

---

[8] Dillwyn Parrish Wall, curiously shares this unusual name with the father of Maxwell Parish, artist; the Parrishes are located in Philadelphia. This shared name begs for further exploration.....

Dot Wolf, *Clearfield friend.*

Dottie Clymer, *married to Dave; daughter Doddie (Bellefonte).*

Dottie Oakes, *Drexel.*

Dr. Arnette, *Drexel campus physician.*

Dutch Waite, *Drexel.*

E. Barklew, *friend of Mary Alice's "back home." She corresponded with him.*

E. Harris, *friend of Cecil Wall in Philadelphia.*

Ed Benson, *a friend Mary Alice ran into at the Sesquicentennial Exposition in Philadelphia.*

Ed Howard, *Clearfield friend.*

Ed Walton, *Drexel friend, yearbook photo, 1926.*

Eddie Hile, *Clearfield fellow Mary Alice dated occasionally, long-term friend.*

Eddie Howes, *just another guy with a group of fellows she knew at a dance in Clearfield.*

Eddie Miller, *this name may be held by two different friends, one in Bellefonte who might have married M. Hill in Phila. and one in Curwensville who seems also to be in Pittsburgh. She writes to him. Mary Alice knew many young men by the name of Eddie and, this being a personal diary, she did not always include last names.*

Eddie Powers, *Philadelphia; Mary Alice danced with him at two different Court[9] Dances at Drexel.*

Edgar Newton Rosenbury, *Drexel.*

Edith (Edie) Walker, *Drexel. Mary Alice attended her wedding shower.*

Edith Knabb, *Drexel '26; President of Women's Student Government; member of Key Club; Yearbook staff.*

Edith Newton, *friend at Drexel, mentioned numerous times; 1927 Student House Board; roommate of Mary Alice, 1926-27 schoolyear.*

Edith Sawtelle, *Curwensville High School '22, often part of the group of friends; family lived on George Street. Mary Alice also records an Edith Satelle and Edith Satille in the Diary, but after combing yearbooks and lists of Curwensville citizens, there is reasonable confidence that the person throughout is Edith Sawtelle.*

Edith Shaw, *Drexel friend and friend of the Thorn family in Clearfield.*

Edna Chasen, *shared an apartment with Edith Shaw in Philly; Drexel students.*

Edna Forney, *Drexel friend and tennis mate.*

Edna Kilpatrick, *friend at Drexel.*

Eileen King, *Curwensville friend, member of group that frequently went to events (usually self-styled) at Greenwood Lodge.*

---

9   As in "courting....." These dances were held as a social opportunity for students to meet those of the opposite sex; may have been a forerunner to what, during the next generation on college campuses, were called "mixers."

Eleanor Steinbauch, *Drexel; friend of Alice.*

Elinor Coen, *Weekend visitor.*

Elizabeth Biddle, *Drexel; upperclassman when Mary Alice was a freshman.*

Elizabeth Dukes, *friend of a friend, Philadelphia area.*

Elizabeth Hoag, *Drexel.*

Elizabeth King, *known as Libby, Curwensville friend; Editor-in-chief, 1922 Echo; she was the force behind the school's FIRST yearbook (in prior years a booklet had sufficed); her father was a physician and VP of the School Board. Siblings included Orville and Sarah. Elizabeth attended Elmira College; Mary Alice saw her when she was home on breaks.*

Elizabeth Koosier, *Drexel.*

Elizabeth Spencer Thompson (Mama), *Mary Alice's mother.*

Elizabeth Wall, *Curwensville High School '22, Class Treasurer; longtime friend (cousin of Mary Alice's cousins); parents are Dillwyn Parrish (DP) and Bessie. Elizabeth's sister is Alice. Elizabeth and Alice's uncle was Charles Wall.*

Ella Radford, *Drexel house/dorm mate; known for her charm, but often was misunderstood by others (as stated in her yearbook profile).*

Ellen Barbara Johnson, *1927 May Queen at Drexel; friend of Mary Alice; VP, Key and Triangle.*

Ellis Keller, *friend in Clearfield, affiliated with Clearfield schools, 1929.*

Emily Cruider and sister May *were on the train with Mary Alice and others, coming back from a Penn State House Party; all were having a good time on the journey.*

Emma Hess, *lived in the same Drexel Home Economics dorm/house as Mary Alice did.*

Enos Derham, *attended the dinner party given as part of Mary Alice's class assignment.*

Estella Buckley *(whose last name in not included in Mary Alice's Diary) is a classmate of Mary Alice's who attended a nursing school in Buffalo, NY; she hosted Mary Alice and others on their trip there.*

Esther Bucklew, *one of the new frosh, 1924, was housed in same residence as Mary Alice; as a sophomore she was president of the Home Economics Club '26 and Representative of the Matheron YWCA.*

Ethel York, *Drexel.*

Evelyn Ogden, *assisted with care of Papa and Mama Spencer, 1929.*

Evelyn Rosenburg, *Drexel.*

Everett Davis, *Clearfield.*

F. Kruesen, *Mary Alice wrote to him.*

Florence Briseby, *Drexel.*

Florence Green, *friend of the William Jacksons in Philadelphia.*

Florence Irene Kreutzer, *friend at Drexel, Class of '26.*

Frances Custer, *Clearfield/Philipsburg area.*

Frances Light, *Philadelphia.*

Frances Sell, *Drexel.*

Francis Schenley, *Clearfield; played the violin.*

Fred Sweeley, *with friends from Scranton, visited Mary Alice in 1929 at a Phi Kappa Sigma event.*

Francis Thompson, *Mary Alice's uncle; youngest brother of her father, H. J. Thompson; Married to Roxie M. Hess; "Tucker" (his nickname), a one-of-a-kind delight, was a professional roller-skater.*

Franklin Steine, *Philadelphia.*

Fred Redden, *Clearfield.*

Fred Robison (Mr. and Mrs.), *Curwensville. (Mr. Robison owned Robison's Printing.)*

Fred Sweeley, *Clearfield friend.*

Fred Wright, *Clearfield.*

Frederick Kittelberger, *son of Mrs. George Kittelberger in Philadelphia. (See family listing.)*

Fredrick Conklin, *Clearfield, friend of the Wall family. He drove a Franklin car and was a frequent guest at Greenwood Lodge.*

G. Johns, *Philadelphia, one with whom Mary Alice corresponded; he mentioned that he liked the Curwensville area.*

Geare Johnson, *Drexel acquaintance.*

Gene McKenzie, *Philadelphia.*

Genevieve, *Curwensville area friend.*

George Biddle, *Curwensville.*

George Custer, *Drexel; Phi Kappa Beta.*

George Eichner, *Drexel.*

George Irwin, *Philadelphia.*

George Proctor, *Philadelphia; Drexel '26; Phi Kappa Beta; voted most popular in the class; athlete and scholar; Captain of the track team; President of the Phoenix Club; Secretary of Society of Mechanical Engineers.*

George Rumsey, *Philadelphia.*

George Shoutz, *Mary Alice's date at a House Party at Penn State; he was from Scranton; also visited her in Clearfield.*

George Stevens, *Drexel, Phi Gamma Delta.*

George Wrigley, *Drexel, Business Manager of the* Lexerd *(yearbook); graduate of Curwensville '22; high school friend of Mary Alice.*

Gertrude McMaster, *Philadelphia.*

Gertrude Stamp, *daughter of the senior John Stamp; sister of young John Stamp, Buffalo, NY.*

Gordon Herrington, *Curwensville area.*

Gordon Kephart, Curwensville. *(brother of Katherine and four other sisters).*

Gordon Miller, *Penn State.*

Grace Johns, *Classmate at Drexel; from Scranton.*

Grace Niles, *Drexel '27; Executive Board of Student Government.*

Grant "Red" Norris, *Dickinson; Mary Alice's date for a House Party there (Carlisle); friend from Curwensville.*

Guerry Brunetti, *Curwensville acquaintance.*

H. Kohrer, *Drexel. (possibly Koeh or Koehier, but I think Kohrer is the correct spelling.)*[10]

Haimie (Haim), *Drexel.*

Haines, *Friends in Curwensville.*

Harold Clark, *Drexel, Mary Alice's date for a Kappa Sigma Spring Formal.*

Harold Keefer, *Penn State.*

Harold Knight, *Clearfield native; professional musician in Philadelphia.*

Harold Strickland, *Curwensville.*

Harold Tatman, *Drexel.*

Harris G. Breth, *Clearfield, graduate of St. Francis High School, circa '23; friend and occasional invited member of "the gang." Also mentioned as part of the group in 1929 at a dinner held for Clearfield teachers.*[11]

Harry Bixler, *Drexel.*

Harry Brown, *Drexel.*

Harry Gardner, *Drexel '29.*

Harry Wilson, *Drexel.*

Hazel McMann, *Drexel.*

Hazel Thompson, *Drexel; girl friend of Carl Gregory.*

Helen (Alice Kay's sister), *Dickinson House Party.*

Helen Bromie, *Curwensville acquaintance.*

Helen Cruse, *classmate from Bellefonte High School and Highland Hall. Both appeared in the high school play, "The Spinster's Convention."*

Helen Decker, *Curwensville; sister of Louise.*

[10] Please be advised that these unfamiliar names are hand-written in Mary Alice's Diary.

[11] Industrial consultant, Member of the Pennsylvania House of Representatives, 1940-1942, 1947-1962; Chairman of the Conservation Committee; Member of the County Industrial Development; Member of the Screen Actors Guild, American Federation of Television and Radio Artists; Outdoor Writers Association; American Wildlife Society; and Pennsylvania Industrial Development Executives.

Helen Ellsworth, *Drexel.*

Helen Kephart, *Curwensville.*

Helen Kohlner, *a longtime friend, who visited Mary Alice in Philadelphia.*

Helen Mumford, *Drexel House Party.*

Helen Nace, *Drexel.*

Helen Shirk, *Curwensville.*

Henry Bixler, *Drexel.*

Henry Miller, *Clearfield.*

Henry Stetina, *Drexel '27; Treasurer of Junior Engineers Club; Drexerd[12] Editorial Staff '26; Senior Class Treasurer '27; rank as Major in R. O. T. C.; Secretary-Treasurer of Drexel's A. S. C. E (American Society for Civil Engineers); Kappa Sigma Delta (most cited fraternity in the Diary). Definitely a BMOC.*

Herb Horn, *Drexel.*

Hev Noll, *Clearfield.*

Heverly(s), *Bellefonte close family friends.*

Howard Chapman, *dated Mary Alice, September, 1929.*

Howard Jefferson (H. J.) Thompson (Papa), *Mary Alice's father (as his mother died when her sons were still young, it is unlikely that H.J. is a high school graduate; this obviously did not deter him from becoming one of the most successful businessmen in Curwensville.[13]*

Howard Vincent Thompson, *Mary Alice's older brother, a graduate of Clearfield High School, June 7, 1922.*

Howd Milligan, *friend of Bill McClure.*

Hugh and Kate Sayers, *with the group at Crystal Springs activities/parties.*

Hugh Norris, *Curwensville friend; graduate of Dickinson College in Carlisle.*

Hugh Quigley, *Clearfield family friend.*

Ida Bromley, *Drexel.*

Irene King, *Clearfield/Curwensville friend.*

Isabel Earhart, *Curwensville.*

Isabelle Ward, *Dickinson, likely a friend.*

J. Bullocks, *Drexel, Bellefonte friend, mentioned several places; Mary Alice attended his wedding.*

J. Clark, *Clearfield/Curwensville friend.*

J. Kirk Hile, *Curwensville.*

J. Martin, *date at Penn Alto (Penn State satellite campus) from Indiana.*

J. S. First, *Clearfield.*

---

[12] College magazine

[13] Also, Cassidy Coal Company, Curwensville Water Company, Strand Theatre, Curwensville State Bank.

Jack Hart's, *tavern and dance hall frequented by the college crowd. Live bands appeared in this popular gathering spot.*

Jack Moore, *Drexel.*

Jack Prather, *one of Mary Alice's social group.*

Jack Reynolds, *worked at the American Store.*

Jack Roberts, *escorted Mary Alice to the Phi Kappa Beta formal and house party as well as having many other dates with her. Class President, sophomore and junior years; photographic editor for the* Lexerd. *At one point Mary Alice and he were pinned.*

Jack Stock, *definitely not a favored beau.*

Jack Thompson, *Philipsburg; Mary Alice ran into him several times.*

Jack Wetherhold, *blind date, Sigma Kappa Kappa.*

Jack, *a professional singer at Cape May.*

Jake Kantar, *occasionally joined the group that went to the private camps and other social events. Family owned Kantar's variety stores, one of which was in Curwensville.*

Jane Clark, *Penn State; several mentions of her when Mary Alice went to a Penn State House Party, invited by Bill Jackson. Jane took her to breakfast.*

Jane Cross, *met Mary Alice in Philadelphia with Cousin Anna; is mentioned only once.*

Jane Heath; *Mary Alice occasionally went with her on double dates with fellows from Delta Sigma Epsilon.*

Jane Kirk, *one of Mary Alice's many friends. Jane was working at the shore the same time as Mary Alice was in 1929. Daughter of Harry Kirk in Curwensville; siblings included Harry, Jr., Richard, and Mary Jane. (Henry Kirk was the father of Alice.) Likely also related to Patty Kirk.*

Jane (and Carl) Murray; *Mary Alice ran into these friends when they were at Atlantic City in the summer of 1929.*

Jane Shaw; *Mary Alice and Bill Jackson double-dated several times with Jane Shaw and Bill Horn, 1927.*

Jane Smith; *Mary Alice, on a date with Bill Jackson, ran into Jane Smith and Tommy Mensch.*

Jane Teats, *with group at Greenwood.*

Jay Holten, *Curwensville, friend of the family; perhaps also the proprietor of a restaurant; the diary entries suggest that there was a place to dance at Holten's.*

Jay Miller, *friend of Miller Preston. On one particular double date, Kathleen was with Jay Miller and Mary Alice was with Miller Preston.*

Jean Whitney, *returning for second semester at Drexel in 1926, was one of several who shared a taxi.*

Jennie Mitchel, *attended a party at Hugh's (likely Hugh Norris) in December 1927.*

Jerel Twiner, *mentioned only once in passing.*

Jerry (female), *mentioned only once as a new roommate of Mim Spardle.*

Jerry McNaul, *one of Curwensville's respectable young men.*

Jerry Miller, *friend of June Frankenfield.*

Jessie Pifer, *classmate, close neighbor, and good friend of Mary Alice, occasionally visiting her in Philadelphia; sister of Catherine (Katherine) who married Mary Alice's brother. Read more about Jessie in the bios., "Jessie, Vamp to Victim" and "All the Gentlemen Caller," available on Amazon.*

Jewel, *mentioned only once as someone who went to Jack Hart's with Mary Alice.*

Jim McNulty, *from Dickinson. Lambda Chi house, Mary Alice met him at Sunbury.*

Jim Norris (Mr. and Mrs.), *relatives of Bill K. Jackson, whose mother was a Norris.*

Jimmy Gillen, *a graduating senior at Drexel when Mary Alice was a freshman.*

Jimmy Grant, *a young man from Curwensville who wanted to take Mary Alice home from a dance during Christmas break in 1926.*

Jimmy Hall, *young man known to the Jacksons in Philadelphia; Mary Alice invited him to the senior-freshman dance at Drexel.*

Jimmy Holton, *another young man she dated in C-ville area; had car trouble on one of their dates.*

Jimmy Johnson, *part of Curwensville's young singles crowd.*

Jimmy Strickland, *Mary Alice dated him, always loved him, Curwensville. His father was Zelotus and siblings were Jeannette, Harold, Earl, and Betty. Mary Alice's parents did not approve of JS. There are numerous mementoes in her high school scrapbook of events she attended with Jimmy, including one at the Dimeling Hotel on April 2, 1923.*

Joe Ellis, *part of the Drexel group.*

Joe Errigo '24, *Curwensville High School, attended U. of Pittsburgh (pharmacy).*

Joe Hipps, *one of the Greenwood group. Remained in C-ville and married Verna McGarvey '29.*

Joe Katz, *one of the Bellefonte young crowd.*

Joe Larnier, *one of the Drexel crowd who was at dinner at the Frankenfields (June).*

Joe Liese, *part of Drexel group.*

Joe Nichols, *Sigma Alpha Epsilon, Carnegie Institute. Mary Alice dated him when she went with friends to Pittsburgh and nearby places on a three-day trip during Easter break, 1929.*

Joe Parrish, *one of the group of young people who went out together when Mary Alice was visiting in Bellefonte for two days in September 1926.*

Joe Rhinehart, *one of the group who attended a wedding together, 1927.*

John Barryman Shearer, *one of the many young men Mary Alice dated at Drexel.*

John Deitz, *a very good friend of Jessie's from Clarion, who attended Penn.*

John Joseph, *a frequent date of Mary Alice; he is mentioned 95 times in her Diary. Attended the Univ. of Pennsylvania in Philadelphia. Nickname is "Joe," which led to much confusion for this writer.*

John Leitzinger, *part of the Clearfield crowd, lifetime friend of Mary Alice.*

John Martin, *dated Kathleen Hill and had a date with Mary Alice in late 1929.*

John McGurish, *one who made a terrific first impression on Mary Alice.*

John Scherer, *dated Mary Alice for only a short time during her freshman year.*

John Schiemer, *a friend of Marjorie Wall.*

John Sidener, *one Mary Alice dated as a freshman; she was not interested in him after that.*

John Spentel, *Drexel; a friend of a friend who was part of a double date.*

John Stamp, *is a son of the family in Buffalo for whom Maude Thompson (Aunt of Mary Alice) worked. He appears in Curwensville and likely the Stamps have family there. Likely his father's name is also John Stamp.*

John Trumpy, *appeared on Mary Alice's social scene during her senior year; she had a few dates with him, including the Senior Ball and Phi Kappa Beta events.*

John Wandall, *Mary Alice met him the fall of Freshman year. He mainly dated her roommate, Kathleen; later John and Kathleen were engaged. An Allentown native, John drove a Hudson Coach car.*

John Wells, *Drexel; attended fraternity dance after the Upsula football game. Appears only once.*

John Wright, *a great guy, friendly, regular part of the "young unmarried" group at Curwensville.*

Josie, *friend of the Thompson siblings and dinner guest at Aunt Mary's (This is Mary Wall who is married to Verne Wall).*

Julia and Bob Keeler, *friends in Bellefonte.*

Julia Bullock, *longtime friend from Unionville, a very small village (population 291 in 2010) in Centre County near, or perhaps now a part of, State College near Bellefonte. Julia appears throughout the Diary even into 1929. She may have attended a college "on the way" to Philadelphia because she rides the train with those friends headed to Philadelphia.*

June Ellis, *Mary Alice arranged for June to have a double date with friends in Philly.*

June Frankenfield, *good friend of Mary Alice at Drexel; June's real name was Naomi May. She lived in Allentown and held a party at her home during Easter break 1926.*

K. Reese, *acquaintance in Bellefonte.*

Karl Rowles, *Clearfielder at Drexel. Mary Alice also ran into him at Cape May, 1929. Karl would marry Alice Wall.*

Karstetter (Sara '20 and Louise '17), *family who had a bakery in Curwensville. Mentioned in the 1929 Diary.*

Kate Smith, *Clearfield/Curwensville friend, part of the social gaggle of young people.*

Katherine (Kate) Howd, *Class of '27, Drexel friend, mentioned several times.*

Kathleen Hill (M. Kathleen), *best friend of Mary Alice at Drexel; mentioned often; witty; made many friends. Spent a lot of time at events at the University of Pennsylvania with John, a steady boyfriend.*

Kathryn Smith, *nee Kephart, Curwensville; friend and classmate of Mary Alice and best friend of Catherine Pifer Thompson; K. Smith had the following siblings, all out of "central casting." The family included five girls and one son: Helen, Gordon, Ruth, Thelma, Elizabeth, and Mary.*

Kathryn/Katherine Thorn ("Tat"), *Mary Alice's best friend in Clearfield, Class of 1922; attended Drexel; they both taught Home Economics in the Clearfield Schools and took a cross-country automobile trip together in the early 1930s.*

Katy, *a woman hired to help with the H. J. Thompson household, particularly tending to and befriending Philip, fourteen years younger than Mary Alice.*

Kay Custer, *Clearfield acquaintance.*

Kay Quigley, *part of the Clearfield-Curwensville young crowd.*

Kay Smith, *a classmate and friend at Drexel.*

Kegerise, *assigned escort/date for Mary Alice at Phi Chi Medical Fraternity party.*

Kenny (Kenneth) Wall, *one of five siblings, first cousins to Mary Alice.*

Kenny Gearhart, *Clearfield friend and date.*

Kenny Johnston, *Clearfield; Mary Alice had several dates with him in 1929.*

Kenny Thorn, *part of the young adult Clearfield crowd; Mary Alice dated him several times in 1927.*

Kirk Hile, *mentioned throughout the Diary; very handsome; Clearfield cohort.*

Kitty Betz (Butz?), *friend of Mary Alice, Philadelphia.*

Kitty Plotts, *Philadelphia friend.*

Kitty Reese, *Bellefonte friend.*

Kochler *(Only part of the name is mentioned in the Diary). Mary Alice danced with him at Jack Hart's, Philadelphia.*

Mrs. Kittelberger *lived in Philadelphia; she was a family friend frequently mentioned; the Kittelberger family is Curwensville-based. (See information in separate section for this family.)*

Laura Reed, *Drexel, member of Sigma Sigma Sigma, and active in the YWCA.*

Lawrence Howe, *part of the Clearfield group of young people.*

Leah Siberon, *chaperone for a group from church in Philadelphia at a weekend retreat.*

Lenore Heller, *a Clearfield friend of Mary Alice's.*

Leo Sutton, *escort for Marjorie. On the way back after Christmas break, they worked a crossword puzzle (these were new at the time), which Mary Alice placed in her scrapbook where it remains.*

Leonard Bland, *likely Drexel; dated friends of Mary Alice.*

Leonard Kantar, *Curwensville High School, Class of 1919; one of the eligible bachelors in the group. Mary Alice attended the Charity Ball with him. Their family owned Kantar's Stores.[14] Father of the family was Isaac; sons were Leonard, Alex, Jake, and Hyman.*

Lester Long, *acquaintance at Drexel.*

Lib Hanes, *Drexel.*

Lib Wall, *multiple references; a cousin of the Wall cousins of Mary Alice. When Mary Alice was teaching she went to many social events with Lib.*

Libby Barnes, *Drexel.*

Libby Kephart, *wife or cousin to Gordon Kephart (see above), Curwensville.*

Lillian Morcey, *Drexel.*

Linn Gramer, *Drexel.*

Lisa Foreant, *Bellefonte friend.*

Liz Fontaine, *Drexel friend who tattled. (Given name likely is Elizabeth)*

Liz Wall, *part of the Greenwood gang. (Likely Elizabeth)*

Lois Hamilton, *Drexel friend of Mary Alice.*

Louise Decker, *Curwensville, sister of Helen. Friends of Mary Alice.*

Louise Satelle, *teaching colleague of Mary Alice at Clearfield Junior High School, 1929; part of the Clearfield group who helped decorate the Children's Home for Christmas.*

Louise Taylor, *Drexel friend who, as did others, left college to be married. Lived in Bellefonte.*

Lucinda Clark, *Drexel friend.*

Lucy Nichols, *Marjorie Wall's roommate at West Chester.*

M. Jane Mundy, *a friend Mary Alice met at an education meeting at Lock Haven Normal School.*

Mabel Dale, *Curwensville friend, 1925 social events.*

Mabel and Tom Forcey, *along with Winfield Sykes of Curwensville, visited Mary Alice at Drexel. (The Forceys likely were related to Francis Thompson through his wife Belle.)*

Mabel Phillips *was part of the group of friends who were on a jaunt to Ebensburg, summer 1925.*

Mae Crider, *Drexel.*

Magdeline Sunday, *part of a group of friends in a local Bellefonte excursion.*

Mahlon Robb, *friend in Philadelphia, likely Drexel.*

Mama (Mary Alice) Spencer, *the grandmother of our Diarist for whom she was named.*

Mamie Higgins, *at Jack Hart's. (May have been part of a small group from Clearfield who attended together.)*

Margaret Ardary, *see above with Mamie Higgins.*

---

[14] Kantar's Department Store in 1922 was located across from the National Bank. Mr. Kantar later built a large store on the same side of the street; managed mainly by Jacob and Leonard. A mainstay of the community and favorite destination.

Margaret Kelley, *part of the home crowd (Clearfield-Curwensville).*

Margaret Leitzinger, *one of the several collegians on the same train going home to Clearfield from various points, beginning in Philadelphia; she went on to Bradford.*

Margaret Rhodes, *one of the Curwensville gang of friends. Later would marry Joseph Errigo.*

Margaret Sharp, *another of the Curwensville gang.*

Marge (Margie) Irvin, *one of the "college crowd" from Curwensville. Attended West Chester.*

Marge Davis, *another of the gang from Curwensville.*

Margie Thorn, *sister of Mary Alice's good friend, "Tat" Thorn*

Marguerite Reichenbach, *a teacher of Latin at Curwensville High School and a friend of extended families—the Robinsons and the Walls.*

Marguerite Thorpe, *originally from Clearfield County, married Cecil C. Wall.*

Marian Haim, *Drexel.*

Marian Newgold, *entering freshman colleague, Drexel, Home Economics.*

Marie Bower, *Bellefonte friend.*

Marie Hobbs, *suspended indefinitely from Drexel.*

Marie Sloan, *a friend at Drexel; sister to Alveta.*

Mariella Redding, *Bellefonte friend.*

Marjory Hill, *friend at Drexel who left college to be married; Mary Alice continued correspondence with Marjory and saw her in Bellefonte.*

Marjorie Pifer, *wife of Clyde.*

Marjorie (Marge) Irvin, *Curwensville; attended West Chester, friend of M. Wall.*

Marjorie Miller, *visited Mary Alice after car trouble in Downingtown.*

Marjorie Wall, *Curwensville Class of '23, first cousin and best friend of Mary Alice; attended West Chester (later, career teacher in Norristown).*

Marjory, *an alternate spelling.*

Mark Hunter, *friend in Bellefonte.*

Marnie, *friend at Drexel.*

Martin Ardrey, *Curwensville acquaintance.*

Mary Gongler, *from Scanton, attended a House Party Mary Alice was attending, November 17, 1929.*

Mary and Vernon Wall, *Aunt and Uncle of Marjorie Wall (and, of course, of her brothers).*

Mary Churchill, *among the group who went to Drexel Lodge, a private hall/camp near Wayne belonging to Drexel Institute.*

Mary Conklin, *friend of Alice who visited the group at Greenwood Lodge.*

Mary Cunningham, *third year student at Drexel dismissed for stealing money.*

Mary Elizabeth, *part of the Curwensville gang (no last name found).*

Mary Frances, *Drexel.*

Mary Gordon Miller, *from Butler; Mary Alice met her at the Tyrone train station where the destination of both was a house party at Penn State.*

Mary Lou Warner, *Mary Alice ran into Mary Lou at the Kappa Sigma House, same house party at Penn State noted above; Junior Class President; Senior Class Vice-President.*

Mary Parish, *friend from Bellefonte.*

Mary Rider, *worked for Mary Alice's family. (Mary's home was in Sykesville; she was a friend of Katy, who also worked for the Thompson family.)*

Mary Shirk, *Curwensville friend.*

Mary Taylor, *with the group at Drexel Lodge.*

Mary Wolf, *sister to Cora, Curwensville; friends of Mary Alice.*

Matt Storey (or Florey), *Drexel; occasionally seen at Jack Hart's.*

Maude Allen, *acquaintance at West Chester.*

Maude Ann, *daughter of Fred Thompson; cousin to Mary Alice; niece of Maude Ann Thompson Davidson.*

Mauvis Wall, *wife of Kenneth Wall.*

May Crider, *Drexel.*

McDonald twins, *from DuBois; occasionally seen in Philadelphia.*

Mildred Larkin, *Drexel Class of '26, with group from Drexel Lodge (See* Lexerd*).*

Mildred Leib, *Curwensville friend whose father was a druggist.*

Mildred Starner, *Drexel friend, transferred from Dickinson College for only her senior year at Drexel.*

Mildred Stout, *Drexel, Home Economics '26, member of Key and Triangle Club.*

Miller Preston, *Mary Alice dated him at Drexel.*

Millie, *friend at the shore, 1929.*

Milly Laskin, *Drexel.*

Milton Bloom/Blume, *Clearfield, 1929.*

Mim/Min Rodrick, *Drexel, Thanksgiving, 1926; Student House Board '27.*

Mimsey Book, *Drexel; involved in the Home Economics Practice House.*

Min Spardle, *Drexel; male friend of John Joseph.*

Miss Alice, *proprietor of tea room at the shore where Mary Alice worked.*

Miss Cruise, *person who had a Tea Room at the Jersey Shore; Mary Alice worked there at the end of her freshman year at Drexel.*

Miss Margaret, *an adult who worked at the shore tearoom with Mary Alice.*

Miss May, *guest or worker at the shore tearoom with Mary Alice.*

Mitch Akers, *good dancer at Jack Hart's.*

Mitchell, *attendee at Clearfield teachers' dinner, 1929.*

Mitzie, *classmate who had a role in the play "The Madcap."*

Mr. Beezer, *attended (with Marjorie Wall) one of their Camp parties, likely at Greenwood.*

Mr. Beggs, *Mary Alice had dinner with him after picking up a junior high basketball team and taking them back to the school, 1929.*

Mr. Byington, *Philadelphia; he took a number of students for a ride after church.*

Mr. Clancy, *date for Jane Heath with group at Devon Park Hotel.*

Mr. Kochler, *Mary Alice danced with him at Jack Hart's.*

Mr. Strickland, *owned cottages for rent at the shore when Mary Alice was working there.*

Mrs. Cruise (aka Grandma), *family member of those who owned the tea room where Mary Alice worked. Part of Mary Alice's duties was to care for this elderly lady. (My summation is that this is a professional family that includes Dr. Cruise and Miss Cruise, who is the proprietor of the Tea Room at the shore.)*

Mrs. Erbert, *cook or housekeeper for the Thompson family.*

Mr. Hare, *a date at the shore, 1929.*

Mrs. Harper *from Beaver, family friend of the Thompsons.*

Mrs. Haverly/Heverly, *family friend.*

Mrs. Ilrisher, *family friend who managed a rooming house in Philadelphia.*

Mr. and Mrs. Jim Norris, *Philadelphia, relative of the Norris Family in C-ville; Bill Jackson's mother was a Norris from the Curwensville area and it was through this connection that Mary Alice first met William Jackson.*

Mrs. Robinson, *aunt of Alice Wall.*

Mrs. Scott, *house mother, Drexel, Home Economics dorm.*

Murray Clark, *part of the gang of Clearfield/Curwensville friends; Class President, Curwensville '25. (My copy of the 1925 Echo bears his signature of ownership.)*

Naomi Machless, *friend of Mary Alice, 1929.*

Nate Smith, *paired with Mary Alice at a wedding in Clearfield they both attended.*

Neema Clarentine, *among the group who had Memorial Day parties in Philadelphia.*

Nellie Coleman, *Drexel.*

Nelma Smith, *Bellefonte, part of group who partied in Philadelphia, Memorial Day 1927.*

Nelson Harris, *friend of Mary Alice at the Jersey shore, 1929.*

Nelva, *part of the party group, Memorial Day '27 in Philadelphia.*

Neville ("Bugs") Smith *from Cleveland, date, Philadelphia, fall of 1926.*

Newton Clark McCullough, *date, fall of 1925, Drexel.*

Olive Eckert, *Curwensville High School, Class of 1922, part of the group who camped at Anchor Inn.*[15]

Orlie Norris, *related to Mary Alice through her mother.*

Orvil King, *one of a group of friends picked up by Mary Alice and others who then took the hikers back to camp at Greenwood.*

Orville Johnson, *attendee at party at the Legion in Curwensville, Christmas 1925.*

Orvis (last name may be Thompson, son of William), *friend of Jimmy Strickland and others of the group.*

Pat Latimer, *appears at social events/camping excursions as part of Drexel crowd.*

Pat Wotimer, *attended a Spring 1927, Drexel-sponsored camping event.*

Patty Kirk, *appears at several events at various places, likely a daughter of one of the Kirk brothers. Lives in Clearfield or Curwensville.*

Paul "Piggie" Burr, *invited Mary Alice to the Sophomore Hop at Drexel, 1925; Dreserd Advertising Staff; Phi Kappa Beta. Appears throughout. Mary Alice dated him a number of times.*

Paul Johnston, *Kappa Sigma; Mary Alice had a few dates and attended a dance with him.*

Paul Lutz *(Altoona), Overbrook Gold Club, a Drexel dance, Freshman Fall.*

Paul A. Zetler, aka P. A. Z., *a science teacher at Curwensville High School, noted as being Marjorie Wall's date both locally (Curwensville) and in Philadelphia (according to this Diary).*

Pauline Allen, *attended the Acorn Club for New Year's Dance, 1925.*

Pauline Snyder, *friend from Punxsutawney; Mary Alice rode home with her family at the end of freshman year after meeting Pauline on the train to Tyrone.*

Pearl Todhunter, *date of Kenny Wall.*

Peg Alexander/Alexandria, *freshman, lived in an apartment, impressive perk from Mary Alice's perspective.*

Peg Bean, *Drexel friend; one of three girls who attended the Court Dance, then went to Jack Hart's to dance.*

Peg Hartel, *Drexel Phi Kappa Beta dance.*

Peg Leitzinger, *friend at Drexel.*

Peggy Lou, *brought before the House Board for an infraction.*

Perdita Ardrey, *Curwensville Class of '22, Yearbook staff, Curwensville. Mary Alice attended her bridal shower.*

Pete Barney, *Curwensville friend.*

Pete Chase, *Clearfield friend, 1929.*

Pete Pross, *Phi Delta; Mary Alice went to the Sophomore Hop with him.*

---

[15] The author remembers her as a very earnest grocery clerk.

Pete Martin, *M.A. dated him in 1929.*

Phil Johnson, *Curwensville friend.*

Philip Bell Thompson, *much younger brother of Mary Alice.*

Phyllis Weinberg, *Drexel; dated John Joseph.*

Pifer family *who lived directly across from the Thompsons in Curwensville. Jessie, Catherine/ Katherine, and Jean Pifer were all in high school at the same time as Mary Alice during the 1920s.*

Porter, *Bellefonte friend.*

Ralph Fleming, *Curwensville friend of John Stamp.*

Ray Wiley, *friend in Clearfield, 1929.*

Raybold, *acquaintance at Dickinson.*

Raymond J. Holten, *part of the young crowd, Clearfield/Curwensville.*

Raymond Maurey, *Clearfield area. Mary Alice dated him.*

Rayonner, *a member of the Clearfield set of young adults.*

Reba Frank, *freshman friend at Drexel.*

Rebecca Ardery, *Curwensville friend.*

Reece, *Mary Alice corresponded with him; no indication of dates recorded.*

Rice (Mr. & Mrs.), *part of bridge group including Mary Alice, 1929.*

Richlens, *Bellefonte friends who shared an interest with H.J. in the new theatre there, the Richelieu.*

Ronald Feioli, *fellow who once escorted Mary Alice home from Jack Hart's.*

Rose Bloom, *Curwensville friend, member of the young adult crowd.*

Roy Strickland, *part of the Curwensville group of friends.*

Roy Taylor, *Mary Alice met him at the shore, Cape May 1929.*

Rufus Newcomber, *Curwensville crowd, friend of Stricklands.*

Russel Price, *part of group who went to the Clearfield County Fair together, 1925.*

Ruth K., *one of a group of students who attended Drexel Lodge for orientation, fall 1924.*

Ruth McCullough '25, *(new London, Ct.) steady date of Sammy Jones, Drexel.*

Ruth Miller, *Drexel.*

Ruth Parker, *graduate of Drexel.*

Ruth Rarsary, *friend of Mary Alice throughout the years at Drexel.*

Ruth Stout, *long-time friend through years at Drexel.*

S. Bennett, *Drexel friend, Home Economics.*

Sally Schaffer, *Drexel.*

Samuel (Sammy) Jones, *steady of Ruth McCullough; President of Phi Kappa Beta; Men's Student Council; Chairman, Senior Ball; popular and, using Mary Alice's favorite description, "sweet."*

Sara Bennett, *Drexel friend, a Junior who signed Mary Alice's Lexerd.*

Sara Paishall, *Drexel friend; active member of Key and Triangle Club: Drexerd Editorial Staff; Alpha Sigma Alpha, Panhellenic Council.*

S. Taylor, *Friend in 1929 in Curwensville.*

Sara Thompson, *Drexel friend, Home Economics, like most of Mary Alice's close pals; House President of Home Ec. House.*

Sarah Ann Sutliff, *Drexel friend, group who went to Drexel Lodge.*

Sarah King, *part of the group at Greenwood Lodge.*

Saul Merkin, *Clearfield fellow, on the same train as Mary Alice on one of her trips home from Philadelphia.*

Scott Ammerman, *one of the Curwensville fellows at the Legion Party, Dec. 1929.*

Selma Shanabe, *Drexel friend.*

Shorty, *fellow from Beaver College.*

Sidney Korb, *Curwensville Class of 1923; brother, but not twin, to Mildred Korb, also CHS '23; Mary Alice dated him.*

Snowden Ebling, *brother of Mary Alice's friend Virginia; lived in Malvern.*

Speed Bland, *member of fraternity near the Home Ec. rooming house.*

Stella Robinson, *Philadelphia, related to Jacksons.*

Steve McKenzie, *Curwensville.*

Sue Krusens, *Drexel student who lived with her parents in their home off campus.*

Susie, *cousin to Kathleen, Mary Alice's best friend at Drexel. Susie lived in the area.*

Sutton Hamilton, *Penn Medical School; Mary Alice had a date with him.*

Ted, *(last name never mentioned), Glen Campbell area; Mary Alice dated him extensively during 1929.*

Ted Bowes, *attended Curwensville Legion Party, December 1929.*

Thelma Kephart, *one of the large family of Kepharts (See Kathryn Smith above.)*

Thelma Sykes, *Drexel friend.*

Theo Jordan, *Clearfield friend.*

Thornton Hile, *Clearfield friend.*

Thornton Morris, *good dancer from Penn; Mary Alice met him at Jack Hart's.*

Tom Betts, *friend from Curwensville/Clearfield.*

Tom Dolan, *Mary Alice ran into him at the Jersey shore, 1929.*

Tom Murray, *Clearfield; Mary Alice dated him in 1929, including Christmas Day.*

Tommy Mather, *Drexel cheerleader and friend of Mary Alice; Editor-in-Chief of new newspaper on Drexel campus, The Drexel Hexagon '25-'26; Kappa Sigma Delta.*

Tommy Mensch, *Clearfield friend; attended Penn State.*

Tony, *Mary Alice wrote to him from Drexel. No last name.*

Ty Cobb, *friend at Drexel.*

Uncle Charley Wall, *father of Marjorie and her four brothers; Mary Alice's uncle.*

Vernon Wall, *Charles' brother.*

Viola, *friend of Mary Alice, 1926.*

Virginia Ebling, *Drexel friend, Malvern, PA.*

Virginia Murray, *Curwensville classmate.*

W. Hill, *Curwensville or Clearfield; Mary Alice corresponded with him.*

Walter & Lottie Thompson, *uncle and aunt of Mary Alice. (The name "Lottie" likely a nickname for Charlotte, her given name.) Walter is the oldest of the four Thompson brothers.*

Walter Haim, *Drexel; endured a long hospitalization in 1927.*

Ward Ebling, *brother to Virginia; perhaps to Snowden as well.*

Warren Steel, *Drexel; dinner date with Mary Alice.*

Wasson, *Drexel; friend of John Joseph.*

Wes(s) Sauter, *Clearfield; dated Dot Dimeling.*

William Kittelberger, *Curwensville '23, went to Lehigh College. He is the son of Harry Kittelberger. See extended information on the Kittelbergers.*

William S. Hutchins, *Penn Dental School; Mary Alice met him at Jack Hart's.*

William Spundle, *date with Edith on double date with Mary Alice and John Joseph.*

Willis Hile; *Harmie dated him at Drexel.*

Wilson Norfleet from Cuba; *Mary Alice took a fancy to him at Jack Hart's.*

Wilton Wright '28, *Drexel. Mary Alice dated him a number of times. Phi Kappa Beta,* Triangle *staff.*

Winfield Sykes, *Curwensville; visited Mary Alice at Drexel with Tom and Mable Forcey.*[16]

---

[16] (Sykes is on the cover of this author's book *All the Gentlemen Callers*). His family lived at 423 Thompson Street. Father was J. W. His siblings are Irene and Catherine. (Allegedly, Irene Sykes is the one who gave Jessie singing lessons that appeared to have damaged her very fine singing voice.)

Home Economics Faculty at Drexel

Adenia Chapman, M.A., Associate Professor of Home Economics

Agnes C. Brown, M.A., Instructor in Home Economics

Amanda Ebersole, M.A., Program Supervisor in Home Economics; mentioned often

Anna C. Moe, B.A., Instructor in Home Economics

Beatrice O. Jones, M.A., Instructor in Home Economics

Bernice L. Chellis, B.A., R.N., Instructor in Home Nursing

Emily D. Parker, B.S., D.I., Instructor in Home Economics

Florence M. Turner, A.M., Instructor in Home Economics

Grace Godfrey, M.S., Professor of Home Economics

Helen L. Argar, B.S., Instructor in Home Economics

Janet Myers, PhB., Instructor in Home Economics

Marion Crawley, Instructor in Physical Education

Marjorie Sims, A.M., Instructor in Home Economics

Mildred Burdett, B.S., Instructor in Home Economics

Miss Bergen, Substitute House Mother, Drexel

Miss Dashiell, Supervisor of the Home Economics house

Miss Illman, Supervised the stay at Drexel Lodge

Miss Worrell, Instructor; Mary Alice had dinner at her home.

Mr. Croyle, Instructor, Drexel

Nellie M. Lotz, D.I., Instructor in Home Economics

Nina I. Miller, D.I., B.S., Instructor in Home Economics

Orrel T. Baldwin, B.S., Instructor in Home Economics

Rose T. Baker, M.A., Asst. Professor of Home Economics

Ruth A. L. Dorsey, Dean of Women

Ruth Burwash, M.A., Instructor in Home Economics

Ruth Michaels, PhB., M.A., Assistant Professor of Home Economics

Additional Local Persons likely related to Mary Alice

W. A. Thompson, 612 State Street

Orvis Thompson, 428 Thompson Street

William Thompson, 428 Thompson Street

Mrs. Clara Thompson, 435 Thompson Street

James Thompson, 430 Thompson Street

Mrs. Kathryn Thompson (Aunt Kate), a centenarian, 430 Thompson Street

H. B. Thompson, Heating and Plumbing, 551 State Street

Josephine Thompson

Mrs. H. Philip Thompson (Helen Louise and Harold Philip, friend of Mary Alice's brother Philip)

Good Friends of Mary Alice Who Became Teachers in the 1920s

Edith Sawtelle '22

Elizabeth Wall '22

Jessie Pifer '24

Kathryn ("Tat") Thorne '23

Kathryn Kephart '24

Kathryn Pifer '25

Lois Vaughn, '22

Margaret Kelly '24

Margaret Rhodes '24

Marjorie Murray '22

Marjorie Wall '23

Mildred Korb '23

Mary Alice Thompson's
Scrapbook & Photo
Sampler

M.A.T.

277

The Drexel Institute

No. ....

THIS IS TO CERTIFY THAT

Mary Alice Thompson

IS A MEMBER OF THE

**DREXEL INSTITUTE
ATHLETIC ASSOCIATION**

FOR THE COLLEGIATE YEAR OF 1924-25. SUBJECT TO
THE RULES AND REGULATIONS THEREOF, AND IS NON-
TRANSFERABLE.

№ 145   1924-1925

NAME *M. A. Thompson*

DREXERD

No Drexerds will be issued unless this card is presented

♦ ♥ ♦ ♣ ♠ ♣ ♠   8

Freshman Year

Official Handbook

OF

Rules and Regulations

FOR THE USE
OF STUDENTS

⁂

The Drexel Institute

I'M A
FRESHMAN

Mary Alice Thompson

Curwensville

Pa.

DREXEL · INSTITUTE

ADMISSION
$1.00

FRANKLIN FIELD
Wednesday, Oct. 1st, 1924

Drexel Institute

Delta Upsilon, Penn State

Jack Prather

Annual Banquet

OF

Methodist Students in the City of Philadelphia

NOVEMBER 3, 1924

THE RITTENHOUSE

GIVEN BY THE WESLEY FOUNDATION

—

Menu

Fruit Cup

Puree of Tomato Soup

Roast Sirloin of Beef, au Jus

Rissolee Potatoes   Early Peas

Coleslaw Mayonnaise

              Fancy Cake

Neapolitaine Ice Cream

Demi-tasse

Toastmaster

-:- PROGRAM -:-
"Cap and Bells"

Auditorium, Drexel Institute, February 27, 1925

8 P. M.

Auspices of Y. W. C. A. and Y. M. C. A.

A.
"AN EVENING IN THE CABARET OF THE ZUZUS"
Freshman Girls

2nd page   _With Jack Prather_

B.
"AT THE BAR"
Freshman Engineers

C.
"INSUFFICIENT SWEETIES"
Sophomore Girls

D.
"A BIT OF FOOISHNESS"
Junior Engineers

E.
"TWO ROWES CAUSE A TOUGH TIME"
Sophomore Engineers   _1st page_

F.
"ON PARTIES"
Senior Girls

G.
"NONSENSE"
Senior Engineers

H.
"FINISHED PRODUCTS"
Junior Girls

Dance
Women's Student Government
of
Drexel Institute
at
Overbrook Golf Club

October 25, 1924.

8:30 p. m. $2.00

Went with Paul Lutz

Annual Dance

Pennsylvania Epsilon
Phi Delta Theta

HERTZLER HALL
Carlisle, Pennsylvania

FRIDAY, FEBRUARY SIXTH
NINETEEN HUNDRED TWENTY-FIVE

BASKET BALL
SCHEDULE—1924-25

University
of
Pennsylvania

NORMAN L. PANCOAST............Manager
H. LEE JONES.........Associate Manager
WILLIAM H. KNEASS.............Captain
ROBERT A. EICHELBERGER....Asst. Manager
MAURICE A. GILMARTIN, JR...Asst. Manager

Mary Alice

Women's Basketball Team - Drexel

280

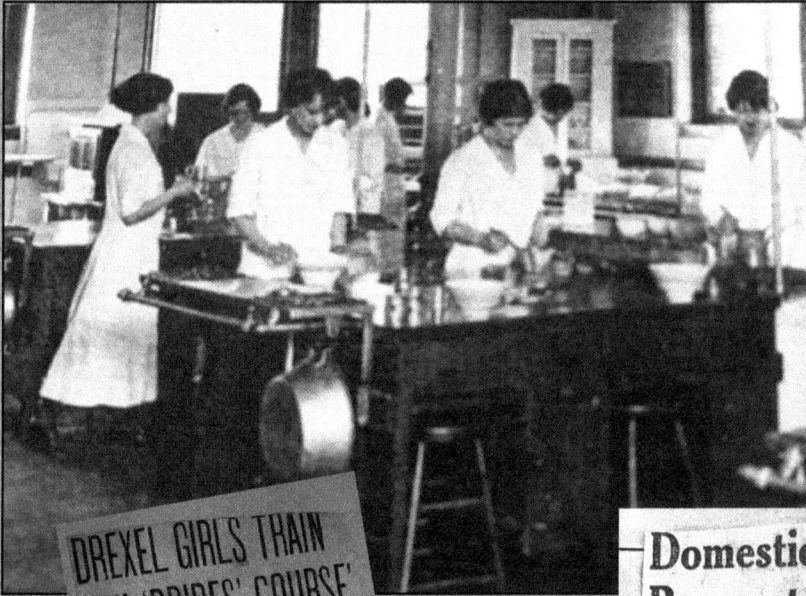

DREXEL GIRLS TRAIN IN 'BRIDES' COURSE

4 Seniors in Home Economics Classes Announce Engagements

Four girls, seniors in the home economics courses at Drexel Institute, are engaged, and following their graduation in six weeks, will be married, it became known yesterday.

This as well as other similar instances in the past, has resulted in the home economics courses becoming known as "brides' courses."

The four students who have announced their engagements are Miss Margaret Schwab, of Harrisburg, Pa.; Miss Irene Elizabeth Manon, of Charleroi, Pa.; Miss Mildred Leola Kutz, of Massillon, O., and Hannah Belle Dewitt, of Falls, Pa.

They will graduate from the school with what is calculated to be the best possible training for marriage. They will know how to keep house, how to make their own clothing and millinery, and how to economically spend their husbands' salaries.

Among the many facilities of Drexel for making the courses effect-

Domestic Science Dept. Banquets School Board

The Domestic Science Department of the Junior High School, under the direction of Miss Kathryn Thorn and Miss Mary Alice Thompson, served their annual dinner to the members of the school board and their wives in the Junior High Monday night at 6:00 o'clock. Eighteen of the directors and their wives were present to enjoy what was claimed by them to be the best dinner ever served by the students at this annual affair. After partaking of the bounteous feast they were unstinting in the praise they bestowed on the members of the classes and their instructors. The girls were congratulated on their ability to prepare and serve such a highly pleasing dinner.

275

Mary Alice   Jessie Piper

James Strickland

Jimmy

HENRY JOHN STETINA
WEST PHILADELPHIA HIGH SCHOOL
PHILADELPHIA, PA.
Class Treasurer, 2, 3, 4.
Secretary-Treasurer, A. S. C. E. 4.
Manager of Track, 4.
Drexerd Staff, 2, 3, 4.
One of the rarest qualities in all the world is
originality. "Stet" is to be particularly commended,
therefore, on the possession of a considerable quantity
of it. This characteristic has displayed itself in the
birds'eye maps of Philadelphia that have graced the
Drexerd on several occasions, as well as the page of
timely comments in the same publication, edited by
this illustrious individual.
Stetina has been blessed with as pleasing an address, as fine a personal appearance as any one could
wish for, so it is only natural that he should count a
goodly number of conquests among his social achieve-
ments. However, he has never forgotten that his
aim is Civil Engineering that is really Civil.

"Dance"
Auspices Junior Woman's Club
Clearfield, Penna.
Hotel Dimeling
Monday evening, April 2, 1923
at nine o'clock
"Jokers Orchestra, of Ohio"

Assessment
Dancing $1.50
Cards   .75 } including refreshments

LADIES MAY OBTAIN TICKETS FROM MEMBERS OF THE CLUB

May 20, 1925.

The Student House Board has decided that you must for-
feit your privileges from May 23 to May 28 inclusive. You
have certainly been here long enough to know the rule regarding dating when you have conditions, and we feel it
necessary to make you realize the importance of this rule in
the future.

Harriet E. Clafey
Secretary,
Student Gov. Association

2

CARL VICTOR GREGORY
LATROBE HIGH SCHOOL   LATROBE, PA.
ΦKB Fraternity, President 4.
Blue Key Fraternity.
A. S. C. E.
Basketball 1-2-3-4, Captain 4.
Men's Student Council 2-3-4, Secretary 4.
Triangle Staff.
Captain R. O. T. C.
Chairman of Military Ball.
There is a reason for the thinness of the hair adorning
Greg's head. For four years now he has been inaus-
piciously searching that elusive degree in Civil Engineering
which in itself is enough to make any man's head become
devoid of decorations.
Naturally a good student, though not predisposed to
overstudy by any means, he has created an enviable record
for himself in both the scholastic and social world. Carl's
short stay with us has justified any praise that we may
write of him, and as virtue is its reward we believe that
he may look no fear of the future.

THE DREXEL INSTITUTE

EXAMINATION BOOK

Name Mary Alice Simpson
Date
Subject

93

282

Took John Joseph

DREXEL INSTITUTE PHILADELPHIA
1892

Senior Dance
Class 1925
Drexel Institute
—
Friday evening
April the seventeenth
1925
—
8.45 o'clock
—
Georgian Room
Pelham Club

Wegman   Subscription
Five $2.50

DANCE PROGRAM HOUSE DANCE

Φ Γ Σ

Ω Δ Ε
TEA DANCE
WEDNESDAY - 4 TO 6
ART GALLERY.

SNAPPY STORIES
FEB 26
TAX - $2.50

SOS

DON'T FORGET!   JUNIOR
DREXEL ~ COURT   PROM
PICCADILLY '8'

Interfraternity Ball
Under the auspices of
The Interfraternity
Council
of
The University of
Pennsylvania

Penn Athletic Club
March the twenty fifth
Nineteen Hundred and Twenty Seven

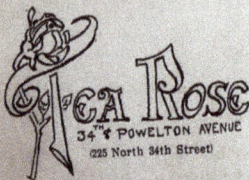

PENNSYLVANIA
RAILROAD COMPANY
PHILADELPHIA, PA. to
CURWENSVILLE, PA.

Via Tyr...
Good for One Passage beginning within
THIRTY DAYS in addition to date of issue,
stamped on back.
Subject to tariff regulations.
(1083 A)
Form M

The President of the Drexel Institute
and
Mrs. Matheson
request the pleasure of your company
in the Picture Gallery
Thursday, October 30
Four to five-thirty o'clock

Thirty-second & Chestnut Streets
Philadelphia

BIRTHDAY
GREETINGS,
to my NIECE!

To You your birthday means an added year.
To Me it means a thing to make me glad.
For had you never had a birthday, dear.
A niece like you I never should have had.

Aunt Maude

Forrest Theatre
Thos. M. Love, General Manager

POSITIVELY TWO WEEKS ONLY
BEGINNING MONDAY, OCTOBER 26, 1925
Nights at 8.15. Matinees Wed. & Sat. at 2.15
Final Performance Saturday Night, Nov. 7

FLORENZ ZIEGFELD
Presents the 20th of the Series
ALL MADE IN AMERICA
of
The National Institution

Ziegfeld Follies
OF 1925
Staged by JULIAN MITCHELL
Dialogue by
J. P. McEvoy, W. C. Fields and Gus Weinburg
Lyrics by Gene Buck
Music by Raymond Hubbell, Dave Stamper
and Werner Janssen
Orchestra under direction of Charles A. Prince
Produced by F. ZIEGFELD

Red Lights Denote Exits

We have been told—our repaint job is better
than the original—Dorham.

Chestnut St. Opera House
WEEK BEGINNING MONDAY MATI
FEBRUARY 22, 1926
Matinees Monday, Wednesday and Satu

THE MESSRS. SHUBERT
Present

MAY FLOWER

The Stanley
NINETEENTH AND MARKET
CONTINUOUS—11 A. M. TO 11 P. M.
FIRST SHOWING ANYWHERE

RUDOLPH
VALENTINO
in
"THE EAGLE"

Supplemental Feature Program
FRANK FARNUM
AND HIS DANCE REVUE
Solos by the Baritone
TANSY McKENZIE
STANLEY ORCHESTRA—LOCAL NEWS

Broad St. Theatre
Frank Nirdlinger, Business Manager

SECOND WEEK
BEGINNING MONDAY, FEBRUARY 15, 1926
Nights at 8.15. Matinees Wed. & Sat. at 2.15

DAVID BELASCO
Presents

"Ladies of the Evening"

Sam S. Shubert T
BEGINNING MONDAY, OCTOBER 12th, 1925
Matinees Wednesday and Saturday

ARTHUR HAMMERSTEIN Presents

"ROSE-MARIE"
A Musical Play
(A Romance of the Canadian Rockies)
Book and Lyrics by
Otto Harbach and Oscar Hammerstein, 2nd
Music by Rudolf Friml and Herbert Stothart
Production under Personal Supervision of
Arthur Hammerstein

Chestnut St. Opera House
Beginning Monday Night, October 19, 1925
Matinees Wednesday and Saturday
MESSRS. SHUBERT Present
THE SECOND ANNUAL EDITION

ARTISTS AND MODELS"

FROM ELEVATED — South & West-bound

AM 2 3 4 5 6 7 8 9 10 11 PM 12 1

Sunday NOV. **16**

041355

This Transfer Ticket Receivable ONLY—on route, in direction and at junction point as designated on reverse side of this ticket—for a continuous trip of person to whom issued—within time punched—on date printed hereon. *E. Davis* TREASURER

A MISDEMEANOR—The sale, barter, or transfer of this ticket, or its presentation for passage by anyone other than the person to whom issued, constitutes a misdemeanor under the laws of the State of Pennsylvania, punishable by fine or imprisonment or both. Act approved June 13, 1911. P.L. 503.

M 3 4 5 6 7 8 9 10 11 | A.M. NEXT DATE 12 1 2

TALLY

3 A 16
ROW SEC. NO.
Reserved Seat

THE CORNER Restaurant

The Corner Restaurant in State College, Pa

FOX THEATRE

Market at Sixteenth Street
Philadelphia Pa.

SUPERIOR PHOTOPLAY PRODUCTIONS

WILLIAM FOX
Circuit of Theatres

"The Pride of Philadelphia"
FOX THEATRE GRAND ORCHESTRA

ERNO RAPEE
MANAGING DIRECTOR

PAY TOTAL OF FARE AND EXTRAS
SEND TICKET WITH ANY COMPLAINT TO

Yellow Cab Co
LOCUST 7200 RACE 4241
FARE   EXTRAS
No. 1632
030 APR 28   2779   —

EAGLE

Eagle Theatre, Montgomery, Pa

HIGHLAND HALL
HOLLIDAYSBURG, PENNSYLVANIA

My First RECITAL *& Last*
if possible
GIVEN BY THE
DEPARTMENT OF MUSIC.

SATURDAY EVENING AT EIGHT O'CLOCK, JANUARY

PROGRAM

Musette — Bach
Water-sprites—Barcarolle — Neidlinger
Isabelle Warford

Gondoliera — Reinhold
Hungarian Dance
Mary Alice Thompson *forgot this—played it over—then tried trying to get it right.*

Invention, C major — Bach
Maria Conradi

To a Wildrose — MacDowell
Scherzo — Gurlitt
Dorothy Stafford

Heimweh — Schumann
Romance
Marguerite Rice

Canzonetta — Hollaender
Spirit of Chivalry — Burgmuller
Katherine Books

Barcarolle — Scharwenka
Gertrude Toner

Scherzo — Schubert
Helen Nichols

Love Song
Martha Dickerson

Waltz, D flat
Marie Rodkey

"MISS SOMEBODY ELSE"
(Directed by the High School Faculty)
CAST OF CHARACTERS

Constance Darcy · · · · Margaret Rhodes
Celeste · · · · Jessie Pifer
Ann Delavan · · · · Helen Martin
Mildred Delavan · · · · Alice Wall
Mrs. Blainwood · · · · Frances Hooven
Fay Blainwood · · · · Jeannette Strickland
Alice Stanley · · · · Kathryn Kephart
Freda Mason · · · · Dorothy Bixler
Mrs. Herrick · · · · Mildred Leib
Susan Ruggs · · · · Estella Bulkley
Cruger Blainwood · · · · Joe Errigo
Ralph Hastings · · · · Orville Hipps
John · · · · Victor Grande
Jasper Delavan · · · · Sam Cross
Sylvester Crane · · · · Kay Wrigley
Bert Shaffer · · · · Gunnard Olson

SYNOPSIS

Act I. — Time: Present
Act II. — Time: Ten Days Later
Act III. — Time: A Few Weeks Later
Act IV. — Time: In the Evening
The scenes take place in the Tuxedobrook Club House.

SECOND ANNUAL
CAPE MAY
JUVENILE JUBILEE
Cape May, N. J.   August 29, 30 and 31, 1929

CURWENSVILLE
LABOR DAY
1924

WESTERN UNION

The Penn State Thespians
and
Glee Club
present
"VARIETY"

houseparty-moderne number
Fall 1931 - Bill Stiles - Phi Kappa Sigma

TIME   the penn state froth   IMPO

The Penn State Thespians
PRESENT
As Their 32nd Annual Production
June 1930
House Party Bill Johnson
"The Duchess in Dutch"

The SOPHOMORE HO
MARCH 14, 1930

CURWENSVILLE
HIGH SCHOOL
ALUMNI
ASSOCIATION

41st Annual Reunion
and Banquet

Locust Street Auditorium
Curwensville, Pennsylvania
Thursday evening, May 29th
1930

Jessie Pifer

Mary Alice

Mary Alice

Jessie Pifer

Cloches and Coats!

Post = Card

FOR CORRESPONDENCE

FOR ADDRESS ONLY

PLACE
ONE-CENT
STAMP
HERE

The places I marked are the windows of our room. We have a wonderful room, we see everything that goes on

Highland Hall

DREXEL INSTITUTE 1891

Large Celebration held at Drexel

"GREENWOOD" CLUB. "MOUNTAINS NORTH OF CURWENSVILLE"

CAMP ELLIOT BUNGALOWS

L. Taylor, Marjorie Wall, and Mary Alice at Camp Elliot

Mary Alice, far right, with friends, visiting one of H. J. Thompson's mines

College Sweethearts,
Mary Alice Thompson
and Bill Jackson

Mary Alice

Bill Jackson

Delta Upsilon House Party 1927

William K. Jackson

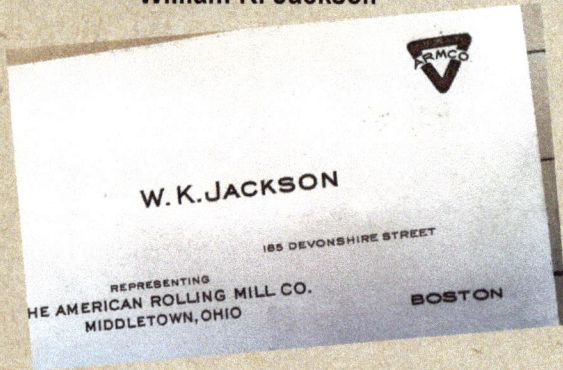

W. K. JACKSON

185 DEVONSHIRE STREET

REPRESENTING
THE AMERICAN ROLLING MILL CO.
MIDDLETOWN, OHIO

BOSTON

BARON & WILSON HOTELS

"SAVANNAH'S BEST"
HOTEL SAVANNAH
SAVANNAH, GA.
"JACKSONVILLE'S LEADING HOTEL"
HOTEL SEMINOLE
JACKSONVILLE, FLA.

HOTEL SAVANNAH
ANDREW A. SMITH
RESIDENT MANAGER

HOTEL SEMINOLE
ROY McCOMBS
RESIDENT MANAGER

WRITTEN FROM THE HOTEL SAVANNAH
SAVANNAH, GA.

Monday

Dearest May-
         I have neglected
answering your sweet letter
in hopes that I might be able
to do it from N.Y. - But have
given up hopes - times are
to hard. The old racket has finally
got me tied up completely - I
guess Hugh must be pretty
well tied up also.
         May I miss you more
then ever - You should be

Radio in Every Room.

Bill Jackson with
Mary Alice Thompson

Merry Christmas
to the dearest girl
in all the world!
Bill

You're my Valentine
now - for always!
Love, Bill

292

Mary Alice Thompson
William K. Jackson

Announce Engagement of Mary Alice Thompson

Mr. and Mrs. H. J. Thompson of Curwensville announced the engagement of their daughter, Mary Alice Thompson, to William K. Jackson of Lansdowne, Pennsylvania, at a family dinner Saturday evening. Miss Thompson was a teacher in the home economics department of the Clearfield Junior High School last year, and has many friends in Clearfield.

The engagement of Miss Mary Alice Thompson, of Curwensville, Pa., to William K. Jackson, son of Mr. and Mrs. William C. Jackson, of Lansdowne, has been announced by Mr. and Mrs. Howard J. Thompson, parents of the bride-to-be.

Mr. W. C. Jackson

Placecards: William K. Jackson and
Mary Alice Thompson Wedding Reception

Mrs. W. K. Jackson

'28 Mary Alice Thompson has announced her engagement to William K. Jackson, of Lansdowne, Pa.

Mr. and Mrs. H. J. Thompson announced the engagement of their daughter, Miss Mary Alice, to William K. Jackson, of Lansdown, Pa., at a family dinner held Saturday evening. Guests at the dinner included the prospective groom's parents, Mr. and Mrs. William C. Jackson, of Lansdown.

Howard J. Thompson home on lower State Street in Curwensville

The Wall Family Home (later the home of "Bubby" and Kate Thompson) in Curwensville

Collection of photographs from earlier, during, and following the 1920s:

Four generations of the Dyers

Young Vincent Ulysses Spencer

Elizabeth Spencer, Grace & Charles Wall with Mama & Papa Spencer

Grace Wall and Papa Spencer

Corner of State and Thompson Streets, Curwensville, Pa.

Elizabeth Bailey Spencer

PHOTOGRAPHED BY
J. W. C. FLOYD   LOCK HAVEN, PA.

Howard J. Thompson

Elizabeth Bailey Spencer (left) and friends (classmates)

Grace S. Wall

Elizabeth Bailey Spencer and Howard Jefferson Thompson
Wedding Party.

Cecil Wall, Superintendent of Mount Vernon, escorting King George VI
and Queen Elizabeth of Great Britain as well as President Franklin D.
Roosevelt and First Lady Eleanor Roosevelt and others during a visit to
Mount Vernon, home of George Washington.

Mary Alice and Bubby
1910

Elizabeth Spencer Thompson

Howard V. (Bubby)
12 years old

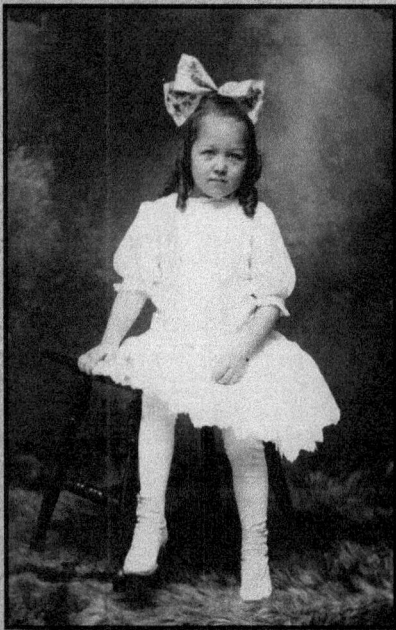

Mary Alice, 6 years old

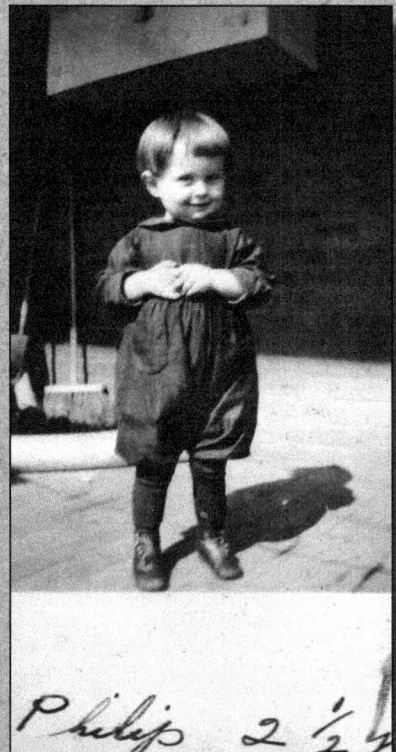

Philip 2 ½

Early Days,
Marjorie Wall and Mary Alice Thompson

High School Graduation
Marjorie Wall and Mary Alice Thompson

Mary Alice College Graduation Portrait

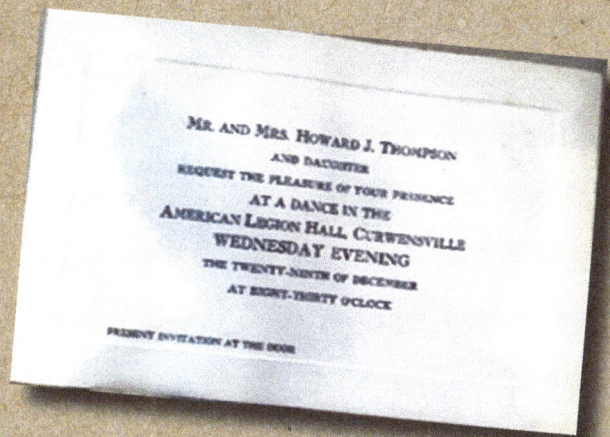

MR. AND MRS. HOWARD J. THOMPSON
AND DAUGHTER
REQUEST THE PLEASURE OF YOUR PRESENCE
AT A DANCE IN THE
AMERICAN LEGION HALL, CURWENSVILLE
WEDNESDAY EVENING
THE TWENTY-NINTH OF DECEMBER
AT EIGHT-THIRTY O'CLOCK

PRESENT INVITATION AT THE DOOR

Elizabeth Spencer Thompson

Howard J. Thompson with Young Philip

"Up a Tree"
Mary Alice (center) with Bubby (right)
and friend (left)

(l to r) Sisters, Katherine and Jean Pifer

Howard V. (Bubby)
Thompson
High School

Bubby and Katherine

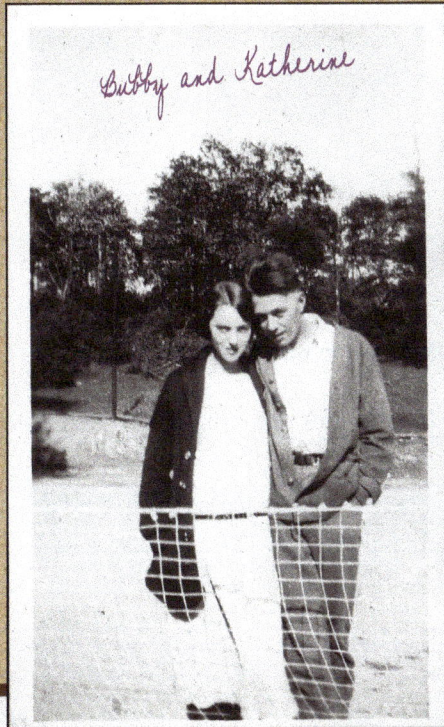
Katherine S. Pifer
High School

Howard V. (Bubby) Thompson,
local tennis champion

"Bubby" Thompson (r) and friend (l)

In front, young Philip Thompson, left to right, unidentified, Mary Alice Thompson, unidentified, Katherine Pifer Thompson, Elizabeth Spencer Thompson and Marjorie Wall

Alice Wall

Wall

Brothers

Jake and Leonard Kantar
Curwensville friends of Mary Alice

John Wright
Curwensville friend
of Mary Alice

Children: Kay Thompson, Bill Jackson and Mary Jane Wall.
Adults: Cecil Wall, Mary Alice Jackson, Marjorie and Marguerite Wall,
Papa Spencer, Charles and Grace Wall

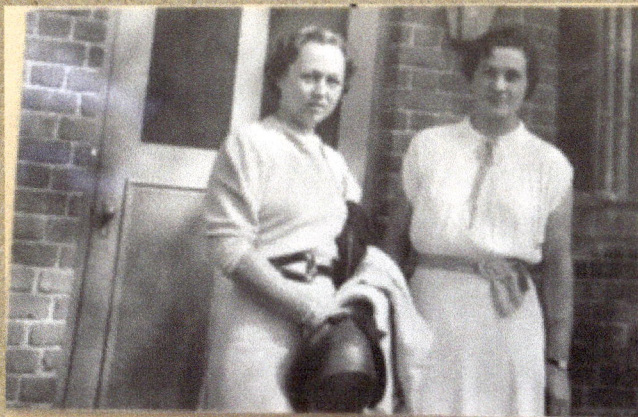

Visit to Mount Vernon, fall 1°

Mary Alice Jackson and Marguerite Wall
at Mount Vernon

Bill Jackson outside in his yard,
August 6, 1939

303

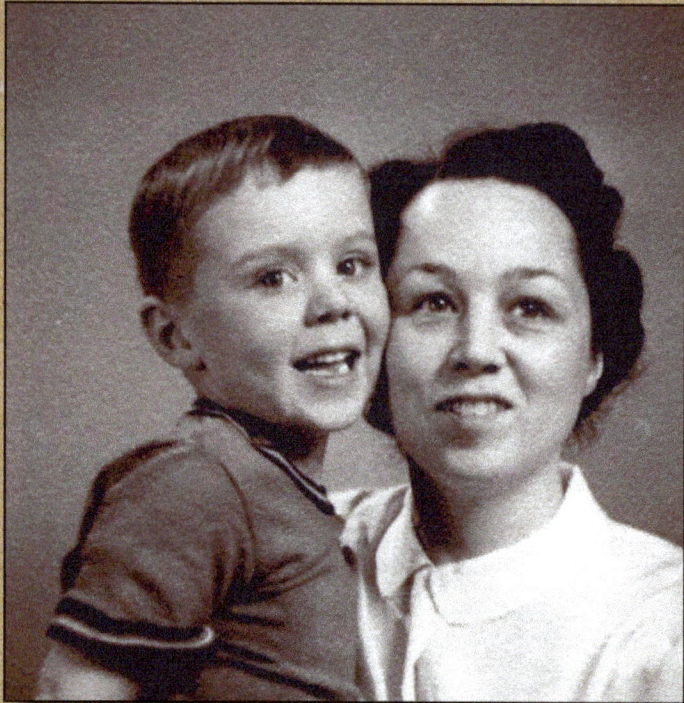

Mary Alice with son Bill

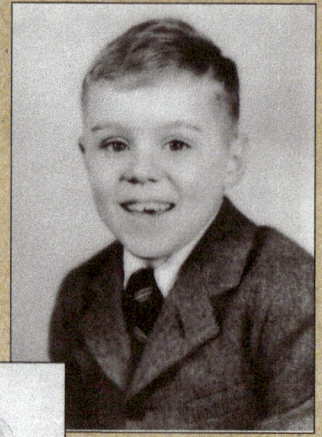

Young Bill in 1942

William Jackson

In front, young Bill Jackson and his father, William Jackson. Back row, Papa Spencer, Elizabeth Spencer Thompson and Mary Alice Thompson Jackson.

Young Bill Jackson working on
his stamp collection

BUY WAR BONDS

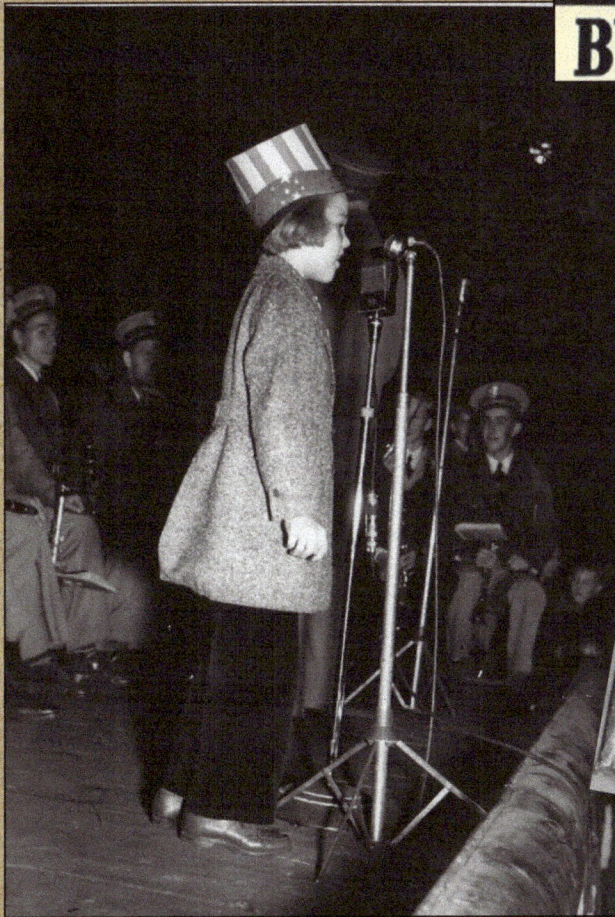

Judith Thompson singing at a
WWII War Bond Rally

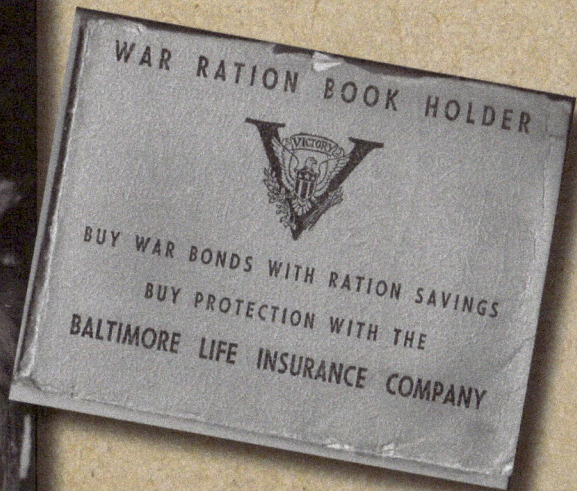

WAR RATION BOOK HOLDER

VICTORY

BUY WAR BONDS WITH RATION SAVINGS
BUY PROTECTION WITH THE
BALTIMORE LIFE INSURANCE COMPANY

May 16, 1943

Dearest Mary Alice,

I type here alongside of you and yet try to throw my mind far into the unknown and imagine you alone reading this very same letter with what I believe will be pleasant, happy and satisfying memories of a husband who has lived the happiest years of his life with you.

You have always been my sweetheart.....and the memories that I will always have of our years together fill me with pride and the swelling joy of having lived life at its best because of you.

Our boy well typifies the manner you have in doing things "just right!" And you have continued to do all else "just right" so you can well recognize that I will miss you.....terribly so.

I love you, Punk, and will love for eternity every treasured moment that we had had together. So chin up and continue the supervision of Bill so that he can "soak up" the best that is in you in the development of his character and well-being. Perhaps this may years hence from tonight apply, too, to a grandchild or two or........? Oh, well! We tried anyway.

My will and insurance you know about, yet I believe it best to ask that you give immediate thought to both in planning: (1) a consistent income for yourself and (2) an education for Bill. Both are of my heart's desire.

Two insurance policies with Provident Mutual (total $15,000) have specific income arrangements covering a period of years. Another policy with Provident Mutual ($30,000) and a policy with Equitable Assurance ($4,000) have no income provision for the reason that I want to give you as much flexibility as possible, feeling that future conditions may dictate your best course of action. It is your privilege, however, to elect any monthly income that you desire, either on a temporary basis or on a life income basis. Such an arrangement is a safeguard against either possibility of dissipation or loss.

Equitable Assurance policy ($2,000) is to start Bill's college days and I am hopeful that you can and will complete them.

Happy days, my girl, and if Mother and Dad Jackson are living and ever in need, remember them with a portion of what you have. And this goes for Mother and Dad Thompson, too.

My love, always,

Bill

United State Army
Middle of November 1944

My darling Tommy and Bill:

Tomorrow will be, no doubt, my first real combat test and the German defense is stiffening. When I think of today being your birthday and of the distance between us, I realize more than ever what your love means to me. Sweetheart, I love you more than words can tell—remembering always to keep you alone in my heart. I trust in tomorrow's push that death does not part us.

Please agree that it has been our duty to try to eliminate the hell of war for Bill sake if nothing else. God alone know how much I miss you both and may the job here be that successful that all threats of war are crushed out of the minds of people for generations. If so, our contribution as a family will have been worthwhile.

My love to you both from a mighty homesick husband and father—may God continue to be with us so that our happiness together will continue forever and ever.

Bill—Dad

P.S. Two weeks now at the front and all is well.
12/3/44

Life is no less, and no more, sweeter to on
man than to another. And, to the bereaved,
matters not whether the casualty—killed in ac
tion—is Bill Jones or Simon Smith. Both give
life—everything. Mothers, wives, children suffe
in the same degree.

Early in this thing we call World War No.
it was a temptation, difficult to resist, to editor
ialize on every sacrifice of a life. We knew th
grief of mothers, wives, sweethearts and childre
at the fateful news. We thought some comfor
would accrue from editorial mention. But, havin
gone through the period of World War No. 1, an
knowing that this journey on which we had em
barked would call for un-anticipated losses, w
retrained.

There is, however, such a thing as a com
munity loss; a loss transcending that of a membe
of the community circle. Not because of the indi
vidual's position in business or in social circles
but because of the value a man has been to th
community, particularly in its war activities.

This brings us to a consideration of the los
of Bill Jackson. In business Bill Jackson was
picture theatre man but until he took his place a
a private in the Armed forces he was the spark
plug of this County's war activities. He organize
our war bond and other war activities and he di
this job so well that what he did has been th
pattern for all succeeding campaigns.

Our natural reaction would be to sing Bill'
praises as an individual, for the fine type o
young man he was, for his willingness to be
good citizen in every sense of the word, but, re
alizing that scores of others are in this category
our purpose here is to make of record his contri
bution to the war effort as a citizen. It was no
an easy job, in the early days of this war, t
make us war conscious, but it was Bill Jackso
who persisted, who worked night and day, t
wake us up, to make us realize our responsibil
ties and our duty. He travelled the length an
breadth of this County preaching the gospel o
"buy bonds". He personally visited hundreds o
people persuading them to serve on communit
groups.

Well, Bill Jackson has gone to his reward.

America will live, thanks to the Bill Jack
sons.

G. A. S

Scrapbook Photographs and Items

277.

- The Diary on the top left is Lavinia's.
- The Diary on the right is Bubby's, shown with his own pen when fountain pens were relatively new. (The pen was a gift from his grandfather Vincent Spencer.)

279.

- Student Handbook
- Athletic season ticket
- *Drexerd* was the school newspaper
- The Freshman tag was required to be worn by freshmen for the first several weeks of their freshman year.
- Admission ticket to the football games
- Original building for Delta Upsilon fraternity at Penn State

280.

- Annual Banquet program for college students (Wesley Foundation)
- Cap & Bells annual talent show
- Women's Student Government dance at the Overbrook Club
- Ticket to the house party event at Dickinson College
- U. of Penn basketball schedule
- Girls basketball squad

281.

- Home Economics classrooms and activities
- Annual dinner, Clearfield School Board Members, prepared by the Junior High Domestic Science Department

282.

- Trend of raccoon coats
- Jimmy Strickland, always special to Mary Alice
- Henry Stetina
- Mary Alice photo booth snapshot
- Junior Women's Club Dance, 1923, J. Strickland
- Loss of privileges notice sent to Mary Alice
- Carl Gregory
- Chemistry exam book, summer 1927

283.

- Drexel Senior Dance, Class of 1925
- Dance Program (Home Economics House Dance)
- Omega Delta Epsilon Tea Dance

- Phi Gamma Sigma Dance Program
- "Snappy Stories" Junior Prom, 1926
- Interfraternity Ball, Penn 1927

284.

- The Tea Rose, popular restaurant near Drexel
- Pennsylvania Railroad ticket, Philadelphia to Curwensville, 1925
- Reception for Freshmen, October 30, 1924
- Birthday card from Mary Alice's Aunt Maude, November 1924
- Ziegfeld Follies, Forrest Theatre, October 30, 1925
- Valentino in person, Stanley Theatre, November 11, 1925
- "Artists and Models," Chestnut Sreet Opera Hourse, October 23, 1925
- "May Flower," Chestnut Street Opera House, February 23, 1925
- "Ladies of the Evening," Broad Street Theatre, February 20, 1926
- "Rose-Marie," Sam S. Shubert Theatre, October 16, 1925

285.

- Ticket on the "El" (elevated train)
- Reserved train ticket at Christmas time
- Dance Tally
- The Corner Restaurant, State College
- Fox Theatre, Philadelphia
- Yellow Cab receipt, April 28, 1925
- Eagle Theatre, Montgomery, Pa., owned by H. J. Thompson

286.

- Highland Hall Recital
- "Miss Somebody Else," 1924 Senior Class Play, Curwensville H.S.
- Penn State *Froth*, Fall 1929
- Cape May Jubilee 1929
- Penn State Thespians, June 1930
- Curwensville Labor Day Event, 1924 (sponsored by the Yellow Dogs)
- Western Union telegram to Mary Alice from her friend, Ark.
- Sophomore Hop, March 14, 1930

287.

- Cloches and Coats

Brief Synopsis of Later Times

Following a cross-country trip in the early 1930s with best friend Katherine (Tat) Thorn, Mary Alice married William K. Jackson of Philadelphia and they became the parents of one child, a son, William Spencer, born in September 1934, to whom they were devoted. The family lived in Springfield, a Philadelphia suburb near where Mr. Jackson, a handsome man, was Assistant to the President of ARMCO, a Philadelphia-based steel company. In 1939 Mary Alice's father convinced his son-in-law to re-locate to Clearfield County and become general manager of Mid-State Theatres and Moshannon Valley Theatres, which together included 15-16 theatres.[1]

The Jacksons returned to Clearfield and moved into a house on Market Street with a large kitchen from which emanated delectable aromas, particularly at Christmas. Mary Alice was an immaculate housekeeper, with never anything out of place, yet her home was always comfortable and inviting, with sparkling white woodwork. It was also the only house up to that time that the young Thompson girls had seen that had a fully finished basement with a workshop and a third floor that provided a spacious playroom for their cousin Bill whom the younger girls stood in awe of—or at least in awe of his array of toys, particularly his large model train set.

Through the years Mary Alice sent us special Christmas and birthday gifts. She always seemed to know just the right item for the right age at the right time. Each gift came beautifully wrapped with a richness of tissue paper enveloping the item in its box from Marshall Field's in Chicago, Best Co. in New York, Neiman-Marcus in Dallas, or Josten's in San Antonio, names that suggested opulence and refinement to the young gift recipients.

Mary Alice also arranged with her mother Elizabeth to make sure that each of us, upon reaching the age of sixteen, would receive one of the heirloom rings that either had belonged to our grandmother or that Mary Alice herself had been gifted by her own mother or grandmother. Because of my keen interest in Victoriana, Mary Alice had also given me a cameo pendant on a densely woven gold chain that had been her Mama Spencer's.

During World War II when new clothing was scarce, I received a rich wool tweed coat that had been Cousin Bill's. I loved it because it had been "his" and because my mother chose to act very "matter of fact" that it was a boy's and not a girl's garment. Occasionally, outgrown ice skates and sleds also came the our way from Clearfield, as well as opportunities for Kay to go on vacation with the Jacksons. Mary Alice included Kay because "she was such a well-mannered little girl and a good influence on Bill."

---

1   The Ritz and Lyric Theatres in Clearfield, Rex in Curwensville, Sherkel in Houtzdale, Dixie in Coalport, Liberty in Madera, State and Plaza Theatres in Bellefonte, and others in Stoneboro, Weedville, Meadville, Sykesville, Reynoldsville, Watsontown, and Montgomery, Pennsylvania.

In early 1944, in the thick of World War II, Mr. Jackson enlisted in the Army, after having turned down an offer from the Navy of a direct commission to run their film distribution system. He was killed in 1945 during the first wave across the Ruhr River in Germany, leaving, as did many of his comrades, a widow and a child.

Two years after the war Mary Alice met Bradford B. Crunk, a veteran and the epitome of the tall Texas cowboy and cattle rancher often seen on the movie screen. Blond, good-looking, intelligent, strong, and gentle, Brad was seen by Kate's girls as the cowboy hero who walked in and swept Mary Alice off her feet. Two years later Brad, Mary Alice, and young Bill moved to a ranch in Texas, but returned to Clearfield in the mid-1950s when Brad became general manager of the theatre chain. He was totally devoted to Mary Alice, the love of his life, during their fifty years of marriage.

In later years, when Mary Alice was living in a skilled nursing facility Nan and I visited her there and found her cheerful and as kind as ever. She was looking forward to going home, while at the same time accepting that she might not be able to return. On visits there was no lack of topics for conversation, as Mary Alice enjoyed her informal status as historian of the family, matching cousins with second cousins and cousins once removed, and she loved talking about events from the past, particularly because, while I hadn't known all of the people Mary Alice had known, I usually could recall the persons about whom she spoke from town history or previous conversations with my Aunt Jessie and my mother, as well as Aunt Mary Alice. Mary Alice's mind was sharp, except for the fact that she often would talk to me as if the two of us had been part of the same era.

Soon after our last visit, Cousin Bill expressed his thanks for my keeping in touch with his mother, adding, "I don't know if you realize how much Mother cares for you and your sisters. You are the daughters she never had."

The Spencer and the Bailey Families

The Spencers

The father of Elizabeth Bailey Spencer (Mary Alice's mother), was Vincent Uriah Spencer, son of Joseph M.[1] and Lydia Griest Spencer. Vincent (May 14, 1854 – January 12, 1950) lived in Bridgeport. He worked on his father's farm, one of the first homes in the settlement. When not working in his father's grist mill, he joined the work of hauling timber out of the woods to Anderson Creek. He once rode one of the rafts as far as Jersey Shore. At the age of 19 Vincent began more than 20 years of teaching. He later served as a school director in Pike Township and Curwensville Borough. During his lifetime he made three trips to the West Coast.

The decline of Bridgeport as a commercial community with its woolen mills and other small industries began with the Johnstown Flood of 1889, when Anderson Creek went on a rampage and caused devastating damage to many homes and other buildings in the lowlands, including areas of Curwensville.

Vincent had two sisters and a brother:

♦ Lavinia (1852–1871), whose 1871 Diary is included in this book.
♦ Rowland (1856–1928) relocated to the West Coast at a young age.
♦ Almina (January 12, 1859–October 1963), who married
  Joseph J. Downing on May 10, 1883 and lived in Xenia, Ohio.
  Her 100th birthday anniversary was celebrated in Xenia.

The Baileys

Joseph Bailey (March 5, 1823–October 7, 1902), son of Daniel Bailey III (July 31, 1795–August 1, 1875) and Jane Passmore (September 11, 1797–August 30, 1877), was a lifetime resident of Pike Township and lived near his father's homestead. He owned several hundred acres of land, including the stone quarry tract. In 1892 he sold the property to the Clearfield firm of Weaver and Betts who opened what became known as the Bailey Quarry, whose stone was prized; notable examples include the chapel at Princeton University and the famed steps of the Philadelphia Art Museum.

---

[1] A successful grist mill proprietor and landowner

Joseph married Sarah Elizabeth Boal (April 11, 1835–October 19, 1877) of Centre County. Their family included the following:

- **Mary Alice** (April 16, 1854–July 19, 1937)
- Martha Jane, (June 13, 1858–March 22, 1945); married Jonathan Ogden
- J. Dorsey (July 6, 1860–February 2, 1923)
- Annie Gardner (January 27, 1863–November 29, 1919); married Charles Boyd
- Charlie (December 17, 1868–February 24, 1950)

(It is the needlepoint handiwork of Martha or Annie which is mentioned in the Dedication of this book and that remains in the family.)

Mary Alice Bailey married Vincent U. Spencer (who in his later years worked as a clerk for his son-in-law, H.J. Thompson who developed and installed electrical units in the towns and villages in Centre County). Vincent and Alice had two daughters, **Grace Cecilia** (July 17, 1879–June 22, 1944) and **Elizabeth Bailey** (September 14, 1880–October 10, 1951). The sisters were of a small minority of women at the time who earned high school diplomas, Grace in 1899 and Elizabeth in 1900; their parents gifted both daughters with class rings embossed with CHS and the date of graduation. Grace was the first of the two sisters to marry.

Grace Cecilia Spencer married **Charles M. Wall,** son of Miles Wall of Curwensville, in October 1902. Their family included five children, four boys and a girl:

- Charles Cecil, June 21, 1903[1]–May 1, 1995
- Marjorie Alice, June 5, 1905–August 16, 1972
- Kenneth Spencer, February 12, 1908–August 8, 1969
- Arthur Russell May 16, 1910–October 18, 2002
- Richard Vincent, September 26, 1912–September 25, 1992

Elizabeth Baily Spencer and **Howard J. Thompson**[2], an entrepreneur–businessman, were wed in her parents' home on June 17, 1903, and her wedding book is still in the family. The union included three children, Howard Vincent, **Mary Alice**, and Philip.

(The Genealogy of the Thompsons picks up at The Thompson Family)

---

[1] Which explains why Grace does not appear in her sister's wedding party photograph of June 17, 1903.
[2] Richard V. Wall (author) in his *Family Remembrances*, refers to Howard J. Thompson a "the town's richest citizen."

a Quaker Courtship in the 1840's

ROMANCE TRIUMPHS OVER
TIME AND DISTANCE IN THIS
STORY REVEALED IN THE
LETTERS OF TWO
PENNSYLVANIANS

315

James Boswell and Carl Sandburg spent long, tedious years chronicling the lives of two famous men, Samuel Johnson and Abraham Lincoln. So I hope it won't seem frivolous for me, a casual family historian, to spend a brief time reminiscing, in these pages, about two non-famous but very special people -- my great-grandparents.

Circumstance has focused my attention on these two, Joseph M. Spencer and Lydia Ann Griest, among my eight great-grandparents. For it happens that only Joseph and Lydia have handed down to me an enduring record of their thoughts and activities. This legacy is a beautifully hand-written transcript of 35 pre-marital letters which nurtured their Quaker romance over a 4½ year span in the 1840's.

Lydia lived in York county, Pennsylvania--nearly 200 miles distant (almost a whole world!) from Joseph's home in the sparsely settled Grampian hills of Clearfield county in west-central

Joseph M. Spencer (1821-1889)

Pennsylvania. They met in 1843 when Lydia visited her Aunt Ruth, who had recently married a widower, Gideon Widemire, in the Grampian area.

("I often think," wrote Lydia, "of the time thou wished it was but 20

"Quaker" is used in this account - instead of the more proper designation "Friend" - for a member of the religious Society of Friends. The Quakers were a peaceful, industrious people who relied on the "inner voice" of the spirit to guide them. They were prominent in the early history of Pennsylvania, which was founded by a Quaker, William Penn.

317

miles when I was talking of coming home, and I have been sometimes ready to wish the same thing if it had been of any use.")

Joseph's ill health during long periods kept the lovers from meeting face to face, except a few times, during their long courtship. In fact, doubts about his recovery nearly terminated the relationship.

Meetings ofttimes were planned, in high hopes, but did not materialize. <u>May 1845</u>. "I have had thoughts of taking a tour to your delightful country," wrote Joseph," from some of our coming (Quaker) meetings, but the accomplishment appears doubtful to me at present, as some time ago I promised to take sister Lavina to the Fishing Creek Half Year's Meeting, which promise she appears to claim, and perhaps will hinder me from going any further at that time."

Then he suggested an alternative: "I do not wish to cause thee to have any trouble or inconvenience, but would just suggest that I would be very happy to see a friend of mine there (at Fishing Creek), even if we could only get to say how <u>do</u> you do, and get a pleasant smile from her cheek which one whole year has rolled over since I saw."

Lydia, however, was unable to go to Fishing Creek to show the hoped-for "pleasant smile," as she explained, somewhat tersely, in Letter 8th (<u>July 1845</u>): "I would have been very much pleased if I could have met thee at Fishing Creek but I saw no chance of going and therefore said nothing about it."

But she went on to comment at great length on Joseph's original plan: "No tongue can express the joy I felt when I came to that line in thy last letter when thou sayst 'I have had thoughts of taking a tour to your delightful country etc.' But I hope thou wilt not form so favorable an opinion of this neighborhood as to be disappointed when thou sees it, or of the people in it. My father's what might be termed a poor man in respect to worldly riches. He owns no land, yet he is much respected. He has so far made an honest living, mostly on the loom, although he is much afflicted. The cancer on his nose is still increasing. Mother is also enjoying poor health, yet able to do most of the time with the help of my younger sister.

"I am now at David Cadwallader's in Mechanicksville,* which is often called Braggtown. If thou ever comes this way thou need not look for many houses and those at our end of town are all on one side of the street. It may be I

- - - - -

*A tiny village in western York county, which later became part of adjoining Adams county.

Joseph Spencer's desk has passed down to Charles C. Wall (seated, left). It is possible that this is the same desk at which Joseph was standing when he wrote to Lydia in 1845 (see text below)

will be here for some time, yet I know not how long. This is three miles from father's."

Lydia then proposed that Joseph meet her at her Quarterly meeting in August 1845, one week prior to his Quarterly meeting at Half Moon. This plan very nearly succeeded, but it too faltered, as Joseph explained: "Though at first I knew not how to accomplish it, a way soon appeared to offer that I thought I might accomplish it (which was this): Father and mother proposed going to the Bedford Springs (some 80 miles away) for the benefit of my father's health. They also made the proposition for me to accom-

pany them, which I readily agreed to with the intention of leaving them at the Springs and pursue my journey unto your land, which I was very anxious to see. And not only the land but also an acquaintance of mine who I have not seen until the time appears long . . . Father and mother were going on the buggy and I on horseback, but I had to regret my disappointment, for when I arrived there I was sick, and therefore did not like to undertake the journey alone, and our situation otherwise would scarcely permit me to leave them. I stayed there and abouts for the space of ten days. They appeared to be in pretty good spirits and I was also some better, so I left them and started for our Quarterly meeting. But I caught some cold on the way and was quite unwell during the time of meeting . . . I returned home and (am) standing by my desk this morning to write, yet feel unwell."

Joseph went on to voice fears that, due to his illness and their lack of personal contact, "our affections will diminish and our intimacy eventually cease." But

319

he added: "I hope to have patience and probably the times will change for our benefit."

After nearly a half year's silence, which brought an anguished inquiry from his beloved, Joseph explained in Letter 12th (March 1846): "I have not forgotten thee, neither do I desire to, but since I wrote my last letter I have had some trying times. I think I can truly say that I have not felt well since that time and not at any time did I think myself able to bear exposure, yet nearly all the time able to be about something. My disease is perhaps Neuralgia in my head, caused probably by too close attention to study while teaching school. It being a delightful task made it the more trying to refrain therefrom, which I have had to do for a considerable time, as much as possible. I have become quite reduced in strength and at some seasons of discouragement felt as though I could never recover."

Then Joseph spoke cryptically of a possible journey, but with no prospect this time of seeing Lydia. "I have disengaged myself from business this summer and have a prospect of a journey before me, some distance, though yet kept secret. If it should turn out so, I will be at home yet more than a month and I think I will probably write to thee after I get there. If thou hast anything more to say thou canst write before that time."

In Letter 13th (May 1846), Joseph cleared up the mystery of his intended journey. "My prospect was to go to Philadelphia at Yearly meeting time, but instead of taking such a long journey I went to William Underwood's in Bald Eagle (and) undertook with him under the Thomsonian treatment of medicine. I was there better than two weeks and went through two courses, after which I felt much better and then returned home. I have been at home nine days and feel pretty well satisfied with the course I have taken."

Finally a brief meeting did take place between the two lovers, when Lydia again visited Aunt Ruth and Uncle Gideon in the Grampian hills in the fall of 1846. But apparently this meeting was all too short, and possibly the cause of a misunderstanding. After receiving no communication from Joseph for nearly a year afterward, Lydia wrote in Letter 17th (July 1847): "I feel it to be my lot once more to break this long silence. I know no cause for it, dost thou? . . . Have I written, said or done anything that was unpleasant to thee? If I have, it was not done wilfully . . . Gladly would I have spent more time with thee last fall, if I could. I hope thou hast not taken offense at my staying so long with thy sister the evening we were at Uncle Gideon's. It was caused by my intimacy with *health is I believe as good as when I was in Clearfield, I have not been sick one single day nor at any time had any reason to complain since I left Clearfield, with the exception of toothache sometimes, & I have not been troubled much with that of late, yet I am not as fleshy as I was while I was there but I know no cause for it, I have as easy times as I could wish for and always have had, I have long considered good health one of the greatest favors bestowed upon us. This with a contented mind is of great value. I sometimes think there is nobody gets along easier than I do, I spend some of my time at home & some of my time in sewing or assisting my neighbors in what may seem most needful.*

This excerpt from Lydia's letter
of June 14, 1846, indicates that
she, unlike Joseph, enjoyed good
health

---

her. Little did I think then that time would pass as it has done. But worst of all is thy being sick. And I can never hear from thee. Not one sentence has ever reached my ear concerning thee since thee started to Philadelphia (to attend Yearly meeting) . . . Please tell me the particulars concerning thy health. Let me know the worst . . . When I think of our acquaintance, I cannot help wondering at thee having so little acquaintance with my family connections. If thou art yet able to travel, I would be pleased to see thee spend some time in our neighborhood in order that thou might form some more acquaintance here and that I may become better acquainted with thee."

A month later, still not having received any response, Lydia enclosed a really frantic note to Joseph with a letter sent to his sister: "I am sorry that thou art not able to write once more to me. Gladly and quickly would I fly to thy room that I might spend one moment with thee, and no one know it. But perhaps it would not be thy wish. I do not want to be uppermost in thy mind, for I believe thou hast much of far more importance to think about. I am yet willing to trust in God, for I now feel that there is nothing but His will that can raise thee . . . Ah! how can I think of bidding thee adieu? It is a solemn thought indeed but we must all part sooner or later. But I hope we will be prepared to meet in Heaven, that happy home. It is hard to part, but I now feel resigned to the will of Him who first caused us to become acquainted, and in that tender feeling I can now bid thee an affectionate Farewell."

Six months passed before Joseph could write and dispel Lydia's worst fears. February 1848: "I desire to inform thee that it (my failure to write) has not been intentional, but was caused by indisposition of body. So I think thou wilt be willing to excuse what we could not help. I received thy very acceptable letter when lying on my sick bed. I opened it and read one page and was unable to read any more. I requested my sister Eliza to inform thee of my situation and gave her the letter to lay away for me, which remained until lately. When I read it, I admired the contents very much. Since thou hast been at thy cousin William's I should have loved very much to have seen thee, but I did not feel well enough to cross the mountains. My health now appears to be improving, yet I do not expect to be at the Quarterly meeting. As I have heard that thou hast a prospect of coming out here, I hope thou wilt not feel any delicacy in coming on my account, for I should love to see thee and converse with thee once more . . . There is yet a hope arises which appears to inspire my mind at seasons—that I should not despair, knowing that the Lord is good and kind and that faith worketh patience, therefore let patience have her perfect work. But I must not imagine too great things for us lest we might be disappointed. . . Come out and see us if thou canst."

Finally the long-awaited meeting was to take place, though not in Grampian but in Unionville (Centre county) where Lydia was visiting at cousin William's. First Lydia's buoyant response (March 1848) to Joseph's February letter and his followup three weeks later: "I feel it to be impossible to express the pleasure I felt in receiving thy last letters. . . The same hand writing, the same tender feelings . . . and that same hope or prospect of once more meeting and conversing with thee is again fresh in my mind. But all this seems in some measure new when I think of the last I wrote to thee. I could not help feeling discouraged at that solemn time. Thy sickness has caused a long silence but perhaps this silence has been of use to us . . . Thy most anxious question at present shall here be answered as nearly as I can answer it. I do intend and have all along intended paying you a visit before I return home . . . I intend putting up at my old home (Aunt Ruth's) where I hope we may again meet and have a pleasant interview. I feel very patient but have long ago looked forward to the coming Spring as being productive of a most memorable time but I know not why I have had such an idea . . ."

The Spring of 1848 did produce a "memorable time," for we find Joseph's next two letters penned in Unionville, where he and Lydia presumably were frequently together, and weighing the prospects of marriage. June 30: "How fast the days are rolling away that were intended for our happiness. Four years and more have passed away since that friendship was formed which I believe bound us more strongly than words or promises could have done. Yet if we do not give out before the time appointed for us, we may yet be permitted to enter into that united enjoyment which I have sometimes imagined would constitute our happiness."

Then, as Lydia's time of departing for home draws near, Joseph turned more specific. July 13: ". . . Since our lots have been cast in this place, we have had some pleasant opportunities of conversing together during our excursions on the beautiful banks of the Bald Eagle (creek) and elsewhere, giving us an opportunity to become more and more acquainted with each other. . . And now my dear shall I make so bold as to ask thee how long thou canst be patient under the present

---

Quaker Practices

In addition to its regular religious services, each Quaker Meeting (congregation) holds a Monthly Meeting for business affairs. A regional group of Meetings holds a Quarterly Meeting. The members making up a grouping of Quarterly Meetings constitute a Yearly Meeting.

Traditionally, the Quakers were a self-governed body without clergy. Members voiced their thoughts and beliefs freely in meeting when "the spirit moved them." Elected officials carried out record-keeping and similar functions. The marriage certificate of Joseph and Lydia Spencer, for instance, was affirmed by the Huntington Meeting "Recorder".

privations and trials that appear to attend our prospect of future happiness . . . I did not expect when I commenced writing to have brought the case to so close a bearing, but as it appears to be my train of thought whilst writing, it may perhaps prove satisfactory to us both to have an understanding wrought whilst personally present, seeing that out intimacy is intended and we have never come to such a review before . . . And now I will say that it would have been pleasant to me to have bound the nuptial bond before the conclusion of the coming winter. But perhaps my health will not yet permit me to expect such a change so soon. I should like thee to be satisfied before making such an engagement . . . I might probably write more but conclude to leave this for thee to consider and if thou pleases' and opportunity should offer thou may'st exchange with me a few lines that I may look upon when perhaps we may not have the opportunity of conversing together."

Lydia responded cautiously (Letter 24th) to Joseph's proposal, acknowledging their mutual love but suggesting they should wait "still longer" to decide, because of his delicate health. "And, my dear friend, to be candid, I do not expect to ever see thee enjoying good health, yet it may be much better than it is at present. And the great wonder to me is whether it is

right for us to continue to increase our intimacy, or not be willing to wait until spring for a final conclusion . . . It is hard to part, but it will be the means of proving our attachment perhaps more than anything else . . . And I believe it is right to give our expected near relations an opportunity of some acquaintance with us ere we can expect them to consent to our being joined together. And remember my friend I will expect thee to pay us a long visit this fall if thy health will permit."

There followed a quick exchange of letters on succeeding days (still in Unionville) which erased Lydia's caution and sealed the engagement. First Joseph, though confessing that "thou hast answered my letter as satisfactorily as I could reasonably expect," voiced reluctance to visit her without a prior commitment, for otherwise "it could not be expected for us to get the consent of thy parents." He pledged to keep her informed of his health, and implied that the next move was up to her. Whereupon Lydia capitulated, referring to a prior dream she had experienced in which "thy hand was immediately laid upon my heart." Then her warm acceptance: "I now feel willing to become thy companion through life at any time we can fix upon for this great change . . ."

The Huntington Friends
Meeting House, outside
York Springs, near the
Adams-York county boundary.
The structure, built in
1790, is seldom used today.
Here Joseph and Lydia were
married Jan. 25, 1849

The remaining nine letters set the stage for their marriage, although final details remained somewhat uncertain, partly because Lydia's letter of September 25, 1848, miscarried (it finally was delivered in mid-November). Meanwhile, Lydia's parents consented to the marriage, excusing Joseph from any prior trip. Joseph's parents also consented, and the bride and groom to be proceeded to request the consent of their Quaker meetings. Joseph wrote on December 4: "And I want thee to tell me when your Monthly meeting comes, especially the one that I will be expected to attend

. . . I think it will not be worth my while to come long before the Monthly meeting. If I should make some stay, I would prefer staying after we are married . . . I will perhaps have the company of a couple. Sister Lavina is desirous of coming . . . I cannot tell yet whether brother Miles will or not. And if we have to be accompanied, as is fashionable, with waiters (attendants), I leave thee to choose for thyself and for me, as thou art best acquainted with friends in your parts."

In Letter 34th, Lydia expressed happiness that winter was not being allowed to delay them. "I think thou must be a great deal

325

better or thou wouldst not think of crossing the mountains in the middle of winter. This is an encouraging thought. Do not feel concerned about the weather on my account, but I don't want thee to come with the prospect of finding sleighing here. It is of too uncertain continuance. If thou canst come with a two horse carriage I think we can do very well. I will have a little more than my clothes, but I do not expect to take much from here towards house-keeping."

The final letter (35th) found Joseph still awaiting the preceding letter from Lydia, but assuring her: "But I intend to come at any rate, whether I receive a letter or not, if health permits." Then his concluding lines: "And now, my friend, after a long time of corresponding, if all things are going on straight and nothing turns in the way, unless I receive a letter from thee soon this will be the conclusion--and I do not feel to regret a moment's loss that I have spent in so doing."

- - - - -

On the 25th of the first month 1849 (as Quakers express it), Joseph and Lydia were married at the Huntington meeting, near her home in York county. The official certificate, now in my possession, bears the names of 53 witnesses, all family members and friends.

Their son Vincent, my grand-father, described the marriage scene in a sketch presented at the 100th Anniversary of the West Branch Friends meeting, Grampian, in 1933: "The ceremony was to be held at her home meeting, a diff-icult and long journey (for Joseph.) The end of January. Mid-winter. No cars. No trains. No good roads. Horse and sleigh. Joseph M., accompanied by his brother Miles and sister Lavina, made the trip. (Midway in their trip) the snow was gone--sleighs would not operate. Buggies were procured, and the trip continued. Eventually they returned. The original trio, accompanied by a second lady. The newly-wed established a home at Bridgeport (between Grampian and Curwens-ville), where the young man was associated with other brothers in the carding of wool - later changed to a woolen mill - a saw mill - a grist mill. Surrounded by several hundred acres of wooded land."

- - - - -

Aside from their sentimental interest, the 18,000 words pain-stakingly inscribed by Joseph and Lydia--with crude pens, sometimes under dim lighting, and probably on ill-sized paper--provide a clear picture of "life as it was" in rural Pennsylvania in the 1840's.

Quill pens apparently were used, for Lydia wrote in March

Joseph and Lydia's marriage
certificate. On the reverse
side is the signature of Joel
Garretson, the Recorder

1845: "I hope thou wilt excuse
my bad writing, for my pen is bad
and I have not got our dear little
knife here to mend it." Later
Joseph commented about the paper
he was using: "Perhaps thou
canst understand my short sentences. One sheet of paper is
scarcely sufficient to contain
lengthy ones."

Even when completed, letters
had to be taken some distance to a
postoffice and entrusted to slow,
haphazard delivery by stagecoach or
rider. Lydia's "missing letter"
of September 1848 did not reach
Joseph until November. "It is very
strange how that letter missed
getting to thee," wrote Lydia. "I

intend to speak to our postmaster about it. I know he has been very careless sometimes."

Despite the limited modes of travel, these "plain" Quaker folk were surprisingly mobile. Lydia seemed always on the move, starting with her nine-month visit in 1843-44 to the Grampian hills, nearly 200 miles from her home in Mechanicksville, York county. She commented, after that trip: "I love to travel but it is a fast way of spending money."

Since her father owned no land ("I would be in favor of every family having a home of their own," she wrote, "if it could be so . . ."), Lydia frequently visited with friends and relatives. "I am now away from home (near Rossville, York county) and have been for four weeks," she wrote in 1845, "and I do not expect to get away from here for several weeks yet. They are particular acquaintances of mine that I am living with." Again: "Brother Elisha and I were at York. It was 20 miles from where we started. I spent New Year's Day at a snug party and dined on roast turkey and other things to suit it."

At another time: "I am now at Dr. Edwin G. Vancise's. He is a son-in-law of Joel Garretson (the man who later signed Joseph and Lydia's marriage certificate as Recorder of the Huntington Quaker meeting). I have charge of

his family while he and his wife are gone to Yearly meeting."

Lydia spoke favorably of the neighboring community of Gettysburg which had not yet suffered its bloody hours on the stage of history.

"We had a very pleasant visit at Gettysburg to see brother Allen's," she wrote in 1945. Later she commented: ". . . we are looking for brother Allen and his wife and little son to pay us a visit the last of this month. They are living in Gettysburg. . . I think it is a handsome town."

Lydia's return journey to York county from her long 1848 sojourn in Unionville must have tested her endurance to the fullest. "We had a more comfortable ride to Lewistown than we had anticipated," she wrote. "But when we arrived there our way appeared to be closed by a break in the canal . . . but it turned out that the boat got to town about 9 o'clock the next day, (two hours after) the usual time to leave. And when the boat was ready we started and reached Harrisburg about 1 o'clock that night, and took breakfast on the boat." However, finding no space available on the stagecoach from Harrisburg to York, they had to hire a "private conveyance" which "had us safe at brother Elisha's in about five hours. We had a pleasant ride in a large two horse hack,

A Pennsylvania Canal packet boat approaching Harrisburg (Pa. Historical & Museum Commission photo)

(the driver's) company was middling agreeable and he treated us with respect. My journey cost me seven dollars."

(Note: Lydia's trip on the Juniata Division of the Pennsylvania Canal from Lewistown to Harrisburg occurred at the height of the canal era. Construction of the Harrisburg section of the state-owned Pennsylvania Canal began in 1826, and the entire 400-mile system, Philadelphia to Pittsburgh, was completed in 1834. The passenger-carrying packet boats travelled about 4 miles per hour. Railroads began to supplant canal travel around 1860.)

His letters were variously sent from Grampian hills, where many Spencer relatives resided, and Bridgeport (some five miles away), where his father's mill, and perhaps his home in some period, was located.

The school where Joseph taught was probably the original one-room school near the Grampian Quaker meeting house. Thus, school, church and mill required regular travel by foot, horse or buggy. "I walked to (Quaker) meeting today, across by Uncle Widemire's lane," wrote Joseph in 1848. "They (Aunt Ruth and Uncle Gideon) were both there and appear to be as well as usual."

Joseph was much on the move also, when his health permitted.

329

Beyond these local travels, there were frequent journeys to Quaker meetings in Centre county and elsewhere. The Quaker scheme of weekly, monthly, quarterly, twice-yearly and yearly meetings at designated locations involved much travel, and also accounted for much of the social life of the members. Joseph wrote of attending "Samuel and Elizabeth's" wedding, by appointment of the Grampian Quaker meeting. "Seven buggies and three persons on horseback went over on fifth day (Thursday, by Quaker calendar) to Coopers, where the meeting was appointed at 3 o'clock. The meeting was very quiet. Thirty-three persons present all signed the certificate. And all got home safe on sixth day, with the slight misfortune of John W. getting his buggy shaft broken and Samuel losing a bolt from his, which detained us on our way a couple of times a little. And (they) had their infare (house-warming) at Samuel's own house at 3 o'clock the same day."

As a descendent, it is pleasing to conclude from their letters that Joseph and Lydia, though more coquettish than pious on occasion, were mainly steadfast in their devotion. "Thou art, dear Joseph, my only lover," wrote Lydia, "and I have no wish for any other." Later, she speculated that Joseph and a mutual Grampian friend Eliza were "waiters" (attendants) at a wedding he attended, and asked if he and Eliza "are so intimate that you have both forgotten me? I do not think so . . . ." Joseph, replying, confirmed that he and Eliza had been waiters. "But as for Eliza and I becoming so intimate as to forget all others, it is not at all the case, for I believe I have not had hold of her hand since . . . though not through any disrespect, for I think her a worthy youth . . . I have kept private company but very few times since I took thy leave."

To this, Lydia responded that "I was only joking" and added: "I am far from wishing to prevent thee of the pleasure of enjoying the company of any young lady that thou mayst feel free to spend an evening in social converse with. But to be candid I have felt no inclination to keep private company with any since I took thy leave, yet I have through politeness spent a few evenings in this way."

In one letter Lydia questioned whether she was too free in expressing her feelings toward Joseph. "I am now looking forward with much pleasure," she wrote, "toward that day, that I trust is near at hand, that we may have the pleasure of once more conversing together as we had long ago. Oh, my friend, I know not how I will meet thee. When I think of this pleasure my heart feels almost ready to leap for joy. Please excuse me for expressing myself as I have done. I sometimes think strange of the freeness I have taken when writing to thee, for I never have met with any person that I could write to and converse with as I have with thee."

Not surprisingly, weather and crop conditions were frequent topics in the letters. Lydia commented in an early letter: "Spring with all its inherent beauty is fast approaching. This morning (April 1) the peach trees are in full bloom. When the trees were in blossom a year ago, I was on your hill."

And Joseph, replying (5-29-45): "It is little after sunup and the grass and boards are quite white with frost, which I fear will injure the fruit very much."

Lydia's comment in October 1845 about fruit has special significance because her home was in the still-renowned fruit belt of York and Adams counties. "We have for some time past been middling busy with the fruit," she wrote. "Often when I have been engaged in eating the very best of apples, peaches and pears, etc., my mind was with thee, wishing I could share with thee, who I think had none so good. We boiled apple-butter twice last week, one day for brother Elisha and his wife. They were down and helped us."

In May 1846, Joseph reported: "We have a prospect of a plentiful harvest. The grain and grass look better and appear to be growing

faster than I remember having seen at this time of the year. We have had very wet weather for about three weeks, and floods for the lumbermen to carry away their lumber, and at this time we have a prospect of abundance of fruit."

(Note: From 1840 to 1890, lumbering was the leading industry of Clearfield county. An average of 2,000 rafts descended the Susquehanna river each spring, taking millions of board feet of lumber to downriver markets.)

Three months later, in August, Joseph confirmed that crops and fruit had indeed been abundant. "It is said that hundreds of bushels of whortleberries (huckelberries) have been gathered north of Curwensville. I have not been working much this summer, only in harvest."

Marriages of Quaker friends and relatives were an ever recurring subject, sometimes with humorous overtones. "If thou does not get down before long," wrote Lydia, "I wilt not promise that thou wilt see brother Elisha single. He appeared to fall in love with a little girl that we passed in the road before we got quite home from Centre county. She was then an entire stranger to him. I do not know that this will be a match, but if it is I expect it will be the forepart of the ninth month." Later she wrote that the two were happily married.

In November 1848 Joseph jested about a flirtation between his sister Eliza and a painter who was helping fit out father Joseph Spencer Sr.'s new home: ". . . If Eliza does not be careful she will be caught by the painter. But only for a joke's sake. She might do worse. And it might turn out that we may have them for neighbors." No report of marriage followed in this case.

- - - - -

Joseph's letter of 11-16-48 gave Lydia a preview of the neighborhood she soon would be entering as a bride. "When I came home (from Unionville) I purchased of my father the gristmill property, and made such arrangements for housekeeping as I thought necessary at that time. And now I think that after collecting together some of the necessaries of life we may be furnished with a comfortable home in the little town of Bridgeport. Our town is growing--three houses have been built this summer. Isaac Jones has quite a good store here."

He added: "Today I expect father's will flit (move) into their new house, but I am not there to help them. They have it all finished but a little painting, which the weather would not admit of doing."

From the foregoing it may be speculated that the "gristmill property" which Joseph M. acquired was his father's former home, near the mill. As a youngster, I recall such a dwelling and an adjoining

orchard where my brothers and I gathered apples with our grandfather Vincent Spencer. We also freely explored the gristmill, operated by a friendly man who had purchased it some years before from the Spencers.

Regrettably, it is a common failure of the "generation gap" that everyday facts about our forebears are allowed to escape us. My grandfather Spencer lived to be 95, and I was often in his company through my thirties. Yet I failed to find out from him some facts of my own "roots" -- including the exact site of his parents' home and whether his grandfather had lived there beforehand.

Joseph Spencer's gravestone in the Friends Cemetery at Grampian, Pa. Lydia's epitaph is on the opposite side of this same monument

Seven years after their marriage, Joseph M. Spencer took time to re-copy in rich, clear penmanship, in a bound 7½ by 12 inch folio, the 35 letters between Lydia and himself, which he titled "A Correspondence Before Marriage."

Joseph and Lydia ultimately raised a family of four, two sons and two daughters. Joseph, despite his frail health during his twenties when he was courting Lydia, lived to be 68, dying July 26, 1889. Lydia died at age 62 on September 27, 1882.

The Spencer name is still prominent in the Grampian Hills, where Joseph's grandfather (also Joseph) first settled in 1808. The first Joseph purchased 440 acres between Pennsville (now Grampian) and the Susquehanna river. He divided the land into four farms, one for himself and the others for three sons, one of whom was Joseph Jr., my great-great grandfather.

A D D E N D U M

Although this pamphlet was inspired by Joseph and Lydia Spencer's remarkable pre-marital letters, it seems appropriate to close with a brief reference to my other great-grandparents. All eight forebears had much in common. All except two were Quakers, and all lived in Clearfield county at a time when it was largely forested and very thinly settled. (The county had only 875 inhabitants in the census of 1810.)

Charles Cleaver, a Grampian hills neighbor of Joseph M. Spencer, courted Mary Blackburn of Shellsburg, Bedford county, and brought her to his farm home after their marriage January 13, 1848. (Their daughter, Elizabeth became my grandmother Wall.)

Another great-grandparent, Reuben Wall, came with his father David to the Grampian Hills as a tiny boy in 1812. David Wall's first cousin Jonathon moved to a nearby farm, and Reuben married Jonathon's daughter Sidney Wall, his second cousin, in 1842. (Their son Miles was my grandfather.)

My other great-grandparents, Joseph Bailey and Elizabeth Boal, married 1-22-53, also lived in Clearfield county, in the so-called Bailey Settlement. They were Methodists. (Their daughter Mary Alice married my grandfather Vincent Spencer.)

333

DISTANCES WERE GREAT....
"NO CARS, NO TRAINS, NO GOOD ROADS"

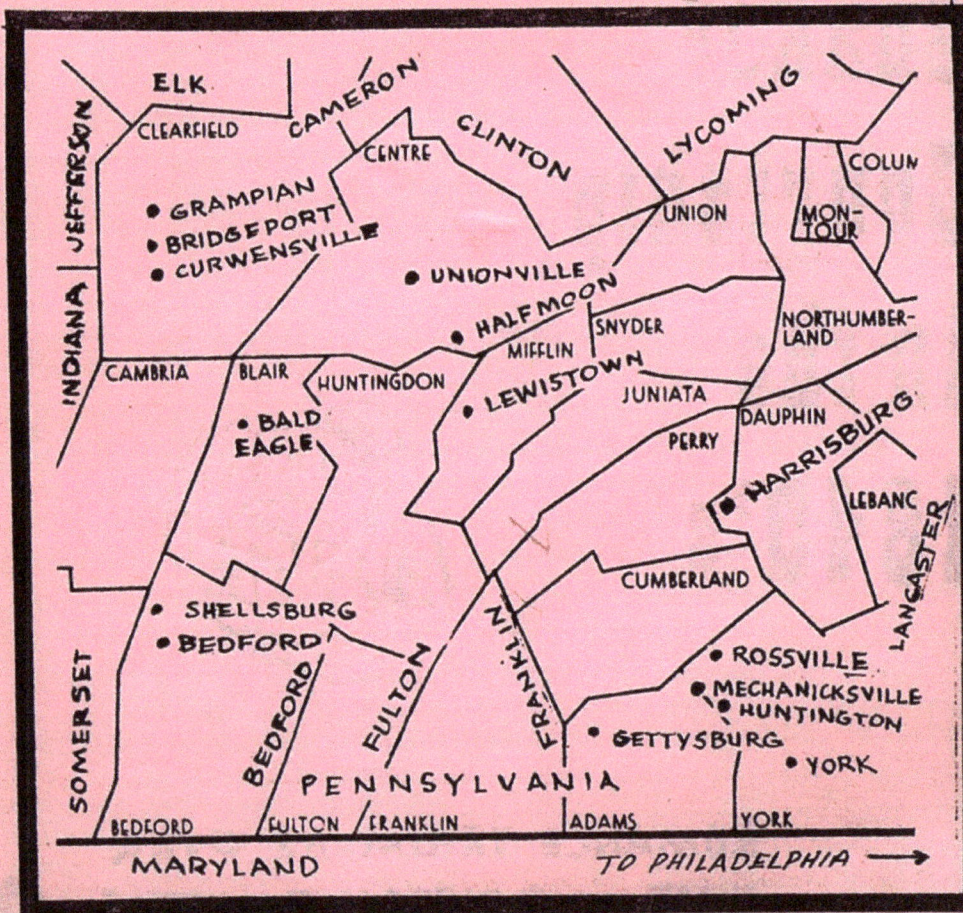

Compiled in 1978, by Richard V. Wall, Harrisburg, Pa.,
with the assistance of brothers Charles C. Wall, Alexandria, Va.,
and Arthur R. Wall, Burlingame, Cal.

ALL are great grandsons of Joseph M. and Lydia Ann Spencer.

Artwork by Nick Ruggieri, Harrisburg, Pa.

334

The Thompson Family

Peter Thompson (May 7, 1748–March 13, 1811) came to this country from Ireland and settled in that part of Bedford County which became Huntingdon County. Peter had come to Pennsylvania prior to the American Revolution and it is believed that he served in the Fifth Pennsylvania Regiment. He married Mary Patterson (1754–1795).

Ignatius Thompson (September 26, 1784–May 27, 1861), a son of Peter and Mary Thompson, served as County Commissioner 1832–1834. He married Mary Norris who may have been a sister of Moses Norris, the progenitor of the Norris families in the Curwensville area.

The family of Ignatius and Mary consisted of three sons and six daughters all who reached adulthood:
- Nancy Ann (1809–1859) married Joseph Straw
- Mary (1811–1885) married Ross Reed
- John D. (1813–1886)
- **James, (b. October 12, 1815 in Glen Richey; died in 1886)**
- Martha (1817–1836)
- Elizabeth (1820–1848) married Elisha Ardary
- Esther (1825–1913) married R.D. Cummings
- A fifth daughter never married
- Josiah William (1825–1900)
- Aloysius (1826), Ann Harriott (1827), Maria (1828)

James Ignatius Thompson, second son of Ignatius, was born October 12, 1815. He helped his father clear their farm. He married Catherine Hepburn (March 7, 1824), daughter of Wm. Hepburn, a native of Scotland.

James and Catherine moved to Curwensville in 1848 where he started what became the family foundry business and worked there until his death in 1886. He was a Democrat and a Methodist. Catherine, born in 1824, lived to **the age of 101**, dying April 23, 1925. She was known throughout the community as Aunt Katie.

James and Catherine had the following eleven children:
- Martha (b. February 11, 1844)
- **Francis Ignatius** (June 2, 1846–December 26, 1909)
- William H. (b. February 14, 1848)
- Samantha (November 12, 1850–1898)
- Mary Alice (b. March 12, 1853)
- Josephine Blanche (June 1, 1855–March 14, 1925)

- Henrietta (b. November 7, 1856)
- Leonora (b. November 15, 1858)
- Frances (b. May 12, 1861)
- Nannie (b. November 17, 1862)
- Jack (April 9, 1865–1897)

Francis Ignatius, eldest son of James Thompson, assisted his father in the foundry. He also engaged to a large extent in the lumber business. He was one of the leading Democrats during his life and served as Constable of Curwensville Borough for many years. On August 6, 1871 Ignatius married Mary Eire Bell (August 15, 1850–March 10, 1892), daughter of David R. Bell and Margery Hoover of Greenwood Township. Mary Eire died in 1892, aged 42 years. Francis Ignatius died in 1909, aged sixty-three years.

Francis Ignatius and Mary Bell (paternal grandparents to Mary Alice) had four sons and two daughters:

- Eire (1872–1872)

- Walter Bell, (January 18, 1874–February 14, 1946) was twice married, first to Edna Rawles (b. 1881) and later to Charlotte Decker (1890–October 1968); Edna and Walter are the parents of one daughter, Irene (b. 1912).

- **Howard Jefferson** (January 12, 1878–January 3, 1968). His middle name, Jefferson, was chosen to honor the name of both his father and of his mother's brother. He married **Elizabeth Bailey Spencer** (September 14, 1880–October 10, 1951).

- Maud Ann (June 10, 1884–September 30, 1958) married Clinton Davidson (b. 1882), was widowed, then lived with and helped to rear the children of the John Stamp family.

- Fred J. (May 16, 1887–December 12, 1952) married Belle Reed Forcey (April 17, 1887–December 19, 1925).

- Francis Ignatius, known as "Tucker" (May 10, 1891–January 1 or Feb. 3, 1962.) Francis married Roxie Hess. Their children are Darl Francis, Robert Walter, Lois May, and William Lee.[1] The daughter of Robert W. and Sarah Buffington married Joseph Geppert in 1963.

- There is some evidence of a daughter who died in infancy in 1892. If so, this might be related to Mary Eire Bell Thompson's death.

---

[1] Bill Thompson should be noted as a talented and respected partner of Richard Jenrette, noted purchaser and restorer of historical mansions in NYC and in South Carolina; Bill served as curator and manager. Richard Jenrette's acquisitions included a series of significant historic American houses, including Robert William Roper House in Charleston, South Carolina; Millford Plantation in South Carolina; Ayr Mount in North Carolina; Estate Cane Garden on St. Croix; the George F. Baker House in New York City; and Edgewater in Barrytown, New York (purchased from author Gore Vidal).

All four sons were said to be mechanically inclined. The three younger sons established the original Electric Plant in Curwensville and assisted with the Clearfield Plant, later branching out into new territory. They sold their interests to the Penn Public Corp. and established other businesses, including real estate, water companies, electric companies, and theatres.

Howard Jefferson, or H. J., as he was known, was engaged in various successful businesses—water, electricity, coal mines, movie theatres, a knitting mill, and banking. He was president of Cassidy Coal Company, Central Penn Light and Power Company, Curwensville Water Company, Curwensville State Bank, Mid-State Theatres, as well as co-owner of a knitting mill. He also ran twice for a seat in the Pennsylvania State Senate.

Elizabeth Bell Spencer and **Howard J. Thompson,** an entrepreneur–businessman, were wed in her parents' home on June 17, 1903; her wedding book is still in the family. The union included three children, **Howard Vincent, Mary Alice,** and **Philip Bell.**

Howard Vincent (b. April 10, 1904 in Clearfield [Fourth Street]; d. January 14, 1964 in Clearfield) married **Katherine[2] Shields Pifer** (b. February 11, 1908 in Curwensville; d. January 31, 1998 in Hershey) on June 20, 1927. They are the parents of four daughters:

- **Matilda Kay** (b. November 1, 1930), who married Albert Brunetti. They are the parents of Mavis Kim Richards (b. September 2, 1952).

- **Judith Evelyn** (b. March 9, 1937), who married Thomas E. Ball. They are the parents of Jean Rochelle Jacobs (b. March 7, 1959 and wife of James Jacobs) and Thomas Ross Ball (b. April 23, 1968).

- **Jo Ellen** (b. November 6, 1938), who married E. Kendall Lorenz. They are the parents of Janelle Corinne Wright (b. January 2, 1969 and wife of Jay Wright) and Eugene Kendall Lorenz, Jr. (b. April 17, 1970; d. January 3, 2013.)

- **Elizabeth Nan** (b. August 19, 1942) who married Joel K. Edmunds (b. August 14, 1942). They are the parents of Shayne Scott Edmunds (b. December 9, 1965 who married Grace Graybill), and Jesse Joel Edmunds (b. November 6, 1979).

  Jean and James Jacobs are the parents of Jordan Ashlee Jacobs (b. April 17, 1986) and Jillian Rochelle Jacobs (b. October 29, 1992). **Shayne and Grace Edmunds** are the parents of Aero Graham (b. April 18, 2004) and Iris Isadora (b. September 2, 2005). **Thomas R. Ball** is the father of Emily Madison Ball (b. July 11, 2002) and Olivia Emerson Ball (b. June 27, 2005). **Janelle and Jay Wright** are the parents of Corinne Catherine Wright (b. May 29, 2001) and Theodore Piers Wright (b. September 30, 2002).

---

[2] Katherine's name appears with different spellings. She was born Katherine Shields Pifer. From the time then met, her husband spelled it Catherine. She always said she didn't mind.

Mary Alice (b. November 21, 1905 in Clearfield, PA (Locust Street); d. April 19, 1998 in State College, PA) first married **William Kitson Jackson** (b. December 28, 1906; d. February 23, 1945), a WWII casualty at Henri-Chapelle, Belgium.

On December 28, 1946, Mary Alice married **Bradford Blueford Crunk** (b. February 16, 1914 in Lockhart Texas; d. May 1, 1998 in State College, PA). They were attended by Mr. and Mrs. Kenneth Wall.

Mary Alice Thompson and William K. Jackson are the parents of one child: **William Spencer Jackson** (b. September 4, 1934 in Philadelphia.) William Spencer Jackson married **Rosemary Keating** (b. January 12, 1937) in 1960. They are the parents of two children: **William Kitson II** (b. August 26, 1962). This son (II) carried the name of his paternal grandfather. **Tracy Keating**, b. February 18, 1967.

> **William Kitson Jackson II married Nancy Louise Witman** (b. February 28, 1964). They are the parents of two children, Sage Marie (b. April 26, 2002) and William Kitson III (b. August 27, 2003).

> **Tracy Keating Jackson married Robert Paul Calvert** (b. January 8, 1966) and they are the parents of two daughters: Kyleigh Rose (b. May 9, 2004) and Chloe Valeria (b. January 7, 2007).

Philip Bell (b. October 20, 1919 in Bellefonte (Lynn Street); d. January, 2001 in Altoona). Circa 1951 Philip married **Eva Hart** (b. June 15, 1922; d. September 4, 2010).

Philip and Eva are the parents of two children:

- **Patricia Ann,** (b. April 25, 1952; d. December 17, 2008)
- **Mark Allen** (b. circa 1954), father of (1) Jessica Sue (b. July 14, 1985; married Christopher E. Walters, May 27, 2005; divorced July 9, 2007; remarried July 8, 2011) and (2) Morgan Rae.

The Wall Family

Members of the Wall family are integral to Mary Alice's story because the Wall children were first cousins to and best friends of Mary Alice Thompson and remained so throughout their long lives.

Grace Cecilia Spencer, mother of five Wall siblings, and Elizabeth Bailey Spencer, mother of Mary Alice and her brothers, were sisters. (Please refer to "The Spencers and the Baileys" for earlier family history.)

The Walls

- Miles Wall (1848-1936) (son of Reuben Wall [1811–1892] and Sidney Waln [1813–1885]) married Elizabeth Cleaver (1849–1932) on September 21, 1871. They lived in Curwensville, two doors from Vincent and Mary Alice Spencer) and are the parents of the following:

- Dillwyn Parrish (known as D. P.) Wall (1873–1950) married Bess L. Wright (1880–1968) and lived at 311 George Street in Curwensville. D.P. was the Office Manager and Corporate Secretary at North American Refractories Company (NARCO). D.P. and Bess are the parents of two daughters, Mary Elizabeth (1902–1983) and Alice Josephine (1906–1998). These sisters married brothers, Claude H. (1894) and Karl T. Rowles (1899–1982), the latter being a graduate of Drexel. Alice and Karl are the parents of Helen Elizabeth Rowles (1993–2017).

- Hannah Mary (1876–1963) married Will Thompson (1866–1948), local Railway Express Agent and son of H. B. Thompson (1841–1925) who owned H.B. Thompson Plumbing. Hannah and Will lived on State St. across from the high school. (Will Thompson's siblings were Frank and Josephine.)

- **Charles Miles Wall** (1877–1945) (see details below)

- Reuben Leslie (1882–1884)

- Verner S. (1885–1963) married Mae Sharp (1886–1961) and lived on Walnut Street, next door to Verner's father Miles. Verner and Mae had two sons, Eugene and Jack.

- Wilbur Lewis (1891–1979), who was the only one of his siblings to earn a high school diploma, married Bernice Read from Clearfield. They lived on Ridge Avenue and are the parents of daughters Virginia Nell, Mary Louise, and Pauline (who was a stand-out at Curwensville High School and who married George Young).

Charles Miles Wall (1877–1945) married Grace Cecilia Spencer (1879–1944). He was the Director of Major Machinery Projects at Crescent Refractories and remained so when it became NARCO. The Wall family lived at 319 Thompson Street.[1] Charles and Grace are the parents of the following, all graduates of **Curwensville High School** and all cousins, friends, and contemporaries of Mary Alice Thompson:

♦ Charles Cecil was born June 21, 1903 in Sadsbury Township, Lancaster County, PA and died May 1, 1995 in Greenwich, Connecticut. (CHS '21)

♦ Marjorie Alice: June 5, 1905–August 16, 1972 (CHS '23)

♦ Kenneth Spencer: February 12, 1908–August 8, 1969 (CHS '26)

♦ Arthur Russel: May 16, 1910–October 18, 2002 (CHS '28)

♦ Richard Vincent: September 26, 1912–September 25, 1992 (CHS '29)

RESIDENT DIRECTOR, MOUNT VERNON HOME OF GEORGE WASHINGTON

Charles Cecil married Marguerite Vaughn Thorp (May 15, 1908–October 4, 1976) on June 15, 1929.[2] In 1935 Cecil was hired as assistant director of Mount Vernon, becoming Resident Director 2 years later.

Cecil and Marguerite Wall are the parents of two daughters:

▪ Mary Jane (1930–) who married James Norman McKean (1926–1984) on September 7, 1951 in London, England.

▪ Patricia Ann (Patsy) (1936–1969) married Lucuis Beasley.

Mary Jane and James McKean are the parents of four children:

• Elizabeth (Ann) Prather McKean (September 12, 1952)

• James Norman McKean (November 4, 1953)

• Charles Edward McKean (September 6, 1956–May 4, 2008)

• Patricia Ann McKean Huebner (January 30, 1958)

---

[1] Howard V. and Catherine Pifer Thompson, parents of four daughters, all of whom are graduates of Curwensville High School, purchased this large house from the Walls in 1946. The Howard V. Thompson family moved from their smaller house on Schofield Street on March 9 of that year.

[2] Marguerite Vaughn Thorpe is the daughter of the colorful Henry Rentz ("Rance") Thorp and Mary Jane Kerr, all born in Curry Run, near Mahaffey in Greenwood Township, Clearfield County.

Marjorie Alice remained unmarried.

Kenneth married Mauvis I. Furey (1907–1933), then Nancie Rawsthorn (1920–1997) in 1945.

Arthur married Gwendolyn Keith; they had 3 children, one of whom is Lynn Keith (1936–1992) who married Gregory W. Barber.

Richard married Margaret Michael (1908–1968) with whom he had a son, Richard, b. 1937.[3] Richard (the father) later married Rita Grottola Gohn (1919-2008).

Trivia: In 1929 Ken Wall was manager of the Richelieu Theatre in Bellefonte, which explains why Mary Alice notes in her Diary that she saw him there. In the same year, Cecil was employed by the Stanley Theatre Company in NYC. Mary Alice remained closely connected with these cousins and their children, as she did with the children of her two brothers, Howard Vincent, Jr. (Bubby) and Philip Bell.

---

[3] Richard and Esther's child, Nancy Ann Wall (b. July 26, 1969.)

The Robisons, The Robinsons, The Kittelbergers, and a few seemingly unrelated Thompsons

The Robison and Robinson Families

For years residents of Curwensville have confused the Robison and the Robinson families of Curwensville and Clearfield. The following may be helpful to this publication, but is not by any means definitive.

There were only 5 Robison names (3 in one family of Robison Printing, plus Paul G. the Principal and one other found in Curwensville listings in the mid-1920s. The name is easily confused with the Robinsons who were more numerous in both Curwensville and Clearfield. There were 75 Robinsons listed as living in Curwensville in the *1928 Echo*, as well as the Reuben Robinson Ladies Store.

The Robisons who were graduated in the early years of CHS include the following, gleaned from the yearbooks, with the understanding that not all yearbooks contained a list of town residents:

- Paul G., Class of 1892, who later served as the Supervising Principal of the school
- Wayne, Class of 1900
- Louis, Class of 1905
- Fred, Class of 1907, who established Robison's Printing Shop; he and his wife had a son, Robert (Robbie) who was a popular ventriloquist
- Mrs. John D. Robison, 423 Anderson Street (Children: Edith, Class of 1913 or 1915 and Bruce, Class of 1917)

Other Robisons without children acknowledged include Mr. and Mrs. Frank P. Robison, 417 Thompson Street; Mrs. Tolbert J. Robison, 514 N. Filbert Street; and Margaret Robison, 312 Thompson Street.

Robinsons who were graduated in the early years of CHS include the following:

- Ruth – 1890
- Ida – 1891
- Isaac – 1910
- Esther – 1913
- Saul – 1907

The Robinsons who were listed as residents of the town in the 1920s yearbooks include the following:

- Mr. and Mrs. Arthur Robinson, 407 Thompson St.
- Mrs. J. P. Robinson, 633 State Street (Children: Emma, Ruth, and Ida)
- Mr. and Mrs. Harry Robinson, 531 Bloomington Ave. (Children: Dema, Florence, Avanell)
- Mr. and Mrs. William Boyd Robinson (Children: Anna Elizabeth, Florence, Rebecca)
- Mr. and Mrs. R. R. Robinson, 712 State Street (Children: Philip, Helen)
- Mr. and Mrs. Will R. Robinson, State Street (Children: Ida and Edith)

The Extended Robinson Family in Philadelphia

- Ann Robinson, enrolled at Drexel, is from the state of Virginia.
- Mr. Arthur Robinson is mentioned in regard to the Robinsons in Philadelphia, yet is named above with a Curwensville address; He appears to be a friend of Mrs. Kittelberger of Philadelphia.
- Mrs. Kittelberger knows Beatrice Robinson of Curwensville.
- Alice Robinson, also a student at Drexel, visits the Philadelphia Robinsons, but doesn't seem to be a daughter of Arthur.
- Alice is noted as the daughter of Bea Robinson in the Diary, May 1, 1926. On that same date Stella Robinson is mentioned along with Marguerite Reichenbach, a Curwensville High School teacher of Latin. ("Alice and Marguerite came up to the house awhile. The rest went out to Robinsons.")
- Ken Robinson is seen at a Legion Dance in Curwensville, as mentioned by Mary Alice; Blair also appears to be a Curwensville Robinson.

The 1922 yearbook (*The Echo*), which provides the names of most residents in Curwensville, gives the name Marjorie as the only child of Arthur Robinson in Curwensville. This could be an understandable error considering this is a student publication.

The Kittleberger/Kittelberger Family

This is a more troubling mystery, as the spelling of this name is not even consistent with a particular person. This book will follow the spelling as found on the grave marker of William Kittelberger (son of Harry Kittelberger) in Oak Hill Cemetery in Curwensville. The author chose this spelling over the alternate as it appears more often. Even in William's own yearbook (*The Echo*) William's surname is spelled both ways.

The following identifying information came from the *1927 Echo*, Curwensville High School's yearbook established in 1922, and from Ancestry.com. For purposes of this book, the family members are being designated as Family One or Family Two.

Family One

Name	Graduation Year	Spouse	Birth Place or Resident
George	1886		Curwensville area

(George later worked in various places and then settled in Philadelphia)

Nan/Nann	1887		no mention
Louise	1891	W.K. Wrigley	Curwensville
Effie	1893	S.L. Daugherty	Curwensville
Harry	1897		Curwensville

Family Two (offspring of Family One)

(George) Frederick	1914	(son of George)	Philadelphia
William	1923	(son of Harry)	Bethlehem
Louise[1]	1925	(daughter of Harry)	Curwensville
Elizabeth S.	1926	(daughter of Harry)	Curwensville

As to the Kittelbergers that Mary Alice mentions in her Diary, I offer the following information (3.2.2020) based on my own research and on Ancestry.com:

After being graduated from Curwensville High School in 1886, George Frederick (b.1869) lived in several different places including Philadelphia where he married Marcia Hendrickson (1871-1938) in 1895. Their son, also named George Frederick (but known to Mary Alice as Frederick) had been born in Curwensville March 20, 1896 and was graduated from CHS in 1914. It is presumed that he and his mother returned to and made their home in Philadelphia. (Frederick died in Philadelphia on January 11, 1975.) Mrs. Kittelberger is mentioned a number of times in the Diary and appears to have formed positive friendships with Curwensville residents, many of whom visited her when they were in Philadelphia.

---

[1] I knew Louise Kittelberger, a classmate of my mother.

Lavinia Spencer's Family Home
Bridgeport, Clearfield County, Pennsylvania

RES. FARM, GRIST MILL, & MILLERS DWELLING OF JOSEPH. M. SPENCER, BRIDGEPORT CLEARFIELD COUNTY, PA.

Lavinia wrote her Diary in the house shown above:

The town of Bridgeport in Pike Township, Clearfield County, Pennsylvania, was founded by early settlers, most of whom farmed; some also worked in lumbering, which was seasonal. The community also had woolen mills and other small industries many of which were destroyed by the devastating Johnstown Flood in May of 1889. The town never recovered.

Lavinia's father was Joseph Moore Spencer (b. March 31, 1821; d. July 26, 1889), the son of Joseph Spencer, Jr. and Lydia Moore. He was described as a leading member of the Quaker sect, of kindly disposition, charitable, and an ideal citizen in every respect.[1] Joseph married Lydia Ann Griest (b. April 20, 1820; d. September 27, 1882) of York County, two hundred miles from Bridgeport. They had met in 1843 when Lydia visited her Aunt Ruth, who had recently married a widower, Gideon Widemire, in the Grampian area, near Bridgeport.

Joseph M. and Lydia had conducted a four-year, long-distance correspondence, as Joseph's ill health kept them from meeting face to face, except a few times, during their long courtship. In fact, concerns about his health nearly terminated the relationship. Finally, after a proposal, hesitation, and then acceptance, they were married at the Huntington Meeting House in Adams County on January 25, 1849. "It was mid-winter with no good roads, just horses and sleigh."[2]

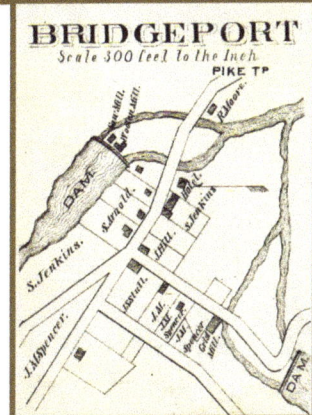

---

[1]   P. 275, *Genealogies*, Straw, 1931
[2]   According to the description presented by their son Vincent at the 100th Anniversary of the West Branch Friends Meeting, Grampian, in 1933.

345

Joseph ran a farm as well as operating a grist mill and is said to have built one of the first homes in Bridgeport. In addition to farming, Joseph taught school in the original one-room school near the Grampian Quaker Meeting House, which explains why he was later comfortable serving in his daughter Lavinia's stead when she was ill and not strong enough to teach at her school.[3]

Joseph and Lydia are the parents of the following children:

- ◆ Lavinia (b. 1851; d. 1871)
- ◆ Vincent Uriah (b. May 14, 1854; d. January 12, 1950)
- ◆ Roland (b. 1856; d. 1928)
- ◆ Almina (b. January 12, 1859; lived past the age of 100)
- ◆ *Jane (unconfirmed)*[4]
- ◆ Amos (dates unknown)

Lavinia Spencer's Diary, 1871 (born 1851)

While Lavinia's name is handwritten inside the cover of this Diary, it may not be in her own hand. More likely the Diary fell into the possession of her brother Vincent who later gave it to his Grandson, Howard Vincent Thompson, who, in turn, placed it in my care.

The first pages of the Diary include the following:

- A table by which to compute interest rates.

- A table showing the number of days from any day in one month to the same day in any other month.

- A listing of the Difference of Time in New York City and other places in the country.

- Rates of Postage, with the information that a letter to any other part of the United States is 3¢; Weekly Newspapers (one copy only) sent to actual subscribers within the County where printed and published: free.

- Several pages of "United States Stamp Duties."

- Sun rises and Moon phases by month; on each of the 12 pages is a listing of historical events with specific dates of the month.

---

[3] *A Quaker Courtship in the 1840's: Joseph M. & Lydia Ann Spencer* by Richard V. Wall & brothers, 1978. This is the account of the courtship of Lavinia's parents, privately published and reproduced in this book, *It's the Berries.*
[4] Not confirmed, only indicated in one of the sources used here.

Diary Entries

Sunday, January 1, 1871

Saw the old year go out and the new one ushered in. It is a beautiful day indeed. Went to the roast; about 20 there, had a splendid dinner, a roast turkey, a goose, and 3 chickens, 3 kinds of sweet cakes and any amount of doughnuts, preserves, sauces, pies. Papa, Mother, and Almina[5] went to meeting and from there to Uncle Will's. We got up a sledload of 14 and went out to Greenville to church. Rev. Wilson preached. We had a lovely ride, such a beautiful evening, got back about half past ten. Had the chance of a beau; do not know who it was, but think it was a Yankee. Of course, I did not accept his company as he was a stranger.

Monday, January 2, 1871

Very cold and windy. Teaching again as usual. The superintendent visited my school this forenoon.[6] There were seventeen scholars present. Lydia S. Porter and Eliza A. Spencer visited it in the afternoon. At the schoolhouse in the evening; wrote a long letter to Jennie Iddings; have not received an answer from the one I wrote to Ellie yet.

Tuesday, January 3, 1871

Quite a disagreeable day; the school pretty noisy in the afternoon. Hope it will be quieter tomorrow & will be. Eliza was up a little while after school and I was down there part of the evening and at the school house some of the time. I cannot get any time to sew. Papa was in town in the morn and took my letter to the office.

Wednesday, January 4, 1871

The thermometer was 6 degrees above zero. The school was considerably quieter than yesterday. Only 16 present. Received two letters this evening, one from Cincinnati, Ohio and one from Cleveland, Ohio, the former from Wilson Winkle and the latter from E. C. Mc Clintock. Have spent the evening at the school house. Amos was up awhile.

Thursday, January 5, 1871

Not so cold this morning and melting some during the day. The grain is beginning to come in from Indiana. Papa bought a couple of loads.[7] One of the men was here for dinner. Aunt Mary went up to see Maggie. She is still growing weaker. Did not go to the school house this evening. Sewed till bedtime. Vincent received a book this evening as a reward for subscribing for a paper.

---

[5]   Lavinia's sister [later referred to as Aunt Minie, pronounced with a long "i" by the Spencer family offspring] and Mary Alice's Great-Aunt.

[6]   It is possible that this is the same school building in which Jessie Pifer later taught.

[7]   Lavinia's father owned and operated a grist mill.

Friday, January 6, 1871

Melted some last night and looks like snowing now. Papa went to Clearfield Town today. Vincent went to town in the evening and got the paper. I read some in it and sewed some. Did not go to the school house in the evening; have completed one and a half months of my school.

Saturday, January 7, 1871

Cloudy all day. Washed some things for myself. Sewed, ironed, and I read in the paper after tea. The School Directors met at our house this evening. They were all present. Drew an order on my first month's teaching but received only nine dollars in payment yet. Heard that Snyder had turned out two teachers in Penn and threatened two more if they did not do better. This is Rowland's birthday. He is 14.

Sunday, January 8, 1871

A very snowy and stormy day. I spent most of it at home. Allie Spencer, Emma Sykes, and Amos were here for dinner and Charlie came up afterwards, then all the others ran off downtown and he asked me to go down to their house. I went awhile then over to Wills. Mary Jane Stage and Emma Hockman were over today. Papa and Mother went to meeting and from there to Wm. Johnson's. Said they had a pleasant visit. Maggie is very poorly, are watching her all the time. Vincent has gone to church.

Monday, January 9, 1871

The coldest day this winter, 2 degrees below zero. Sewing after school. Charlie talked some of coming up to school but I guess he is going to haul timber a while longer. Looked for Uncle Miles to come down but they did not come. We could not have better sleighing than there is now. When V. came home last evening he said he had not been at church.

Tuesday, January 10, 1871

Snowing in the forenoon but did not amount to much. Lucretia Porter visited my school this afternoon. I dismissed early this evening and went up to see Maggie. Papa went over to Uncle Miles to get Espy to come down and drive our team. He came down with us. He only staid[8] until about nine o'clock. Maggie is very poorly; do not know if she will see another day. Mattie Moore and Sally Rigglesworth were going up to stay with her tonight. She knew me as soon as she saw me.

Wednesday, January 11, 1871

Very mild and melting a good deal. Did not hear anything from Maggie today. The school was very quiet and good. Espy got in a little after dark. Amos was up this evening. I did not go up to the school house this evening. Sewed until bedtime. Papa received a letter wanting to know if he was an heir of Thomas Spenser (a man who had served in the War of 1812)

---

[8]   Lavinia uses this spelling of the word throughout the Diary

informing him that if he was, he would be entitled to 320 acres of bounty land at $10 an acre amounting in all to $320, but he cannot claim to be any relation.

Thursday, January 12, 1871

Quite warm and seems some like spring. Papa went to meeting and brought back the sad news of Maggie's death. Her spirit has flown, we hope, to that blessed mansion which is prepared for all the righteous. It is hard to give her up, yet it must be so. His will is not our will; neither should it be. This is Almina's birthday. She is 12 years old. She and Papa and Mother went over to Chestnut Ridge after school and spent the evening. They returned a little after ten. Espy went home this morning. I spent the evening sewing. Lucretia Porter came up after dark and will stay until tomorrow. She is going to get married pretty soon.

Friday, January 13, 1871

A beautiful day but the snow is going off pretty fast. Have finished 16 days of my second month of school. Papa measured up some apples and took them to town. Espy was down at town and came up this way. I got ready after school and he took me up to Cos. Matthew's. Found Ellie Iddings there. She and Warner came down the last 4th day. A good many there in the fore part of the night but they most all went away before 12 M. and all went after supper at 1 o'clock either home or to bed except Ellie, Edith, Joseph White and I who staid up all night, but they all slept part of the time except Joe and I; we did not sleep any. The corpse looks beautiful; it just appears as if she was sleeping and so she is but will never waken again to the sorrow and suffering of this world.

Saturday, January 14, 1871

A pleasant day, but quite warm. Ellie and I fixed poor Maggie's corpse and placed a delicate green vine over her waist and around her head. She had on a fine white dress, trimmed in fine lace. We placed her first rose bud which had just commenced to open on her brow. She had watched so anxiously for the first rose to bloom but never saw it. The Friends met at 10 a.m. to take leave of and to pay their last tribute of respect to the departed one. Indeed it was a solemn occasion. Many were the warnings to turn from the things of this world and commence a new life. This was a large funeral. We came right home and I retired early.

Sunday, January 15, 1871

Commenced raining last night and continued at intervals during the day. Vincent and I got ready to go to meeting but it rained so fast that we did not go. The flat in front of the house is nearly all under water. I spent the forenoon upstairs reading. There is a big flood in the creek now, but the ice has not all gone out yet. Uncle Jerry brought Hettie down to Roberts, then he went back and she started to walk over to her school. Heard that sweet Becky is worse.

Monday, January 16, 1871

Still warm and rainy. The water was running down the main street this morning as if it was a river. Tommy Mills' cellar was full to the joists. There were two families that the scholars could not get to school, only 10 here in the forenoon but 15 in the afternoon. The water fell very fast about noon. Looked some for Ellie and Warner but they did not come.

Tuesday, January 17, 1871

Got very cold this day and had the appearance of snow, but is clearing off this evening. All but two of the scholars present today. Went down to Crist's in the evening to see if I could get his bell for school. Got it. It is not very large but will answer the purpose. Did not go to the school house this evening; baked punkin pies.

Wednesday, January 18, 1871

Some warmer and melting; it is very icy now. The teams have all stopped hauling on account of the ice and for want of snow. Papa and Mother went up to Cousin Nathan's and do not expect to return until after M. M. tomorrow. I received two letters, one from Cincinnati, Wilson Hinkle and "Cos," the other from Alice Way Halfmoon. George Dilman was up a little while after supper and V. went with him to Presbyterian Church.

Thursday, January 19, 1871

Cold and cloudy. May have snow before tomorrow. All the scholars present except one. Papa and Mother came home about 3 p.m. Said Aunt Becky is about same as usual, not entirely bedfast. They had a pleasant visit. Grandma was there. It was proposed at Meeting to change the hour from eleven to ten o'clock and then meet an hour earlier, but they could not all agree and it was left over to be decided next month. Do not think they can make it any better than it is.

Friday, January 20, 1871

Cloudy and dull, but melting some, has the appearance of more rain soon. All of the scholars present but Tommy. Do not expect him any more for about three weeks. Did not go to the school house in the evening. I get tired enough of it in the daytime. Papa is not very well. Vincent has just come up from down town but did not get any mail for Amos and John had not come home from Curwensville yet.

Saturday, January 21, 1871

Snowing a little all day. Very stormy and disagreeable in the afternoon and evening. Papa and Vincent went to Clearfield for a load of rye. The School Directors met in the school house in the evening. I scrubbed, ironed, swept upstairs, sewed and did not retire until nearly eleven. Got the papers this morning containing the Western news. There is an account of a terrible steamship disaster. The SS. McGill destroyed by fire at "Shoo Fly" bar between St. Louis, MO and New Orleans, Lou. Over thirty lives lost.

Sunday, January 22, 1871

A little more snow this morning. There is enough now to cover the ice. The wind blew harder here last night, I think, than it has done this winter. Vincent and I went to Meeting in the sleigh. Stopped at Cos. Nathan's and brought Ellie down with us. The boys were not ready to come yet. E. and I went down to Roberts a little while in the evening. The boys tried to get up a sled load and go to Pennsville to church which would have been easy enough, but failing to get a sled they had to stay at home. Vincent took Ellie up in the eve and went to church up there. He got back again 10 ½ p.m. The coldest night we have had this winter.

Monday, January 23, 1871

Very cold and stormy; snowed six inches or more during the day and drifted everywhere that it can. Finished half of my school. Heard that Sue Bloom had been turned out of her school. Received word a few days ago of Cos. Joseph Underwood's death and it was published in the Carolinian last week. He was only 29 years of age, has a wife and two children. Did not go up to the school house this evening.

Tuesday, January 24, 1871

Very cold but quite calm. The school pretty noisy. Went to the school house and made out the last night's report. Total average 16 and total percentage 84. Helped Vincent work two examples in Arbitration of Exchange and helped Roland some in the Algebra. Irvin Spenser visited my school in the afternoon. Papa spent the day writing for Tommy Hill.[9]

Wednesday, January 25, 1871

A pleasant day and plenty of snow for timber hauling. The teams were out pretty thick. It is twenty-two years today since Papa and Mother were married. I copied a beautiful song this evening. It was entitled "Pass Under the Rod." Did not go to the school house in evening. A good deal quieter today than yesterday. Papa is not done writing for Tommy yet.

Thursday, January 26, 1871

Snowed all day. The snow is very deep now. Several loads of grain came in from Indiana. They contain rye, wheat, and oats. Papa bought over three hundred and thirty bushels of it, including all kinds. I spent the evening sewing. Matthew Shockey visited the school in the afternoon.

Friday, January 2, 1871

Very cold and disagreeable, but I spent the day as usual. Every day it is the same over and over when one is teaching. After recess I had the scholars all spell off the book. I chose for both sides and kept tally. Only spelled one game, had 15 against eight. Sewed some and read some in "The Children's Friend" in the evening and went up to the school house. Intend reading some in the newspaper which V. just brought.

---

[9] Likely this gentleman is not literate.

Saturday, January 28, 1871

Very cold and quite stormy in afternoon and evening. Churned, swept et al in the upstairs in the morning and then got ready to go up to Uncle Will's and got the chance to ride most of the way with William Cleaver; had a pleasant evening. Papa and Almina came up for me in the sleigh. We were only about 15 minutes coming home. Vincent was at Clearfield in the sleigh. It is snowing fast now.

Sunday, January 29, 1871

Not very cold. Amos, Vincent, and I had intended to go out to James Hills but things not pointing favorably to that plan. Vincent and I got a sleigh and went to Uncle Miles and Roland and I got in the sleigh and horse and went to meeting which was quite large. Saw Sallie Iddings. Ellie and Warner only went home yesterday and Sallie came out on the train to see Maggie. She had not heard of her death until after her arrival. R. and I went to Uncle Jerry's and spent the afternoon. No one there but Uncle and Mattie.

Monday, January 30, 1871

Melting some. School small; only 15 scholars present. Vincent did not return until after 11 p.m. this evening. They attended church at Pennsville. Said there were 6 persons forward and about 20 got through. I sent for a photograph album to the dollar sales in New York. Amos is getting up a club. Knit some this evening.

Tuesday, January 31, 1871

Quite warm. The snow is melting fast. The timber haulers are trying to make a good use of it while it lasts. At the school house this evening; helped Roland some in the Algebra. Almina received a letter from Cousin Hannah Cookson. They are all as well as usual.

Wednesday, February 1, 1871

A pleasant day overhead. The snow is melting pretty fast where it lays fair to the sun, but there is plenty of it yet and has the appearance of getting colder. There is a very strong South West wind and I think it will blow up quite cold when the wind changes. There are a great many complaining of colds at present among whom I am included. Did not go to the school house in the evening.

Thursday, February 2, 1871

A good deal colder than yesterday. Papa went to Meeting and I think Robert went along. The boys and Papa went to the debate at Locust Ridge and have not returned yet. Snowing and howling furiously all evening. Papa spent part of the afternoon in the school house. Heard Aunt Becky was no better.

Friday, February 3, 1871

Another week of school finished. This evening always gives me more pleasure than any other during the week. Papa is writing for Tommy Hill today. Lucretia called in a little while on her way to Clearfield, I suppose to get her wedding outfit. Got the *Intelligencer* and the *Weekly Times* both this week. The latest news says the war is over in France and they have compromised.

Saturday, February 4, 1871

Quite cold and has the appearance of being stormy soon. Did chores all forenoon and sewed for a new calico dress for Mother in the afternoon, but did not get it quite finished. We heard that Robert's little girl is very poorly and Papa and I called on them awhile in the evening. We stopped in at Crist's when we came back which was 10 P.M. when we got home. Vincent went to church and George started to go with him but slipped off. There were 6 couples of young folks that came to R. W.'s to stay and went away this morning. They were from Bald Eagle.

Sunday, February 5, 1871

A very cold day. Did up the morning work. Vincent, Amos, Allie and Norah and I went out to Cos. J. Hill's, went in two sleighs. I thought it a great distance but it was splendid sleighing and we drove pretty fast. The country is open and built up nearly all the way, but no very nice buildings. They did not look much like I had pictured in imagination. Got there a little before 12 N. and found them looking for us; had a good visit, but it was not very long. Started home about 5 P.M. Had the best ride coming back that I have had this winter. Saw the moon rising when we were out on the hill; no expectation ever seeing it look so large.

Monday, February 6, 1871

Thermometer 4 degrees below zero in the morning. When Papa came from Meeting he told us that Cousin Nace England was married; he lives in Ohio. Seymour Ross came to drive our team a couple of days. Vincent has just been reading of another Steamship disaster, explosion of the W.R. Arthur. About seventy saved, but some of them not expected to recover. About 60 missing; supposed to have perished.

Tuesday, February 7, 1871

Very cold. The sun shone very brightly in the morn, but cloudy the greater part of the day. This school is much quieter so far of this week than it was last week. Uncle Miles and Aunt Nancy[10] came down about noon. Aunt was in the school all afternoon and uncle and papa were in the greater part: they remained until after tea. Seymour did not come this evening. Can tell no reason.

---

[10] Handwriting has faded; this may not be the name.

Wednesday, February 8, 1871

Middling cold. Teaching today but do not feel much like it. Papa offered to teach in the afternoon but I thought I would put the day through. He finished working for Tommy Hill. Robert B. Way spent more than half of the afternoon in school. He is the first director that has been in yet excepting Papa. He gave me the rem. of first month's wages. I have got my watch all paid for now and $9 remaining. Do not know when I will get the rest. Seymour is here this morning. Whiskey is making a great excitement in our village this evening. Something very unusual.

Thursday, February 9, 1871

Getting quite cold. Very stormy and snowing in morning, but cleared off with the exception of light clouds and very windy since. S. was so wet and cold when he came with the team that he would not stay but went on home. I have been enjoying myself as well as I could in the house today—that is, feeling very badly. Papa was not satisfied to let me teach and said he would take my place till I felt better. Do not think I could have stood it.

Friday, February 10, 1871

I think I feel some better than I did yesterday but not able to teach. Papa took charge of the school again. I have been knitting a little and reading some but cannot read much on account of my head feeling very badly. S. was here tonight. Got the *Intelligencer* and the *Weekly Times.* Several reports of very severe weather in the Northern and Western States. A shower of blood passed over parts of Iowa lately.[11]

Saturday, February 11, 1871

A very stormy day. Snowing most of the time. Felt a good deal better in the forenoon but tired myself too much although I did not do much work but feel quite bad this evening, lay down some of the time. Cousin Hettie came just about dark, was so glad to see her. Rowland took butter and eggs to town, the first we have sold yet this year. Butter 40 cts, eggs 25 cts.

Sunday, February 12, 1871

Very stormy, snowing and blowing furiously most of the day but the storm abated some toward evening. Papa went to Meeting and from there to Uncle Miles, did not return until after dark. Hettie spent the day with us and her company was very pleasant. We had neither one forgotten Halfmoon yet. She gave me a message from Sarah Way that she had sent by her. Vincent took her over. I feel weaker than yesterday but not any worse other ways with the exception of coughing a little harder.

---

11   Information found online: An incident occurred at Peru "...on the bank of a river, in Peru, Feb.4, 1871, a meteorite fell. 'On the spot, it is reported, several dead fishes were found, of different species.' The attempt to correlate is ---that the fishes 'are supposed to have been lifted out of the river and dashed against the stones'. Whether this is imaginable or not depends upon each one's own hypnoses." In *Nature*, it was suggested "That the fishes had fallen among the fragments of the meteorite." (page 303) In the small town of Chico in California, **rocks** were falling regularly from cloudy skies.

Monday, February 13, 1871

Quite cold. Papa is teaching yet and not much sign of getting out of it. I do not think that I am any better than yesterday. Did not do any work. Vincent went to see Dr. Ross to get me some medicine. He took up a load of flour and brought back a load of coal. Read a little but I can't read much.

(Written in another's handwriting is the following in pencil: "Beginning of her breakdown.")[12]

Tuesday, February 14, 1871

Some milder than it has been for several days. Felt better in the morning but very badly in the afternoon and evening. Do not feel that I am improving much. Received a letter from Jennie Iddings this evening which does me as much good as medicine. It was a good letter but could not be as sweet as she is. Have not heard from Ellie since she went home, excepting by others.

Wednesday, February 15, 1871

Feel some better than yesterday. Papa is still teaching but plans to dismiss the whole school this evening for the remainder of the week. Most of the scholars have bad colds now and Papa wants to go to preparative meeting tomorrow and expects to go to Dr.'s the next day but does not know yet how he will go. I tried to sew a little but it was a very little, it makes me so tired to do anything.

Thursday, February 16, 1871

A very changeable day. Had the appearance of being very cold and stormy in morning and melting fast in afternoon and a strong South West wind, then changed quite cold in the evening. Feel about the same as yesterday. Papa went to meeting. The boys about home. Almina is not very well. They all have colds. Aunt Lucy came down to Aunt Mary's and Espy came here to stay all night. They do not know yet how they will go. New neighbors moved to Bridgeport. It is Jim Hills, and Crists have moved into the corner house.

Friday, February 17, 1871

I feel worse all day. My head feels so bad and I am so weak. Aunt Mary and Aunt Lucy came up a little while in morning and Robert was up before I came down. Did not see him. Papa almost gave up going but they finally concluded to go by Railroad and, after eating their dinners early, Vincent and Espy took them to meet the afternoon train. Very windy and stormy in afternoon. (In pencil: meeting in Unionville.)

---

[12] Note from this author/transcriber: Papa (Vincent, Lavinia's brother) used the Spenserian style of writing and this does not look like his handwriting which I have seen. It may be Howard, Jr.'s, as I came into possession of this Diary through Howard, Jr., my father, who also gave me his own diary written when he was sixteen.

Saturday, February 18, 1871

Rained hard by spells last night and very hard once or twice in the morn. Snowing or the sun shining between times. I feel a good deal better than yesterday, and lay down a good while in the afternoon. I suppose Papa has enjoyed one meeting ere this. I would love to be there but try to be contented where I am. Heard there was a stranger, known as Mr. Spencer, who arrived in Bridgeport today or yesterday.

Sunday, February 19, 1871

Snowing in the forenoon but breaking away in the afternoon. Did not get up until after 11 A.M. Seemed lonesome for a while but I feel as well as yesterday. Read more than usual, but can't read very much yet. No one went to Meeting. Sid Porter and 3 or 4 of the little girls and George Dillman were up part of the afternoon.

Monday, February 20, 1871

I feel livelier than I have for some time but not much stronger. Some milder and has the appearance of rain or snow before long. Aunt Mary was up awhile in the afternoon. Vincent has been cutting wood a good part of the time. I read a little. Seymour brought the team back by 4 o'clock and said they had all the time in that was made. Suppose D. Mg.[13] was over before this time.

Tuesday, February 21, 1871

Snowed last night and the trees and woods look beautiful. Do not think I have seen them look so fine before this winter but the snow is falling off fast and not melting on the trees this evening. Feel about the same as yesterday. Almina is not any better. Did not retire until after Papa's return (8 P.M.). He said Darlington Hoopes a minister and Lindley M. Vail, his companion, attended their Q[14] Meeting. They were strange friends within minutes. A very good meeting. Friends generally well. Prof. did not attend. Had school. The school there and at Unionville both doing very well.

Wednesday, February 22, 1871

School did not commence today on account of its being Washington's Birthday. Don't know if there'll be anything tomorrow as it is monthly meeting. It seems like losing so much time and I don't feel much better. Have been out of school two weeks and cannot say that I feel any better than when I left only I don't have much fever now. Papa went to town and has come back. Made some small purchases.

Thursday, February 23, 1871

A beautiful day overhead but melting. Lucretia Porter was married today in Bridgeport. The wedding was at Jim's but they went to Dranker's tavern for their wedding dinner then took

---

[13]   Directors' Meeting
[14]   Quaker

the train for Tyrone where they expect to remain until tomorrow morn, then return on the noon train. I was invited to attend the wedding but was not able. Annie D. and George C. were all the waiters[15] they had. Her husband's name is Hiram Caldwell. No school yet. Papa went to MM [monthly meeting], and said he heard Aunt Becky is not expected to last over another night.

Friday, February 24, 1871

Papa commenced my school this morning and intended to teach tomorrow but we received the bad news of Aunt Becky's death and he had to postpone it to attend the funeral. I would like to go very well, but have no prospect of going. Amos came to get his books. He is not coming to school here any more; intends going at home. Vincent went up along to go to Spelling school and to stay all night. He will not be likely to come back until after the funeral. Kirk Russell is in Bridgeport this afternoon, just came from N.C. and said he left their folks well. The bride and groom arrived about 4 P.M. Jim's got a supper for them. J's children are all very sick. Tommy's very bad; they sent for the doctor last night at midnight.

Saturday, February 25, 1871

Clear part of the day and cloudy a part. Jim's children are not any better. The doctor said he didn't know if Tommy would get well. He proposed that they should send for another doctor and they would meet there this evening but when they met they did not think they could do much for Tommy. Papa went to the funeral, said it was quite large. Vincent was there but did not come home along. Heard of Wash Horn's wife being dead. Robert B. was up awhile in the evening. Received a nice share of the wedding cakes. Feel some better than yesterday. Papa got me more medicine.

Sunday, February 26, 1871

I am about as usual. Papa and Rowland had intended on going to meeting but just as they got ready to start it commenced raining right smart and Rowland did not go. Vincent came home along. He was at Miles' both nights. Not a person excepting our own family here all day. The ice went out of the Lumber City dam and out of the river at Curwensville last night. A smart shower after dark. It came like a summer rain. Tommy is not any better, but think the others are. Mrs. Horn was buried today. The ice gorged in the creek.

Monday, February 27, 1871

Quite stormy. Snowing and blowing all day. Do not think that I feel any better today. Papa commenced school again this morning, only 12 scholars in forenoon. Rowland went to town after school. He got the mail among which was a letter for Papa from George Beatty who now resides in Wisconsin. He moved out there from Bridgeport about 18 years ago. I can remember hearing our folks speak of them different times. The river is very high and part of the water from the creek is running down the pike since dark.

---

[15] witnesses

Tuesday, February 28, 1871

A beautiful day overhead, melting very fast; the road is all bare along here and the people almost entirely in wagons. I have not heard a sleigh bell nor seen a sleigh in two days. Feel some better than yesterday. Wrote to Annie Sillers in the afternoon, but got very tired. There is a splash this evening. I received news from Wisconsin and Clearfield this evening by a messenger.

Wednesday, March 1, 1871

Two months of this year have already passed away and a third one ushered in. It has been very changeable during the day. I believe it rained about daylight and early in the morning the sun shone very bright, then entirely clouded over, sometimes warmer and colder and very windy at times. I feel about as usual; have been out of school three weeks from today; do not gain much strength. Tommy is getting some better.

Thursday, March 2, 1871

Clear the greater part of the day with scarcely a cloud to be seen. I feel a little better but not any stronger that I can notice. Fred B. Caldwell postponed his school today to move into his new house. Tomorrow will be the last day of his school and it would have finished today, but they were too superstitious to move tomorrow. Papa said Tommy was not so well this afternoon. We received a very welcome letter from Aunt Martha. All is well as usual. Nace is at home and his wife is teaching three miles south of them. Josie is teaching a mile from there and Will Broomall is there yet.

Friday, March 3, 1871

Very rainy and disagreeable all day. Papa has finished another week of school for me. He has just taught half a month. Feel about the same as yesterday. Got the papers this evening and one of them contained the death [notice] of Cousin David Spencer of Illinois. He was a first cousin of Grandpa Spencer and quite an aged man. Fred finished his school and treated the scholars; did not hear any further concerning it. I wish that mine was done. He is going to finish the Bailey School to near about three months of it yet.

Saturday, March 4, 1871

A beautiful blue sky nearly all day to look over at the hill, where we can't see any snow, it just looks like summer. Hettie came over before dinner and spent the remainder of the day. Always glad to have her come. Papa went to town and did not get back until we had dined. Lucretia Caldwell came and spent about two hours here this afternoon. Jim's children are getting better and Mary Ellen is some better today. I do not feel any better.

Sunday, March 5, 1871

A middling pleasant day, but very muddy. Papa rode to meeting on horseback; the roads are scarcely fit to go any other way. Studied a good deal about going for the doctor in the morning and had not decided when he started, but afterwards went. The doctor did not discourage me any, but rather encouraged. He said the most I needed was outdoor exercise, as walking or riding, but the weather prohibiting it. Said I should exercise as much as possible in the house without sewing or much work. Left some medicine. Lizzy Crowley and Eliza Ann spent the evening here.

Monday, March 6, 1871

Quite cold and stormy, looks very much like snow soon. Arose a couple of hours earlier than usual. Cousin Suzy Spencer and Aunt Mary came up in the morning, but Aunt went home before dinner. Suzy remained until near 3 o'clock; we had a very pleasant time. Papa commenced school again this week, but is getting very anxious to quit school and go to work. Papa, the boys and Almina spent the evening in the school house, ciphering. Cornelius called in a few minutes.

Tuesday, March 7, 1871

A beautiful spring day; quite contrary to the indications of yesterday. Aunt Phoebe came down early, was here before I had got down stairs, left all the children at home and she remained until evening. I have been growing stronger every day this week, feel quite a difference since this time last week. Papa and Rowland went to town after school; got some mail, only one letter for Papa and some papers. Thomas Bloom called awhile. He brought me a note from Hettie.

Wednesday, March 8, 1871

A beautiful day. The jams are splashing now every day, but have not run any logs past here yet. The raftsmen are very busy now, preparing their lumber for market, not many started yet. Hannah Way came over early in the morning and remained until about three o'clock; had a pleasant time. She visited the school, but they thought I had better not go along and she did not stay very long. I have the headache more than usual today, which makes me feel dull. Uncle Miles made us a call in the evening. Brick Pomeroy passed through here twice in the morning from Luthersburg. He will lecture in Clearfield tonight. Col Walters accompanied him.[16]

Thursday, March 9, 1871

A fine day overhead. I am still improving slowly, sewed a little in the afternoon. We have no visitors today. Mother is washing. Vincent went to Clearfield; he took down 30 bus. of potatoes to Adams and brought back a load of flour. The roads along the river are very bad; nearly impossible to get along, near the bridge. They are dry now past our house. Vincent

---

16   Brick Pomeroy likely was MM "Brick" Pomeroy, a widely known newspaper editor (who earlier had edited small newspapers in New York and Pennsylvania) whose commentary on the Civil War brought him national recognition. Although loyal to the Union, he made bitter denunciations against President Lincoln and the administration's war policies. This reputation would explain the high cost of admission and likely guarantee a full house which is what Miss Spencer's diary entry implied.

said there were near 1,000 persons present at Pomeroy's lecture. He took in about $500 with 50 cts. admission. A smart summer shower in evening and got very dark, then got light again. A little gust after dark and I saw lightning 3 or 4 times.

Friday, March 10, 1871

Another clear day not much colder after the gust. The children are all at school. I helped a little at the ironing and baking, but could not do much. Ann Hill called in the forenoon, on an errand. The first logs ran past here, for this spring. They ran very fast some of the time. There are 8 Yanks down and are boarding at the Hills. Charley went to logging this morning. It will be new work for him. Went to town and has not returned yet. Jack. R. called Jef. B. out of bed the night before last and shot him, but did not mortally wound him. He will recover. The rascal made his escape.

Saturday, March 11, 1871

Pleasant enough overhead, but very muddy again on account of the late rains. Do not feel as much like work as I did yesterday, did not do anything of any note. Mother and Almina are pretty busy. My head aches very badly. Vincent did not return until after I had retired last night, brought the mail with him. I read a little.

Sunday, March 12, 1871

Very rainy nearly all day. Feel better than usual. Washed and wiped the dinner dishes and put them away without any assistance. Almina went down to Jim's in the afternoon. It was so rainy that none of our folks went to meeting but getting quite cold. Papa and the boys went up the creek a couple of miles to see a big jam of logs. They run back for more than a mile and are piled as high as the house. There was a big splash,[17] but not many logs ran as they could not get a break. There are twelve men working on them.

Monday, March 13, 1871

Clear and frosty in the morning but clouded up and rained and snowed together in the afternoon. I wrote to Jennie Fielding but got very tired for I scarcely knew where to stop whence I commenced writing to her. Mother and I have been trying to do the chores but she is worse than I am today and ought not to touch work but she won't give up. Vincent went to haul boards from Kratzers, came home about 3 or 4 o'clock on account of the rain. A few logs run.

Tuesday, March 14, 1871

Cold and dull all day, but a heavy frost in the morning. Got up earlier than usual and Almina combed my hair before she went to school. Mother is some better, but I hardly feel as well as yesterday. Read considerable in some new Sabbath School books that I had never examined before and found them very interesting. Vincent is hauling boards. No splash today.

---

17   "Splash" is the term used when the logs break out of being piled and "stuck" together. When the log jam breaks, it causes a "huge" splash.

Wednesday, March 15, 1871

Quite a gust about daylight appeared to be small hail or sleet with the rain part of the time. Rained occasionally during the day. Vincent is hauling boards. A very large splash and a good many logs run. I feel pretty well with the exception of the headache and sewed a little in the afternoon. Mother is knitting. I have been out of school just six weeks. Expect to try it again tomorrow and let papa go to meeting.

Thursday, March 16, 1871

A very pleasant day, the warmest we have had this spring. Six weeks today since I have been off the porch or stepped on ground. Went to school and got along very well. Got pretty tired. Papa came after P.M. Recess and took charge of the classes. I think the scholars have improved considerably since I left, although the school is greatly diminished. I could hardly put in the time. A splash. Papa attended meeting and a committee.

Friday, March 17, 1871

Cold and cloudy most of the day. Rained last night and in the morning. Papa is teaching again, but I do not feel any worse of being out yesterday. Mother has not been well this week and is scarcely as well today as she was. Sewing most all of the afternoon. Mother is working some. Another splash; they do not get the logs out very fast; about a dozen of the Yanks moved to the camp and will not be at Tommy's any more.

Saturday, March 18, 1871

Cold but pleasant; the roads drying fast. Working some, finished a shirt for Rowland, ironed for Mother, and Almina doing the scrubbing, baking and other work. Papa went to town in the afternoon, where he met Hettie and got her to come up along and we coaxed her to stay until tomorrow. She wants me to assist her some in the mental, for she wants her class to go through the book again before school is out. I will do all I can. The logs run. I have a very weak eye.

Sunday, March 19, 1871

A very pleasant day. I can scarcely stay indoors. The splash came about 10 or 11 A.M. and Hettie and Almina went to the dam to see the logs run. Hettie had never seen them before. Then they went down to Roberts and took dinner. John Blackburn is out there now. Papa went to meeting and Nathan, and Ann with the two little girls came down along with him. Had a very pleasant though short visit from them as they went home in the evening and Mother and Ann were at Robert's part of the time. Hettie came up a little while after dinner. Espy was here awhile but hardly got to speak to him. Vincent was up the creek and says the jam is as long yet as it was last Sabbath. The logs running as fast from above as they can get them. Some came up from Clearfield to see them. There were about 100 up there, coming from all around.

Monday, March 20, 1871

Cold and very windy. Mending for Mother most of the day. My eyes are not so weak as they were for three or four days previous. Papa is teaching yet, will finish his month tomorrow. No splash. Vincent was later than usual coming from church last night; do not know if he got on a new road which was farther than coming directly home or not. Charley Briggs called a few minutes and I had some talk with him. Papa went to grubbing after school. Vincent is hauling boards.

Tuesday, March 21, 1871

Rained and blew last night and dull and cloudy today. Snowing a little occasionally through the day, but not layering. Sewed a little and spent nearly all the afternoon solving mental problems for Hettie. I want to send them to the offer tomorrow; got all but one, which puzzles me some.[18] A great many logs run. Vincent is hauling boards. Papa has taught now one month.

Wednesday, March 22, 1871

A pleasant day, but windy. I taught; did not get very tired; think I can finish the school term now. There are only 7 more days. Sewed till dark after school. Papa spent the day grubbing. Vincent hauling boards. No splash. There was a new dwelling place put up in B. today—it was a bird house. Heard that there were about 300 persons present at the exhibition, at the close of Prof. Andrew's school. The lady pupils all appeared in white. The answers during the examination were all very prompt and correct. The exercises very entertaining.

Thursday, March 23, 1871

Very warm before dinner and the most windy day here this spring. The hollow appeared to be full of smoke, supposed to be winds from the western prairies which are now probably on fire. Papa and Mother went to Meeting which had a good deal of business and did not get home until after 3 o'clock. Heard that Cousin Lydia Spencer[19] broke her leg by being thrown from a horse and Sue buried her baby today.

Friday, March 24, 1871

Clear but quite cold. Papa is grubbing on the hill. Teaching. The logs run faster and thicker and for a greater length of time than they have done heretofore this spring. I feel more tired than usual this evening. Mother washed some in the afternoon. I sewed after school and ironed some. Vincent got the paper and a letter for papa. I am looking for one and hope I may not have to look very long.

---

18   Newspapers and magazines occasionally ran contests. Possibly the problem Lavinia didn't solve was intentionally included to make sure there were no winners.

19   Lavinia's mother's name was also Lydia (Moore) Spencer.

Saturday, March 25, 1871

A heavy frost and ice on the windows. Have the headache quite bad; lay down in the afternoon for a while. Read, sewed, ironed, etc. Mother baked bread, cakes, and custards. Papa and the boys were grubbing, picking and burning brush. Papa caught fire by a spark being blown from the heap and falling on his back, which burned through his vest and flannel; he began to feel hot and asked Vincent if he was afire and Vincent put it out. If the spark had been larger and blazed it might have proved serious.

Sunday, March 26, 1871

Very stormy, snowing all day and about 4 inches deep, on the boards in the evening. Papa went to meeting, said it was a very large group, more people there than had been for a good while. Two strangers that he did not know. I have the headache very bad. Had a good dinner of smashed potatoes, tomatoes and corn. Papa read to me in the afternoon. I love to listen to a good reader.

Monday, March 27, 1871

Snowed about two inches last night and still continues. Several teams went out with sleds to haul timber. I feel worse than yesterday but I am in school again. There was a splash. The logs ran very fast for a short time; they (the Yanks) have got an opening through the jam now. Papa is dyeing a piece of English broadcloth for to make a coat for himself."

Tuesday, March 28, 1871

Quite cold and stormy. Snowing some. No splash, the water is very low now. Never taught before when I felt as miserable as I did today. My head hurt me so badly. Vincent helped me some of the time. Papa went to clear fields, had a load both ways; got 300 flour sacks. Sewed some after school at a new apron for Almina.

Wednesday, March 29, 1871

Much warmer and melting very fast. Feel a great deal better than I did yesterday. Papa spent the forenoon doing chores about the house. Vincent unloading lime, some of it is splendid for whitewashing, must get at it after school is out. Got the *Children's Friend* and a letter. Heard that Hettie had a good spelling school last night, also that John, Frank and Addie Rensell arrived at Clearfield on the train this afternoon.

Thursday, March 30, 1871

Dull and cloudy, rained a little in the morning. I feel pretty well. Teaching yet, but my school term will end tomorrow, and I am not sorry. Vincent is hauling timbers for Hartsock. Papa is doing chores most of the time; he took work up at John Porter's. Milton Kirk and Bertie Port were married this afternoon. The wedding took place at Will Cleaver's. She is now Cousin Bertie. Sykes moved. The girls will stay with their aunts until after school is out.

Friday, March 31, 1871

A beautiful morning, but it got cloudy before noon. I feel about as yesterday. This is Papa's birthday. He is 50 years of age and is busy at work all day. The last day of my school, and 13 pupils present. 2 moved away yesterday. 7 of them spoke pieces. Aunt Mary was up a while after recess. Treated them with two apples and a candy cake each. Received a letter from Ellie Iddings; stated that the people were all well. Says the school does not re-open until the 15th of next month.

Saturday, April 1, 1871

Looks quite wintery, about 2 inches of snow in the morning and snowing fast all day. Mending, ironing, etc. Mother is baking graham bread; it is new business; we never had any baked before. Papa is looking over the account books. Tommy Hill was up in the evening and staid awhile. A splash, not many logs run. Did not get April Fooled.

Sunday, April 2, 1871

Very cold but pleasant overhead. Helping Almina to prepare a letter she is writing to her cousin. Papa went to meeting and from there over to Uncle Miles. Found them well. Grandma sent word for me to come and see her. Mary Ellen, Sid, and Norah were up in the afternoon. Vincent went away after dinner and did not return until after church. Do not know where he went. George was along. I must find out where they go.[20]

Monday, April 3, 1871

A very disagreeable day, raining most of the time. A rainbow in the afternoon. Vincent was hauling all day, got very wet. Mother cut out a fine cloth coat for Papa. I have been sewing nearly steady and do not feel so well. Think I should have run around the house more. Got the mail and Papa read aloud from the *North Carolinian* in the evening.

Tuesday, April 4, 1871

Nearly clear, though very windy. Did not do much to be called work, yet was busy most of the time. Eliza brought her sewing and spent most of the afternoon. Johnson Holden has only been able to go to the barn on his crutches. Mother is sewing some. Papa and Rowland fixing fence. Vincent hauling timber, they finished Hartsock's and talk of helping G. Ross.

Wednesday, April 5, 1871

Warm and windy. Feel very poorly today. Lay on the wood box most of the forenoon. Did not do much. Mother sewed in afternoon. There was a large splash and a good many logs run. Tommy Hill is having the bank below the road cleared off and intends fencing and planting it. It will be a great improvement up town and lies directly before our door. Papa and Vincent sowed one piece of oats. The frogs are croaking loudly this eve.

---

[20]   Likely somewhere with other young people, a prelude to later courting....

Thursday, April 6, 1871

A very fine day, the roads about here are as dry as the middle of summer. Have the sore throat, but feel much better than yesterday; busy all the time, but did not sew any, as it does not agree with me. Made out the last month's report of my school average 11 out of 13 pupils, percentage 84 (Totals). Papa brought me a bottle of "Layne's Expectorant." Thinks it will help my cough, and perhaps it may be beneficial to my head. Sowing another field of oats.

Friday, April 7, 1871

Very warm summer weather. Thermometer about 80° above zero. Busy all day, walked out in the backyard. Mother did a big baking. A splash and a good many logs run. The water fell soon and a goodly number struck in the creek opposite the house. Vincent is harrowing. Papa was chosen by the Court to assist in dividing the farm owned by Irvin and Bilger. Spent the day helping to survey it. He dined at Ed Irvin's. Did not get the mail.

Saturday, April 8, 1871

As warm as yesterday and very high wind about noon. I feel quite poorly again, weak and nervous. Papa went again to assist in the division. Rowland sold 14 dozen of eggs for Easter. Cornelius was up in the morn and Sally Crist and Aunt Mary in the afternoon. Uriah C. is going to start for Kansas next second day. He has a brother living there. Papa dined at Bilgers. Got the mail, two papers and two letters. Snyder told Papa today that the Normal (school for training teachers) would be held in Curwensville.[21]

Sunday, April 9, 1871

A lovely forenoon, but clouded up in the afternoon and a little shower about the time that Papa, Mother, and Almina came from meeting. Rowland remained in the house with me for company while they were gone. Vincent out somewhere, at home a couple of hours. Maria Way, thinking I would be lonesome, brought the children and came up and spent a couple of hours. At half past nine last night we discovered a great light which we supposed must have been caused by a large fire in the direction of Curwensville, but we could not tell if it was so near. Heard today that was the residence of Urban Thompson. It was burned to the ground. Vincent and U. C. went to M.E. Church.

Monday, April 10, 1871

A beautiful day, very warm. Not doing much; do not feel like it. Have been weaker for several days but think perhaps the medicine is the cause of it. Went down to Crist's and spent part of the afternoon. Cornelia took Uriah to the train and had first returned when I started home. Tommy Hill came from the city this evening and brought an Englishman with him to weave. Jesse Dale is married. Got a preacher's daughter (Rachel Clary). Expect she's a little beauty.

---

[21]   She is correct. A Normal School was established in Curwensville.

Tuesday, April 11, 1871

Rained in the morning then cleared off and got very windy before night. Papa finished sowing his clover seed before noon. Feel about as I did yesterday; not doing much. Wrote to Alice Way. Vincent is plowing the potato ground. No splash. The water is very low now and no sign of a flood yet. The maple trees are looking beautiful now.

Wednesday, April 12, 1871

The sun shining most of the day, but very windy. Do not feel at all well. Papa and the boys are hauling stones off the corn ground. Mother sewed a little. There was a gentleman informed me that they intend moving the high school from Williams Port to a more desirable situation. They are now having the subject under discussion, and is some talk of locating in Curwensville. I think the people of our county will do all they can towards getting it here as we need such a school.[22]

Thursday, April 13, 1871

A couple of showers in the morning, then cleared off and got very windy. Feel some better than yesterday. A splash, but not many logs run. The boys are hauling. Papa walked to meeting, says Hettie is going to Halfmoon. He planted about a dozen cherry and a half dozen of plum trees around the yard and near the house this afternoon. There was a large grist mill near Clearfield burned to the ground this week. A beggar woman stopped and got supper for herself and husband. She had come from Scotland to America before she was 11 years old. Was taken and raised by a family of a friend in NJ. (In Vincent's handwriting in the margin: "I remember this.")

Friday, April 14, 1871

It is beautiful out of doors, but a very cold, disagreeable wind. Feel better than I have for some days. Doing chores. Papa is repairing the garden railing on the lower side. Have not made any garden yet and it is getting pretty late. Most of the neighbors have some made. Got the papers but did not read much. Mary Ellen was in a little while. Lucretia is living at Fred B. Caldwell's. Harry has his new house nearly finished.

Saturday, April 15, 1871

Very cold with heavy frost, though clear and beautiful during the day. Did not feel so well in the morning, but got better pretty soon after. Cousins Hettie and Nathan stopped here about an hour. H. was on her way to Halfmoon to attend the school and came this way to see me before leaving. I did not like to see her go and I have to stay, but must try to be content. Know she will enjoy herself; she gave me a present of a nice lace collar; said she was perfectly satisfied with the questions. Jimmy Moore is not very well.

---

[22] Curwensville did offer schools from a very early date. It might be debatable as to when education at a "high school" level was offered as records of graduating classes began only with the class of 1886. However, "upper grades" were offered in the 1830s, although a "night school" was offered in 1828. The date for an official "graduation" is 1886.

Sunday, April 16, 1871

A beautiful day, but very cold and some wind. Feel better than yesterday. Papa went to meeting and said it was quite large. Cecilia Irvin from Luthersburg; her son and daughter attended; the former spoke in meeting three times. Rowland, Almina and I rode up to Johnson Holden's in the carriage; met with his brother and sister, also Amanda Cleaver. Had a very pleasant visit, returned about 3:00. The first I have ridden out anywhere for 11 weeks and things are greatly changed since then, the ground being all covered with snow, and not beautiful spring weather. Uncle Miles, Aunt Luci and three of the children were here in the evening. Vincent went to Chestnut Ridge Sabbath School in the morning, from there to town. Again at noon when he saw some people being baptized. Jane Harley was the only one he knew. Said there were a great many out from Clearfield. He did not come home until after Church.

Monday, April 17, 1871

Pleasant, but very cold for the time of year. Stirring around and do not feel any the worse for my ride yesterday. I think if only the weather gets warm and pleasant it would do me good to go out. Suppose Hettie has experienced one day of school. Papa finished the garden pails. Vincent is working for Jason. Tommy Heil got the rest of his goods this afternoon. Heard that there was a family going to move in with Whitakers intending coming tomorrow.

Tuesday, April 18, 1871

Some warmer than yesterday. Very smokey; there is fire out up the creek. Saw the Northern Lights plainly about 9 o'clock last evening, two broad red bands across the sky nearly east and west. Papa cleaned up the gardens and they burned the brush after supper. Grandmother MacDowel came and spent the afternoon and staid until after tea. Papa and Vincent at town in evening. Mother washed before dinner.

Wednesday, April 19, 1871

Dull and cloudy with showers of rain in forenoon. Papa dug and made most of the early garden in the afternoon. Feel quite poorly, almost good for nothing. The boys are both on the sick list today. The trees are being covered with leaves and the early flowers are beginning to wither and die. Nothing more of importance.

Thursday, April 20, 1871

Clear and pleasant until 11 A.M. when it suddenly clouded up and a heavy rain with thunder and very high wind on the hills. Not much wind here. Before 1 p.m. not a cloud to be seen and a beautiful afternoon. Papa and Mother went to M. Meeting. This is Mother's birthday; she is 51 years of age. Rowland took marketing to town and got caught in the shower. Feel some better than yesterday.

Friday, April 21, 1871

Cloudy most of the day, but the sun shone out some times very brightly. Papa commenced plowing the corn ground. Vincent is about the house, helping some; he is not well. I feel about as usual; thought I would walk out after dinner but before I got ready there were three ladies from town called to spend the afternoon with me. It was Mattie and Minerva Bilger and Ella Laporte; they had just heard a few days previous that I was ill. I got their mail but I did not read the news.

Saturday, April 22, 1871

Cold and cloudy with rain in the afternoon. Papa out plowing. Vincent is some better. He is working about the house. Mother and Almina are doing the seventh day's work, and I am lying around not doing much of anything. My head is so bad again today. Cannot think of any more to write at present.

Sunday, April 23, 1871

A beautiful day but windy in the morning. Do not feel any better, but rather worse than yesterday. Papa went to meeting, pretty large. He saw Addie Russel who said she wanted to come down soon. It seems so lonesome to be shut up in the house this beautiful day. No visitors here. When Aunt Mary came home she said Hil was some better. Spence came back from N.Y. the first of last week. George Frantz went through here this evening and brought his wife, daughter and daughter-in-law in along and left them to visit… he was on his way home again.

Monday, April 24, 1871

A beautiful day. Some warmer than it has been for the past week. Some better than yesterday, yet I do not feel as if I can work much. Spence's father was still living and about the same when he left as when he went there. Went to the mill and got weighed; have lost 16 ¼ lb. since last autumn. I weigh only at present 83 ¾ pounds. Stopped at Jim Hill's a few minutes and saw some of Tommy's goods. A little splash.

Tuesday, April 25, 1871

Very pleasant in the morning, but got very windy before noon. I feel much better than yesterday; planted two boxes of choice flower seeds in the morning and have another box planted in which the flowers are beginning to come up nicely. Mother washing in the afternoon. Papa and Vincent are plowing and Robb Moore is helping them today. They want to finish as soon as possible. Vincent received a package containing seven of the "People's Literary Companion," and an order they have not sent the picture yet, but perhaps they may in time.

Wednesday, April 26, 1871

Another very fine day. The peach and pear trees are coming out in blossom nicely now. Feel like running around, but was not out of the yard today. Rowland was helping our folks to plow and they finished soon after dinner, then Vincent went to help Jason in return. Papa cut potatoes in the afternoon. I am getting anxious to hear from Halfmoon as I want to know what is going on there.

Thursday, April 27, 1871

Commenced raining about midnight and continued until after noon. Some prophesy a flood and some none. There is not rain enough yet. Serving some of the time; have the headache. The boys were here reading most of the day. Vincent took a load of chop [chopped wood] to town. Papa cutting potatoes. Espy came down to the mill and will stay all night; said they were all well as usual. I would like to see Grandma.

Friday, April 28, 1871

Pleasant overhead, but cold and muddy. A remarkable heavy gust between 11 & 12 P.M. last night and a pretty good flood in the river this morning. Will be a good many rafts to start a splash. There is another jamb up the creek about as large as the other and in nearly the same place. Vincent went to Lumber City with a load of flour. Papa was making a shaft for the carriage and got it finished. I got a letter from Hettie stating she arrived safely and liked the school very well. They have 24 pupils and expect more.

Saturday, April 29, 1871

Got quite cold and disagreeable in the afternoon. Mary Ellen came up about 10 o'clock and staid until nearly one; she had only been gone a short time when Uncle Andy and Aunt Margaret came here from town, but they went away about 4 o'clock down to Robert's, so we could hardly call it much of a visit. Papa and Vincent took a load to Clearfield and got one back to Curwensville and were home before three o'clock. There was another splash. Have not been doing much and do not feel much better.

Sunday, April 30, 1871

A beautiful day but cold. Feel pretty smart again. Papa and the boys went to meeting, not a very large attendance. Sarah Spencer and Aunt Mary were here in the forenoon and Addie Russel (from N. Carolina), Lizzie Crowley, Bertie Kirk, Allie Crowley, Lizzie Spencer and Addie Spencer were here in the afternoon. It was the first time I had seen Addie since she came out. Think she has not changed much in looks; appears to be right hearty. Right glad to see her here again.

May 1, 1871

Quite pleasant and much warmer than yesterday. Sewing a little, have a headache. Aunt Mary, Jane Frantz[23] and Addie Russel came up just after dinner. Jane is on a visit from Elk County; she and her family moved from this place 8 years ago. The first two did not stay long. Addie remained until dusk. She told me many things about the South—their manner of living, amusements, etc. She expects to stay north until Autumn, but will not listen to coming back here to live. Mary and Martin and Mattie Spencer are at home now at their father's. Mary lives in Arkansas and Mattie has been down spending the winter.

Tuesday, May 2, 1871

Warm and pleasant. Feel pretty smart and did several chores and wrote a long letter to Ellie Iddings. Warner's Menagerie & Circus went past here early this morning. Did not see the elephants and camels (two of each) as they were driven past here in the night. They will exhibit in Luthersburg today; several persons went but have not returned yet. Vincent is plowing for Jason. Mother made a kettle of beautiful soap this afternoon. Papa, Rowland and Almina planted the potatoes; they finished and have quite a patch. Looks like rain now.

Wednesday, May 3, 1871

Damp and a slow steady rain the most of the day. Had intended going to Lumber City if the weather had been favorable, but gave that up as soon as I got up. Do not feel quite so well. Vincent tried harrowing a little while in the afternoon, but soon got tired of it; thought he would prefer dryer work. Rowland commenced Normal School; said there were only 21 pupils, including himself. The Superintendent and an assistant are both teaching, have the north room. I copied some mental answers in a new book.

Thursday, May 4, 1871

Very heavy rain after daylight and showers through the day. The people are in hopes of a flood. There was a big splash. Do not feel much better. Baked some cakes and did other little things. Had three more scholars at their (Normal) school. Papa and Vincent doing chores. Not much of importance for today.

Friday, May 5, 1871

Still continues to rain by showers. Papa talked of going for the Doctor, but gave that up and went to Curwensville. Vincent went down in the morning and did not return until evening; said he was going down the river if he got a chance, but do not think he will. None of us would be satisfied to have him go. The river is low, but a good many rafts starting. Reuben Wall paid us a short visit in the afternoon. There was another splash. Feel about as yesterday. Read an account of the death of Samuel Cornman (?). He resided in Baltimore and was 78 years of age. I had the pleasure of meeting him at his own residence and dining there.

---

[23] Some of the capital letters in Spencerian handwriting, taught and used at this time, are difficult to distinguish one from the other. Spencerian was a style of handwriting, not in reference to this Spencer family in the Diary.

Saturday, May 6, 1871

Still continues to be wet. Vincent at the river until noon; the flood is getting very low, not many starting now. Papa is working in the shop. Felt quite poorly in the morning, but better in the afternoon. John Russel made a short call this afternoon on his way to Curwensville, but is coming back to B--- tonight (Bloomington?). Would love to attend the First day of school tomorrow, but will not be able to go out much until the weather changes for the better.

Sunday, May 7, 1871

Almost clear, though very cold and windy. J. P. spent the early morning with us. They all went to Firstday school except Vincent and I. They left me at Aunt Mary's until then returned after meeting. Vincent was there some of the time. Got my dinner. Addie was there and I enjoyed myself pretty well. Papa was appointed on a committee which met after meeting and did not return until evening. He walked all the way up and down again. Dined at Cos. Kathryn's, brought me a lovely yet sad present, a photograph of Maggie.

Monday, May 8, 1871

Cold and very windy. Have the headache pretty badly. Sewed some. Mother and Almina are busy at the housework. Rowland at school, about 15 new scholars in the morning who came a short time to see about enrolling. Vincent is harrowing. Papa made calls in the forenoon, shelled his seed corn in the afternoon. Has the appearance of being a very cold night. There are fears of the fruit being very much injured if it is not already.

Tuesday, May 9, 1871

A very hard frost; the fruit could not possibly escape all being frozen, 1 degree below zero. Freezing here and colder other places. Heard that there was ice one inch thick in Brady [later Township] this morning. Do not feel so well as common. Addie Russel made a morning call. She is going to leave here today and expects to start for Cameron [County] the first of next week. Vincent commenced going to school; 2 new scholars. I guess he likes it pretty well, for one day's experience. Papa was hauling and cutting wood most of the time. Got some notions from a peddler.

Wednesday, May 10, 1871

A very pleasant day, cool in the morning, but got quite warm soon in the day. Papa took a load of chop to town early and when he came back I was nearly ready to go to Lumber City and he was not long getting ready. Found the Doctor at home and dined with him. Got acquainted with his wife. She appears to be a fine woman. The doctor did not discourage me any and I feel better after my ride, only I got pretty tired. He gave me some more medicine. Mother cleaned part of the kitchen while I was away.

Thursday, May 11, 1871

Right pleasant. Papa talked of going to meeting and taking me along as far as Uncle Miles where he would have me wait until he came from meeting, but it was so warm he concluded it would be best to get the corn ground and get ready to plant the corn. I think I caught a little cold yesterday but do not feel much worse. There was a splash. The boys are at school. I would like to be able to attend also.[24] They have about 45 pupils at present. Mother made another kettle of soap.

Friday, May 12, 1871

Very clear and pleasant. Papa finished harrowing before the boys came from school, then went to engage corn planters. Got the promise of half a dozen. Doing a good many turns and feel very tired this evening. Almina hemmed a fine handkerchief for herself and did it nice enough to beat anything except a good sewing machine. The Yanks took their boat down past her on the wagon and are going to put it in below the bridge. Will have only one more splash past here.

Saturday, May 13, 1871

Almost clear but very windy. Our folks went to planting corn. There were nine hands altogether, Three of them here for dinner and only one for supper. Mason and Martha Bloom came about eleven o'clock and remained until near three. It was their first visit since they were married and the first time he ever was here. Our town is quite alive with Yanks this eve. The school directors met in the school house; got all of my orders, but no more money yet.

Sunday, May 14, 1871

Very windy and cold. All of our family excepting myself went to school and meeting and all came right home but Vincent. I think he went to Uncle Miles. I staid at Christ's while they were gone. Had a right pleasant visit. Received a very nice present from a poor neighbor this evening. It was two fine large trout which he had just caught, the first fresh fish I have had this summer. This is Vincent's birthday; he is 17. He was at Uncle's. There were about a dozen visitors there for dinner. Sophia Hill spent part of the evening with me. I am pretty well today.

Monday, May 15, 1871

Very warm before night, but quite windy in the afternoon. Papa is planting corn for Jason's. I feel stouter today than I have since I got sick; did not sit much of the time. Mother is washing some. I wrote to Hettie. Sold 50 cts. worth of sweet milk to the Yanks. They run the last of their logs past here that will go past this spring.

---

[24]   She likely is referring here to attending the new Normal School.

Tuesday, May 16, 1871

Very fine until about noon when it commenced to cloud over, but broke away again; about 2 o'clock there came up a heavy gust but did not last long. Papa, Almina, and I went up in the morning to see Grandma. Started home as soon as the storm was over. Felt very tired. Three of Uncle Miles' little boys came down this evening to stay all night and see the show go past tomorrow morning. The winter grain looks pretty well but the oats look poor. Think the rain will help it.

Wednesday, May 17, 1871

A very pleasant day. I chose early to see the show go past. Saw all of it and it was quite a sight. Hear the parade in Clearfield was an even grander sight than the show [was]. The best was outside; counted 57 wagons and buggies belonging to them. Saw the 2 elephants, 5 dromedaries. 1 camel and 6 Shetland ponies. Such beautiful horses. Miles' boys started home early. Nathan Cleaver spent part of the forenoon here and Nathan, Ann and the little girls stopped here on their way from town about 1 o'clock and stayed until after supper. Do not feel so well.

Thursday, May 18, 1871

A very fine day, not windy. Papa and Mother went to Monthly Meeting. The boys at school and Almina and I were here alone, but got along very well, Jason was in a few minutes and Allie Spencer and Emma Sykes brought the *Times* up. Hannah Holden was here in the evening.

Friday, May 19, 1871

Very pleasant, no wind and signs of its being warmer soon. Papa came up to my room this morning and talked to me a while. He is thinking some of writing to a doctor in New York. Feel weaker than yesterday. Papa was at Clearfield. Talking some of getting a girl to help about the work, and sew. Got the *Intelligencer*.

Saturday, May 20, 1871

Pleasant and still, but very hot. Could not keep cool enough to be comfortable all the time. I feel much better than yesterday, took a ride in the afternoon, enjoyed it very much but it was very hot. Cecelia Leonard's mother made a call in the afternoon. Robert came up to see me and paid me another month's wages on my teaching. Papa and Rowland sheared the sheep and Vincent opened the breakers on the hill in the forenoon. Papa went to town towards evening and got me some things, among others, a pair of slippers.

Sunday, May 21, 1871

Warmer than yesterday. The thermometer at 88° above zero about 2 o'clock. As well as yesterday, but suffer with the heat. Louisa, Willie, Mary Ellen and a couple of the children were here in the forenoon. Papa, Almina, and Rowland went to meeting in the carriage and

Vincent rode Dolly. Vincent slipped off and was not about after meeting and Rowland rode her home and Papa brought Grandma down along. Uncle Jerry came along, too, but he had his own carriage. Aunt Mary and Cousin Jennie were here in the afternoon. When Vincent found his horse was gone, he dined at Nathan's, then went to Pennsville.

Monday, May 22, 1871

Much cooler, raining a little in the forenoon. Uncle Jerry remained here until after dinner, a very heavy shower soon after he started and a gust went around. Will freshen up the things some. About like yesterday. Do not feel much encouragement. Papa is working on the Saw Mill. Mother quite busy at most everything. Got a box of pills from Philadelphia. Papa sent for them last sixth day. (Saturday)

Tuesday, May 23, 1871

Clear and cool after the rain with a pretty white frost early in the morning. Do not think anything was injured. Have the headache very bad. No visitors here but Grandma. She will probably stay a week or more. Papa is sawing longs on the sawmill.

Wednesday, May, 24, 1871

Some warmer but a little frost. Feel nearly as bad as yesterday. Aunt Mary was up in the forenoon. Jason came up about noon and took Grandma down to his mother's. Caleb and Elizabeth Way were here for tea, had a very pleasant time with them. Thomas Bloom made a call.

Thursday, May 25, 1871

The warmest day yet for this summer. 92° in the shade, but a good deal of air going. Did not arise until very late but felt refreshed and lively when I did. Hannah Holden dined here and Lydia Porter took tea. Had intended riding in the evening and the wind arose so high that I was afraid to go, as a heavy gust went around.

Friday, May 26, 1871

A couple of showers in the morning and one about noon will help the things very much. Our shade trees look very nice now. Vincent took the horses to the shop when he went to school and brought them home at noon and ate at home. Too damp to ride out.

Saturday, May 27, 1871

Very hot, but no rain. Papa finished the logs that were on the way in the morning and did not saw any more after that. Vincent went to Clearfield for a load of corn. Grandma came up in the morning. Elisha Davis, wife and child, also Cousin Nathan Moore and Jimmie Moore were on a visit. Felt pretty well. Took a short ride in the evening.

Sunday, May 28, 1871

Very hot again. Uncle Miles, Aunt Lucy, and a couple of their children, Aunt Eliza Spencer, Spencer and Mary, and Mary Ellen and children, Aunt Mary, Maria Way and Robert and Children, Caleb Way and Lydia Ann Way were all here during the day. Felt worried. Papa took me to ride in the eve, and I felt refreshed afterwards. Caleb took Grandma out there. Lydia will stay at Roberts tonight, expects to be up again before she goes home.

Monday, May 29, 1871

Warm as yesterday, air passing most of the time. Papa is sawing. L. A. Way came up in the morning and concluded to stay all day and sew. Got word from Ross he sent a vial of number six and directions how to make another medicine. Papa came to take me out to ride, but it commenced to rain. We had a pleasant shower. Thought it too damp afterwards and did not go. Mary and Jennie Dale were down most all day.

Tuesday, May 30, 1871

As warm as common or a little warmer. As high as 89° after the boys came from school. Did not feel very smart in the morning, but got better pretty soon. Rowland went out with me in the evening and we had a beautiful ride. Everything appeared to be in its best appearance. I do enjoy a ride this time of year and feel thankful that I am able to go out. Heard that Cousin Emma S. was not expected to last many days. Nancy P. was here a few minutes in the evening.

Wednesday, May 31, 1871

As hot as ever; no rain here yet. My cough has been bothering me more today than usual. Papa is plastering the corn, says it needs rain very badly. There was a man hauling past the house and in locking his wagon the whole weight of it came down on his finger, tearing loose the nail and crushing it to the first knuckle. He came to the pails and got it dressed; made him very sick, came near to fainting a couple of times but the cold water prevented it. A blind man and boy stopped. They were selling ballads of the blind, price 7 cts.; bought one. (A note from Vincent is written here: "I have this poem.")

Thursday, June 1, 1871

A gusty day, but no rain here except a few drops. Papa started very early and went around by Lumber City to get me a bottle of Hall's Balsam. From there to meeting and home. He cultivated corn after dinner. Ruthanna brought Grandma over just as the boys had started for school. Maggie and Susan Bloom came from school and spent the evening. Received a very interesting letter from Alice Way who is now teaching at Powelton. Heard that Prof. and Hettie are getting along fine.

Friday, June 2, 1871

Very hot, the clouds arose early in the day and got very heavy before night, but no rain. Papa working at the corn, the boys went to assist as soon as they came from school. My cough is very troublesome and side sore today, the former looser than usual. Got three more boxes of the Anti-Canker Pills. Also a letter from Ella Laporte and a pretty lively one. Cornelius down to Aunt M—'s and some other places.

Saturday, June 3, 1871

Cooler in the morning, a little rain, but not enough to settle the dust. Have more pain in my side than usual, but feel pretty strong. Grandma did not come back until this afternoon. The boys setting up the corn. Papa at town most of the day. Vincent went down this evening.

Sunday, June 4, 1871

We had a very fine rain last evening after I had retired. Vincent saw the gust just as he was going to start home and remained in town until the hardest was over. Much more pleasant today, not so hot. Papa went to meeting and took Grandma along. She is going home. Essy came around by John Dale's to see Cos Erma, then on down here; she was still living. Papa and Almina went over to see her in the afternoon. She is just skin and bone, no flesh to be seen. How some have to suffer while I enjoy so many blessings. Maria Way and her mother-in-law made us a pleasant call in the afternoon. I had a pleasant walk out to the orchard fence. Feel much better this afternoon.

Monday, June 5, 1871

Very hot and gusty clouds passing. Feel pretty well with the exception of more headache than I've had for several days. Papa is working the potatoes. Almina washing and churning in the morning; Mother helped finish. Almina and I changed our bedroom today; do not know how we will like it, but think it will be more comfortable. Took a ride. Do not think Vincent is coming home tonight.

Tuesday, June 6, 1871

Clear with a strong east wind nearly all day, cooler than it has been for several days. Exercised a good deal in the forenoon and felt tired in the evening. Rowland took me a ride after school. Vincent was out at Thomas Bloom's last night. Papa working at the potatoes until late in the afternoon. Mother busy at the work as she always is.

Wednesday, June 7, 1871

A fine rain in the morning, cool all day. Stirring around in the forenoon, but felt like resting during the latter part of the day. Mother fixing some on one of my dresses. Papa went out the pike before dinner and worked in the garden and washed the wool after. Almina and Rowland got a nice parcel of strawberries, found them in the orchard. Did not ride.

Thursday, June 8, 1871

Quite cool and very windy. Papa went around by Miles and on to meeting. Uncle Andy was here a few minutes in the afternoon. Brought me a present of a sugared strawberry cake that was sent from John Dales. Feel about as well as usual but did not exercise very much in the forenoon as I intended and did go to town to the Bank, it being the day our notes were due. I deposited $31.75 now and with what my old note called for, it made the new one $100. Papa took Almina and I, and we rode down.

Friday, June 9, 1871

A very pleasant day, cool and windy in the afternoon. Papa working the corn for the second time. Almost cold enough for frost this evening. The corn was frozen several years ago about this time of year. Hanna Holden was here in the forenoon and Uncle Will in the evening. Think I must have caught cold yesterday while riding, feel quite poorly, not able to ride today.

Saturday, June 10, 1871

Cool and pleasant. Do not feel much better than yesterday, better in some ways and worse in others. Tommy Kirk was here for some time but did not stay to eat. He is just returning from a visiting down at U.C. Left most of the friends well and some quite poorly. Mother and Almina baked bread, cakes, custards and strawberry and rhubarb pies. Papa and the boys working at the corn. Isaac Thompson called on business; he is nearly 82 years of age.

Sunday, June 11, 1871

A heavy rain accompanied by wind between 11 and 12 p.m. last night; cool in the morning but got pretty warm, a pleasant shower in the evening. Feel considerably improved. Papa and Almina went to meeting and L--- C--- dined at Uncle Harrison's. Vincent was buggy riding the girls. Mother, Rowland and I at house all day. Hannah Way and Sue Bloom called to see me in the evening and Aunt Mary was up awhile.

Monday, June 12, 1871

Rain and sunshine, cold and warm also windy. My head feels bad, as well as I was with that exception. Papa went to see if he could get Lib. Norris to come and help a couple of weeks, but she could not be spared from home. They said they were in need of help themselves at present. Have no idea where to go for one now. Got another paper of crackers and some candy. Mother is fixing up upstairs this afternoon and was lying up there part of the time. Nathan Cleaver was here. Robert paid my 3rd month school order.

Tuesday, June 13, 1871

Very cold and windy for the time of year; was obliged to keep the doors and most of the windows closed to keep comfortable. Papa finished hoeing the corn in the forenoon and the school directors met in the afternoon, agreed to build the house down in the bottom. Our folks killed a young sheep and I have good mutton to eat now.

Wednesday, June 14, 1871

Still cold and windy. Feel better than yesterday. Moving around some and trying to exercise. Papa visited the Normal School in the forenoon, and appeared to be pleased with the proceedings on the saw mill after dinner. He sold three of the sheep, have four yet. Keeps too cold to ride. When the boys came from school they brought me a letter from Hettie and Rowland brought me a present of two oranges. It did me good to get them.

Thursday, June 15, 1871

Cool and pleasant in the forenoon, a shower in the afternoon which prevented me from riding. Papa went to meeting and afterwards moved clover until it rained. Was working in the garden after the rain. The boys got The Times. Feel better than yesterday. Louisa and M. E. here.

Friday, June 16, 1871

Frost, but did not show here excepting on the boards and bridges heavier some places. Still continue to feel better. Got warmer and Papa took me riding after I got my dinner. When we came back we drove around to the Mill and I was weighed again. Have lost 6 ½ lbs. since I was down before, only weigh 77 ¼ lbs. The ride tired me some, but I enjoyed it.

Saturday, June 17, 1871

A beautiful morning, but soon clouded up and rained towards evening. I feel about the same as yesterday. Papa and the boys doing chores in forenoon. Papa and Vincent went to help raise Uncle Will's house but V. did not stay long. He came back and took in a load of clover hay before it rained. Aunt Phoebe sent me some rice cake but it is too rich to eat much at a time. Will not ride today.

Sunday, June 18, 1871

A showery day. Papa and Rowland went to school and meeting and returned. Espy and Em Moore came here about ten o'clock on their way to Chestnut R. and wanted Vincent to go with them He wanted to study, but consented to go. Mother and Almina at home. Eliza, Job, Mary Jane, and Maria Way were here in the afternoon. Could not get my rest as usual and feel worried. Jason here in the evening.

Monday, June 19, 1871

A pleasant day. Papa on the saw mill most of the time. He took me out to ride about noon. Feel better in some ways, not so well in others. Have been taking more medicine today than usual and think that is probably the cause. Mother washing some and Almina sewing at her new dress. Kirk Russell was here in the forenoon. He has got to be almost a young man and has grown considerably since he went down south. Will remain out here and clerk for Ross now.

Tuesday, June 20, 1871

Rainy during the greater part of the day. Papa took some potatoes to Clearfield and sold for $1. per bu. And brought back a load of corn to the Mill to sell. Z. McNaul and two older lady friends went out the pike today and we thought they would probably make us a call on their return, but they did not. I expect the rain prevented their stopping. Mother doing almost all kinds of house work.

At a later date:

In Vincent's handwriting: "Lavinia died in August of consumption, aged 20 years."

Nothing more written.

1920 Diary
Howard Vincent Thompson

The following is a transcript of the 1920 Diary of Howard Vincent Thompson,
Mary Alice Thompson's older brother.

Review of 1919

Christmas Presents Received:

Aunt Grace – book
Cecil – tie
Kenneth – handkerchiefs
Mama – slippers, shirts, stockings, gloves
Papa – pair of shoes
Sister (Mary Alice) – tie
Mrs. Heverly – silk handkerchief
Aunt Maude – book and handkerchief
Uncle Francis – pocket book
State C. El. Co.[1] – pair of plyers
Papa Spencer – fountain pen[2]

Cards Sent:

Cousin Anna
Bobby Custer
Mrs. Allen Wrigley
Audrey Hyde
Uncle Francis (Thompson)
Andrew Runkle
Mark Hunter
Louise Miller
Minot Willard
Foster McGovern
Miss Marion Harm
Lois and Doris Young

People I gave Presents to:

Mama – Casserole and handkerchief
Papa – Linen Handkerchiefs
Sister – Writing paper and cologne
Brother – comb
Mama Spencer – Pyrex dishes
Papa Spencer – cigars
Pauline – box of candy
Aunt Grace – Talcum powder
Aunt Maude** – Writing paper
Cecil* – book
Kenneth* – puzzles
Mable Musser – table set
Mrs. Heverly – cards
Arthur* – whistle
Richard* – tool set

* Cousins, the sons of his Aunt Grace
Spencer Wall, who was sister to his
mother Elizabeth

** Sister to his father

[1] Likely the Pennsylvania Electric Company, since Howard worked for his father who owned the local electric company in Curwensville, and earlier in Bellefonte.

[2] Howard's first fountain pen which I still have. Fountain pens were just then coming into fashion despite the criticism of them by President Wilson.

1922 Sophomore Class (1919-1920)

President – Linn Bodle
Vice-president – Joe Parrish
Secretary – Alice Whitaker
Treasurer – Elizabeth Williams

Contests between the Reds & Blues, 1920

Reds 878 points; Blues 1018 points
Total amount for A.A. $474.00

1922 Junior Class (1920-1921)

President – Joe Parrish

Vice-president – Andrew Runkle

Secretary – Raymond Brooks

Treasurer – Mark Hunter

Information

(1) Area of Rect. = length x breadth
(2) Area of Rect. divided by length = breadth
(3) Area of Parallelogram = base x altitude
(4) Area of Triangle = base divided by ½ altitude
(5) Area of Triangle divided by base = ½ altitude
(6) Area of Trapezoid = Sum of p x ½ A. sides
(7) Circumference of a circle = Diameter x p
(8) Circumference of a circle divided by p = diameter
(9) Area of a circle = p R2 or circle x ¼ diameter

$(b=a+ (N-1) d)$

Arith. Prog $(s = n/2 (s+l)$

$(l=dr (N – 1)$

Geog. Prog $(S=a-6 (? – 1)$

On the next two pages are the basketball[3] games and scores from Bellefonte High School where he attended until his junior or senior year when the family moved to Clearfield, the high school from which he was graduated. Also included are the Preliminaries and Finals at State College.

The following page is titled "Things I need and want." Recall he was 15 at the time.

Need art holder (OK)

Next in the Memoranda section is a list of "People I owe" and "People who owe me." The amounts have been erased with the exception of "Mama" to whom he owed $5 reduced to $2.00.

The next several pages are filled with maps of the continents.

The last page of Memoranda lists the following Birthdays:

Mama – September 14
Sister – November 21
Papa – January 12
Howard (self) – April 10
Anna Rich – September 7
Louise Miller – August 31
Margaret Bower – March 18
Pauline Sasserman – August 29

Entries begin with three of the last four days of December 1919:

Sunday – Useful information:

1 gal water weighs 8 lb.
7 ½ gal = 1 cu. ft.
1 cu. ft. of water weight 62 ½ lbs.

Monday – Pressure of water in tank equals the no. of ft. in depth times 434.

Tuesday – C. Building and Loan Stock

-2-Series 28 –Mat. 400

Got on Aug. 21, 1916

[It should be noted that young Howard most likely wanted a handy guide as he also did work for his father's water company.]

1920[4]

Beginning in January 1920

Jan. 1: Took inventory of old plants in morning. Awful cold. Tubby and Dave helped. Sorted cards.

Jan. 2: First day collected, took in over $412. Coldest weather. We beat Hollidaysburg by a close score. School on Monday.

Jan. 3: Collected money today. Went to pictures. [movies] Mama Spencer coming home tomorrow. Took her (P.S.[5]) home from pictures.

Sunday, January 4: Took bath in morning. Went to Sunday School and Church. Missed papers as they were gone after church. Played games.

Jan. 5: First of school since Dec. 19. Paid $18.10 for 2 weeks work. Cold and clear. Worked after school.

Jan. 6: Worked in morning till 11 when I went to Latin. Bad cold. Mama Spencer home. Worked also after school.

Jan. 7: Worked in morning. Through collecting money. Got $760.90 for December. Have sore throat bad. Took R. B. Taylors' meter out. But he paid and it was put back in.

Jan. 8: Raining icy and slippery out. Papa and Papa Spencer went away to Millersburg. I'm doing P.S. work. Fixed pump chart.

Jan. 9: Trouble on Port H/W/M line so I missed school; was there all day, no dinner. Basketball game Friday BHS (Bellefonte) Girls – 7; L.H. (Lock Haven) H.S. – 31.

Jan. 10: Worked at office. Went to pictures in evening. Friday the BHS Boys beat L.H. HS, 36–25. Saturday they beat LH. Normal School 31–19. Cold and icy.

Sunday January 11: Went to Sunday School. 30 above. Fixed pump chart. Fine dinner. Went out on Howard [name of a small town nearby] line in afternoon. Papa and Papa Spencer came home.

Jan. 12: Went to school. MT[6] 1st and 2nd periods; 3rd vacant; 4th Latin. Have History, English, Latin and Algebra to make up by Tuesday.

Jan. 13: Snowing. Made up all my lessons. 5th period Alg; 6th, vacant; 7th History; 8th English. Snowing and blowing in evening. $13.60 for ½ month pay.

Jan. 14: Clear & colder. Went to school. First, second & third periods vacant on all except Mon. & Thurs. Got reports: All Cs except one B.

---

4 Note that this is being reviewed in January 2020
5 Likely Pauline Sasserman.
6 Manual Training

Jan. 15: Went to school. MT 1st & 2nd periods. Game and dance tomorrow night. Got hair cut after school. Card Party at our house. Ice cream.

Jan. 16: Went to school. Snowing out. Mid-year examinations 28, 29, & 30th of this month. First three periods vacant.

Jan. 17: Didn't work at office but I cleaned the old plant walls. Went to pictures in afternoon. Loafed in eve.

Sunday January 18: Went to Sunday School. Went to Mussers with his paper. Had chicken for dinner. I helped pick (pluck the feathers) it.

Jan. 19: Went to school. Went to dentist in afternoon after school. Got my pay. Deposited $10 for suit in Spring.

Jan. 20: Worked in morning running service. $.50. Went to school. Got tickets to sell for Athletic Association at .15 each.

Jan. 21: Business Men's meeting this evening. Going to put up a big silk mill where the planing mill was situated.

Jan. 22: Went to school. Got off from 1:45, on account of the death of Mrs. Dr. Locke. Went sled riding. Played basketball.

Jan. 23: Went to school. Latin 4th period, Algebra 5th, vacant 6th, History 7th, English 8th. Snowing out. Went to Basketball game in eve.

Jan. 24: Shoveled walks. Went to dentist. Went to pictures in afternoon. Won box candy. We beat Mt. Union 19–41 on Friday.

February 1920

Sunday, February 1: Went to Sunday School. Got papers. Stayed home in afternoon & evening. Studied for examinations in evening.

Feb. 2: Had Algebra exam in A.M. Had English exam in P.M. Sorted cards after exam was over. Got out at 3:30 p.m.

Feb. 3: Manual Training exam in morning. History in P.M. Collected in evening. Studied this morning after exam.

Feb. 4: Had Caesar exam in morning. Collected after exam and in afternoon as I was through. Played in snow in eve.

Feb. 5: Been snowing all day yesterday & today. Got 33% in Manual Training exam and 95% in Algebra. Collected money.

Feb. 6: Collected money in morning. Went to school. Finished collecting in evening. Tubby got more than I did. Mr. Coldern was helping.

Feb. 7: B. H. S. beat Army & Navy, 33-17 and beat Renova 33–21, the last being the hardest game this year. Worked at office in morning. Went to game in evening.

Sunday, February 8: Went to Sunday School. Home the rest of the day. Philip in high chair part of the time. Went to bed early.

Feb. 9: Went to school. Through working for a while. Dance, game, and social Friday the 13th. Have cold. Regular lessons.

Feb. 10: Went to school. Regular lessons. Snowed some last night. Flunked Caesar and M.T.[1] so far. Made up lesson today.

Feb. 11: Went to school. Got no more marks yet. Everybody has the Flu. Got last period in morning for receiving health inspection.

Feb. 12: Lincoln's birthday. Last period in the afternoon had speech by Dr. McKinney about Lincoln. Went to dentist in evening.

Feb. 13: Went to school; had dance and social in the evening at high school. Pauline has the Flu. So I hadn't any girl.

Feb. 14: Worked at office today. Payroll goes in on Monday. I have $4.60 coming. Went to pictures this afternoon. Helped clean a chicken.

Sunday, February 15: Went to Sunday School. Had a fine dinner. Lights were out last night. They fixed them this morning. Awfully cold out. Studied in eve.

Feb. 16: Went to school. Sec. Lansing resigned as Sec. of State.[2] People say Wilson isn't all there. Cold at school, registers 58 (inside).

Feb. 17: Went to school. Weik still home. Pauline still sick. Had speeches in English in auditorium. She missed me.

Feb. 18: Went to Opera House tonight to see "Mutt and Jeff," fairly good. Worked some at office this eve. Had homemade ice cream.

Feb. 19: Went to school (Weik back and things running smoothly). It is at the end of the 3rd period that I'm writing this. I sit in seat B-A in school.

Feb. 20: Went to dentist. Went to concert last night at high school. Regular lessons. Papa went away yesterday.

Feb. 21: Went down to Tubby's in morning gotten it (?) fixed. Went to pictures last night. Took M.B.[3] home. Put up wireless aerial in afternoon. Cleaned chicken in eve and shoveled snow.

Sunday, February 22: Went to Sunday School. In afternoon Tubby, Margaret and Sara came up and we went for a walk & took pictures.

1   Manual Training
2   Having been appointed counselor to the Department of State by President Woodrow Wilson in 1914, Robert Lansing took over as Secretary of State in June 1915 following the resignation of William Jennings Bryan. Lansing was involved in various initiatives, including interventions in Haiti, the Dominican Republic, and Russia. Wilson asked for his resignation following Lansing's convocation of a cabinet meeting — without Wilson's approval — during the period in which Edith Wilson presided over her husband's affairs.
3   Likely Margaret Bower

Feb. 23:Went to school. Go to Centre Hall to read meters tomorrow. Reg. lessons. Joe Katz said 50 lines before the school today.

Feb. 24: Went to Centre Hall on 6:00 train. Had easy day of it. Dave helped me. Had dinner at a restaurant.

Feb. 25: Went to school at 11:00 a.m. for Caesar. I flunked Caesar and Manual Training. Went in P.M. and read meters.

Feb. 26: Sister went to Philipsburg today. Read meters in afternoon. The girls play PA over there today.

Feb. 27: Went to school. Read meters. Went to game tonight between B. H. S. Boys & Girls and Huntingdon. Boys score 20-40 our favor and Girls score 7-19 their favor.

Feb. 28: Went to Port Matilda in morn and Unionville afternoon reading meters. Went to pictures and eve.

Sunday, February 29: Went to Sunday School. Sorted cards in afternoon. Had ice cream for dinner. Studied lessons in evening.

March 1920

Monday, March 1: Went to school. Re-examinations rest of week. Tubby thinks he is sick today. Had lines for History.[4]

Mar. 2: Went to school. Had Caesar re-exam in morning. Collected money in evening. Said lines in history tonight.[5]

Mar. 3: Collected in morning. Went to school. Collected in evening. Very near through. RR passed into private ownership Monday.[6]

Mar. 4: Finished collecting this morning. Tubby back on deck. Went to school. Made up Algebra today.

Mar. 5: Went to school. Had Spelling Bee between Freshmen Boys and Girls. 2 games tonight. Boys and Girls play Tyrone. Lois and Doris Young are staying at our place.

Mar. 6: Got 100 in M. Training re-exam Friday. We beat one game and lost other last night. Boys score 13-31; Girls 6-3.

Sunday, March 7: Lois and Doris are going home this evening.[7] Tubby took some pictures today of the girls. I went to the train with them.

Mar. 8: Went to school. Made up History in evening. Took some negatives up to Mallory's to get developed.

---

[4]   Likely Tubby was not prepared for his recitation.
[5]   Possibly a public performance?
[6]   The Transportation Act, 1920, commonly known as the Esch–Cummins Act, returned railroads to private operation after World War I, with much regulation. Passed on February 28 and went into law March 1, 1920.
[7]   A separate notation lists their home as in Howard, PA.

Mar. 9: Went to school. Made up Caesar at noon. Got 67 in my Caesar re-examination. Tubby up to my place in eve.

Mar. 10: Went to school. Regular lessons. Now 11:12 or the 3rd period. Got pictures from Mallory's.[8] Stayed home in evening.

Mar. 11: Went to school. Mama has trouble with her eyes. I don't know what. Elizabeth is able to be around now.

Mar. 12: Got off at 3 to see Basketball team go to Mt. Union and Huntingdon. High water at the Plant has over 5 ft. of water.

Mar. 13: Street lights off last night and Bellefonte crested. Fixed bicycle in morning. Rain yesterday and snow today. Rode bike in snow. Went to pictures. Good.

Sunday, March 14: Went bicycle riding in afternoon. Water has gone down. Snow melting some. We won both games. Mt Union 30-32; Huntingdon 24-26.

Mar. 15: We are ahead of the league. Boys are getting pictures taken today. Only 2 more league games and the States on 9 & 10 of April to play for the championship of League.

Mar. 16: Went to school. Bad day. Raining out. Had bike out after school. Got re-exam marks. M.T., B. Latin, D.

Mar. 17: Went to school. Streets dry. Cloudy out. Snow about all-gone. Yea! Snowed some at noon. Went to dentist after school. Studies in eve.

Mar. 18: Went to school Mr. Menold talking of starting a class in cement. Nice day. Sun out. Going to take Bab's picture at noon.

Mar. 19: Boys having game with Hollidaysburg tonight. Party and dance given by Junior Class at school tonight. I went and had a good time.

Mar. 20: Boys got best of Hollidaysburg 22-40. First league game lost this year. Tonight we played Lock Haven Normal and beat them 30-20. This was a hard game.

Sunday, March 21: Went to Sunday School. Went to Milesburg on bike in afternoon. We are still ahead in the league. Game on Fri.

Mar. 22: Went to school. Don't feel very good. This is the 2nd day of Spring. Sun out and everything bright. Got basketball picture.

Mar. 23: Went to school. Took 4 pictures of the baby[9] at noon. We play Lock Haven high Thursday night. Nice day.

Mar. 24: Another nice day. Took pictures of Milesburg Plant yesterday Then working on aerial last night. Trying to study Caesar now.

Mar. 25: Reading meters in Bellefonte. Nice day. Helen Jack family is moving next door today. Basketball game tonight with Lock Haven High.

---

[8]   Mallory Studio in Bellefonte; evidence found up to the mid-1930s with the possibility of as late as 1942.

[9]   His brother Philip, younger by 15 years.

Mar. 26: We beat LHHS[10] last night 19-15. Game tonight B.H.S. girls and Philipsburg girls. Reading meters. Another nice day.

Mar. 27: The girls got beat 4 to 9 today by PHS. I went to Port Matilda and Unionville to read meters on train. Walked back to Bellefonte from Unionville.

Sunday, March 28: Went to Sunday School. We got our reports on Friday. English, B; History, B: Algebra, A; M.T., B; Caesar, C. Went to Milesburg in afternoon.

Mar. 29: Read meters before school. Dr. Beach is teaching History. Got pictures of Basketball team. Read meters in eve.

Mar. 30: Read meters in morning. Nice day. Renova challenged. BHS to play them for the championship of Central Pennsylvania to be played at Lock Haven.

Mar. 31: I don't think we will play them. Through reading meters. We play Houtzdale Fri. day or nite.

April 1920

Thursday, April 1: All Fools Day. My day! Went to school. Get off Fri. Kids bringing Hoopster contributions today. Nice day.

Good Friday. Worked collecting all day. Went to the last game of the season tonight. BHS won from Houtzdale 38-30.

Apr. 2: We get the championship of the Mountain High School League of Central Pennsylvania. Went to pictures. Worked in morning. Got my first suit of long trousers today. Cost $40. Got hat also.

Easter Sunday, April 4:

Easter Sunday: Went to Sunday School. Raining. Had my new suit on. I like it. Stayed home this afternoon.

Apr. 5: Finished collections today. Went to school. Friday and Saturday we go to States to decide the championship of Pennsylvania.

Apr. 6: Wearing my other good suit to school. New girl started to school. Freshman and pretty. Snowed last night. Cold today.

Apr. 7: Snowed hard this morning. 2nd period (10:09) just now. Getting our winter coal now. Baby got his 1st pair of shoes and stockings today.

Apr. 8: First champion game played Fri. night. Admission 25¢. There are going to be 14 teams playing. Cold today. No English teaching today.

Apr. 9: Snowed again today. Dick Herman is sick; don't think he can play. Didn't have a lesson all morning. Going to States.

---

10   Lock Haven

Apr. 10: Went to states on Friday eve. We played Williamsport and got beat, 19-18, a close score. Lost championship. Harrisburg Tech won the Championship. Went to "Katcha Koo" at Opera House.[11]

Sunday, April 11: Went to Sunday School. Saw P. [Pauline] in afternoon. Took her home from church. Belleview played Harrisburg Tech and got beat 34-38.

Apr. 12: All the boys that played are back home. Now in 3rd period. New fellow started to school.

Apr. 13: Sun was shining. Boys get Football picture taken this afternoon. Getting new girl to work for us (in the family home). Base Ball season began yesterday.

Apr. 14: Orchestra and Girls BB team got pictures taken also. Getting some pictures of the baby at noon. Went for a walk with P. last evening. Nice day.

Apr. 15: Started to make concrete walk along side of commons. Went to B.Ball practice last eve. Went down to see P. last eve. Nice day. P. not at school.

Apr. 16: Raining today. Went to Base B. practice last eve. Staid home in eve. Went to dentist tonight. Didn't have practice tonight. Raining.

Apr. 17: Bad day. Worked at office. Went to pictures this eve. Didn't see P. tonight. Two B.B. games next week, State College & Huntington.

Sunday, April 18: Went to S. School. Went down to the plant in afternoon to see them start new turbine. Pauline S. came up to my house to see Baby in eve.

Apr. 19: Went to school. Nice day. Put cannas flowers in. Went down to dentist. Stayed in in evening. Play ball at home.

Apr. 20: Went to school. Raining this afternoon. Played ball some. School closes on June 3, yeah! Now 2nd period in afternoon.

Apr. 21: Went to school. Baby six months old yesterday. Took P.S. home from pictures. Worked around house after supper. Got paid.

Apr. 22: Went to school. Boys going to play Lock Haven Normal today. We got beat 7-0. Nice day. Going to dentist this evening. Read meters Monday.

Apr. 23: Went to school. Worked around house in evening. Went to dentist. Go again Wednesday. Was out for half an hour tonite.

Apr. 24: Worked at office in morning. Went to game in afternoon between B.H.S. and State College H.S. We won 19-4. Went to pictures in eve… P. home.

Sunday, April 25: Went to Sunday School. Took pictures of the plant after dinner. Saw P.S. Walked home with her in evening. Nice day.

Apr. 26: Went to school. Nice day reading meters in Bellefonte. Going to start concrete walk tomorrow morning alongside of school.

11   Katcha Koo was an "Oriental American musical comedy" produced in high schools in their auditoriums or the local opera house, popular with local audiences.

Apr. 27: Read meters till 11:15. Went to school. Bad day. Raining. I am reading Book 3 in meters. First time I read it. Now 2nd period in P.M.

Apr. 28: Read meters in morning. Went to school. Cold out but not raining. Started to make my English notebook. Went to dentist.

Apr. 29: Went to school. Worked on concrete walk. Nice, cold windy day. Get Friday off. Worked reading meters tonight. Cold.

Apr. 30: Went to school in morning. Had English examination on Book. Went to Unionville in afternoon to read (meters); supposed to go to dentist.

May 1920

May 1: Finished reading meters today. Didn't work in afternoon. Went to pictures early. Didn't take P. home.

Sunday, May 2: Went to Sunday School. Sorted cards in afternoon. Took a walk. Went to church in evening. Took P. home from church tonite.

May 3: Finished sorting cards today. Went to school. Worked on cement walk. Getting along fine. Studied in evening.

May 14: Collected money till 11:00. Went to school. Collected money after school. Stayed home and studied lessons.

May 5: Collected money. Went to school. My check hasn't come yet. Got off tomorrow to work on walk in afternoon.

May 6: Worked on walk all morning and all afternoon. Went to school. Got home to eat after we were through.

May 7: Went to school. Collected money today. Went to High School Play, "Green Stockings"[12] at Opera House tonight.

May 8: Fooled around home all morning. Went up to Pointe McCoy in afternoon with Ly, Margaret, Edna, Bobby, Pauline, Alice and May. Went to pictures in eve. Took P. for a walk and then home.

Sunday, May 9: Went to Sunday School. Cecil came over and I went for a walk with him. Kept baby in eve. P.S. came up after church.

May 10: Went to school. Didn't work on walk, but on my drawing. School will soon be over. Stayed home in evening. Arthur stayed over.[13]

May 11: Went to school. Worked on walk there three periods. Raining today. Stayed home this evening also. Too bad!

May 12: Went to school. Worked on walk 2nd period. Talked to P. after school. Went down to her house in evening. Took Bobby Stevenson home. Yea!

12   A popular play for high school groups.
13   Possibly his cousin, Arthur Wall.

May 13: Worked on walk all morning. They are getting ready for the Junior reception. Mama and sister[14] went to a social.

May 14: The juniors put their flag up and the seniors took it down. Went out in the evening with Porter and Joe Katz. We were with six girls—E, M, A, S, H, M. Got half brick of ice cream at Jr reception.

May 15: Worked around home today. Wasn't allowed to go downtown in evening as I was out too late last nite. Dave Newcomer is the one who took down the Junior Class pennant.

Sunday, May 16: Went to Sunday School. Went for a walk in afternoon. Went to church in evening. Took P. home from church. Yea!

May 17: School will soon be over. Worked in garden tonight. Went to dentist after school. Working on my English notebook for exhibit.

May 18: Went to school. Worked on concrete all day. Got off at 3:00 to go to game. We were beat by Lock Haven Normal 7-8.

May 19: Went to school. Seniors are having final examinations. Worked on walk in morning. Worked on notebook in evening.

May 20: Don't have to study much. Finished MJ sheet. Mama had a party in evening. Worked in garden. Put in beets and peas.

May 21: Worked on walk and finished it. I put last load of concrete in. My last regular day at school. No English or Algebra today.

May 22: Worked on bike. Went over to Philipsburg in afternoon. Had strawberry shortcake for supper (first). Came home eve.

Sunday, May 23: Went to Sunday School. Saw P. in afternoon. Went to church in evening. Took her home from church.

May 24: Read meters at Centre Hall and Pleasant Gap. Put 11 hours in. Final exams begin tomorrow.

May 25: Read meters in Bellefonte all day. I had no examinations today. Worked on notebook tonight.

May 26: Read meters in Milesburg this morning. Found jam in John Shultz's meter. Had Latin exam this afternoon.

May 27: Had History examination in morning. Read meters in Bellefonte in afternoon. Then down to (indecipherable) in evening.

May 28: Had English exam in morning. Went to Unionville in afternoon to read meters. Took P. home from last day of school.

May 29: The whole family went away for Decoration Day. Worked in the office all day. Took P. home in eve. She was up to my place in eve for a while.

---

[14] This would be Mary Alice.

Sunday, May 30: Fixed pump chart. Got dinner at restaurant. Good. Went out and saw them put circus tents up. Turned on lights.

May 31: This is circus of Memorial Day. Fixed chart. Worked in garden. Saw part of parade. Went down to P. tonight. Mama and family came home.

June 1920

June 1: High School picnic today. I went at 10 a.m. and home at 7 p.m. Took Pauline. Went down there in the evening.

June 2: Went to work on Beech Creek line putting guys up (as in guidewire). Pretty hot work. Went to concert at high school in the evening. Go to dentist.

June 3: Worked on line today. Went to Commencement exercises this evening. I got $5. from A C. Mingle for the best history exam paper.

June 4: Worked on line today. New fellow working. He is just learning to climb. We are now in Eagleville.

June 5: Worked in Bellefonte. Collected money in afternoon. Went to pictures. Took P. home this evening.

June 6: Took bath. Didn't go to Sunday School. Went to Church in evening. Took Pauline home from church. Last time I went with her.

June 7: Worked around Bellefonte today. Worked on gutter job in the evening. Bought some clothes. Gave Mama $5. to pay what I owed her.

June 8: Worked around Bellefonte today. Saw Marion Marn; Weik is working for State—Center as meter man.

June 9: Worked around town. Went down to band concert this evening. I was going to take Pauline home but Cryder Rockey took her home.

June 10: Worked around town today. Mama went to Beech Creek to see Uncle Francis. Went to bed.

June 11: Worked today (early). Put in transformer at Milesburg Brick Plant. Finished my concrete curb.

June 12: Worked around town. Worked in office in the evening. Went to pictures. Not very good ones.

Sunday, June 13: Worked all day at Center County line on putting in substation. Didn't get done till 9 o'clock. Had supper there.

June 14: Worked on Beech Creek line. I was ground man for siding for a new fellow learning to climb. He is slow as molasses.

June 15: Worked same place. Was climbing some after work. Mama Spencer came home. She said Cecil made $5. a day for 2 weeks.

June 16: Raining out. I don't feel good. Have bad cold and cough. Not working. Was climbing a little this morning. Went to doctor.

June 17: I worked on the Beech Creek line and around Bellefonte all summer.

June 18: I got 25¢ an hour. I drove the Ford truck a lot the later part of the summer.

June 19: Worked on the Centre Hall line up in the mountains. Worked on line across from Hof's.

Sunday, June 20 and June 21: I did a little climbing. I cared for street lights, brought in meters to be tested, read meters all over the territory. I was not away from home all summer. I did most any kind of work around.

June 22: Kept track of all material lying along Beech Creek and Center Hall line. Tubby Runkle was working, too.

June 23–26: I worked some of the time with Tubby, Johnnie, Bunny, Sam, John, Bill, and Marx. I've plugged pot holes, anchor holes, put up berms, stripped poles, tied in wire, distributed material, put in meters, pulled out wire. I know everything a lineman needs to know. I could almost build a pole line, I think. In fact, I enjoyed my vacation very much. I made quite a lot of money, but spent almost all of it.

> Note: There are no entries from this point until August 29th except for a listing of football scores with only three games (with Williamsport, State College, and Lewisburg) noted, all of which Bellefonte scored nothing. A fourth game—with Lewistown—has a line through it with the notation "Cancelled." This is followed by the message (in print which is what Howard used for lists of games and scores): "Football season closed because Edward Miller had his leg broken in practice."
>
> Two entries on Basketball are noted, along with the list of opponents and scores of games, but it is not likely that the entries are specific to the following dates:
>
> **Wednesday, August 4:** "Hollidaysburg game was forfeited to BHS 2-0 because they had illegal players." [not uncommon in those early years of high school football]
>
> **Thursday, August 5:** "Mt. Union won the championship of the League. Bellefonte is tied with Tyrone for 2nd place."

August 1920

Sunday, August 29: Pauline was up in the evening. Last time I was with her. I gave her a box of candy. Her birthday.

September 1920

Wednesday, September 1, 2, 3, 4: Each entry has only "10 hrs." We can presume this was hours at work before school resumed.

Sunday, September 5: Mama and Papa went to Curwensville. Loafed around all day. Made some candy this evening.

September 6: Loafed around all morning. Went to Hecla (Likely Hecla Park in Mingo Ville near Bellefonte [1894 – mid-1950s]) in afternoon. Went to skating rink in evening. Had good time.

September 7: First day of school. It starts at 8:45. I take English II, American History, Health, Ins. M.T., Plane Geometry, Caesar, and Chemistry.

September 8: School Today. Haven't got all my books. Nice day. Started to study, 1 ½ hrs. this eve., oh, boy!

September 9: Rained in afternoon. Family went to Granger's Picnic. Aunt Grace and Uncle Charley are here. 1 hr. study time.

September 10: Sit in E-7. Have my books. State College E(lectric) Co. sells out Merchandise end today. Rode in new truck this eve.

September 11: Worked on Beech Creek line. Finished it up today. Drove truck (Ford) all of 10 hrs. the time there.

Sunday, September 12: Went to Sunday School. Went for ride with Uncle Charley (Wall) to Hecla Park. Family went over to Curwensville today.

September 13: Sorted out Book 2 & all ready for new ledger. Got a haircut. Felt bad. Practice started. (2 hours.)[15]

September 14: I gave Mama box candy and playing cards for birthday. Nice day. Drove truck to Milesburg this eve (1 hr.) Mama's birthday.

September 15: Seat E-7. Nice day. Weik gave experiments in Chemistry. Went to pictures.[16] Great! Class meeting after school about things. (1 ½ hr.)

September 16: Rain in morning. Had experiments today. Mama & Papa & the baby came home tonight. May Crider was over then. 1 hr.

September 17: No English today. Miss Taylor is sick. Went to skating rink this eve. Mr.& Mrs. Wall and daughter Alice, Mr. & Mrs. Conklin were here.

September 18: Trimmed arcs today. Drove Ford to Howard [nearby town] with Mr. Weik to fix meter. Went to pictures. Got check for $16.75. OK. (9 hrs.)

Sunday, September 19: Went for a ride to Penn's Cave for dinner, then to State College and home. Had nice time. Studied in evening.

September 20: Have bad cold. Nice day. Went to the pictures, "Male & Female." Good, best I have seen for a while.

September 21: Mama went away this eve for Middleburg with Philip. Sister went to pictures. I went to bed early.

September 22: Feeling better. Fixed bike up and started to fix sister's. The IOS[17] had a

---

[15] I believe these hours here are hours worked a particular day.

[16] Reminder that pictures here mean movies.

[17] Possibly a nascent political group. There were many at the time.

meeting at our house tonite.

September 23: Start chemistry experiments Monday. Nice day. Went to Opera House tonite. "Jim's Girl" was on. Pretty good show.

September 24: Went to pictures and then to skating rink to see the fancy skater. Mama and Papa came home with a new Franklin car.

September 25: Read meters in Centre Hall. Went to skating rink. Got pictures I took last Sun. (9 hrs.)

Sunday, September 26: Went to Sunday School. Rally Day. Went for ride in new car after supper. Got my lessons.

September 27: Read meters after school. Mr. and Mrs. Heberly were up in the evening. I read magazines, etc. (1 ½ hrs.)

September 28: Start school at 8:40 now. Have 1 hr. training. Nice day. Read meters in evening. Sprinkled some this eve. (1 ½ hr.)

September 29: Mama and Papa went to Curwensville today. Nice day. Recited in Caesar for the first time. Read meters. (2 ½ hrs.)

September 30: Read meters in morning. Raining out. Start M.T. today. Tubby got fired at the office. Still reading (3 hrs.)

October 1920

October 1: Still reading meters. Cold, dreary day. Went to pictures this evening. Cold out. (1 hr.)

October 2: Read meters in Port Matilda and Unionville. Walked home from Unionville. Went to show tonight. "Polly and her Pals" was on.[18] Good.

Sunday, October 3: Got up at 10 o'clock. Got papers. Went for a walk to Fairyland[19] as it is called with Phil, Ray, and Jimmie Mayer.

October 4: School again. Nice day. Have cold. Rained in eve. Loafed around after school. Ran around. Went to bed early. (1/2 hour)

October 5: Contest at school to raise money for a A.A.[20] Reds and Blues. I am a Red. Mama & Papa came home this evening. Pd. $8.25.

October 6: The Blues won. I worked around the house after school. Studied my lessons in eve. Did my Chem. experiments today.

---

[18] Originally a comic strip, Polly and her Pals featured a pretty young girl, a flirtatious child of the Suffragette movement and a precursor of the Jazz Age 1920s flappers. Over time, the center of the action changed from Polly to those around her, and thus the title changed to Polly and Her Pals—though the "pals" were in fact members of her family: her parents and cousins. Evidently a movie was produced based on this comic strip. I was unsuccessful in finding relevant information.

[19] No suggestion as to what this might be.

[20] Likely Athletic Association.

October 7: Had chem. experiments. Took Mama's checks around this eve. Got $2.00 from Mama this month. I didn't feel good. (1/2 hr.)

October 8: Have bad headache. No History today. Game at State College tomorrow. Sold my chances[21] and went to the Dr.

October 9: Worked at Mussers garage with Harold. Went to State in afternoon. Saw last half of H.S. game. We got beat. Saw (Penn) State beat Dartmouth 7 to 11. Went to pictures.

Sunday, October 10: Sunday School, papers, etc. Stayed home in afternoon. Got my lessons in evening. Sister made candy.

October 11: Nice day. Still have headache. I went to Dr. on Fri. eve. Some of the Football players are quitting on account of nothing.

October 12: Cut grass in evening. Watched Football scrimmage. Studies in evening. Went to bed early.

October 13: Hauled wood after school for Papa Spencer. Put lights on. Studied lessons in eve. Don't know what to write about.

October 14: Had Chemistry test this morning. I wrote good English story. Handed in my time for first half 13 hrs.

October 15: Started political campaign in high school. Nevin Robb, chairman of Republicans and Foster McGovern, chairman of the Democrats.

October 16: Worked trimming arcs in morning. Had academy boy helping me. Worked up at Musser's afternoon. Pictures in eve. Mr. Musser time, 3 hrs.

Sunday, October 17: Ran around town for Papa in morning. Worked at plant in afternoon fixing boiler. I was used inside, hot as the dickens. (9 hrs.)

October 18: Democrats had three speakers this morn. Mary Sebring, Musser Gelting and Mary Yorks. Kept in for being late at noon.

October 19: Republicans had 3 speakers this morn. Thomas Mench, Harold Wion, and Mary Dale. Bought Philip a comb for birthday.

October 20: Got paid $4.20 total. Democrats had platform today. Mary Sebring and Marilyn Decker spoke. Not very good. Philip's Birthday.

October 21: Rep. had platform. Mary Chambers, Marjorie Hill, and Warren Cobb spoke. Sister went to club meeting tonight.

October 22: Had open forum this morning. Dr. Brech spoke. Mr. Stoche and others. Going to vote now. Harding won in the straw vote.

October 23: Went on 6:00 train to Center Hall and read meters. Came home at 4:30. Went to pictures at Opera House this evening. Good. We got beat in football by Lewisburg, 13-0.

---

[21]   Likely related to the Athletic Association.

Sunday, October 24: Went to Sunday School. Counted money. Walls came over after dinner. Mama and Papa went to Curwensville when they did.

October 25: Went to school. English re-exam this morning and mathematics this afternoon. Read meters some in the evening after school.

October 26: History re-exam this morning and French and Latin this afternoon. I took Latin exam. It was hard. Read meters. Went to pictures.

October 27: Raining this morning. Read meters in evening. Wrote short story for contest this morning. Raining out.

October 28: Cold day. Had test in Chemistry. Edward Miller had his leg broken in practice this evening. Read meters. Went to pictures eve.

October 29: Cold day. Built a fire. Decorating for party tonight. Went to party. Read meters in eve. Going to Port Matilda in morn.

October 30: Read meters in Port Matilda and Unionville. Cold day. Mama & Papa came home today. Went to pictures in eve. State beat Penn 28-7 and Penn State Freshmen really beat (Bellefonte) Academy 27-0.

Sunday, October 31: Bummy and I trimmed arcs early in morning. I stayed at home in afternoon. Sister made fudge. Mr. and Mrs. Heverly[22] were here.

November 1920

November 1: Read meters. Big time in evening parade. I dressed up fancy. Didn't get home till 11 o'clock.

November 2: Election Day. Finished reading meters. Papa going away. Went downtown till 10:30 in evening to get returns.

November 3: Papers say Harding won. Worked putting in meter and fixing street light after school. Cold day. Stayed home in eve.

November 4: Nice day. Had chemistry experiments. Had to stay in for being tardy. Big parade tomorrow nite for Harding. $15.30.

November 5: Nice day. Chemistry experiments. Went to pictures in eve. Republican parade this eve. Pretty good. Papa came home.

November 6: Went to Eagleville to work ten hours putting in meters. I put in 13. Went to open house in evening.

Sunday, November 7: Worked nine hours at Beech Creek sub-station today. It rained in afternoon. I have 25 lines to set on Tuesday morning.

November 8: School today. Football men handing in uniforms today. Ordering hooks, pliers, and dinner pail from State-Central.

[22] Friends of the family, mentioned numerous times in Mary Alice's Diary.

November 9: Set lines this morning. Bad day. Papa went away. School was closed second period because a girl had scarlet fever.

November 10: School again. Chemistry experiments this morning. Track and Basketball meeting after school. Worked reading meters after school.

November 11: Had school half day, marching with B.H.S. in parade. Armistice Day. Went to football game. Army and Navy 7 and American Legion xxx.

November 12: Chemistry experiments today. My report was sent home by mail. Fixed arc after school. Worked in cellar in the evening.

November 13: Trimmed street arc with Stock. Cleaned up arc room and took out meters for Weik for nine hours. Got my report. Papa came home. Chemistry, B; English, C; Deportment, C; History, D; Geometry, D. Manual Training, D.[23]

Sunday, November 14: Went to Sunday School. Stayed home in afternoon. Sister made candy. Studied lessons in evening.

November 15: Snowing hard all morning. Wore long pants to school for first time.[24] Handed in time (35 hrs.). Lights off about 5 o'clock.

November 16: School. Snowing today again. Stayed home in evening and studied.

November 17: Papa went away today. Capt. Richard Hobson talked in the morning at school. Ran some errands in eve.

November 18: Not snowing today. Had music this afternoon but I didn't take it. Helped fix street lights this evening.

November 19: School only in morning. Local institute in afternoon. Fixed street lights all afternoon. Went to bed early.

November 20: Went to work at 6:15 a.m. Went to Beech Creek and we put in 34 meters. I worked 10 hours. Went to pictures. Bought new suit: $50 reduced from $75.00.

Sunday, November 21: Went to Sunday School. Got papers. Studied in eve. Mary Alice's Birthday. Gave sister a dollar bill for present.

November 22: School again. Freshmen and Sophomores are training for game on Thanksgiving. Studied in evening.

November 23: Have examinations today. We had test in History today and have another tomorrow. Oh, ye gods and goddesses!

November 24: Had chemistry exam this morning. Kept in for Clubs this eve. Papa took out insurance for me. Cleaned up cellar in evening.

November 25: Went up to game between Freshmen and Sophomores. Sophomores winning 19-0. Went to pictures 2 times.

[23] Did anyone consider that work and absences for work could be a cause? My mother told me Howard was very bright and his heart was broken when his father would not send him to Penn State, only Williamsport Business School.
[24] Most young men were wearing knickers.

November 26: Read meters at Center Hall. Got up at 5 o'clock. Stayed home in evening and studied. Bad day. Raining out.

November 27: Trimmed street arcs. Johnnie helped me. Went up and read meters at Port (Matilda) and Unionville. Snow, sleet and rain; bad day. Went to skating rink in evening.

Sunday, November 28: Went to Sunday School and got papers. The Johnson boys were there. I stayed home rest of day. Ate dinner at M.S.'s.

November 29: Have chemistry vacant period today. Kept in for not having problems (finished). Handed in experiments in both. Read meters in evening.

November 30: School Chem. Extended 3 periods this morning. Went to Star Course Entertainment. Very good, funny.

December 1920

December 1: Through reading meters. No experiments today. Dentist two weeks from now.

December 2: Loafed around after school. Basketball practice has begun. We are in the Mountain High School League again.

December 3: I went to basketball practice tonight. After that I went to pictures at Opera House. Pretty good.

December 4: Paid $12.30. (10 hrs.) Went to work at Beech Creek. I patrolled line from Howard to Beech Creek in morning putting on notices. Nice day.

Sunday, December 5: Worked on street system today. There was a ground on it. Other fellows worked at Howard sub-station. Studied in evening. (10 hrs.)

December 6: School today. Saw in paper where Clearfield High beat Tyrone High 45-21. Rebecca Rhoads house burned down today.

December 7: Have three vacant periods today. Elected 2 basketball managers for boys and 2 for girls today. Have lines to say. Don't know them.

December 8: Didn't say lines. Studied them in evening. Mama went to pictures in evening. The lights were low this morning.

December 9: Said lines this morning but have to say them again because I didn't know them. Made HCl acid today. Basketball game.

December 10: Said lines this morning. Boys Basketball uniforms are bright red pants and jerseys. We beat Houtzdale, 29-18.

December 11: Went to Beech Creek to finish up. They have lights now and we put in meters, etc. The street circuit was off all evening. I worked till 9.30 on them. (Christmas party)

Sunday, December 12: Patrolled street system in morning. Found a lot of bad places. Some of the lights—about 257—were out tonight again. (9 hrs.)

December 13: The line crew fixed up the street lights today. They cleaned the post lights on Allegheny and Linn Streets.

December 14: Basketball team has special practice tonite. Play Tyrone Friday. Start in Caesar tomorrow in Latin.

December 15: George Showers got a job reading meters, etc. at office last night. "Fifi's" is on at the Opera House tonight.

December 16: Snowing again today. The ground has frozen. Class going to "Fifi's" tonight. On Jan. 3rd we have 1st class at 8:40.

December 17: Snowing today. I got 95 in Chemistry exam. Last day of school this year. Seniors give presents this eve.

December 18: Boys team got beat at Tyrone last night. Worked at Julian[25] today. (9 hrs.) Helped raise some 20 & 25 foot poles and distributed up as far as Materson's farm.

Sunday, December 19: Went to Sunday School. Got mail and papers. Went up to Mussers. Went to church in evening.

December 20: Worked around office today. Getting ready to take inventory. Other fellows at a line. (8 hrs.)

December 21: Worked around office today. Went to dentist yesterday and today. Have another date for tomorrow. (8 hrs.)

December 22: Still working around town. Went to dentist. Finished except cleaning. Went to pictures tonite. (8 hrs.)

December 23: Trimmed street lights and washed shades today. Finished at dentist. I am to stop in at Easter vacation. (7 hrs.)

December 24: Read meters in Centre Hall today. Charged new rate of 11¢ for first 100, 9¢ for next kw. Went to pictures in eve. (11 hrs.)

December 25: Worked changing meters in the morning. Went to pictures in evening. Got a lot of presents. (1 hr.)[26]

Sunday, December 26: Went to Sunday School. Got papers. Went to church in evening. Snowed some.

December 27: Read meters in Pleasant Gap all day. Went to pictures in evening. Showers. Working in Bellefonte. (11 hrs.)

December 28: Read meters in Milesburg all day. I came out $3. short. Went to pictures this evening again. (10 hrs.)

December 29: Read meters around town, Coleville, American Line, Center Count, etc.

---

25 An unincorporated community and census-designated place (CDP) in Centre County, Pennsylvania, United States. It is near and viewed as a part of State College.

26 So, young Howard worked on Christmas Day changing meters....

Went to BB game tonight[27] at State College & BHS. We beat State College 28-4.

December 30: I hurt my knee last night at playing basketball. Read Port (Matilda) and Unionville. Bad day for me; not feeling good. (9 ½ hrs.)

December 31: Read meters in Bellefonte. Mr. Stock was back yesterday. Basketball team got beat at Philipsburg, 29-31. (9 hrs.)

January 1, 1921

Took inventory of old plant all day. Went to pictures in evening. 9 ½ hrs.

Following the above Diary entries are the following:

- Several telephone exchanges
- Howard's class schedule

In the inside cover of the back is written:

Catherine S. Pifer
411 Thompson St.
Curwensville, Pa.
Saturday, June 30, 1923[28]

(This information of my mother's name, address, and date would have been written later (1923) than the date of this Diary (1920). The Diary entry struck me with a sadness, perhaps because of the unexpectedness of finding this information in a Diary three years old when Catherine had just completed her Sophomore year in high school and Howard would have been a year beyond high school graduation. It also may be viewed with some interest that the Diary itself was written during Howard's own Sophomore year in high school. This realization was immediately followed by the thought of Catherine and Howard's being young and just meeting and having hopes and dreams with no idea of what their future together would hold.)

---

[27] Spelling of "tonight/tonite" is inconsistent throughout.

[28] One can only surmise that he had kept this diary on hand and it was the closest place in which to write my mother's name and address, along with presumably their first date. In contrast, the only thing my mother kept is the first Valentine Howard sent her.

Excerpts from 1920s High School Yearbooks
From Clearfield and Curwensville

The Breeze 1921, Clearfield Yearbook

- This issue included graduate Robert Kurtz, Founder of Kurtz Brothers. Ads in this yearbook included the Susquehanna College of Music, to which the Pifer daughters took the train to their violin lessons; H. Clark Thayer, Proprietor.
- Theatres in Clearfield included the Driggs and the Liberty.
- Mitchell Milling was owned by the father of Clark Mitchell, later friend of Mary Alice's son, Bill

The Breeze, 1922, Clearfield Yearbook

- The book includes graduate Howard V. Thompson, brother of Mary Alice.
- The Les Shull Studio of Clearfield, beginning a dynasty.
- The notable "lifetime faculty member" of Clearfield High School, Amy Reno, who marked her fifth year teaching in 1922.
- There was no football game played between arch rivals Clearfield and Curwensville in the fall of 1921.

The Echo, 1922, Curwensville Yearbook

- This first yearbook for Curwensville High School featured a section on Alumni, noting that of the 14 graduates from the Class of 1922 that the yearbook staff could track, 10 of the 14 were in enrolled in a college.
- Josephine Pifer (the oldest of the five Pifer sisters that included Ruby, Jessie, Katherine, and Jean) married Droz Hamilton and the young couple lived with his parents, Mr. and Mrs. Frank Hamilton at 421 Meadow Street; Droz and Josephine named their son Noel Franklin, CHS Class of 1952.

The Echo, 1923, Curwensville Yearbook

- William Kittelberger, Editor
- David McKinley, Class President
- Marjorie Wall, Joe Hipps, Sidney Korb, Hugh Norris (Noted in the Diary)

- Popular young male teacher, Paul Zetler
- Mary Alice was in the Junior Class; there was a lot of moving between classes. Jessie was also in this Junior Class; Kate Pifer was a Sophomore.
- Mildred and Sidney Korb, siblings but not twins, were in the same class.
- General Patton Literary Society Programs
- November 10, 1922: Vocal Solo by Jessie Pifer
- February 1, 1923: Piano Solo by Mary Alice Thompson
- During their Freshman and Sophomore years, several members of the Class of '24 advanced to the next grade. Two of these entered the class of 1923: Hugh Norris and Mary Alice Thompson: "Deciding at the last call to enter the Class of '23 and leave us heartbroken, Mary Alice was graduated last year but came back to us again this year in order to take up special work." Her graduation photo is in this yearbook.

The Echo, 1924, Curwensville Yearbook

- Mary Alice started this school year in the Junior Class, but had credits enough to be graduated with the Class of 1924.
- Jessie Pifer was graduated this year.
- Gordon and Kathryn Kephart, siblings, were in the same class after Kathryn advanced for having credits enough to be graduated early.
- Elizabeth King '22 is noted as attending Elmira College.

The Echo 1925, Curwensville Yearbook

- Cora Wolf '22 was attending Beechwood School, as were a number of young women from the Clearfield-Curwensville area.
- Elizabeth Wall '22 was said to be enrolled in a school in Florida.
- Elizabeth King '22 was said to be attending Bucknell University.
- Joseph Errigo '24 was attending the University of Pittsburgh.
- Orville Hipps '24 was at Grove City.
- Joe Hipps '23 was attending the University of Pittsburgh.
- William Kittelberger '23 was attending Lehigh College.
- David McKinley '23 was at State College, later known as Penn State.
- Hugh Norris '23 was attending Dickinson College.
- Mary Alice Thompson '24 was a freshman at Drexel Institute.
- Marjorie Wall '23 was enrolled at West Chester State Normal School.

The Echo 1926, Curwensville Yearbook

- Alice Wall was attending Beechwood School; Edith and Lucy Brunetti both were attending Columbia University; and Hugh Norris '23 was at Allegheny College.

The Echo 1927, Curwensville Yearbook

- Seven Juniors, including Margaret Jean Pifer, joined the Senior Class.
- The Debate Topic for Assembly was "Which of the following has been of greatest service to mankind—Gasoline, Electricity, or Steam?"
- Class Night – the first mention of this event to appear in the yearbook, so it likely was the first one held.
- Note that most of the elementary teachers in the Curwensville schools were graduates of the high school and not from out-of-town.
- Under the section on Alumni News for the class of 1924, Marjorie Wall was listed as teaching at (but was only attending) West Chester and Mary Alice Thompson was attending Drexel.
- Joe Errigo was working as a druggist (He had attended a pharmacy program at the University of Pittsburgh).
- Jessie Pifer was teaching in Hyde City.
- Alice Wall was a student at Beechwood College (absorbed by Beaver College the year Alice enrolled.) She was also listed in the 1928 *Echo* as a student in Jenkintown, PA, which is the location of Beechwood.
- Of the Class of 1926, Elizabeth Kittelberger was noted as "being at a school" whereas Park and Elmo Erhard were listed for Allegheny College.
- Murray Clark '25 was in NYC and Katherine Pifer was teaching at Driftwood.

The Echo 1928, Curwensville Yearbook

- This yearbook took on the name *L'Echo* in celebration of the non-stop flight of Colonel Charles A. Lindbergh to France.
- There was a huge Editorial Staff and an additional Directory Staff for a section on Alumni, Directors, Teachers, Curwensville Population.
- Irvin Park Dam Committee was a school club formed as part of the effort to raise money for building a dam at Irvin Park.
- This was the first year for a Glee Club to be officially organized.
- Anna Kittelberger was in Philadelphia.
- Arthur Wall was Class President.

- There is strong evidence throughout the yearbook that Margaret Jean Pifer and Chet Bloom were closely devoted to each other. No surprise they married right after graduation.

- In this yearbook is the first view of anklets (on sophomore girls) being worn rather than silk stockings.

The Echo 1929 (Grant Norris Memorial Edition)

- Another giant size yearbook staff (likely this was an inside joke as there were 30 members of the staff, from a graduating class of 30)

- Ambitious class plays! Bravo!!

- Junior Year: "The Whole Town's Talking," a comedy written by Anita Loos and John Emerson.

- Senior Year: "The Importance of Being Earnest," a 19th Century comedy by Oscar Wilde (written only thirty years prior to the graduating of this class).

- The fund-raising efforts (see above) of the Class of 1928 paid off:

- "...a dam was built across the river, thus affording much deeper water and consequently better swimming. This is the one big asset to the park, and accordingly, the big drawing card. ...in the spring of 1922 the "Yellow Dogs" had built a large Kennel with a hard wood floor and here many happy hours are passed by those who indulge in this pastime. ...then, too, baseball has risen to a major part in the activities and through its advancement has made possible the enjoyment of many afternoons. Luncheons and confections of all kinds are sold on the park grounds... ."

- "With the addition of swings, see-saws, and sliding boards, children may have their own fun. ...Large benches are also provided. This is Irvin Park...for the hundreds of people who visit there each year."

- Football was king in high schools with only two defeats for this team, while the sweetest victory was Curwensville's outclassing and outplaying Clearfield and triumphing on Thanksgiving Day.

- Under "Class Notes" is found, "Mary Alice Thompson is teaching Domestic Science in the Clearfield Schools" and "Alice Wall is private secretary to the Principal of the Lititz School for Girls."

- ...Foot-ball and Basket-ball were still hyphenated words and CHS had both Lettermen and Letter Girls.

For State Senate

From the Clearfield County Daily Newspaper 1930:

HOW'D J. THOMPSON BIDS FOR DEMOCRAT STATE SENATE POST

Howard J. Thompson, candidate for Democratic nomination for State Senator, is widely known through business interests in both counties of the district. Though now a resident of Curwensville and the only Democratic candidate in Clearfield County, he has resided in Clearfield, Philipsburg and Bellefonte as well.

Mr. Thompson is a life-long Democrat, the son of F. I. "Nace" Thompson, one time sheriff of Clearfield County under Jim Mahaffey. He served for twelve years on the Board of Trustees of Huntingdon Industrial School, an appointive position, and is a member of the Board of Directors of Clearfield Memorial Hospital.

Coming to Clearfield in 1901 from his native town, Curwensville, Mr. Thompson was associated for eleven years with the late A.W. Lee in the electrical business. When this firm was taken into the Penn Public system, he moved to Philipsburg as an associate with Mr. Lee, John W. Wrigley and ex-Governor Fisher in the business of that company.

Mr. Thompson next lived in Bellefonte, where he supervised the erection of electric lines through Centre County. He still retains business relations there through his connection with Richelieu Theatres in that town.

Himself a large tax-payer, Mr. Thompson is stressing government economy and reduction of taxes in his campaign. He is owner of the Curwensville Water Works, president of the Board of Directors of Curwensville State Bank, and president of Erdman Hosiery Mills and Clearfield Amusement Company. He also is president of the Wiley and the M. and N. coal mines.

Friends of Mr. Thompson expect support of his candidacy by farmers in this section as a result of his efforts in getting Sheffield Farms to locate a milk station in Curwensville. He also was instrumental in attracting the Box Factory to that town.

The business card below confirms his support by the Democratic Party.

For State Senate

Howard J. Thompson
Curwensville, Pa.

4

Subject to the Rules of the Democratic Party at the Primary
Election, Tuesday, May 15th, 1934

The Mid-State Theatres

In 1920 Fred and Francis Thompson, uncles of Mary Alice, purchased the land upon which to build the Strand Theatre, the first movie theatre in Curwensville and likely an ominous threat to the Opera House. This was not a surprise, as the Thompson brothers were industrious. Seeing the interest the new theatre engendered, in 1924 their older brother Howard J. Thompson, even more of an entrepreneur than they, began to explore this new theatre trend and in 1924 he began acquiring a number of theatres scattered throughout central Pennsylvania, with one as far away as Meadville.

In the fall and winter of 1924-25 he purchased and refurbished a theatre in Bellefonte, renaming it the Richelieu. On March 20, 1925 Mary Alice wrote in her Diary that she "went through the new Richelieu Theatre." In July 1925 she noted that her father and mother "went to Pittsburgh with Mr. and Mrs. Richlens from Bellefonte to select the picture (movie) to be shown the opening night of the new theatre in Bellefonte."

On August 19, 1925 Mary Alice wrote in her Diary that she was attending a movie in Bellefonte, likely the very one selected for the ribbon-cutting of the opening of the new theatre. "Shore Leave" was the movie with Dick Barthelmess, later cited as one of Motion Picture Magazine's "Best of 1925 Movies." In 1929 H.J. Thompson acquired ownership of the Ritz Theatre in Clearfield. Mary Alice's Diary recorded her attending its official opening and later taking her students (as her guests) from the nearby school to a special after-school matinee.

In 1935 Mr. Thompson purchased the fire-destroyed Strand Theatre (Curwensville) from his brothers Fred and Francis. He had it remodeled and updated, expanding the building in the rear to use as storage for his various holdings. He renamed the theatre the Rex, the name it retained. This theatre had small dressing rooms both off-stage and in the lower level of the building, accessible from backstage as well as from stairs in the theatre lobby which also led to the men's restroom in the lower level.

By 1946 the small dressing room offstage of the Rex Theatre, accessible by a short set of stairs, was claimed by my sister Jo Ellen and me as a playhouse, a plan rather short-lived because not only was it almost a block from our house, but the general area back stage was dark and somewhat foreboding. In addition, my mother thought it unwise for us to be there alone because the workmen from H.J.'s other businesses had free rein of the area. Nonetheless, I was crushed when some years later a new wide screen and sound system were installed, claiming the space we once had coveted, and we were told to remove the doll furniture.

H. J.'s holdings later would be known as the Mid-State Theatres, a chain of as many as 23 theatres. Below is a listing of those this writer could confirm.

- Academy Theatre in Meadville
- Adelphi Theatre in Reynoldsville
- Brockway Theatre in Brockway
- Dixie Theatre (1935) in Coalport
- Eagle Theatre in Montgomery
- Liberty Theatre (1930s) in Madera
- Lyric Theatre (1929) in Clearfield
- Park Theatre (1922) in Meadville
- Plaza Theatre in Bellefonte
- Regency/Regent Theatre in Reynoldsville
- Rex Theatre (1935) in Curwensville
- Richelieu Theatre (1925) in Bellefonte
- Ritz Theatre (1929) in Clearfield
- Roxy Theatre in Clearfield
- Sherkel Theatre in Houtzdale
- State Theatre in Bellefonte
- Stone Theatre in Stoneboro
- Sykes Theatre in Sykesville
- Valley Theatre in Weedville
- Watson Theatre in Watsontown

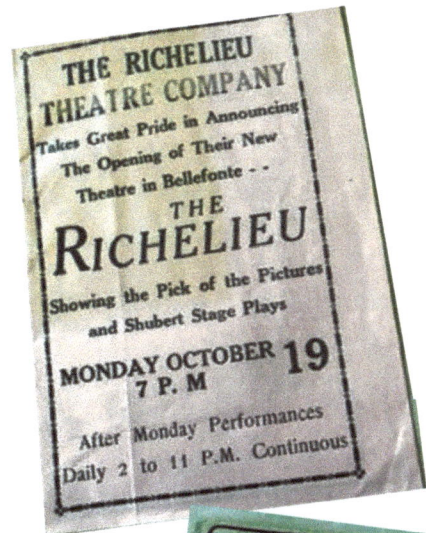

Mary Alice Thompson Jackson Crunk

With a name like a melody, Mary Alice was soft as a breeze in springtime. ♪ ♪♪

Scheduled to graduate with the Class of 1924, she finished her classwork early in order to graduate with the class of 1923. To show how flexible the schools were in those days, Mary Alice returned the following year, as the 1924 Echo states, "in order to take up special work." Her picture is in that 1924 yearbook sharing the page with her cousin Alice Wall and with Jessie Pifer, her friend and my maternal aunt. "Tommy" will join "Jebbie" later today on the hill above Curwensville, not far from where their high school once stood.

Mary Alice was one of the few young women from her small town to have the opportunity to attend college — and her parents selected one of the best for her. She always spoke fondly of Drexel and I never travel to Philadelphia but what I don't think of her as a young co-ed in much safer times. It must have been her experience there that led to her generosity some thirty years later when she made it possible for me to also pursue higher education.

To this day I remember Mary Alice's wonderful Christmas cookies; I can still recall the aroma from that large kitchen on Market Street. Even more than the Christmas cookies, however, was her immaculate house. There was never anything out of place, yet her homes were always comfortable and inviting. Even as a child, I knew that someday I wanted a large two-story house with white woodwork.

Christmas and birthday gifts from Aunt Mary Alice were the most special one could imagine. She always seemed to know just the right item for the right age at the right time. Each gift came beautifully wrapped with a richness of tissue paper enveloping the item in its box. Marshall Field's in Chicago, Nieman-Marcus in Dallas, and Josten's in San Antonio. When I had an opportunity as an adult to travel to these cities, I headed straight to those stores. Not because I like to shop, but because I felt I wanted to actually "be" in those places from which came those glorious gifts of childhood.

Gentle, fair, kind, and reserved. That was Aunt Mary Alice. I never heard her raise her voice or speak ill of anyone. We were too young to remember very well William K. Jackson, but I do remember he, too, was welcoming to the Thompson sisters. Brad I remember more vividly as the tall Texan who came into our lives and seemed even larger than life. His were the first genuine cowboy boots we had ever seen and we were in awe of his presence. A gentleman always, we saw Brad as totally devoted to the love of his life. He was her soulmate and her protector.

Mary Alice was an important part of my life and my future in that she underwrote the cost of my education at a time when paying for college would have been an impossibility for our family. I hope she knew just how much I have appreciated that. Fortunately I had the opportunity to tell her personally as well as put it in writing in letters and in a book dedication.

Mary Alice was the historian of the family, matching cousins with second cousins and cousins once removed. I enjoyed our long visits in which she would reminisce about family and friends. I think she liked to talk to me about those days because I usually could recall those about whom she spoke. Many of them I had not known personally but I knew about them from town history or from conversations with Aunt Jessie or my mother. Mary Alice's mind was sharp, except she often would talk to me as if I had been part of her era. I remember a couple of years ago when she had been talking about stopping at a little store on the way home from high school. She asked me the name of it – a store that did not exist in my own experience. However, I said, "The Sweet Shoppe," and she nodded, as if of course I would remember. During that same conversation she asked me if the woman who worked at R K Way's was his sister. Combing the corners of my memory, I tried to recall a time before I was born. I said, "I believe so." I was so pleased to verify later that the woman in question was, indeed, Miss Way.

Because of her close ties to Curwensville, perhaps the final verse of the Class Poem of 1924 best summarizes our parting:

> And here's to the class of '24
> And all the classes of the past.
> The classes that are soon to be
> And the colors on their mast.
> With hopes we leave the High School
> Where we lived, and loved, and trod.
> To enter other fields of actions,
> To live and love and honor God.

May God bless you, dear Aunt Mary Alice Thompson Jackson Crunk.

Your love and make You happy – the rest of my life will be devoted to just that; there is so much love and affection stored up inside me for you I am sure there could never be an end to it, instead it seems to grow larger all the time. Perhaps other people have said the same thing and thought they felt the same way, but darling, I know how I feel and I have been waiting a long time for you.

I feel secure in your love and promise now and darling, please believe me, you will never regret it. I am fully aware there are things in our path that necessitate our waiting, even though I am very sure how we both feel and love each other now, and it hurts me to even wait a day, still for the welfare of those who must be considered, and to be sure they understand. I am willing to wait. But still darling, I dislike to see a day or night pass without being with you, the though always sticks in my mind that there is never the chance to relive a day once it has passed and each such day is one less for us to be together.

Oh Darling, I do love you so much, so very very much and I thank God I found you and waited for you – May nothing ever

412

happen to seperate us again.

I don't know what I have ever done to deserve anyone like you and your love, but whatever it was I am glad I did it and just hope I am always worthy of you – I will die trying darling.

Thank you very much for the nice Goodnight kiss after You got in the car. That meant an awful lot to me, more so because you wanted to kiss me in the presence of the others, it was rather like telling them and me at the same time that you loved me and wanted everyone to know it – I do want everyone to know I love you – everyone! We are going to be so happy, so very happy darling.

You should be almost home now and this room is still dark, cold and very lonely – but not nearly so lonely as it would have been had you not been here tonight. I am going to bed now, I hope I can dream and may all these dreams soon be true.

Thank you for loving me darling and by the time you read this I will soon be with you. Goodnight darling and I love you always.

Always

Bob

BRADFORD B. CRUNK

During my growing up years, our family owned a chain of movie theatres known as Mid-State Theatres where we had the chance to see every movie that ever made it to small town, Pennsylvania. Musicals, comedies, and dramas. *Gone With the Wind* where we cried with Scarlett over Ashley Wilkes, *The Snake Pit* which I never should have been allowed to see, and on Saturday afternoons, the westerns, especially all of the Roy Rogers westerns with the broad-brimmed hats, the chaps, the spurs, and, most of all, those cowboy boots. (Some of you heard me two weeks ago speak of our first impression of Bradford Crunk and his cowboy boots.) At that time there were no cowboy boots to be had in Clearfield County, but once I became a young adult, I bought a pair in every color available, including gold. I don't think I ever put those boots on without thinking of Brad.

Brad epitomized that tall Texas cowboy and cattle rancher in the Saturday matinees. Blond, good-looking, intelligent, strong, and gentle. He was the hero who walked into our lives and swept Aunt Mary Alice off her feet, just like in the movies. And Cousin Bill got to move to Nixon, Texas, and live that life we could see only on the silver screen. Did you know, Bill, how we began to also view you as a western hero? You had a good role model in Brad who never tried to take your own father's place, yet always regarded you as his son.

I have never witnessed a couple more devoted to each other than were Brad and Mary Alice. Fifty years of marriage, and I don't believe an angry word was ever exchanged between them. They were a wonderful couple, true partners who loved each other. Brad, God speed you to her side. She is waiting for you.

A Texan died today. It was not unexpected they said, for his heart was broken.

He fell, they said. I think rather that he just didn't want to stand alone.

He lost the one person in this world who meant the most to him, and in losing her he lost the will to live.

The stars at night
Are big and bright
Deep in the heart of Texas

Well, there is one star now that has fallen from that Texas sky and I would guess that if we were to stand on that hill in Curwensville we would see that star brightly shining down on Brad and Mary Alice, two people with hearts at least as big as Texas.

415

www.ingramcontent.com/pod-product-compliance
Lightning Source LLC
Chambersburg PA
CBHW061231150426
42812CB00054BA/2564